JEAN, LADY HAMILTON

1861–1941

A Soldier's Wife

CELIA LEE

JEAN, LADY HAMILTON
1861–1941

A Soldier's Wife
(wife of General Sir Ian Hamilton)

A biography from her diaries

For

Chris Read

Best wishes

Celia Lee

2/5/02

CELIA LEE 2001

First published 2001 Celia Lee
London SE13 5LP

ISBN 0 9539292 0 5

A CIP catalogue record for this book is available from the British Library.

Typeset by Phoenix Photosetting, Chatham, Kent
Printed and bound in Great Britain by
Mackays of Chatham, Chatham, Kent

Dedicated to

John Terraine
for his work on the First World War generals

and

Kathy Stevenson
for her work in the Western Front Association

*A special note of thanks to my husband and editor, John Lee,
author of A Soldier's Life: General Sir Ian Hamilton 1853–1947*

Contents

Acknowledgements

Mr Ian Hamilton (Literary Executor, the Hamilton papers), and his wife, Mrs Barbara Hamilton. Miss Helen Hamilton. Mr and Mrs Alexander and Sarah Hamilton. Elizabeth, Lady Muir. Sir Richard Muir and his wife The Lady Linda Muir. Miss Anna Muir. Mrs Fiona Goetz. Mr Robert Muir. Mrs Katherine Cobbett. Mrs Griselda Maffett. Lord Kilbracken. The Honourable Christopher Godley. The Duke of St Albans. Lord Lambton. Mrs Cowan. Miss Kitty Falzon. Mr Robin Cruickshank, ROR Intl. Ltd. Sarah, The Duchess of York. The Lady Soames. The Honourable Celia Sandys. The Marquess of Northampton. Lady Frances Campbell-Preston. The Duke of Beaufort. Professor Brian Bond MA, FRHistS, FKC and his wife Mrs Madeline Bond. Patricia Methven BA, DipArch, FKC, Director of Archive Services; Kate O'Brien BA, DipArch, Assistant Director of Archive Services; Alan Kucia, Assistant Director of Archive Services; Geoff Browell Ph.D., Archives Assistant; Robert Baxter BA, MA, DAA, Archivist; Pat Kelly; Alison Price, Archives Assistant; Elizabeth Selby, Archives Assistant; Beverley Ager, Senior Clerical Assistant, The Liddell Hart Centre for Military Archives, King's College, London. The staff of the Library, King's College London. Professor Ian Beckett, Head of Deptartment of History, University of Luton. Major-General Julian Thompson. Professor Peter Simkins, formerly IWM. Mr Tony Cowan. Mr Chris McCarthy, IWM, Sec. BCMH. Mrs Jane Carmichael, IWM. Mr Bryn Hammond, IWM. Mrs Bridgeen and the late Mr Colin Fox. Mr Peter Robinson. Prof. Tony and Mrs Cis Morris. Dr Stephen Badsey, RMA Sandhurst. Dr Keith Grieves, Kingston University. Mr Len Sellers. Mr Ian Stirling. Mr and Mrs J. Chambers, Kiftsgate. Mr Michael Bloch. Mr Sandy McMillan, Postlip Hall. Mr David Coombs and the Staff of The National Trust, 'Chartwell'. Mrs Josephine Lamb. Mrs Joan Schlewinski. Mr Jim Blaney. Jill M. Banks, Archivist, The National Trust, Kedleston Hall. Miss Pamela Clark, Dep. Registrar, The Royal Archives, Windsor Castle. Lewisham Library. Manor House Library, Lewisham. The Royal Society for Literature. The Central Library, Edinburgh. City of Westminster Archives Centre. The National Army Museum. Welcome Institute For the History of Medicine. The Tate Gallery. Barbara Thompson, Witt Library, Courtauld Institute of Art. Mr Ian MacKenzie, Admiralty Library. The Management and staff of NatWest Bank: Mr Nicholas Harod, Mr Alan Fuller, Mr John Search, Mr Peter Farnham, Mrs Joanne Smalley, Mrs Carol Donovan, Mrs Stella Roderigues, Mr Richard Laughlin. The Management and Staff of Adecco Alfred Marks, Fenchurch Street, and Devonshire Row, London. Chris Gibson, Fiona Carpenter, Karla Jennings and Derek Askem all helped greatly with the production of the book and its illustrations.

Quotations from the Hamilton archives are made with the kind permission of The Trustees of the Liddell Hart Centre for Military Archives.

List of Illustrations

SECTION ONE

San Antonio Palace, Malta
Major Ian Hamilton, c. 1887
Jean Muir in her wedding finery 1887
The Muir family 1986
The Hamilton family 1987
Mary at Langside by Greiffenhagen
Valetta Harbour, Malta
Sheep at Cap Martin
Garden at San Antonio Palace, Malta

SECTION TWO

Jean Hamilton 1900
Lord Alwyne Compton
Stirling Castle, Simla, India
No. 1 Hyde Park Gardens, London
Winston and Clementine Churchill 1908
Deanston, Perthshire
Blair Drummond Castle, Perthshire
Miss Janet Hamilton 1922
Mrs Katharine Cobbett
Roly, Bro. Hugh Cobbett and Susanna Avery
Gideon, Rachael and Chloe Avery
Staff at the Liddell Hart Centre, King's London

Front cover: Miss Jean Muir on her wedding morning 1887
Back cover: Jean, Lady Hamilton (1896) wearing a cloak designed by
Worth of Paris.

Foreword by Prof. Ian Beckett

Historians have tended to dismiss the army wife as an 'incorporated wife', subordinated to her husband's institution and, therefore, something of a victim in playing a predetermined role. Additionally, feminist historians have seen such a woman's status as deriving entirely from that of her husband, with any potential influence over the husband's career represented somewhat negatively. While it is recognised that women might enjoy considerable authority in the private domestic sphere, there has been an assumption that even women with apparent influence in the public sphere, such as the great political hostesses, lacked power. Increasingly, however, it is becoming clear that, in common with many aristocratic and middle-class women in civilian life and, especially, politics, the wives of leading soldiers often played a highly significant role behind the scenes. The incorporation of women in the army through marriage neither automatically implied their subordination, nor constrained their ambition. Thus, as Frank Prochaska has remarked, 'We are perhaps too prone to see limitations where the women of the past saw possibilities'.[1]

As Celia Lee's study demonstrates, Jean Hamilton was of immense significance at important moments in the career of her husband, General Sir Ian Hamilton. A wealthy woman with literary and artistic talents, Jean Hamilton moved comfortably in the world of Edwardian hostesses. Though often separated from Hamilton for long periods while he was on campaign and, at times psychologically distanced from him as a result, Jean Hamilton remained a loyal wife, working assiduously to cultivate the well connected on his behalf. Her efforts to secure him official observer status during the Russo-Japanese War, and to defend him as the Dardanelles campaign began to go tragically wrong, are especially striking. This is a valuable addition to our knowledge of the role of women as army wives in Victorian and Edwardian Britain, and it is to be hoped that it stimulates further study of the wives of other leading British soldiers.

Ian F. W. Beckett.

Preface

A Voyage of Discovery

On a summer's evening some years ago, John, my husband, and I sat
round the living room of Professor Brian and Mrs Madeline Bond discussing military history. It was the night before Brian and Madeline were
due to leave on a week's holidays and John and I were there to take care of
the cat. John's biography of General Sir Ian Hamilton was already under
way and Brian and John talked of the failed battle at Gallipoli during
World War I, which has become synonymous with the names of Hamilton,
Kitchener and Churchill. Someone mentioned that Lady Hamilton's letters
were in the Liddell Hart Centre for Military Archives at King's College,
London, where John was researching his book, but that no one could read
her handwriting. Being a commercial secretary, I volunteered and a month
later went with John to King's. The letters they wanted read were those
that Jean had written to Ian during the Boer War in South Africa but,
though they were listed in the catalogue, they were missing. Kate O'Brien,
Assistant Director of Archive Services, said: 'Why don't you have a look
at Lady Hamilton's diaries?' – or words to that effect. Up to that point no
one in the world of military history had ever heard of Lady Hamilton's
diaries. Patricia Methven, Director of Archive Services, arranged for the
diaries to be brought up and when we removed the lid off the box there
were eight reels of film inside, containing much of Lady Hamilton's life
story.

Several months later, John advised me to write Jean's biography from
her diaries and Professor Brian Bond approved. Some six years later,
when my manuscript was looking like it might become a printed book, my
next task was to try to trace the Muir and Hamilton families. Tony Cowan,
who works for the Foreign Office and who is a friend of my husband, was
home on leave from Hong Kong. We went to the pub for the proverbial
pint and an Indian meal afterwards and discussed our books. When Tony
went to his parents' home he told his mother who said she knew Vereker
and Lilian Hamilton's granddaughter, Helen Hamilton, who had been her

friend from school days. Mrs Cowan gave Tony Helen's address and when he returned to Hong Kong he emailed it to another friend of John's, Chris McCarthy, of the Imperial War Museum, who is also Secretary of the British Commission for Military History and Chris gave the details to John.

Thus begun a voyage to discover more of the past generation from the present Muir and Hamilton families. Helen invited John and me to her thousand-acre hilltop farm in Innerleithen, Scotland. Having travelled all day we arrived in the late evening, to be greeted by Helen at the door. In the gloaming, I could see the striking resemblance she bore to her famous great-uncle Ian – the high Hamilton forehead. Next day, Helen took us to meet her eldest brother, Alexander, and his wife Sarah at their home in Roxburghshire. In the true Hamilton tradition we were given a good lunch, after which Alexander produced large quantities of unpublished papers and letters belonging to General Sir Ian and his late father (affectionately referred to as 'little Ian'), who wrote General Sir Ian's biography, *The Happy Warrior*. The present generation, Alexander, Helen, Ian and the late Mary Pearce are the children of 'little Ian' and Constance (*née* Crum Ewing). Against a background of the enormous fresco of Mary Queen of Scots at the battle of Langside, an oil painting by Vereker of 'the Storming of the Cashmere Gate' and many photographs of past and present generations, we spread the papers out on the drawing room floor and spent the rest of the afternoon browsing through them. Alexander provided me with a full account of who Jean's family were, her parents, sisters and brothers, which information had been painstakingly put together by his late father, and has proved invaluable ever since. We spent a splendid holiday with Helen who showed us the belted galloway cattle they still breed on their farm, the descendants of the first herd which was begun by General Sir Ian at Lullenden farm, purchased by the Hamiltons from the late Sir Winston Spencer-Churchill, who was his lifelong, cherished friend.

We arrived unannounced at Deanston, Jean's former home, nestling in the pretty countryside at Doune. It is now an old people's home and a wonderful respite for the elderly with views over beautifully kept gardens. The present owner, Mr Ian Stirling, treated us to more warm hospitality and, over tea in his office, told us a good deal of the history of the house. The gothic pillars in the hall have been painted with a clever marble effect that is so convincing as to pass for the real thing, an idea Jean brought to her London house. He also told us that Deanston caught fire around 1912 and the tower was badly damaged. Mr Stirling directed us to Sir Richard Muir and his mother.

John telephoned Sir Richard at Blair Drummond, who very kindly saw us early in the morning, at very short notice, despite his being about to fly out to Vietnam on business. Sir Richard and his wife, The Lady Linda, provided us with interesting family histories and the history of James Finlay's tea company, where Sir John Muir, Jean's father, made his money. Their daughter Anna took us out to their business premises; Blair Drummond is now a safari park. Anna and Kitty Falzon, who works in the office, made photocopies of letters and other items of interest about the family. Kitty gave me a copy of the safari park brochure with a photograph of Blair Drummond Castle, the former home of Sir Alexander Kay Muir, Jean's eldest brother, which Kitty explained is now a home for autistic children. Kitty is from Malta and knows well the beautiful San Antonio Palace where Jean and Ian lived when Ian had the Mediterranean Command there. She says they call it St Anthony's Palace.

Sir Richard's mother, Elizabeth, Lady Muir, who lives close by, then courteously received us. Her youngest son, Robert, who is a landscape gardener, treated us to tea and showed us a wonderful black and white print of Singer Sargent's painting of Jean. Lady Muir loaned me her copy of *Jean: a Memoir*, the book General Sir Ian dedicated to Jean and which is personally inscribed to Lady Muir.

Lady Muir gave me the address of her daughter, Mrs Fiona Goetz, who lives in London, and back on our own doorstep, Fiona invited me to tea at her house and we had a cheerful afternoon, eating delicious home-baked cake with Fiona telling me many stories of family history. Fiona provided me with an invaluable Muir family tree which she, herself, drew up, a considerable achievement as Sir John and Margaret, Lady Muir had ten children, of which Jean was the eldest. Helen and Alexander had given me the address of their brother, the present Ian Hamilton, in Berkshire, who is the Literary Executor of the Hamilton papers. Our next call was to lunch with Ian and his artist wife Barbara (Basia). Ian is the third genera-tion of Ian Hamilton and there is a wonderful photograph of the three Ians together. Over lunch with Barbara and Ian, their two sons, Felix and Max, and Laura, daughter of Sarah and Alexander, and her prospective husband, Lionel Mill, Basia told me that General Sir Ian's brother, Vereker, had written a book called *Things That Happened*, about the coincidences which took place in the Hamilton family. John and I have had our share of coincidences while writing our books. Basia is an outstanding portrait painter and, the previous week, I had attended her exhibition at the European Academy, courtesy of an invitation from Helen, where there were wonderful portraits of members of the royal family, the Churchill family and an excellent portrait of Ian, her husband, who like Helen and Alexander, bears a striking resemblance to his famous great uncle Ian. Basia arranged for John and me to dine with His Excellency the Turkish Ambassador and his wife at their London house in Portland Place. Sixteen of us sat down to dinner and enjoyed exquisite Turkish cuisine. The one good thing that came out of the dreadful events at Gallipoli in 1915 is that the British and Turkish peoples have become so much closer to each other. Each year large numbers of British people visit Gallipoli to see the place that claimed their fallen ones. Basia and Ian have given me a great deal of support whilst writing this book, and Basia most especially with the art-work.

Helen also provided me with the address of Mrs Katharine Cobbett, whose mother, Mrs Janet Leeper (Vereker Hamilton's youngest daughter), preserved Jean's diaries. We enjoyed an excellent lunch with Katharine at her home and she provided me with a Hamilton family tree and has been enormously helpful on family history. She has three children, Brother Hugh SSF, Roly and Susanna (Mrs Avery). We met Roly, who resembles General Sir Ian. Katharine and Roly discussed with us the artistic talents of Vereker and Lilian, and showed us the medal Lilian made of Field Marshal Lord Roberts. Katharine and her mother lived at General Sir Ian's London home for a while after Jean died, to keep him company. During the wartime blackout Katharine remembers climbing the dark staircase to the bedrooms on the second floor.

Katharine also put me in touch with other members of the family. Vereker and Lilian had two other daughters, Elizabeth (Betty) and Marjorie (Margot). I am indebted to their children, Lord Kilbracken, and his son the Hon. Christopher Godley, and Mrs Griselda Maffett respectively, for their painstaking letters and telephone conversations providing me with family details.

Ian and Basia had introduced us to the Hon. Celia Sandys, grand-daughter of the late Sir Winston and Baroness Spencer-Churchill, and recent author of *Churchill: Wanted Dead or Alive*. Celia put me in touch with her aunt Mary, The Lady Soames, who is the only surviving child of Winston and Clementine. Over afternoon tea at her home, Mary gave me an insight into the life of her mother, who was a friend of Jean's, and gave me copies of her books: *Clementine Churchill*, a biography of her mother, and *Speaking for Themselves*, the personal letters that passed between her parents, and a photograph of them in 1908 on the day they became engaged to be married. I am indebted to Lady Soames for her guidance and letters on matters relating to her parents, as friends of Jean and Ian Hamilton.

It is rare for a diary to contain such deep psychological insights. Jean Hamilton used her diary to explore her innermost feelings. It gives us a more complete picture of her as a woman living through some of the greatest events in British history than we could normally hope for.

Celia Lee,
'Middlemarch',
12 Longhurst Road,
London SE13 5LP

January 2001

CHAPTER I

A Whirlwind Romance

"Ian *is* here. Ian is in this world. Ian is in my life and we are to be together all the way now.... Every morning and evening I thank God for my gallant, gay, fearless Ian." [5th Dec. 1886, Calcutta]

Little did the fun-loving, stunning beauty Jean Muir think what lay ahead of her as she danced a cotillion at the Viceregal Lodge ball with Major Ian Hamilton. Could she have but known that war after war would take him from her, only to return him a stranger that she would have to learn to know all over again. Or that his career as a professional soldier, painstakingly built up at great sacrifice to herself, would be laid in ruins before them thirty years later, the outcome of the now infamous Gallipoli campaign. But away with these horrors and let the reader dwell for the moment on a young couple falling in love at a ball, the very stuff that Jane Austen novels are made of.

The night is young and Jean's tall, slender, hourglass figure glides round the ballroom in his arms. Her green eyes look innocently into the blue of his and the dashing young major is instantly in love with her. The time, summer; the place, Simla in India; the year, 1886.

Male partners jump through paper hoops, snatching the ladies of their choice. Ian, dazzled by Jean's great beauty, suddenly decides to catch her. One minute he shoots through the hoop like an arrow and the next he is gallivanting with her in the mazurka.[1]

Jean often recalled those early days of their courtship and life in Simla in her later diaries, and she says they met by chance: "... My first meeting with Ian, going out in my rickshaw on a wet Simla night, to dine with the Cunynghams, and a rickshaw with the hood up went up the steep drive before me – fate – I wondered who was in it, and out of it stepped Ian straight into my life. What an enchanting dinner, and a heavy blessed thunderstorm that kept us stranded there for so long we thought we should have to stay the night...." [31st August 1921]

In true Jane Austen style, Jean's father, Sir John Muir, was a gentleman and, like Elizabeth Bennet in *Pride and Prejudice*, Jean was a gentleman's daughter. Jean's mother was Margaret, daughter of Alexander Kay of Cornhill, Lanarkshire, a partner in James Finlay & Co. Shortly after their marriage, John Muir became a partner in the company and by 1883 was sole proprietary partner. He established a flourishing jute industry and tea plantations in India from which he made his fortune.[2] In 1892 he became a baronet and Lord Provost of Glasgow. Deanston, built by John Burnett and nestling on the picturesque banks of the River Teith in Doune, Perthshire, was Jean's family home, until a holiday abroad led her to a chance meeting with the man who would become the love of her life.

Born on 8 June 1861 and christened Jane Miller, Jean was the eldest of a traditionally large Victorian family of ten children: six daughters and four sons. Jean's sisters were also great beauties. Elizabeth (Betty or Bess), married, in 1883, Harry Moncreiffe. Margaret (Nan) married Alexander (Allie) McGrigor of Cairnock in 1886. Agnes (Aggie) married William Coates in 1888. Edyth (Edie), whom Jean considered the most beautiful, died young and unmarried in 1909. Heather married Colonel Stephen (Peter) Pollen in 1905. Alexander Kay (Kay), married first, in 1910, Grace, the widow of Henry Villiers-Stuart, who died in 1920, and second, in 1924, Nadejda (Nadia), the daughter of Dimitri Stancioff, a Bulgarian diplomat. James (Jim) married, in 1909, Charlotte (Chattie), daughter of Joseph Turner. John (Jack) and Matthew William (Willie) married sisters who were also cousins, Heather and Clara, the daughters of John Gardiner Muir. Jean's eldest brother inherited his father's title in 1903 and became Sir Alexander Kay Muir, second Baronet, 1903–1951, residing at Blair Drummond Castle. Jean and family members always referred to him affectionately as Kay.[3]

Ian Standish Monteith Hamilton was born on the island of Corfu on 16 January 1853 and entered the Army in 1872. His father was Colonel Christian Monteith Hamilton. Both Ian's parents were dead, his mother, the beautiful Maria Corinna, having died of consumption in 1856, when Vereker, Ian's younger brother was five months old. The boys were brought up by their aunt, Mrs Camilla Caldwell, whose brothers were George and Harry Hamilton of Skene. Harry became the Minister of Dunblane.

Vereker married Lilian (Lily), daughter of Edwin Swainson, Assistant Secretary to the Admiralty. Vereker and Lily were artists and had met whilst they were studying together at the Slade School in London.[4]

Vereker became well known as a painter of battle scenes with such stirring titles as *The Storming of the Kashmir Gate at Delhi* and many delightful ballet pictures and still life studies. Lilian, known as 'the Slade Baby', having won a scholarship before she was nineteen, was a sculptress and medal maker and won first prize at the opening exhibition of the Society of Medallists for her design for a medal for University College.[5]

In October 1885 Jean Muir arrived in India to spend a holiday with her sister, Betty (whom she sometimes calls Bess), and brother-in-law, Harry Moncreiffe. Accompanying Betty to Simla the following summer, she found herself in the midst of all the gaiety and social whirl of the Simla season. Jean had been in love with Lord Alwyne Compton, third son of the 4th Marquis of Northampton, and she was devastated when he became engaged to another. "...**I know he meant to ask me to marry him when he travelled across India to see me at Jaipur and I was not there. Father had despatched me to Bombay with Betty to see Harry ...**" [March 6th 1905] Whilst in India, news reached Jean of Lord Alwyne's impending marriage to Mary, daughter of the millionaire Robert Vyner.

Jean's first diary entry closes the chapter of her unsuccessful first love: "**... The first volume of my life is closed ... the romance of A.C. It has enchanted and ruined years of my life already.**" [Sunday, 1st August 1886, Melrose, Simla, India]

Thereafter, Jean kept a photograph of her rival in love, the beautiful Mary, in her diary.

Another had taken Lord Alwyne's place in Jean's life. At the time she met Major Ian Hamilton, Jean was about to become engaged to Prince Louis Esterhazy, whose mother was Lady Sarah Villiers. Louis was a feudal Prince of the old Austro-Hungarian Empire and related to the royal families of Europe. In the days when a diamond headdress was the ultimate symbol of beauty and power, the thought of a crown was enough to turn any young girl's head. But Louis' peculiar kiss seems to have been too much for Jean to bear, even for a royal crown: "**... How I hated it when he kissed me. I felt sick. ... Why, why did Louis kiss me in that horrid way? It disgusted me.**

The thought of the nice Major H. is such a comfort and rest to me ... it was cosy sitting by the fire and I showed him my poetry book ... and I found he loved the same ones ... 'Our Spirits Rushed Together' but *not* at the touching of the lips.[6] **He would not have thought of trying to kiss me.**" [Sunday 1st August 1886 Melrose]

In the days of the Victorian ballroom, when young girls wore white ball gowns and diamonds and the gentlemen were in formal dress, it was customary for men to send bouquets of flowers to the ladies they admired. Jean received two, and an unexpected proposal. " . . . **Last night was a powder dance night at the Club, the last of the season. I wore my white dress with the pansies. Two lovely white bouquets came for me, one from Major Hamilton, with some verses – one from Louis Esterhazy, with a most sad little note. . . .**

Towards the end of the evening there was 'Trompete', and I asked Major H. what it was and he asked me to dance it with the man who 'loved me best in the room.' I laughed and teased him saying he had no idea who that was. I was thinking of Mr. Crawfurd who pursues me with his unwanted love. . . .
We did not dance 'the Trompete' but went upstairs and sat in a box looking down on the dancers. . . . We tried to talk a little at first and when the Trompete came to its noisy end and our dance was over I leaned over the box to look if my next partner, Capt. Leonard Gordon, one of the Viceroy's A.D.C.'s, was there . . . . Major Hamilton said in a choked sort of voice behind me:—

'When shall I see you again?' I turned and he added: 'Or shall I never see you again. You know I love you, Jeannie. You must know I love you,' and after an agonised pause, 'Will you marry me?'

I shall never forget his look as he desperately said this. My heart stopped beating and I clasped my hands and cried out:—

'Do not say that. You must not,' but of course it was too late then.

Then I tried to tell him how things were with me, that I was more or less engaged to marry Prince Louis Esterhazy and that I really did mean to marry him as I was very much in love with another man whom I could not marry, and did not now care whom I married. Major Hamilton said instantly:—

'I can make you far happier than Esterhazy, and if you give me the chance I am not afraid of the other fellow.'

I did not know what to answer and felt in despair. I could not bear to say I would not, as I *do* like him tremendously and feel I might love him, but I am confused and don't quite know how I feel yet. We sat on in the box till the ball was over and talked and talked, but came to no conclusion except that I promised to think it over. He pleaded his cause very fluently, was really very eloquent, but somehow or other

the word *'however'* slipped in and is engraved on my mind, making me aware he won't break his heart if I say No. This provokes me to go on. Cheeky devil! How dare he say 'However' as if it did not much matter. Louis always said he would die if I gave him up. It was lovely having Major H. as a friend, so comfy to tell all my troubles to and he helped me, but I never thought he would wish to marry me. I am more than astonished as he had told me of Miss Hughs Hallet, a girl he was in love with, and of Betty Lytton, and I thought he still loved her, and I don't quite believe he is awfully in love with me yet, but I know I can make him more so, and that I could make him happy as his wife – *his wife!* I feel frightened. . . .

Last Wednesday I had a tragic letter from Louis . . . [who] begged and *implored* me to write him even if only a line, once a month. Poor Louis, must I now write him the letter he is so dreading to get? Do I care enough for Major H. to give up what I have always longed to be, very grand and romantic, to be a Princess would be wonderful at the Austrian Court near the beautiful Empress Elizabeth, and Louis is fond of travelling – *but* he is terribly jealous and his companionship dull." [4th August 1886 Melrose Simla]

These days of courtship, grand balls and bouquets remained ever precious to Jean and years later, when someone brought her a bunch of daffodils, it evoked memories of the time " . . . when I was having grand florist bouquets sent by Ian and Mr. Crawfurd for every ball. . . . 'Give me a flower,' I can hear Ian's voice of emotion across the years. We were sitting out between dances and I was holding his flowers then.' [7th February 1930 London]

Nora, Lady Roberts (Lady Bobs), the wife of Lord Roberts, Ian's Commander-in-Chief, had the reputation of dominating her husband in both army and domestic matters. Sir Garnet Wolseley wrote at his retirement when Roberts succeeded him as Commander in Chief: 'that he was clearing his office "where she can job and dispense favours to her heart's content, dreadful woman" '.[7] There was an attitude amongst the army hierarchy that marriage produced children, and wives and children were a hindrance to a young officer's career. As soon as Lady Roberts arrived in Simla, she ' . . . was busy on a scheme for providing skilled nursing for military hospitals, and later "Homes in the Hills" as health resorts for nursing sisters. . . . All of the Chief's staff bore testimony to the way she treated them as if they were her many sons. . . . '[8] Perhaps Lady Roberts'

maternal approach explains why she and her husband tried to prevent the
Hamiltons' marriage. The Robertses may have felt they had the right to
decide whom Ian should marry or whether he should marry at all. Lord
Roberts wrote to Ian on 15 August 1886, asking him to postpone his proposal of marriage to Jean. Ian replied:

> . . . you have altogether misunderestimated . . . the strength of my
> feeling. . . . you imagine I could go on eating my heart out in uncer-
> tainty for an indefinite period. . . . I would ask you Sir what Lady
> Bobs would have thought of you – or what you'd have thought of
> yourself – . . . if after falling in love with her . . . you had withdrawn
> to a distance to think over the matter in a cool business like way for
> four months! . . . I venture to assert that she'd have refused you . . .
> and quite right too! . . . on Tuesday, with luck, I'll ask her to marry
> me.[9]

Ian, whose army nickname was 'Johnny', wrote to Jean, telling her
of Lady Roberts' interference. **"I had a letter from him this morning
telling me Lady Bobs had overheard someone say: 'the kind of girl
Miss Muir is, she rides out to Mashobra with Johnnie Hamilton,
spends several hours there with him and they return hours after
dark.' He begs me to be nice to Lady Bobs as he says so much
depends on this and says: 'the best way to do this is to meet her
advances more than half way.' However, she does not seem likely
to make any and if she does I can't meet her *more* than half way.
As well ask me to jump over the moon; she terrifies me. But if I
decide to marry Major H. she will just have to 'lump it' – I quite
think I will. . . . He told me last night all about his love affair with
Miss Hughs Hallet and sent me a long letter he had had from Miss
Gathorne Hardy. She assumes he is still in love with Betty Lytton.
[Sunday 15th August 1886 Melrose]**
    Lord Roberts ordered Ian, at an hour's notice, to Dehra Dun for a fort-
night to prepare the camp from which he intended to start his winter tour
of inspection. When Ian returned at the end of August 1886, Jean had
made up her mind to accept him. They were deeply in love and Jean
planned an autumn wedding. But once again, the army had prior claim and
Lady Roberts' kiss may be taken with a pinch of salt! **" . . . Lady Roberts
came to see me this morning and was ever so nice. She kissed me and**

told me I had got the very nicest man she knew. It was generous of her to come as I know she hates Ian marrying me, and she and Sir Fred have done their best to prevent it." [8th September 1886 Simla]

For Jean, it was a love that would last for ever. From this moment, her life would be packed full of her admiration for her 'darling Ian'. Jean's fame and beauty had already spread far and wide and the present Elizabeth, Lady Muir remembers being told that when Jean made her début at the Western Meeting at Ayr in 1881, aged twenty, people stood on their chairs to stare at her.[10] Ian courted Jean in the old-fashioned, romantic way, getting up at cock-crow and galloping to Mashobra to pick a bouquet of lavender-coloured asters that grew on the hill above. When Jean came down to breakfast her ayah presented her with the flowers. The Simla gossips put a story around that her ex-lover Count Louis Esterhazy had been seen climbing out of her window at midnight. But Jean says that Ian was jealous of a Major Dalbiac, who had been paying her attention and whom she found fascinating in a 'devilish' way, and Ian blamed Dalbiac for spreading the story.[11]

There were unexpected changes at both political and military levels. The Earl of Dufferin had succeeded the Marquis of Ripon as Viceroy of India in March 1885 and in July Sir Frederick Roberts succeeded Sir Donald Stewart as Commander-in-Chief. Powerful influences at home supported the claims of Lord Wolseley, but Gladstone's administration fell in June and was succeeded by that of Lord Salisbury, with Winston Churchill's father, Lord Randolph Churchill, as Secretary of State for India. Lord Randolph had been greatly impressed by Lord Roberts and had insisted upon his appointment and Roberts took up his new command in November. Hamilton, who had been on campaign in the Sudan, was mentioned in despatches and given the brevet rank of major, as well as a medal with two clasps and the Khedive's Star, and returned to India as one of Roberts' aides-de-camp.[12] In October 1886 the Viceroy suddenly ordered Roberts to Burma to take over command of the Burma campaign following the death of General Macpherson. Jean was desolate at the prospect of parting from her betrothed for six months at the very moment when she was planning her wedding. The course of true love was not to run smooth and Jean and Ian's courtship continued by letter. Ian wrote to her: 'I am sorrowful at the thought of this separation. It is a hard world. I never thought seriously that we could have been married, now, in this little space of four days . . . and even to write the word almost brings the tears from my heart to my eyes.'[13] But Jean pledged never to say, do, or write anything to conflict with Ian's military service.

Ian believed Lord and Lady Roberts did not want him to marry anyone.[14] When Roberts and his staff left early in November, Jean returned to Calcutta with Betty. If the Robertses thought to end the romance by sending Ian away they could not have been more wrong. Absence made the heart grow fonder on both sides, further strengthening the bond. Jean filled her days with pouring out her innermost thoughts in her diary: "**. . . Ian *is* here. Ian is in this world. Ian is in my life and we are to be together all the way now. . . . Every morning and evening I thank God for my gallant, gay, fearless Ian." [5th December 1886 Calcutta]**

Ian was in Burma where, under Roberts, an extensive reconnaissance was taking place. With the rest of his party, Ian rode on horseback through thick bamboo jungle, over mountains, along goat tracks, through the Shan states towards the Yunnan provinces and to Mogok, the ruby-mine capital, across a plateau, 6,000 feet high, encircled by even higher mountains and through a steep forest. They were heading towards an area with the largest ruby mines in the world. In a little village in the middle of the paddy fields, half-worked gravel cuttings remained. Ian saw it as his chance to dig out some rubies for Jean to wear on her wedding day. He set to work, washing the gravel in his handkerchief in a puddle of water and collecting the coloured stones. At the end of two days' work in the pouring rain he had some topaz and bad sapphires but no true ruby – and his friends all laughed at him. But he knew of a beautiful, black and gold lacquer figure of the seated Buddha in a deserted shrine. He went there by night with an escort of the 5th Gurkhas through the jungle and swamps and took the Buddha.[15]

Jean whiled away her days in Calcutta, and on lonely Sundays wrote in her diary of her beloved Ian. **"The thread of my every day is spun on the thought of Ian. He is always there, close there. . . . Never in all my life before have I felt so peacefully, contentedly happy. No ghost even of past pain and loss troubles me now, the past is dead and I feel glad now of all that unhappy time. If it had not been for *that*, I might be married now, have met Ian too late and life gone all awry.**

I did not dream when I was first engaged to Ian I should or could love him as I do now. He has become all my life and I am frightened sometimes to think how happy I am. Life is so dangerous. I cannot now think of anything I wish to be different and love the life I see

stretching out before us. I delight in the uncertainty – the excitement of that shared with Ian. . . . [12th December 1886, Calcutta]

It is said that perfection in love is savoured in small measures and uncertainty aroused apprehension in Jean before her wedding day. **"I want passionately to keep his love after I am his wife and not let the dull routine of every day dim and make it a matter of course. But it will in time; how can it be otherwise? If the real love remains, is always there, will it matter? Yes it will, I will always want to see and feel the radiance and the warmth of it. I can't exist if I am not loved. No: I just *won't* be taken as a matter of course.** . . . [12th December 1886 contd.]

Doubts began to creep in, the more so since Ian was not there to reassure her. Beyond the spiritually pure bride to be, swathed in white, her face veiled, lurked a frightening reality, something that could only be experienced after the wedding in the marriage – sex! Victorian morality decried the very mention of the word before wedlock. **"I am so wretched to-day at the thought of marriage. I must write it out and see if I feel better afterwards. I feel enraged that life is arranged in this vile way. Why must love, so lovely and holy, be dragged through the mire of lust. Why! Why! Why!**

How humiliating to be a woman, to have a ring put on your finger to show you belong to this man in this way – it's too disgusting to think the whole human race comes into the world in this horrible way.

I feel in a wicked, vile temper to-day and so rebellious and horrid I am afraid of myself and wonder if it would be better if I did not marry Ian. I am afraid of spoiling his life, but other women don't seem to feel as I do about this side of life. Anyway if they do they conceal it well.

I do love Ian with all my heart so perhaps everything will be all right. But I wish I could see us a year hence, as I sit here to-day in this vast room. . . . I . . . [am] afraid I may not be able to play up and do my part if I quarrel with the facts of life. . . . Anyway I *can't* give Ian up; life would not be worth having without him so I must go on and find courage. . . . [14th December 1886, Calcutta]

Jean took the sensible step and consulted her married sister. **" . . . Have had a long talk with Bess and I feel much better now. She is a dear and has a practical, clean, sane outlook on life."** [14th December 1886 contd.]

The unknown held a kind of fascination of adventure: "... **I have plenty of weapons in store and I see there will be many excitements in married life after all – if I am to keep that flighty man's love. 'Johnnie head in air' is his nickname.... Anyway I am his now for grief, pain or pleasure. I could never unlove him now. He is entwined in my life for ever."** [22nd December 1886 Calcutta]

It was only when Ian got through his arduous day's work for Lord Roberts that he could 'find time for my daily letter to Jean',[16] a practice he continued faithfully, through every campaign and posting, in future years.

In anticipation of Ian's return, Jean again made plans for their wedding and sent him a telegram. The post office babu misread Jean's handwriting, mistaking 'Hamilton, Mandalay, Burma' for 'Hamilton, Malabar, Bombay', and Bruce Hamilton, son of Colonel 'Tiger' Hamilton, who was ADC to the Governor of Bombay at Malabar Point, received Jean's proposal by mistake: 'Will Wednesday 23rd suit you for our wedding in the Cathedral?' [1st February 1887 Calcutta]

Jean's family, 'a ship load of Muirs', as Ian described them, arrived in December 1886 to attend the wedding but there was no one on Ian's side. **"... Ian's Father and Mother are dead – he has only an Aunt Camilla who brought him up, to write to. His Mother died when he was about three and he lived with his grandmother at Hafton."** [8th September 1886]

Vereker was himself about to be married at that time in England, so Ian invited his friend and fellow soldier, Colonel Reginald Pole-Carew (Assistant Military Secretary to Lord Roberts), to be best man at the wedding.

The arrival of her family, and particularly her mother and sisters, brought Jean great joy. **"... They came yesterday – Father, Mother, Aggie. It is most wonderful and exciting to have them here and Mother, Aggie, Bess and I have done nothing but talk, talk, talk all day long. It seems so strange and unreal having all my home ones with me again. I long to carry my little Mother off with me, just she and I, to visit Agra and Delhi."** [24th December 1886, Calcutta]

But the Muirs' arrival was premature as Ian did not return to Calcutta until 9 February of the following year.

The wedding date was set for Shrove Tuesday, 22 February 1887. Jean's favoured date was the 23rd, but it was Ash Wednesday and the clergy in the Cathedral at Calcutta would not allow it. **"... Two days now**

till our wedding day. Ian is as adorable as ever. I could not ever have faced marriage and all its threats with anyone else – with him I have a heart for any fate." [21st February 1887 Calcutta]

The final touches were being put to the wedding details. The reception would be at Betty's house, 16 Store Road, Calcutta. Jean stood patiently for hours to have her wedding dress fitted and then danced away her remaining hours of freedom at the Government House ball, despite the attitude of Lord Roberts and his party that she ought to be grateful to Ian for marrying her at all. **[21st February 1887 Calcutta]**

At last Jean walked down the aisle in her white wedding gown and veil, diamonds adorning her head and neck. In the presence of the Viceroy and the Commander-in-Chief, surrounded by her family and five brides-maids, one of whom was her sister Aggie, the beautiful, blushing bride made her wedding vows.

Years later, Ian recalled: 'Throughout Christendom and indeed beyond it a wedding is the glorification of the Bride, the bridegroom play-ing the part of the Ugly Duckling. My mind humming with confused images, behold me driving back amidst cheers and confetti . . .'[17]

The viceregal motor-launch whisked the bride and groom away to Lord William Beresford's villa, which he had lent them, in the lovely, romantic surroundings of Barrackpore. Under a velvet blue, star-studded, Indian sky, their love was sealed – or so it *seemed*.

The wedding day would remain ever dear to Jean: **" . . . I think of Barrackpore, the flowers, and my sweet, shy hubby. . . . I stayed up to all hours because of the difficulty of saying, or not saying, good-night, till he grew so tired he asked with a visible effort, 'Aren't you ever going to your beddy-bye?' " [23rd February 1904]**

Next day the newly weds travelled by train in a reserved carriage to Darjeeling, where they continued their honeymoon. At one of the stops, a drunken tea planter tried to open the carriage door and when Ian told him the carriage was reserved for a lady the tea planter shouted to his friends: 'Hi! You chaps, I've found a bearded lady!'[18] At the next stop Ian put his head out of the window to take stock of his surroundings when a lady's voice that he recognised shouted to him from another window in their coach. Unfortunately Jean's earlier plan to show her mother the sights had backfired. She had forgotten to tell Ian, who now found to his horror that his mother-in-law would be accompanying them on the rest of their hon-eymoon.[19]

It was with such hilarity that the young couple began their married life. Jean wrote of her happiness at being Mrs Ian Hamilton: **"We were married two days ago (on Tuesday) in the Cathedral in Calcutta. I felt all day in a dream, rather like the old woman in the nursery rhyme: 'This surely can't be I'. . . as I walked down the aisle with my darling Ian a dear old lady stepped out of her seat and said:– 'I congratulate you on your handsome husband', which pleased me very much. Polly-Carew who was our best man said 'Look at that bold bad woman throwing back her wedding veil!' "** [25th February 1887 Barrackpore]

When Ian was a small boy in his prayers each night he told the Father in heaven he hoped he would find him 'a good wife'. Ian believed his prayers were answered 'for I did get Jean'.[20]

Jean did not keep a diary again until the Hamiltons returned to live in England but she recorded much information about those years from recollections in her later diaries. Whilst in India she wrote a short story, 'Tale of the Princess with a heart of stone', a novel, *Hetty Burton*, and a critique of Benjamin Kidd's *Social Evolution*, none of which were published, but her ghost story, 'Till we meet again', was published in *Chapman's Magazine* (1897).[21]

CHAPTER 2

A Soldier's Wife

"It's a pity I can't knock about with him like another man and leave my maid at home." [26th January 1908 Tidworth]

Jean's life was greatly determined by Ian's career. For the first ten years of their marriage they lived in India. In 1898, Ian received an offer of a job at Hythe, Kent, and they came to live in England, occupying the commandant's house. The Boer War (1899–1902) broke out and Ian went to South Africa, where he completed two spells of duty. During the first spell, from September 1899, he was first on the staff of Sir George White, commander of the British troops in Natal, and later a significant battlefield commander under Lord Roberts, and returned a war hero on 2 January 1901. He then became Military Secretary to Lord Roberts at the War Office. During that year, Jean had taken their first London house, 3 Chesterfield Street. In November 1901, Ian unexpectedly returned to South Africa, as Lord Kitchener's Chief of Staff, not returning home until July 1902. He continued his post as Military Secretary to Lord Roberts, and in early 1903became Quarter Master General at the War Office. When this job was coming to a close in 1904, he set off to Japan in search of a new one. During the time he was there, the Russo-Japanese War (1904–5) broke out and he became an official observer in Japan. After his return, he took up the Southern Command at Salisbury in 1905 and they went to live at Tidworth House, which was owned by the government. In 1909, Ian became Adjutant General to the Army at the War Office and they returned to London and rented 6 Seamore Place. In 1910, the Mediterranean Command took him to Malta where, for the first time since India, Jean went overseas, to live with him at San Antonio Palace. In 1914 they returned to London, Ian having become Commander in Chief, Home Forces. They bought No. 1 Hyde Park Gardens but the house was only just decorated when the First World War broke out. Ian went to Gallipoli as Commander-in-Chief of the Mediterranean Expeditionary Force, from

March to October 1915. After that time, he was never again employed on active service. In 1918, after years of failing to have a family of their own, Jean fostered two orphan children, Harold Knight (Harry) and Phyllis Ursula James (Rosaleen/Fodie), whom she adopted in 1919. In the same year, the Hamiltons first rented and later bought Winston Churchill's house, Lullenden, in Sussex, as a country home, whilst retaining No. 1 Hyde Park Gardens in London.

At the time of the Hamiltons' marriage in India, Ian was a major with the 2nd Gordon Highlanders and, though he was employed on the staff in India, his regiment was in Guernsey. Jean wanted to live in England, not least to be near her family in Scotland. " . . . **I would not like that** [Guernsey] **at all, and wish he would exchange into the Guards. I want to live in London – he seemed to think he might do this, and after a year or two in London he might be made Military Secretary to Sir Fred. I don't think he is sure about the Guards but think he said it to please me." [8th September 1886, Simla, India]**

In this Jean may have been right, as Ian seemed content to serve Sir Frederick Roberts in India. Jean was happy there though she suffered from asthma and came home on holiday every second year, for her health, to her beloved family at Deanston. Jean and Ian first lived in a bungalow, Stirling Castle, in Simla, the Indian hill town that was like an idyllic Surrey village. Later they moved to a large house, The Retreat, and their homes were always fully staffed with servants.

Jean and Ian experienced some of the mishaps that might befall a young married couple. Their first dinner party was a disaster. They invited 'several society leaders – Lady Thullier, Jock Cunningham, the Foreign Secretary.'[1] The outcome was a good story that Ian liked to tell: 'At that period there was a fashion of emptying the sherry into the soup. Jean led the way.' The guests 'followed suit but what was my agony . . . to observe that one taste seemed to be enough for everyone. And then, seeing that I was about to sample it for myself, the khansamah confessed! He had filled the wine glasses with whisky instead of sherry!!' Then came 'the savoury. There is a fish in India known as Bombay Duck. Down there they don't cook it at all but just dry it in the sun which lends it a pungent flavour all of its own. It ought only to be taken in minute quantities with curry. The cook, however, had pounded up a number of Bombay Ducks and had made a substantial dish of them . . . the smell was so pestilential that we rose from our seats on one impulse and bolted for the door. Poor Jean who had meant to make everyone so happy was sadly mortified by these mishaps, but the guests were very jolly about them. . . .'[2]

One embarrassment followed another when, after dinner, Ian was putting some kindling on the fire and Jean was bending over it warming her hands and one of her curls brushed against his face. 'Being very much in love I caught the curl between my lips; she pulled her head away and lo! the curl was dangling from my mouth!' Jean, like other ladies, was in the habit of mixing in pieces of false curls amongst her own to counter the effect of the damp climate on her hair. 'And Lady Thullier had congratulated her on her curls and she had accepted the compliment. . . . We never forgot our first dinner-party'.[3]

Praising Jean and thanking God for sending him such a 'good wife', Ian admits that 'time after time' he 'taxed Jean's patience but her patience and understanding were always forthcoming in full measure and truly only once . . . was she really hurt by my behaviour.' He had written some poems and given them to Jean for her response. 'At that time I was in constant touch with Rudyard Kipling. Every Sunday I lunched with him at the house of Lord "Hatband" Russell, (afterwards Duke of Bedford)'. Kipling 'knew about these verses and was keen that his sister Trix, a charming girl and favourite dancing partner of mine . . . should take a look at them before she went back to England. Jean was out so I nipped the MS. off her table and sent it to Trix. . . .' The outcome was their first row and Ian experienced the wrath of Jean's Celtic temper: 'speaking as a husband . . . give me a storm on the ocean.'[4]

Some years later Trix Kipling, then Mrs Fleming, wrote to Ian of Jean that she was 'the beautiful lady who fascinated me . . . she was the loveliest girl I had ever seen. She has always lived in my thoughts as *the* one fair beauty . . . I have been privileged to see. . . . You both looked so happy together, I used to think the phrase "Gallant and gay" might have been invented for you. . . . '[5]

Jean and Ian had been married only a month when tragedy struck. Betty's husband, Harry Moncreiffe, died on 26 March, after just four years of marriage. Betty, only twenty-four years old, was left a widow with two small boys, Guy and Gerald. It was a tragic end to the sisters' fun-loving days together in London, before they were married, which Jean recalled many years later. They had lived at Albert Gate, Hyde Park Corner, near Knightsbridge, one of the most fashionable parts of Victorian London and were eager to launch themselves in London society. They gave a ball and

Albert, Duke of Clarence (Prince Eddie), eldest son of Edward, Prince of Wales and a future heir to the throne was there. She wrote: " . . . **we wanted to have some fun and enjoy London. . . .**" The Moncreiffes helped Betty " **. . . to give a ball as they said that was the only way we would get invitations – Prince Eddie was a friend of Betty's then and George Holford of mine. . . .**" Jean wrote to her father and got him to pay half the cost of the ball. There had been a disagreement between Jean and Betty, as friends of Betty's: "**Georgina Dudley and Mary Montgomery said to Betty it would be much better if her name alone appeared on the invitation cards and not mine – it obviously being easier to launch one woman and not *two*. Betty rather shame facedly repeated these remarks to me; I said 'Certainly, but in that case I would not pay anything or have anything to do with the ball.' Betty was ashamed and I heard no more of it and got over my fury and thoroughly enjoyed our dance, Betty continuing to dance with Prince Eddie and I with George Holford long after our other guests had departed, in Mary Montgomery's lovely house which she had lent us for the dance. . . . [28th February 1932]**

In the autumn of 1888, Jean came home on holiday to Deanston and then spent the winter in the Riviera with Betty, who left India after her husband's death and went back to live in Scotland, which must have been a great loss to Jean. The friendship with George Holford and Prince Eddie continued after Jean and Betty were married. Ian quoted from a letter of Jean's, when she was staying in London in the spring of 1890, 'that one day, when she was visiting the Holfords at Dorchester House, Prince Eddie had come in and had called out to her in a most decided way right across the room, "I hear Sir Fred [Roberts] is going to stay another year in India." So she said, "Is he, Sir, I didn't know of it," to which he replied, "Yes", he will like that won't he?" '[6] Sadly, Prince Eddie died young, in 1892, aged twenty-eight, and his brother acceded to the throne, as King George V, in 1911.

Ian's brother Vereker and his wife Lily came out to India, in August 1889 and stayed with Jean and Ian. Vereker had painted a portrait of Ian, *An Aide-de-Camp*, which was exhibited at the Royal Academy. On arrival at Simla Vereker

' . . . was set to work under the personal supervision of Sir Fred Roberts on a large picture of the battle of the Peiwar Kotal in

Afghanistan.' His Highness the Maharajah of Kapurthala, one of the richest princes in the East, was being installed on his throne and he commissioned Vereker and Lily to commemorate this event. A large suite of apartments and a studio were placed at their disposal and Vereker painted a portrait of His Highness in 1890. Whilst the King was sitting for his portrait he was ' . . . festooned with many strings of enormous pearls. One day, at the end of a sitting, when rising from his chair a rope of pearls broke, so the huge pearls went rolling all over the floor. Vereker and Lily were down on their knees . . . and began gathering them up but the Maharajah serenely waved his hand, indicating that the matter was of small importance and that they were not to trouble. Lily, however, knew very well that the State Treasurer had an exact count of all the royal jewels and that, if one happened to be missing, suspicion would attach to them for ever afterwards. So the two of them refused to leave until the Treasurer had been summoned and all the pearls safely collected and checked. Lily . . . did careful pencil drawings of His Highness and from them made a medal. The reverse, she felt, must be an elephant. All the state elephants were therefore ordered to parade and she selected the chief state elephant as model. . . .'[7]

Jean and Ian and Lily and Vereker set off for Kashmir, taking few clothes, 'as we were dying to shake off the trappings of civilisation.' Along the way Ian and Vereker did some shooting. The scenery was picturesque, Ian retaining 'one or two vivid memories of Srinagar; the Chinlar trees, gold and green: the magenta of the Woolar Lake with no reflections'. Jean was sketching when they discovered she was 'within twenty yards of a wounded bear.' Jean and Lily wore 'short skirts, puttees, little gloves on their feet with the big toe separate and grass shoes. This to them at that time was an extraordinary emancipation.' The grand barge came sailing down 'from the Resident old Parry Nisbet.' They were invited to dine on the barge and Jean surprised everyone by appearing at dinner wearing a 'red silk tea gown which against the agreements and rules she had tucked away into a bag' and which was 'uncreased' because the servant had kept it pressed by passing it 'over a lamp.'[8]

One night on the barge, when, having blown out the candle, Ian got into bed and 'felt with horror something warm. I leapt out with my hair positively standing on end and said to Jean "There is a rat or a cat or a snake in my bed." The candles were lit; more candles were brought in; Jean got hold of the top of the bed clothes with both hands and I stood close by with an enormous broomstick. On the word, "Now!" . . . the clothes were whisked off; the broomstick descended on a hot water-bottle – and burst it.' Ian had been 'threatening a cold' and Jean had 'put a hot water-bottle in my bed – an article I had never had communion with before. . . .'[9]

Later, Vereker's son, 'little Ian', wrote that Jean 'never quite hit it off' with Sir Frederick Roberts but that his mother, Lilian, 'who was much more demure and self-effacing and a very sweet person, got on with him like a house on fire.' Over a meal, when Lilian and Sir Fred were 'deeply engrossed in conversation', Jean was heard to exclaim from the other end of the dining-table: 'What *do* they find to talk about!'[10] Whilst befriending Lilian, Roberts side-lined Jean, who never forgot his attitude towards her: **" . . . Lord Roberts, who, when I asked him a question about India used to reply, 'I went fully into that in my *Forty-two Years in India*, Chapter VIII, page 12' . . . ." [16th October 1927]** (Jean's memory was playing a small trick on her here, as the book referred to is actually *Forty-One Years in India*.) Whilst referring to most of her other titled women friends by their first names, Jean only ever referred to 'Lady Roberts', and occasionally 'Lady Bobs', but never 'Nora'.

Years later, when Ian was writing his book *Listening For The Drums*, he wanted to include a particularly amusing episode from his early days in India when the Robertses thought he was falling in love and sent him away to Ootacamund. Janet Leeper was helping him and she wrote to the Roberts' eldest daughter, Aileen, who replied: 'the first time Ian's name' appeared in the visitors book was 'July 1882 – then on and off for many a day – at *Snowdon – Ootacamund* – and elsewhere . . . ' Making light of how they interfered in Ian's love life, Aileen said her

> recollection of the episode of his being sent up to Ooty to take care of my mother . . . places it some time later than when he first 'joined up' with us. At a time when my family had discovered a propensity of falling in love. And on this occasion . . . thinking that matters were getting rather serious – advantage was taken of the fact that my mother was going to join Edwina and me and my governess 'Prydie' at Ooty – suggested that Ian should go and look after her. The legend in my mind and Edwina's, is that my mother's kit or Ian's was lost on

the rail-road journey to the hills . . . that when they drove up Ian was wrapped up in a fur cloak of my mothers. . . . Of course Edwina and I were just of an age to be horribly inquisitive on such matters. More especially as I think Edwina looked on herself as engaged to him (aged 8 or 9). . . . [11]

In his biography, Lord Roberts says he met and married his wife, Nora Bews, in County Waterford, Ireland, in 1859, and she returned with him to India. They had two children who died. Of their surviving children Aileen was born in September 1870, Fred in January 1872 and Ada Edwina in March 1875.[12] Roberts wrote of his wife's illness and loneliness whilst he was away, and of their loss at the deaths of their children during the early years of their marriage. It would seem unfeeling of them to have objected to the marriage of Jean and Ian, considering the difficulties they had experienced in married life within the army. When Ian took up his post as Roberts' aide-de-camp in 1882, Aileen was twelve years old and Edwina seven, and at the time of the Hamiltons' marriage, Aileen was coming seventeen and Edwina was twelve. It may have been that Lady Roberts thought one of her daughters would have made an eligible marriage partner for Ian.

Vereker and Lily returned to England in early 1890 and their first child, a son, also an Ian Hamilton, was born in October of that year. Aileen Roberts, who 'had considerable talent' and who had come to England to study under the care of Lily and Vereker, became 'little Ian's' godmother. When Sir Frederick Roberts 'came home he was a frequent visitor to St John's Wood and took a great interest . . . in Vereker's pictures'. Lilian made a very fine portrait medallion of Roberts.[13]

Vereker and Lily had three further children, Elizabeth, Marjorie and Janet. All four children grew up to be gifted and talented. Their son Ian, always referred to in the family as 'little Ian' ('big Ian' being General Sir Ian), was educated at Wellington College. He was commissioned into the Gordon Highlanders and served in the First World War. After the war he became a reputable architect, building flats for the St Pancras Housing Association to replace slum clearance, which later stood up well to the onslaught of Hitler's bombing. He married Constance Crum Ewing and their daughter, Helen, today lives in a house, the dining room of which was designed and built by her father and which enjoys an exquisite view of the purple, heather-clad southern uplands of Scotland.

Elizabeth (Betty), their eldest daughter, born 1892, went to Norland Place School in London and was interested in poetry and writing. Betty was a very fine poet and author and did some amateur composing. She wrote two books, *Green Outside*, a book of verses for children, and *Women's Work In Wartime*. Betty married first, in 1914, Wing-Commander Neville Usborne, RNAS, who was in command of the Air Station at Kingsnorth, near Chatham and captain of the airship the *Astra Torres*. He was killed in an experimental flying test in 1916. Betty married, second, the Hon. Hugh Godley, a barrister, whose father was Lord Kilbracken. Hugh inherited his father's title and they became Lord and Lady Kilbracken.

Marjorie (Margot), born 1894, went to Kensington High School and the Royal College of Music, where she studied the violin. She became a ballet dancer and was a member of the corps de ballet of Diaghilev's Ballets Russes when they came to London in 1911. Margot was offered a job in the corps de ballet of Pavlova's company touring South America in 1913, but Vereker and Lily would not allow her to go as it was considered socially unacceptable and too dangerous for a young girl unnchaperoned at that time. In 1915, she married Felix Warre, a captain in the King's Royal Rifle Corps, who was the fifth son of Edmund Warre, Head Master and provost of Eton College. When Felix retired from the army he became a director and later Chairman of Sotheby's.

Janet, born 1898, also went to Kensington High School, followed by Queen's College, Harley Street. During the First World War, she worked for a time in the naval workshop at Chatham, making the rigging and cables for the coastal airships of the airfleet. She had composition lessons with John Ireland at the Royal College of Music and published several songs, some of which were performed. In 1921, Janet married Allen Leeper, who had gained a First in Greats at Balliol and was a member of the Foreign Office, where he later became Head of the Western Department. After his death in 1931, Janet took up writing and was the first radio and television critic for *The Times*. Her books *English Ballet* and *Edward Gordon Craig* were published by King Penguin books.

Jean and Ian did not have children, and it is apparent that during the first ten years of their marriage in India, Jean did not want any. Like other women of her social circle, Jean was vain and figure-conscious, and child-bearing could expand the waistline and hips. Throughout her life, as told in her diaries, she was constantly preoccupied with her looks and appearance and in her photographs and portraits her figure was even slimmer in the years following her marriage.

Many years later, Jean rediscovered an extract from an old letter she had written in 1890 to her aunt, Nora Anderson, which provides an extraordinarily vivid understanding of her state of mind, just three years after her marriage. It describes the reflections of a young woman endowed with a poetic intellect, obliged to follow the strict social mores of high Victorian society, which was all the more repressive in the case of army wives, living in British India.

"September 13th, 1890. Simla
Why did I not enjoy the Burns Court dance? I suppose I was not
appreciated and liked enough, that must have been it; that so often is
at the bottom of our disappointments and weariness of the world – it
must often happen to me, I am so very, very often tired and sick of it
all – '*utterly weary of it all*' as you say. . . .

I often long to 'break free.' Yet what would be left then for a but-
terfly like me – nothing – I could not, – never will except for change
and by way of contrast. . . .

I wish often I were a better woman or a worse one, had more heart
or less, more intellect or less, more everything or less than I have – it
is so heart-breaking and fatiguing that mid-way attitude of mind,
never decidedly anything, the midway road must be always beset with
regrets whether it leads to good or bad; it is impossible it could be oth-
erwise except when the sun comes out at moments so dazzlingly that it
turns . . . "

" . . . I was going to tear this up – it fell out of an old diary. I don't
know if this letter ever reached Nora Anderson – so I had these moods
even in life's gay morn – I put it in here because I see 'Plus ca change
plus c'est le même chose.' [The more things change, the more they stay the same.] **I care less or control these moods better now."** [28th **February 1932]** That Jean could hardly remember if she actually sent the original letter and that this may have been a copy, does nothing to detract from its interest.

Sir Frederick Roberts offered Ian the post of his Assistant Military Secretary in Ireland. Although Ian wanted to return to the UK, he did not want to go to Ireland but felt awkward in case he would offend Roberts.

He refused and 'wrote instructions to Jean' as to what to tell Roberts. Lady Roberts wrote to Ian 'secretly, begging him not to betray her, probably exaggerating what Roberts was saying about him to her privately, and practically accusing him of ingratitude and disloyalty.' Ian 'wrote . . . offering . . . to come home on half pay as Roberts's private secretary to help him with his book.' In the meantime, Ian was offered the prestigious post of Deputy Quartermaster-General in India. 'He telegraphed to Roberts to ask if acceptance of this was approved. Roberts pretended that the telegram was meant for Jean and sent it to her.' Jean, who was at Deanston in Scotland, 'saw the position perhaps more clearly that he did', and wrote to Ian:

> What I fear has happened is that Lord Roberts is insulted by your supposing him capable of such selfishness as to allow you to come home on half pay so as to help him; that you should suppose him capable of exacting such a sacrifice from you – I feel in his place I should feel this; also the little man was fully persuaded in his own mind that he was doing you as well as himself a good turn by asking you to come as his A.M.S., and to find you despised his A.M.S.-ship so much that you would rather come home on half pay to serve him than help him in that way is of course a nasty pill for him to swallow.
>   . . . and of course being A.M.S. to him does not mean what it would mean in Lady White's household. Lady Bobs manages her household *entirely* herself . . . .

Ian accepted the appointment of DQMG but came to England 'on a flying visit to make his peace with Roberts.'[14] Any hopes Jean may have held for a return to England were dashed and the Hamiltons continued to live in India for the next three years.

It was at Simla that Ian was popular with Lord Lansdowne, Viceroy of India (1888–94), whom Lord Roberts approached to have the Government of India grant permission to train the Indian Army in Hamilton's methods of 'straight shooting' and 'fire control'. A friendship developed between Jean and Lady Lansdowne, Vicereine of India, which would prove valuable at a much later date.

In March 1898, Hamilton received a cable from Sir Evelyn Wood, adjutant-general to the forces, offering him the post of Commandant of the

School of Musketry at Hythe, Kent. Jean had finally got her wish and in April the Hamiltons came to live in England. The high Victorian era was in full swing, with Britain at the height of her imperial glory. Jean entered fully into high society; a world of women fashionably dressed, 'steel-bound and whalebone-lined', as Irene Clephane described them.[15]

In the domestic sphere, Jean did no housework or chores of any kind. She managed her household but a team of servants did the work. Her maid, McAdie, looked after her personal well-being, dressed her and went with her everywhere.

Jean's first glimpse of the house provided by the army at Hythe, when she went there with Edie, was that " . . . **I hated the Commandant's house**" and " . . . **said I would not, and could not live there. . . .**" But when they could find nothing better, Jean set to work and the challenge of the place brought out the artist in her. She transformed the house: " . . . **I had pulled down walls and rearranged it all and I liked it, and could see the sea and sailing ships from my bedroom window, and the drawing-room was lovely. I remember even Lord Salisbury looking at it and saying what a lovely room it was, with the four large panels of printed Persian cotton on the walls. Lord Salisbury was going through a course of musketry and billeted in a cottage at our gates – we saw a lot of him and I liked him immensely. Alice S. told me when we were in Seamore Place afterwards, I was the one woman in London he ever went to see, which pleased me mightily.**

The day Lady Randolph [Churchill] **and Lady Sassoon called there** . . . **Nancy** [Bateman] **was staying with me, and we had one or two nice boys from the Musketry School with us who had been lunching, and we were sitting grouped half in the garden and half on the low window seat. I had on a picturesque hat I had invented. I suppose having nothing special to do on Sunday afternoon, while their men played golf, they thought they'd like to come and see what I was like – Winston** [Churchill] **had written so much about Ian to his Mother.**

I did not know at first who Lady Randolph was, and she was amazed that I should not. I suppose she thought not to know her argued oneself unknown, which I suppose was true. . . . we afterwards had dullish depressing dinners there. Aline Sassoon made a glancing brilliant, but very disconcerting hostess, always breaking up conversation with any continuity in it by going off at a tangent to something

else. She always made me think of the line: 'Sounding the timbral o'er Israel's dark wave. . . . ' " [15th August 1915]

But Jean's home life with Ian was short-lived, and eighteen months later he was appointed Assistant Adjutant General to Sir George White in Natal. On 16 September 1899 he left for the Boer War in South Africa. Ian's safety was a permanent worry to Jean and her friendship with Lady Lansdowne during their days in India provided her with a valuable confidante to whom she could turn for reassurance. " . . . **When the Lansdowne's were in power, during the South African War, when Lord Lansdowne was War Minister, Lady Lansdowne always told me the latest news of Ian, and I could go and lunch with her any day I liked and always ask her. . . ." [30th June 1915 London]**

When, in 1900, Winston Churchill published his Boer War dispatches under the title *Ian Hamilton's March*, Jean asked Winston to dine. She later told her family over dinner at Deanston about the reply she received, which read: " **. . . as Mr. Churchill is so much engaged by his political work I write to say he is sorry . . . and signed by a secretary. I was furious at this impertinence, and had it framed and placed in my drawing-room. . . . " [27th April 1902 Deanston]**

Jean resumed her writing, producing an allegorical one-act play, *Merely mad and silly ass – a plagiarism from Maeterlinck* (1898), two novellas, *Mrs Monckton's flirtation* and *The strange journey of Mrs Arlington*, and a novel, *A fragment from life*. These are mostly undated and none appears to have been published.

After his return from the war, on 2 January 1901, Ian was knighted for his heroic service and they became General Sir Ian and Lady Hamilton. Later that year Jean began writing a diary, which she took with her almost everywhere, recording events as they occurred. There are probably several reasons why she decided to start a new diary, one of which may have been the rediscovery of her old diary amongst her personal possessions in the move from India. The diaries of Samuel Pepys had influenced her when she read an essay by Stevenson: " **. . . the idea he gave me of Pepys' sank into my mind. . . . the points Stevenson notices are what I like – 'As I was writing of this very line', the bellman cried, 'Past one of the clock and a cold frosty windy morning', it makes me shake hands with the man across all the years and changes since he lived, it is the want to do this makes one write down the moment, as one feels it; it is of ones** entertaining self one wants to write, of how everything affects one-self." [Tuesday 21st November 1905, Rookaby Park]

On the day that Jean began writing her new diary, Monday 7 October 1901, the Hamiltons were the guests of Lord and Lady Albemarle (the eighth Earl), at their Norfolk country estate, Quidenham Park, Ian being part of a shooting party there. The Earl's younger brother, George Keppel, married Alice Edmonstone, who, as the Hon. Mrs George Keppel, became famous as the lover of Edward, Prince of Wales, later King Edward VII. Alice, in turn, was the great-grandmother of Mrs Camilla Parker Bowles, close friend of the present Prince of Wales. The Hamiltons had travelled up to Norfolk by train. Queen Victoria was recently dead and Jean, who was dressed more in keeping with the character of Scarlett O'Hara from the novel *Gone With The Wind* than a woman in mourning, found herself in the carriage with the Duke and Duchess of Teck, who boarded the train along the way. " . . . **I felt worried to see her still in deep mourning for Queen Victoria, as I was attired in blue serge lined with bright scarlet. . . .**" [7th October 1901 Quidenham]

Jean shared in Ian's fame as a South African war hero. They now moved in the highest society, a written record of which, for a literary person like Jean, must have been irresistible. Remarks by Count Metternich may also have encouraged her: " . . . **Count Metternich . . . told me he was sorry he had not kept a diary when he was younger, he had feelings then he would have liked to put down. . . .**" [11th October 1901, 3 Chesterfield Street]

Jean desperately wanted to have a child but Ian was exhausted when he returned from the war and Jean would recall: " . . . **his careless kiss and then stretching himself on the hearthrug going to sleep. . . .**" [20th April 1905] Along with his heroic reward, Ian brought home with him the psychological and physical effects of battle, and was ill and possibly impotent. " . . . **I have been thinking again, with bitterness, of the time when he came back to me almost from the grave, from Ladysmith, how I longed and longed that we might be more to each other, and that we might have a child. . . .**" [August 19th 1908] Ian was promoted to major-general and on 9 November 1901, rested and recovered, went back to the war in South Africa. A normal family life with Ian as a full-time husband, complete with children, was not to be. For Jean, the parting was traumatic and depression followed.

Jean filled her days by going abroad on holiday with a friend, Nancy

Bateman. For two months the two women lived in luxury, touring from one hotel to another: the Élysée Palace Hotel, Paris; the Hotel Bristol, Beaulieu; the Villa Stephen, Cannes; the Riviera Palace Hotel, Monte Carlo; the Paris Ritz. They "... **were met everywhere by bowing officials. . . . I never knew before how important it was to be Lady Hamilton. . . .**" At Beaulieu, the day broke with: "**. . . A lovely sunny, morning, sea and rocks bathed in gold mist; orange trees covered with oranges – I can see them from my window – a smell of India in the air – enchanting. . . .**" Nancy went to Monte Carlo and Jean stayed with Henrietta de Labrosse and her mother, the Vicomtess, at the Villa Stephen, Cannes. They gave: "**. . . rather a boring party. . . . The Grand Duke Michael and Countess Torby were there. I was introduced to her and liked her. . . .**" The Vyners' garden, next day, was beautiful. "**. . . I am in love with the sunshine, sweet as Eden is the air.**" They "**. . . gathered me a lot of violets. Lord Alwyne has often told me of this villa. . . .**" Jean joined Nancy in Monte Carlo, they gambled in a casino and Jean "**. . . made some money at the tables. . . .**" But Nancy was prone to fits of temper and they argued frequently. [**9th and 14th February; 4th, 5th and 10th March 1902**]

The horror of war could not be blotted out and whilst they were at Beaulieu, the news broke that Lord Methuen had been wounded and taken prisoner by the Boers in South Africa. The threat to Ian's life loomed before Jean and she "**. . . woke up screaming again last night, it's almost as though the terrible days of two years ago, when this horrid hateful war began, had returned. My heart misgives me about Ian. I read yesterday 'some men, having once heard, cannot live without the siren song of a bullet,' and I know Ian loves danger and to be in it. . . .**" [**11th and 12th March 1902**] Tired of Europe and Nancy, Jean's mind turned more and more to her absent Ian. "**. . . Lord Methuen has been released with a broken leg and is on his way home now. . . . Negotiations are in the air and I begin to hope this terrible war will end at last. I am longing to have my darling man back again, life is empty without him. How thankful I am that he is Chief of Staff to Lord K.** [Kitchener] **and so comparatively safe.**" [**28th March 1902, Riviera Palace Hotel, Monte Carlo**]

Leaving Nancy behind, Jean returned to London, bringing with her a new dress of soft and dark flowered chiffon, designed by Worth of Paris. Next day, accompanied by Puppy, her dachshund, she arrived at

Deanston, which she would frequent during the rest of Ian's time in South Africa. " . . . **It was sunny and bright when we reached Dunblane and I loved Scotland with its distant soft blue hills – snow capped mountains and the peaceful undulating fields with sheep and lambs – my homeland – it is like nothing else. Little mother was on the steps to meet me; waiting there as soon as the carriage came in sight and father was there too.**" [**5th and 6th April 1902 Deanston**] Deanston was always home to Jean and her brother, Kay Muir, was always very dear to her. " . . . **Kay interests me. I keep thinking about him. 'Caviar to the people' he will always be.**" [**27th April 1902 Deanston**] Much as Jean liked the colour scheme of her own home it could never compare with Deanston. When she stayed there she preferred to sleep in the bedroom that had been hers during her 'bachelor' days, and when she was moved to a bedroom in the State apartments she felt less comfortable. " . . . **I have the tapestry room which I love, but with a new paper it seems strange and I have not got accustomed to it yet and miss the old fashioned one with the trails of ivy. This one has strips of roses. Chintzes with roses cover the chairs and make the curtains – it is gay!**" [**20th April 1903**]

Sometimes she brought branches of the gaen tree from Deanston to her London home, 3 Chesterfield Street. Adding her artistic touch and love of nature she could feel, " . . . **the drawing-room looks delicious, I am in love with it again – full of white blossoms and green, lovely against the brown walls.**" [**6th May 1902**] But the house was empty and Jean, feeling deserted, turned to her diary as a vessel for her outpourings: " . . . **if I write at all it must be a true tale of what I am, not of what I would wish to be, also it helps to get rid of the blue devils when I confess to my diary.**" [**May 30th 1902**]

Jean in loneliness was a restless spirit and she set out on a round of visits to her friends. Staying at Arlington Manor with Lady Jeune, they " . . . **sat in pine woods . . .** " and Jean " . . . **read Matthew Arnold. . . .** " Dorothy Allhusen organised parties and they were joined by Austen Chamberlain, the Duchess of Montrose, Lord and Lady Beauclere, Madeline Stanley and Anthony Hope, with whom they had long conversations. They visited Newbury Towers, " . . . **a lovely Elizabethan house where we sat in an old garden, smoked cigarettes and discussed how we should like to die.**" [**22nd June 1902 Arlington Manor**]

When the Boer War ended, Ian sent Jean a cable containing a coded message that the Boers had signed the peace, so she was one of the first to know. **" . . . 'Hymn 135.' I looked it up and it was: 'The strife is o'er, the battle done; Now is the Victor's triumph won.' This means that the Boers; fierce old De lay Rey, Botha and all the rest have signed the peace. Clever of Ian so to have conveyed to me the great secret."** [2nd June 1902] In anticipation of Ian's return, Jean was depressed but tried to count her blessings: **" . . . Here I am with a beloved husband on the eve of starting home to me, covered with honour and glory, a lovely house in London which I have always wanted, nice servants, plenty of money, good looks still, plenty of friends and an adoring family – and yet I think of lying still and dead with passionate longing."** [20th June 1902]

At the railway station, Lady Roberts and Betty, her sister, waited with Jean on the platform for the homecoming train. Ian returned triumphant, Edward, Prince of Wales was there to greet Lord Kitchener. Ian got out of the train, **" . . . looking handsome and gay in his Staff uniform . . . "** and, along with Lord Kitchener and General French, boarded the waiting carriage, which set off at the head of the procession to Buckingham Palace. Jean and Betty followed in a carriage behind. The great procession wound its way through the streets of **" . . . wildly cheering people. . . . It was most exciting, all the waving, hurrahing multitudes . . . beautiful it was driving along the Serpentine and I felt proud of my wonderful husband and so happy."** Ian dined at the Palace and Jean prepared a happy homecoming for him: **" . . . I opened the door for him and drew him into his little study and kissed him, and sat and talked to him . . . then he went to the kitchen to say 'How do you do' to all the servants."** [12th July 1902]

Back together in society, Jean and Ian were being wined and dined and their friends (or at least Ian's friends) were full of adulation. The Boer War brought fame and their movements were the subject of press coverage, the newspapers referring to Jean as Lady *Ian* Hamilton, an appendage of her husband. William St John Brodrick, Secretary of State for War (1900–03), **" . . . gave a wonderful luncheon in Londonderry House. All the loveliest women in London were there to meet the bravest men – crimson roses massed on seven round tables. Ian sat between Lady Helen Vincent and Lady Castlereagh."** [14th July 1902]

Lord Roberts and Lord Kitchener were given the Freedom of the City of London, and Jean, Ian and Betty went to the Guildhall. " . . . It was a wonderful sight. Lord Bobs and Lord K. were tremendously cheered – Lord Kitchener was the most popular. . . .

I felt so proud of my Ian, everyone cheered him. I felt as if we were being married again as we went together in the procession with everyone cheering us, and I could hear 'There is Ian Hamilton' as they pressed forward to greet him." [August 6th 1902]

" . . . We dined with the Howes to-night – a gorgeous dinner, all the loveliest women and most distinguished men in London there, and a heavenly band playing during dinner. I could scarcely eat or talk for listening to it – the programme carefully selected by little Lord Howe. . . . I sat between Mr. Wilson and Lord de Grey and Lady Sarah [Wilson] sat on his other side so that when I talked to Lord de Grey Lady Sarah and her husband sat silent, which was a bore, as I rather liked Lord de Grey. Lady de Grey looked magnificent: dressed in white satin with a Medici collar of lace; with her great height and flashing dark eyes: she looked a magnificent specimen of the *grande dame:* she does extinguish other women. . . . Prince and Princess Christian were there and after dinner Princess Christian discoursed to me at great length on Princess Louise's unfortunate marriage. 'Fancy,' she said dramatically, 'the sufferings of that beautiful creature': the beautiful creature was prancing before us at that moment in Kitchen Lancers, looking uncouth rather than royal, with a wreath of great pink roses on her head." [August 8th 1902]

Jean and Ian dined at the Vagabonds' Club; Sir Arthur Conan Doyle, the famous writer of the Sherlock Holmes detective stories, was there. " . . . 450 Vagabonds. It was amusing . . . they looked like an Anglo-Indian gathering . . . The Chairman, Anthony Hope, took me in to dinner and I sat next Sir Arthur Conan Doyle. Conan Doyle, talking of South Africa, told me an incident about Ian, how at Elandslaagte, what had steadied the troops more than anything else was to see him calmly light and smoke a cigarette before the attack. He admires Ian. . . .

. . . After dinner Mr. Harrison Hall sang a song about Ian with a catching chorus and everyone sang 'Here's to Ian Hamilton, the bravest of the brave,' and indeed I felt proud of him. . . ." [November 28th 1902, 3 Chesterfield St.]

With Ian at home, Jean was happy and hoping for a little curly headed son. But reminiscences years later reveal that all was not well with the intimate side of the Hamiltons' marriage. " **. . . we went to Skene together and I for a moment sitting there alone in the field, seemed to see life open out before me human and tender, and I felt at last this is what life may still give me, and then that terrible disillusioning walk in the afternoon, all my air castles tumbling about me again – the impassable barrier between us, the aloofness against which my needs, my wishes, my longings beat in vain. I think I realised then once for all it was hopeless – I cannot reach him, am not at home in his heart. I wonder does he never feel the loneliness and want of comfort – a woman's love and comfort himself?"** [August 19th 1908 Deanston contd.]

Jean also recalled, years later, how her happiness was marred after the Boer War, when she found the women were besotted with Ian and jealous of her. " **. . . Everyone was running after Ian the good-looking South African war hero, and I felt myself to be the unwanted wet blanket he sweetly dragged about with him."** [9th May 1919]

Ian became godfather to the baby of a friend of Jean's, Muriel Beckett, an occasion which only added to Jean's anguish: " **. . . Muriel's baby, Pamela Thetis, was christened this morning. Ian is her God-father. . . ."** The second godparent, Muriel Wilson, could not come and at the last moment, Jean had to stand in for her. " **. . . I had been suddenly called upon to be proxy God-mother . . . I had to vow all sorts of things for the poor little mite, and then held her in my arms to be baptised. I wished she was my own little daughter, and when the clergyman bathed the tiny . . . head in water the tears came to my eyes. . . . Pamela Thetis wore a lovely lace robe and her nurse was very pleased when I admired it. . . . "** [March 18th 1903]

Life as a soldier's wife was many-faceted, especially following Ian's rise in esteem after his service in the Boer War. Much of Jean's time was taken up with entertaining. Her dinner parties were an opportunity to socialise and keep herself informed of the current affairs of the day. She was ambitious for her husband and missed no opportunity to further his career, maintaining contact with leading politicians, including the various Prime Ministers of the time, and the hierarchy of the British army. Jean emerges as a woman doing a great deal behind the scenes for which she received little or no recognition, let alone a mention in the pages of the history books. For if ever there was a woman 'hidden from history', it is Jean Hamilton.[16] Her elevated social status precluded her from paid employment and whilst she was staying with the de Rothschilds, she quoted a passage from a book she was reading, *Felix*, of how women filled the void, having no meaningful work to do: " . . . **Lady Caroline Hunt says, 'Modern Women take to morphia as having no profession and no religion they find their lives empty and unbearable – the morphia dream makes life possible to them.' . . .** " [February 9th 1903 Ascot Wing]

In the glamour of London society, dressed by the leading fashion designers, Worth of Paris, Chanel, Ravel, and wearing their gowns in white, blue and pink satin, black silk and velvet, adorned in diamonds and fake pearls, thinking real ones unlucky, Jean's tall, elegant, slender figure glided through an endless succession of dinner parties, balls and public functions. Her nephew, 'little Ian' Hamilton, remembered 'she always looked beautiful'.[17]

There were lengthy holidays in France, Rome, Venice, and Monte Carlo. Jean's beauty was much admired and the present Elizabeth, Lady Muir remembers that all the artists of the day wanted to paint her portrait.[18] John Swan first painted her when she was still a bride, and other sittings for famous artists would follow. When Sargent painted her portrait in 1896, the bubbly young girl in her mid-twenties of Simla days had become a serene, intellectual beauty. Her fair hair, changed to blonde with highlights, was cut into a sleek, shorter, layered style, and she wore a floor-length gown of shimmering white satin. She confided to her diary that she now thought **" . . . a reputation for beauty would become a bore, just as Royalty must be if it went on. . . ."** [8th June 1904]

Jean moved in a circle of society hostesses: Lady Jeune (later Lady St Helier), and Lady Roberts, both of whom were known to influence their husbands' army careers; the beautiful American, Lady Randolph Churchill, mother of Winston, whom Jean says she adored; Clementine Churchill (later Baroness Spencer-Churchill), Winston's wife, who was highly acclaimed for her charity work; the Hon. Alice Keppel, the stunningly beautiful mistress of Edward, Prince of Wales; Lady Diana Manners; Maud, Lady Cunard, an American heiress; all frequently graced Jean's table or were her companions to the theatre and the opera. Winston Churchill became a life-long friend of Ian's: the two men were like brothers, and Winston was always about the Hamiltons' house. When Jean and Ian decided to buy a country home, Winston obliged by selling them his, Lullenden in East Grinstead, Sussex.

Jean was not only 'accomplished' in the Jane Austen sense of the word, she was highly cultured and widely read, could converse on philosophy, literature, drama and art, and spoke French. Her great love was poetry and several of her poems were published, including her wartime verses about Gallipoli. She was very artistic and produced many fine pastels. Her time at Malta (1910–1914) was particularly productive. The painters John Singer Sargent and Charles Furse were amongst her friends: **"... went to a Private View, Academy – A *Furse* year the papers call it. I am glad of that, his lovely picture of the Waterfields (a romantic couple) is splendidly hung; knowing Charles as I do – and for so long – I feel almost as if I was included in his triumph." [1st May 1903]**

Recreational activities included, dancing, skating, tennis and golf, and in the drawing room Ian sang German lieder to her, as she accompanied him on the piano.

Jean hated blood sports and during a shoot at Quidenham she told Ian how she felt. **"... At dinner I told Ian how much I had suffered seeing the poor little partridges shot this week: one moment flying overhead so happy and alive, and then bang down on their poor little backs in mortal agony, with their delicate thread-like legs quivering in the air, no one to pity their pain – none of the charming men and women all around paying any attention to their utter woe. If Ian saw a bird killed by an animal writhing like that in agony he would be dreadfully distressed, he is so tender-hearted about pain, but I felt sorry I had said it as it made him sad and spoilt things – he had had such a happy week and had thoroughly enjoyed it." [October 7th 1901 Quidenham]** Count Metternich was horrified when Jean exclaimed she **" ... would rather set a light to a well tarred Christian Martyr than shoot a lark. I love larks singing in the sky and he loves larks well *baked* in a pie." [13th June 1903 Esher]** When Ian was again part of a shooting party at Quidenham, Jean found herself in **" ... a perfectly savage mood, and seize my Diary as a safety valve...."** It made her **"... long to cry to see the little tender fluffy birds come quivering down in death agony. I long to pick them up and nestle them in my breast...." [12th October 1905]** Attending a charity dance brought back memories of when they lived in India and she had to suffer **" ... the purgatory of Hunt balls ...." [9th May 1919]**

Their marital relationship was competitive and it is apparent from a conversation with Winston Churchill that Jean preferred it that way. **" ... We discussed matrimony from his point of view, touched on love very** slightly, and discussed 'strife and life' at some length – I maintaining 'that the one meant the other and that when a thing was perfect it was finished and over'." [Christmas Day 1903 Gopsall]

Jean suffered from asthma and depression and her mother told her the depression was hereditary. An asthma attack would last for days, though she always fought it off and bounced back. In times of depression she thought of Ian as being indifferent to her cares and needs. But it cannot have been easy for him to have such a fragile wife who could be in perfect health and sparkling one moment, and ill and in the depths of depression the next. She could not accompany him to a country where the climate was likely to cause her to suffer constant asthma attacks. When Ian went away to war or on a commission she was alone in a large house for long spells and the shock of his departure, sometimes unforeseen, left her frustrated and disorientated. But Jean was determined to make the best life she could for herself, always having her literary and artistic interests to sustain her, along with her many friends, not least Lord Alwyne Compton, whose marriage had broken down. When she went to the theatre or a dinner party or to stay with friends, there was no shortage of male admirers to escort her and pay her attention.

The chance of conventional family life and, above all, Jean's need for the joy of having children was sacrificed for the battlefield or duty in some far-off country. Ian would drift into her life one moment and be gone the next. Not having children was the most painful disappointment of all and in this her greatest romantic expectation of married life had not been fulfilled. Such disappointment was hard to bear, along with her occasional doubt if Ian even loved her any more: "... I dreamed last night that my beloved Puppy turned into a darling little baby boy, with delicious soft baby arms – I was being photographed with him, and Nan [her sister] said how perfectly lovely he was, and I felt so proud and pleased, and kissed him again and again on his fine white and rosy skin – then I awoke, and my arms felt empty indeed." [January 11th 1904, 3 Chesterfield St.]

CHAPTER 3

Edwardian High Society

"I hear after the King died, Queen Alexandra standing with Alice
Keppel beside the bed and looking at him said: 'We both loved him.' "
[12th May 1910]

Two years after the Hamiltons returned to England from India, Queen
Victoria died, on 22 January 1901, and King Edward VII and Queen
Alexandra took the throne. The Hamiltons were not rich but were very
comfortable on Jean's handsome annuity from the business of her millionaire father. Jean had been painted by Singer Sargent at his Chelsea house,
where he entertained her during the sittings to recordings of Wagner's
music. When her portrait was finished, " . . . he said to me – "I am not
content with it, but it is as near you as I shall ever get. I want you to
look *un*satisfied – not *dis*satisfied." [16th April 1925] Always exquis-
itely dressed in expensive clothes, Jean now 'moved in the highest society
with the old aristocracy, statesmen, politicians and prominent men.'[1]
    In early August 1902, the Prince and Princess of Wales were
crowned, the coronation having been delayed because Prince Edward
was ill. General Sir Ian Hamilton, as a knighted war hero of the Boer
War, rode at the head of the coronation procession to Westminster
Abbey. " . . . Coronation Day. – London's great day come at last. I
started for the Abbey about 8-30 and was shown to my seat by
Capt. Peter Pollen – looking like the Knave of Hearts in his fantastic dress. I had been allotted by some mischance two seats, one in
the gallery and one in the Nave – the one in the Nave was excellent
so I stayed there and saw the procession splendidly though I could
not see the services at all.
    It was wonderful to see the pomp and splendour of these ecclesi-
astics handing on and supporting the Queen and King as they passed
on to be crowned; the conjunction of Church and State struck me as
curious and extraordinary. A puppet show – a Church which has no

real influence on the State, a Church to which we still pretend to listen, but whose precepts have no real influence now on the nation.

A Church which tells us that we are but pilgrims here, strangers journeying to a better land, that all our efforts are to be directed towards making our citizenship of that eternal city sure and abiding, and that we are to despise and renounce this temporal life; crowning a State which devotes all its energies to improving and embellishing this life, making this world happy and comfortable for the human animal, banishing as much as possible all thought and wish for the world to come.

It seemed some huge, childish game played in the beautiful old Abbey – the solemn Peers carrying their glittering toys and taking it all so seriously – the beautiful peeresses in their velvet and ermine robes – the gaudy ecclesiastics, then the dignified strained King with his lovely Queen, the princes and princesses with their great long trains sweeping after them.

The thought of little insignificant me in white chiffon and pearls looking on at all these magnificences amused me greatly but I was seated next to Lady Jane Taylor and gradually I began to feel sick as she smelt like a stuffy old goat. I suppose I looked faint as a kind man (Sir William Devereau) sent a bottle of smelling salts across the aisle. . . . it was very cold, and I had got terribly chilled, and was so ill when I got home I could not go up to Scotland with Ian to-night, which was disappointing. I longed to wake in Scotland to-morrow and see the blue hills. I had not seen him at all as he was riding in the procession. I expect he finds his wife rather dull as all the lovely Social crew are in hot pursuit after him, he is the last and smartest thing 'the man of the moment,' his wife a terrible handicap in their eyes. Even the somewhat scattered remnants of 'The Souls' entice him to their select parties and have to put up with me as he *won't* accept invitations unless I am included.

I had an awful drive home with the crowd pressing up to the windows – there were no blinds on my brougham windows, and they stared in at poor me sick and faint and alone inside; pressing their horrid faces against the glass as we had to go very slowly, stopping every now and then. The long fast, the cold, and this slow jolting movement of the brougham drawn by our old horse Gold completely did for me." [Saturday August 9th 1902, 3 Chesterfield St.]

In October, the royal procession of the new King and Queen took place through the streets to London. " . . . **Ian was riding in it, but I felt** too illish to go to the Horse Guards to wait for such a long time to see it pass and had resigned myself to bed and a lonely day; however, Lord Alwyne arrived with two seats on the House of Commons stand where he could take me after lunch at 2-30, straight, with no wait, so I went with him and he was very kind and looked after me delightfully. The Queen looked a lovely Queen talking away happily to the King as they passed. I hope it is true that she is happy with him at last. Very stately and grand looked the procession at Westminster, with a lovely background of softly tinted sky, the clouds breaking up all over it and peals of great bells clashing as the King and Queen passed.

It was curious looking on, beside Lord Alwyne at Ian so handsome and grand riding by in the procession. My Ian looked splendid in his blue coat which spread out behind him from his shoulders over his horse – he had his conquering air on. . . . " [Saturday 24th October 1902]

Afterwards, Jean went with Lord Alwyne Compton to his house, 5 Balfour Place. " . . . he showed me all the lovely old furniture he bought at Dieppe. Mary is away and as I sat and waited for him in the hall I wondered what life would have been like had I married him as I once longed to do and am so thankful now that I did *not*." [Saturday 24th October 1902 contd.]

With the coronation of the new King and Queen, the fashionable Edwardian era, as it was known even then, was ushered in. The moneyed elite, the power base of Britain and the Empire, entertained lavishly. Part of the season was spent going from one house party to the next, the largest of which would conclude with a ball. Guests stayed overnight or remained in the house for several days, each with their own entourage of servants. A typical scene was when, after dinner, the ladies retired to Mrs Paget's (later Lady Paget's) bedroom to prepare for a ball. Several royal princesses were there, including Princess Henry of Pless, wearing "**bright blue**". Lady Helen Vincent, wife of Sir Edgar Vincent, a Conservative MP and daughter of the 1st Earl of Faversham, looked " . . . **exquisite in silver and blue**". Mrs Paget's bedroom was " . . . **a wonderful scene of extravagant exaggerated luxury – the French bed with twenty different coloured pillows, the dressing table crammed with gay boxes of paint and powder, huge cut glass bottles of essence and scent of every description, and a cluster of lovely women with hand glasses and powder puffs doing up their faces like a gorgeous flight of humming birds** chattering and scattering the wildest gossip in every direction, shattering to shreds the character of every one and every thing." [July 23rd 1902]

From the time of Ian's return from South Africa, the Hamiltons were much in demand at fashionable dinner parties. Joe Chamberlain was a Liberal MP and Secretary of State for the Colonies in Lord Salisbury's Government. " . . . **Dined at Claridge's with the Duke and Duchess of Somerset to meet Joe Chamberlain and his wife – just we six.**

We discussed Buckle's 'History of Civilisation' also from the point of view of being able to foretell history by the past; then he and Ian began to discuss the South Africa question, this was the real object of the dinner party as Ian was anxious to have a talk with him before he (Joe Chamberlain) went to South Africa. Ian was defending the Boer Generals' action in going abroad to ask for money, making excuses for it, which Mr. Chamberlain would not have. Ian described how sad they were about the necessity, they are now so poor, all their farms and homesteads have been burned, etc., and especially spoke strongly in favour of General de La Rey and the great influence he has in South Africa, which Ian thought we could rely on if we trusted him, but Mr. Chamberlain said he would not trust any of them an inch, and that he would not see one of them without a shorthand writer being in the room; he said they were now begging for a private interview with him. I seemed to see the man so clearly as he spoke, clever, clear, incisive and rather mean – no enthusiasm or generosity at all. I loved Ian for what he said and he looked fine as he held his own with the great Joe; generous and full of pity and also full of praise for a brave enemy.

Mr. Chamberlain said he had been making enquiries and that General Botha's character in his financial dealings before the war were not without reproach; he said he knew what they wished to say in his interview, to urge breach of contract and faith and to say now Lord Kitchener was safely on the sea that he had promised them an amnesty. Ian said 'Well, Lord Kitchener did hold out hopes of amnesty,' and Mr. Chamberlain replied 'Well I shall say to them "He hoped and you hoped, but your hopes are founded on nothing."

Mrs. Chamberlain is a little dear. I wonder if she loves him? His teeth are very black and he looks cunning, no ideality about him at all, but he has force and character." [3rd November 1902, 3 Chesterfield St.]

Prince and Princess Christian, the parents of Queen Alexandra, invited Jean and Ian to visit, which Jean did not much look forward to but Helen Dyck Cunningham advised her that the invitation was looked upon as a royal command. "... **We arrived here at tea-time to-night. Ian wanted to walk up but a Royal carriage had been sent to meet us and Lord Rowton, who drove up with us, dissuaded him – said the Christians would not like it.... at tea I felt rather shy; having to say 'Ma'am' and 'Your Royal Highness' bothers me. Ian described various amusing incidents which had happened to the German officers accompanying the Kaiser, who landed at Folkestone this morning. Ian had gone with Lord Roberts to meet him, wearing his new Order of the Prussian Crown with its lovely blue ribbon which matches his eyes. . . . he dashed into my room and made me execute a war dance with him, I in very scant attire and he in all his grandeur.**

Princess Christian roared with laughter over his stories and threw up her fat hands at the misfortunes of the poor Germans, saying, 'Oh, I know them, I know them well! not one is to be trusted, not one,' in guttural German tones." [Saturday 8th November 1902 Cumberland Lodge]

Jean made a courtesy call on Mrs Botha, wife of one of the greatest of the Boer generals, Louis Botha, who was staying at Horrex's Hotel in the Strand, London. "... **I called out to Ian from the stair as we started, to ask if the Botha's farm had been burned and thought he said 'no'. She was very dignified and rather charming and was quite nicely and simply dressed, with pretty hair. Presently I said General Botha had been telling me about their beautiful farm and she asked if I would like to see it and brought me three photographs, one of the charming farm with the flowers and pampas grass round it, the next a thick volume of smoke and the next a heap of ruins; it gave me such a shock I could scarcely bear it and I said so and my eyes filled with tears till I could no more see the photos. But once started she seemed to like to talk of it and told me they lived there for 14 years and planted every tree and flower themselves there and that all their family papers had been burned." [11th November 1902]**

The Hamiltons tried to foster good relations with the defeated Boers. Amongst their guests for lunch was Winston Churchill, who had been taken prisoner and made an historic escape with the aid of John Howard, Manager of the Transvaal and Delagoa Bay Colliery at Witbank. The

Boers had offered a reward for Winston's capture which they put out on posters 'Wanted Dead or Alive'.[2] " . . . **We had a most interesting little luncheon party here to-day; General de la Rey, the Bothas, Ian Malcolms, Madeline Stanley, Winston Churchill and Frank Mildmay. I was dismayed when we first sat down to luncheon as the silence was profound, no one seemed inclined to break it and it was really painful till I laughed and said foolishly 'Angels must be passing round the table' and then talk began. Botha told us Spion Kop had been the most disastrous engagement for them, and that they had been quite unable to understand our evacuation of the position. Winston told us many details of his escape, the Bothas listening with round excited eyes. Mrs. Botha called out once across the table 'Oh, I always knew he was a traitor' when Winston mentioned the name of the man who succoured him after his escape. Winston hastened to defend him."** [12th November 1902]

Whilst staying with Marie and Leo de Rothschild (he was a million-aire banker) at Ascot Wing, near Leighton Buzzard, Jean met the new Prime Minister, James Arthur Balfour, who had succeeded his uncle, Lord Salisbury. " . . . **having a delightful conversation at dinner last night with the Prime Minister did elate and send me happy to bed. I have always felt enthusiastic about him;** *everything* **about him is charming and stimulating.**

Mr. Balfour started by saying to me that he thought any class or set of people struck one unfavourably *en masse*, **whether they were politicians, artists or soldiers, I said, 'Yes, you mean when you get to know them personally their individuality impresses you.' I ought to have said 'When you get to know them individually their powers impress you** *through* **their personality and they can be dealt with,' but I think he knew what I meant. He seems depressed on the subject of large bodies of men; they must indeed be difficult to manipulate; often a solid mass of stupidity. I asked him if he did not think we were pro-gressing as life led us on, that the tendency was on and up by degrees. I was thinking of Watts' 'Progress,' which he did not know, and then we talked of Burne-Jones and Rossetti; he told me of the Persian series of Burne-Jones' pictures which he has.**

I told him I had fallen in love with a man to-day, a man I was sorry to have missed by 50 years – Douglas Jerrold, whose engaging face I saw in the National Portrait Gallery to-day. I made him laugh by

telling him the story of the dull bore who said in the hearing of Jerrold, that a certain tune always carried him away – 'Can no one whistle it?' Douglas Jerrold remarked.

The old Duchess of Devonshire is here; everyone seems much afraid of her, she is indeed fearfully and wonderfully made up. . . . no women are born now-a-days like this, she is 'the last of the Mohicans.' Her wig and rouge are affronting, 'no deception, gentlemen,' but what character in every look and gesture. We sat in the sun together this morning and talked for quite a long time. I asked her how she liked Mr. Sargent's portrait of her granddaughters I said 'You did not approve of his idea of painting them in their shooting costumes,' and she snapped out, 'No, however did you know of that?' I discreetly did not reply, for it had been my suggestion to Mr. Sargent. I had told him how interesting and picturesque they had looked in their shooting costumes. Lady Diana, short-skirted with her gun had struck me very much at Knowsley and Mr. Sargent was delighted with this idea, and when he went to Knowsley made a sketch of the three girls in their shooting dresses. The old Duchess was furious, Sargent told me, and said, 'My granddaughters will not go down to posterity in that fast costume,' so they are now grouped under an orange tree all in virgin white. . . ." [Sunday 8th March 1903 Ascot Wing]

Mrs de Rothschild insisted that Jean should play golf with the Prime Minister. " . . . I feel faint still when I think of it. I protested that it was impossible, as I was only a beginner and could not play, but she insisted, so to my horror I found myself in front of a ball, a driver in my hand and Arthur Balfour my partner. At once I drove the ball into the nearest bush, to his speechless disgust. I made, however, a very good putt afterwards: and felt better when I had told Mr. Balfour how terrified I felt; as yesterday I had been warned not even to mention golf to him as he abhorred women on the golf links. Mr. Balfour laughed and asked who had said this, and I told him Nellie Sellar [Ian's secretary], and he said that was thanks to his sister-in-law, Lady Francis, who insisted on palming off her own dislike of women playing golf on him. I enjoyed the game immensely and we came off all square with Mrs. Leo and Lord Wolverton.

It was a lovely day, and after lunch I played golf with Ian, which I loved. Mr. Balfour took me into to dinner. We discussed Chesterton's Essays, 'London Types,' which I am reading now; Mr. Balfour said he remembered little of them, but thought that was in their favour, as 'essays of that description ought to be evanescent like good conversation.' " [Sunday 8th March 1903 Ascot Wing contd.]

As a guest of Lady Sarah Wilson, daughter of the seventh Duke of Marlborough, Jean dined for the first time with the newly crowned King Edward VII. Alice Keppel, the King's lover (and great-grandmother of Camilla Parker Bowles), was there, and another great favourite of the King's, Mrs George West, formerly Lady Randolph Churchill (and mother of Winston Churchill), whose husband, Lord Randolph having died, was Lieutenant George Cornwallis-West. Lady Sarah was a sister of the late Lord Randolph Churchill. " . . . We dined with Lady Sarah Wilson to meet the King to-night: wore my black and silver dress, an old one. None of my other dresses seemed suitable but I felt nervous in case I should be looked on with disfavour by Lady Sarah, as I know the King hates black. However, I was reassured when I saw Muriel Beckett in black velvet; a gentle little dove she looked, soft amongst all the smart hard dames. I sank down beside her and with a sigh of relief she turned to me and said, 'Thank God something *human* has come into the room. Mrs. George West, Mrs. Keppel, Lady Howe and dear dowdy Lady Cranbourne were there, her peace of mind disturbed by the lovely Worth dress of oyster satin worn by Mrs. George Keppel. . . . she has no idea of clothes at all. She confessed to me the memory of Mrs. George Keppel's would crush her for some time to come. Beautiful gowns in a room like Lady Sarah's *are* a great joy, and Mrs. George Keppel's gave me pleasure to remember.

I have never met the King at a small party before and all the little curtseys and the very deep ones amused and interested me: Then Lady Sarah walking up to him, dipped, and taking his arm walked off to the dining room, and we straggled after.

This is the King's first dinner party since his operation and everyone was astonished at what he drank. First sherry with soup then champagne *ad lib*: after the savouries, tumblers of strong, dark-brown Edinburgh ale were passed round; the King, to Ian's stupefaction, drank two! Old brandy followed with coffee; then followed a succession of whiskies and sodas throughout the evening. Ian told me all this. I did not notice what he drank: After dinner and a talk with Alice Keppel, the King came and addressed a few words to me, asked me if I had gone to South Africa, and when I said I had not as my husband did not wish me to go, he said, 'Quite right, quite right,' in very guttural tones. Presently he asked if I played Bridge, and I said I had no brains for Bridge, and could never remember the cards which had been played, which seemed to surprise him unpleasantly; not thinking much of me he departed to his Bridge whilst we had to sit yawning and amusing ourselves as best we could till one o'clock in the morning. About twelve, hot soup was handed round, and Jennie West complained too loudly, to Lady Sarah, 'My dear girl, if you feed him on condiments he will never go.' I was buried in a deep sofa with a boring man who would admire my wonderful pearls, and they are imitation!

When H.M. had departed Ian said to me in a tone of deep and loud relief, 'For Heaven's sake, old girl, say good-night and come home *now*.' " [16th March 1903]

In May, Jean had her first Royal **"private entrée"**. Wearing a magnificent gown of oyster satin, undoubtedly influenced, if not entirely copied, from Alice Keppel's, Jean presented Gwen Kitson at Court. " . . . **it was most amusing; I made my curtsey immediately after the Diplomatic Corps, and was shown to a seat beside Lady Lansdowne, just opposite the King and Queen, where I had a capital view of all the curtseying ladies. How ungraceful they were, a nightmare of ungrace, not one graceful curtsey did I see, and most of them looked plain, even lovely women like Lady Balcarres – she looked too dark – I did not recognise her and thought she must be a Native Princess of some sort, the light was so unbecoming. The King and Queen looked imposing. The Queen visibly smiled at some of the women's get-up; one woman had on a sort of muslin curtain with a piece of whalebone at the end to keep it out, it looked like a sail. The Queen had smiled rather sweetly at me as I made my curtsey, and I could not help smiling back – then I suddenly got self-conscious and began to wonder if I ought to turn my back on their Majesties, and half turned round again after I had walked on. I saw several women seized by the same panic and it looked horrid, as if they were familiarly looking round to show how much at ease they were, and to see if they could see any more Royalties. We could see from our raised seats all the ladies being marshalled through a distant door to pass on in their turn; with their plumes and bouquets they looked like parterres of flowers when seated, and very mysterious like floating ghosts with their long veils as** they moved along the long row of seats being emptied one after another.

Mrs. Henry Lawson all in black looked more picturesque than anyone, and Gwen Kitson, whom I was presenting looked charming in spite of her paint – she is staying with us. It is such a pity she dyes her hair red-yellow now, and paints most shockingly. I could never have recognised her; looking at her it's difficult to believe she can be still the same demure cynical little maiden I knew so well at Simla.

My dress was lovely, I was highly pleased with it, so was Ian – oyster satin, trimmed with old silver lace, a tight fitting bodice and long sleeves after the style of Charles II., a transparent tissue train covered with ecru chiffon and caught up with gold flowers. We had supper afterwards at the Palace, and the Chinese Minister . . . told Ian he admired his poetry and always repeated some of it before he went to sleep – so we both came home happy." [Sunday 10th May 1903]

Not all encounters with the gentry were a success, many were boring failures and one, at least, was not what Jean was accustomed to, when she and Ian visited Admiral Lord Charles Beresford and his wife. " . . . In the afternoon we drove to Ham to the Charlie Beresford's; found Lord Charlie in bed with gout and she [Lady Beresford] surrounded with fat dark men, singers and sculptors of sorts; she gave us atrocious cold bitter tea and despatched me to the bedside of Lord Charlie, where I found Margie Orr Ewing beguiling him with horrible tales. I made one or two futile efforts to get away, stopped by Margie, who pointed out that if I left so must she; as Lady Charlie would object to her sitting alone with Lord Charlie. He told me I had such a lovely voice that even if I were sitting behind a screen he could sit and listen to it for hours. Although he is so very Irish, this did astonish me. In spite of the flattery I felt wretched, sitting there laughing at what made me sick; his first story of getting into bed with the Bishop of Winchester, instead of with his last love – as he mistook her bedroom door and crept into his bed in the dark – did make me laugh but as, encouraged by our applause, he proceeded after that to tell us all that ever he did – nausea crept over me.

Margie always manages to make conversation centre round sex, and with Lord Charlie, of course, she had no difficulty whatever, he chuckled with delight at her every allusion. She is very attractive and it seemed to excite her that Lord Charlie said broadly every now and then 'How fascinating you are, Lady Margie, what fun you are.' Finally I escaped – went to cool my burning cheeks in the cool pure air and gasped with relief to find myself alone in the garden." [Sunday 5th June 1903]

Dinner with the Humphrey Wards and a ball afterwards made up for the experience. Jean " ... sat next Humphrey Ward, who had to fly off immediately after dinner to write an article on the murder of Queen Draga and King Alexander of Servia, which has shocked Europe to-day ... " Then on to Wimborne House, where Jean danced the hours away with George Peel and Mat Ridley and went to supper with Margie Orr Ewing. [11th June 1903] Next day, a "brilliant dinner" at Clinton Dawkins produced " ... lovely rooms, lovely music, lovely women, lovely food and drink, and lovely was my expensive Empire gown of white and gold, which shimmered between Austen Chamberlain and Sir Pom McDonald. It was *embarras de richesse*, and I thoroughly enjoyed myself. After dinner, seated on a divan discoursing about golf with Arthur Balfour, and listening to beautiful cello playing. . . ." [12th June 1903]

Jean and Ian were staying with Lord and Lady Wimborne (Ivor and Cornelia Guest). Lady Wimborne's maiden name was Spencer-Churchill, and she was an aunt to Winston Churchill. Also staying were Viscountess Alice Guest, who was married to the Wimborne's son, Ivor, and Viscountess Rosey Ridley, the Wimbornes' daughter. " ... We arrived in the dark, and I saw only a part of the house from my window – it looks picturesque – in the Elizabethan style; the inside is very lovely and comfy, masses of richly coloured flowers everywhere, principally red geraniums.

. . . A huge party here – mostly Free traders. Ernest Beckett took me in to dinner last night; he obviously did not want to which was damping, and I sat next Sir Edgar Vincent. . . . however I got on with them both and enjoyed myself – in fact had an exciting talk with Ernest Beckett, who is really delightful to talk to, though terribly ugly, with his awful ears, which I noticed the first time I met him with Jack Poynder in India years ago.

Sir Edgar Vincent would discuss the War Office with me, feeling it ought to be my subject, and that he might pick up something useful, which needless to say, he did not. There was a terrible draught blowing from the door where the food came in – I was seated at the end of the table and suffered much from this.

Such lovely women here – Lady Helen Vincent, Pamela Lytton, Mrs. Ivo Guest, Lady Chesterfield, etc., but Lady Helen makes them all look insignificant. Sir Edgar told Lady Donoughmore last night that beauty in women did not appeal to him, which is blasphemy, seeing he is married to the loveliest woman in Europe – she gives but him, and can give him nothing more, rumour says.

I am reading 'Anna Karenina' again for the fourth time – its wonderful genius does surprise me afresh: the pictures of Russian smart society might be pictures of London to-day – all types are identical – Muriel Beckett lives and moves in his pages, and how well one knows 'Safo' in London, and the way of her adorers, and Princess Betsy rather like Lady Sarah Wilson. 'The smart set then had to hold,' Tolstoi says, 'firmly on to the Court with one hand, in case they should be mistaken for the *demi-monde*, with whose ways and tastes, these were absolutely identical. . . . " [December 2nd 1903 Canford Manor]

Many of these social gatherings were an opportunity for the men to discuss politics in private, behind closed doors. A debate raged in Parliament for years over Free Trade, whether the Imperial economy should be protected by tariffs or whether it would improve with completely free trade. " . . . We have been engaged to come to this party for *four* months – it was really an absurdly long invite, and I fancy has some political significance. Winston, Ian's friend, arrives to-morrow, he is always full of mischief.

Lady Helen Vincent, I find, makes the party here rather difficult, as Pamela Lytton and Lady Chesterfield, Rosy Ridley and Alice Guest, although not her friends – in fact I think, hardly knowing her – are all determined to be with her, especially Pamela and Lady Chesterfield, and if not with her, at least with one another and they, even in one day, have decidedly separated themselves from the rest of the party, and constituted themselves the smart brigade – the dowdy brigade surrounds our hostess, Lady Wimborne, Lady Lucy Hicks Beech, Miss Elliott, Mrs. Seeley, Miss Hicks Beech and Lady Donoughmore; I play about between the two. Pamela, Rosy and Alice Guest, if they are for a moment left out by their own party, put up with me.

. . . Alice Guest is delicious, fresh and spontaneous – not yet spoilt by the 'contagion of the world'. . . ." [December 3rd 1903 Canford Manor]

Pamela Plowden had been an old girl friend of Winston Churchill's, and had recently married the second Earl of Lytton. " . . . I was glad for Pamela last night; she had a triumphant moment when Winston Churchill arrived and came up to shake hands with her just before dinner; she was standing before the fire, looking very lovely in white satin, her wedding dress, I think, trimmed with fur and diamonds, she was talking to Lady Helen Vincent and me – he was so overpowered by her beauty he quite forgot to say 'How do you do?' to Lady Helen, who teased him about this and he hastily rectified his mistake, but his eyes went back to Pamela, and I remembered the little scene she had told me about with such bitter tears, when in a ballroom he had gone up to her, and brutally asked her 'if she had no pride, because he had heard she was going about saying that Winston had treated her badly.' She did not speak to him: I was glad of that, and he fell back and stood beside her husband – such a contrast, these two men! One delicate, poetical, priggish – the other full of animal force, vital, brutal.

Lord Wimborne took Pamela in to dinner as Countess of Lytton, and she swept triumphantly past them both in her loveliness, as they stood talking there. . . ." [December 3rd 1903 Canford Manor contd.]

In winter society women wore fashionable tweed suits. " . . . I had bought a new tweed dress for this party, though I knew it was extravagant, but felt I must. Alas! when I put it on yesterday it looked so terribly common and it was quite impossible to appear in it, and I hastily put on an old tweed cloak, and a hideous hat. I felt so dowdy with all those lovely women in smart tweeds, it depressed me all day, and depresses me still to think of it. . . .

Later. Lady Helen has just been sitting with me; rather exciting this, for me, but alarming. I *adore* her beauty: we discussed Tolstoi in the 'Kreutzer Sonata' – she is against his doctrine and finds it monstrous; she is very determinedly human and determinedly optimistic, I had to leave my vague chaotic world, and step into such an orderly definite one when talking to her. She accepts everything as all right – no kicking against the prick there – Spring, Summer, Autumn, Winter, all right in their right times, and also she thinks the lower you strike your roots the higher you can soar (this with reference to human passion, which she defends with regard to D'Annunzio and Duse); I find her exquisite, but too dogmatic. . . ." [December 3rd 1903 **Canford Manor** contd.]

The women also got involved in discussing political matters. " . . . **Rosy also came and sat with me. I found she had been discussing Fiscal policy with the Free Trade ladies, and evidently been worsted, and she was annoyed. Very delightful of them both to come and amuse me, I feel very gratified.**

Last night after dinner Winston Churchill told me how Mr. Brodrick had been confiding in him about his new appointment at the India Office, and how strange he felt there, whereas at the War office everything was at his fingers' end. I wanted to say, 'As well might poor Mr. Brodrick have soothed his sorrow with a rattlesnake, or rested his head on a porcupine,' I always long to say something rude to Winston." [December 3rd 1903 **Canford Manor** contd.] St John Brodrick's move to the India Office was to prove remarkably fortunate for the Hamiltons before too long.

Jean had a cold and the drafts at Canford did not help so Ian gave up his day's shooting and brought her home. They travelled by train and shared a carriage with Helen Vincent and Pamela Lytton, both of whom got out at Vauxhall. " **. . . I could hear Lady Helen saying, 'he [Ian] is charming, but I don't care much about her – affected and gives herself tiresome airs, and I fancy rather selfish,' and Pamela agreeing. . . .** " It is interesting to hear someone else's opinion of Jean, and needless to say Pamela and Helen went down somewhat in Jean's estimation and she was glad to be home. " **. . . I am glad to be back in my own nest, these visits are full of vanity and vexation of spirit; but there was more in this party than that – it was a deep long planned Free Trade conspiracy against the Conservative Party. After Winston arrived a big confab took place in the billiard room, from which everyone of doubtful opinion was excluded: no doubt Joe and Arthur Balfour would tremble in their shoes if they knew of these going on; Sir Michael Hick Beech [sic] is the moving devil – Ian Malcolm is in it too.**" [December 4th 1903]

Jean and Ian broke with tradition and instead of spending Christmas 1903 and the New Year of 1904 at Deanston with Jean's family accepted invitations to the country houses of their friends, moving from one distinguished household to another, and meeting up with the fashionable sets of the time.

On Christmas Day they were the guests of Lord and Lady Londonderry, at historic Wynyard, in County Durham. In October, King Edward VII had held a meeting of the Privy Council there and the documents connected with the Council were headed 'At the Court at Wynyard'.[3] Other guests assembled for the Christmas festivities: the George Becketts, the Majoribanks, Geengie McDonald, the Grenfells, and Muriel Beckett. " . . . I don't like being away from my own people to-day.

Lady Londonderry, sad and distrait to-night, full of thoughts of dead Harry White – I feel sorry for her.

'Thou wilt not love to live, unless thou live to love;' I tried to say these lines to her, but could not quite remember them – they are very *apropos* to Nellie Londonderry she certainly lives to love.

Ian stayed for Communion after the Xmas Service in the chapel this morning; he came and told me shyly he was going to stay, and I thought, hoped I would; his dear head looked lovely as I looked regretfully back at him from the church door, but I *could* not go. Afterwards he came and took me on his knee, and asked why I did not go with him, and said we would go together on New Year's Day. . . . " [Christmas Day 25th December 1903 Wynyard]

There was the customary exchange of gifts, and the George Becketts gave Jean " . . . a slight gold ring with a single diamond which I can easily wear with my other rings." Jean read lines by her favourite poet: " '. . . This one heart gave me all the Spring' – I read this exquisite line in Browning's 'Pompilia' this morning. Ian has gone hunting. This place rather depresses me, and Lady Londonderry's atmosphere is not sympathetic. [December 26th 1903] Ian was opening a rifle range for the Londonderrys and giving out prizes but Jean was bored and eager to leave: " . . . I hate this black country. . . ." [December 28th 1903 Wynyard]

The conversation was not sophisticated enough for Jean. " . . . Mab Beckett and I were walking with Lady Londonderry the other day, and discussing 'Anna Karenina', and Lady Londonderry maintained a woman who had a love had much better stay in her husband's house, and not break up the home by going off with him, and Mab supported her. I felt I was on very delicate ground but defended the women who did and said I admired her for giving up everything without calculation – it might be stupid, but was fine. We got quite hot

about it. . . ." Lady Londonderry quoted an instance of someone she knew **" . . . and said, 'No doubt she did not think herself any worse than other people, and considered that she was harshly treated, but she, Lady L. considered it was quite right, if she chose to proclaim her affair to the world, the world must take notice.' I admitted there was some truth in what she said, but maintained it was better for the character of the woman to go away openly with her lover, if a lover she must have, than to stay on in her husband's house, living a double life.**

Lady Londonderry interests, and repels me. I feel when I am with her I can only listen, never could I make her see my point of view – she would only feel, 'All your passions matched with mine are as moonlight unto sunlight, And as water unto wine.' " [December 29th 1903 **Wynyard**]

On 30 December Jean left Wynyard on her own, without telling Lady Londonderry she was going, and arrived at Gopsall, the home of Lord and Lady Howe. Lady Georgina Howe's maiden name was Spencer-Churchill, another aunt to Winston. Lord Howe (the fourth Earl Howe) was formerly Richard George Penn Curzon, a Conservative MP. In her room, Jean sat scribbling in her diary of her apprehension at the thought of facing the party downstairs and she did not have Ian's arm to lean on. Her experience earlier that month whilst staying with Lord and Lady Wimborne at Canford Manor seemed to have undermined her confidence. Her clothes had not been as grand as the other ladies', she had not been the focus of attention and, worst of all, she had accidentally overheard the disparaging remarks being made about her on the return train journey. Edwardian high society in England was a far cry from her Simla days, riding about in a rickshaw, her ayah by her side. **" . . . I am rather frightened to get up and go downstairs, these women are very alarming to me. . . . they are all terrific, and Lord Howe will be away shooting. . . . "** [31st Dec. **1903**]

Other guests included Alice Keppel, now at the height of her power as King Edward VII's lover; Lord Stavordale and his wife, Helen, nicknamed Birdie, formerly Lady Vane-Tempest-Stewart, daughter of Lady Londonderry; Lord Bertie Vane-Tempest; Mrs George West; Lady Sarah Wilson, sister-in-law to Mrs West; and Prince Francis of Teck. Lord Stavordale (Stavey) was an old boyfriend of Alice Keppel's. The moment of truth had arrived: Jean had to go downstairs and she would be either a success or a failure in 'society'.

In October 1903, Jean's father, Sir John Muir, had died, leaving the James Finlay company with assets of 74,000 acres, 70,000 workers and well over £4 million in capital.[4] Sir John's will was published in the newspapers. It was now public knowledge that Jean was independently wealthy, though she was completely unaware of her elevated status. Downstairs, Jean was a great success and enjoyed herself " . . . **quite immensely. Everyone was so charming to me – at the shooting lunch Prince Francis sat next me and made me laugh a great deal. Ian tells me he was asking all about my sisters, and saying 'They are a wonderfully pretty family'. Ian says it was because he saw Father's will in the papers, and was astonished how much money he left, and that he was asking if there were any of us still unmarried."** [31st December 1903 Gopsall** contd.]

Alice Keppel, who was a close friend of the Howes, possessed a pleasant nature and was never heard to say an unkind word to anyone. Many parallels have between drawn between Alice and her great-granddaughter, Mrs Camilla Parker Bowles. Just as Alice was to say of her affair with the King, 'My job is to curtsy first . . . and then jump into bed',[5] over half a century later, the young Camilla Shand would charm the present Prince Charles at a London nightclub haunt of The Beatles with, 'My great-grandmother and your great-great-grandfather were lovers. So how about it?'[6]

Alice greeted Jean warmly and Jean was charmed by her. They became friends, both being of Scottish origin, and Alice would later frequent Jean's dinner parties. A great beauty, with 'a natural hour glass figure, large turquoise eyes and light chestnut hair', Alice was 'soft spoken and graceful' in her manner.[7]

There was a rare glimpse of the Keppel children, Violet aged ten and Sonia aged four. Violet would become the famous lesbian lover of Vita Sackville-West, and marry Denys Trefusis whilst continuing her affair with Vita. Sonia married Roland Cubitt, heir to the Cubitt fortune and title, third Baron Ashcombe. " . . . **Mrs. Keppel's little girl, Sonia, came in at tea time, dressed as Admiral Keppel, every detail correct, medals and all: she looked a duck, and Mrs. Keppel tried to make her come and talk to me; she told her 'Here was quite a new lady', – but she evidently did not fancy me, and was quite rude – looked at me with deep distrust . . . ."** [New Year's Day 1904 Gopsall]

Prince Francis of Teck took Jean into dinner and she sat between him and Lord Howe. " . . . **We had great fun singing songs, and making speeches.**" Mrs George West, Winston Churchill's beautiful mother, whose maiden name was Jennie Jerome: " **. . . stood on a chair and sang a merry song –**

> **'Ruby lips, ruby lips -**
> **Oh, who will kiss these ruby lips,**
> **When I am far away, far away?''**

the choruses were shouts –

> **'Some other man,**
> **I don't care a ———**
> **Some other man.''**

there were many verses . . .

> **'Who will pay these little bills?' etc.''**

At the New Year's Eve ball Jean danced with Sir Charles Hartopp and told him she had been unable to come to Gopsall the previous Christmas because she had been ill. With her usual sense of humour she said she thought she was going to die " **. . . and I *very* nearly said, 'I felt convinced the heading in the "Daily Mail" next morning would be "The Hartopp Case" – "Death of Lady Hamilton".' I danced quite a lot, and enjoyed myself vastly. I have not laughed so much for a long time. Lord Bertie Vane-Tempest is perfectly splendid fun, clever and amusing. . . ."** [New Year's Day 1904 Gopsall contd.]

The belle of the ball was undoubtedly Alice Keppel. " **. . . Lady Sarah and Mrs. George West danced the cake walk . . . . George West dances quite beautifully. Mrs. George Keppel, to my surprise, fascinates me – sometimes she looks beautiful – she is absolute woman, fully developed, strong and capable. In her soft, long, chiffon, tea gown she looked beautiful at tea, but at dinner, in a very low blue satin, with purple and green grapes wreathed in her hair, I did not admire her. She has beautiful shoulders, and her dress is cut very low at the back to show a brown mole in the centre of it, I could not help wondering how many men had kissed that mole? . . . "** [New Year's Day 1904 Gopsall contd.]

Alice's husband, George Keppel, was a fellow soldier of Ian's, in the

Gordon Highlanders, which may explain why Ian now refrained from kissing his wife. " . . . **Alice Keppel made us all stand outside for luck, to bring in the New Year. We all took hands and sung 'Auld Lang Syne' as the clock struck 12, and then everybody kissed everybody else, and to my surprise Lord Bertie Vane-Tempest kissed me, but Lord Howe only kissed my hand, and reproached me for being glum. I heard Lord Bertie boasting, 'I kissed Lady Hamilton'. Ian kissed everybody except Mrs. Keppel. I'd much rather have kissed her than anyone else had I been he; then we all drank hot punch, went back to the ballroom and danced again. I danced with Lord Howe, who dances badly, then Lady Howe proposed bridge, and poor Alice Keppel very weary, was dragged reluctantly off to play a rubber – it seemed a pity to begin the New Year so, and Lord Howe was whispering this to me when Lady Howe, a little deprecatingly I thought, came up and said, 'George, we will just have one rubber before we go to bed.'**

Mrs. Keppel looked sad and beautiful when they were singing Tosti's 'Good-bye' to-night – I wonder what she was thinking? . . . ." [**New Year's Day 1904** contd.]

Winston Churchill, now a youthful twenty-nine-year-old, arrived late and joined the spectacular New Year's Eve party. Jean could not like Winston or feel comfortable in his company but acknowledged that he furthered her husband's career. Of Winston, Ian said: ' . . . nobody, not even Lord Bobs in all his glory, has touched my life at so many points as Winston Churchill. . . . '[8] In years to come, Jean and Winston would find each other's company more interesting and agreeable. Winston had been Ian's closest friend since 1897, when they met on the North-West Frontier in India, and from that time they were like brothers. Winston is probably mentioned more often in their lives than anyone else. But for the moment, his extrovert personality was too much for Jean and conversation with him was always difficult. " . . . **Lady Warwick said once at dinner to Winston and me that she would rather be in bed with a dead horse than with Count Metternich: we had been discussing who was the best looking man we knew and I suggested Count Metternich! After that Winston announced 'I would not change my own face for those of any man!' I said something disparaging and he replied, 'Ah, you say that after an exhaustive study of my profile.' I replied, 'Yes, I have had an exhaustive study of your profile, *often*; but I infinitely prefer the back** of your head!' which made Birdie Stewart rock with laughter, and as Winston at that time meant to marry her he was wild." [14th June 1903]

" . . . Winston Churchill . . . after wandering all round the table was obliged to come and sit by me, as his name was placed there; I laughed and said: 'What a painful surprise for you'. He had only his cousin Francis (Lord Curzon) on his other side however, and he condescended to make himself quite agreeable, even delightful; and for the first time I felt how really attractive he could be, in a very dominating sort of way. . . .

. . . We had a perfect feast of music to-night. Mr. Frank Shuster sat by me, Lord Howe was on my other side, and Ian lay on a couch, reading poetry; it was close on 1 o'clock when we came upstairs, the strains of the Liebestod sweeping through me." [Later and still New Year's Day 1904 Gopsall]

On her way to bed, Jean found Ian in her room, " . . . sitting by my fire, rather excited and quite affectionate. I suddenly felt chilly, and sat down opposite him on the rug, and described the Goya engravings I had been looking at in Mrs. George West's book – they hurt and frightened me, they are so brutal, yet so wonderful. 'Sans Remede' haunts me, the criminal woman riding with a look of still proud agony on her face, and surrounded by such pitiless brutality – . . . . Why did I press him with this, he hates tragic sad things.

I could not sleep – I dreamed of Winston and his Mother – she *is* clever . . . . I skated with her yesterday afternoon, she skates beautifully – she does everything well. Winston told me last night his Father proposed to her the second day he saw her, and that he made up his mind to marry her the first moment he saw her. . . . " [Later and still New Year's Day 1904 Gopsall contd.]

Lord Howe took Jean round the gallery in his house, showing her the works of art hanging on the walls. They strolled along the historic landing and steps where the King was reputed to have first met and courted Alice Keppel, in 1898, when he was Prince of Wales.[9] " . . . Tonight after dinner I looked at all the pictures with Lord Howe, and discovered many beauties hidden away – A Ruysdael behind a screen – a Gainsborough landscape of great beauty, Claudes and Guypskiedell mixed up with rubbish, and many lovely pictures whose authors I could not guess. I begged Lord Howe to get an expert down, to catalogue and number them, and get them hung properly; many of them we could hardly see, one lovely Murillo hung high above a door. He promised he would, he showed me many interesting things, Admiral Howe's sword presented to him after the glorious 1st June, and the two little ships of wood each on fire, with the name of the battleships he had conquered.

Leo Shuster was playing the while lovely music – last night he played Dr. Elgar's 'Apostles', which I much liked, and the words I thought lovely – 'What are these wounds in Thy Hands?' 'They are the wounds which I received in the house of my friends.' " [Sunday 3rd January 1904 Gopsall]

Alice Keppel was always the focus for curiosity because of the powerful favour she held with the King. In private, Mrs West told Jean: " ... Alice Keppel seemed very anxious to be well informed, and to pass for a clever woman . . . it was shocking how initiated little Violet Keppel is. . . . " On Christmas morning, Mrs West said to her: " ... 'What a lovely brooch – is it a Xmas present? Who gave it to you?' Violet looked carefully all round the room, then whispered 'the King'. . . . " [Sunday 3rd January 1904 Gopsall contd.] Mrs West was herself a great favourite of the King's. On his Coronation day, she sat with Alice Keppel in the King's box at Westminster, laughingly dubbed 'the King's loose box'.

CHAPTER 4

Japan (1904–5)

"I felt furiously bitter, lonely and deserted, feeling my youth, my womanhood was all passing away – and why? When I was still young and loveable should I wait and wait and wait for Ian, when we were always 'strangers yet'." [16th September 1919]

Ian's letters to Jean, and her diary entries between February 1904 and 1905, concentrate on two important promotions in his career, and Jean's personal role in helping secure them for him.

When Ian wanted to convey his opinion at official levels he wrote to Jean, partly because she could intervene unofficially. If, for instance, Ian had approached his Commander-in-Chief, General Roberts, directly, about a commission, it would have been an official enquiry. Instead, he wrote to Jean who could follow up his enquiry with Roberts' wife, or his daughter, Aileen. It was in this unofficial way that women married to officers became involved in their husbands' careers in the army.

Jean helped Ian become an official observer of the Indian Army to the Japanese Army, though his mind had been originally set on becoming the British Army's official observer to the Japanese. The command of the Second Army Corps at Salisbury in England was being negotiated whilst Ian was in Manchuria and he would secure this also, with Jean's help.

Ian's tour of duty as Quarter Master General of the British Army at the War Office in London was coming to its normal end when Arnold-Foster became Secretary of State for War. There was a major reform of the War Office and many office holders were dismissed, some quite abruptly and with no immediately available new postings. Ian was one of these but agreed not to make a fuss with the promise that he would be given one of the prestigious new Army Corps commands. He expected to eventually receive the Second Army Corps (the Southern Command), at Salisbury. In the meantime he sought employment and, foreseeing the outbreak of war between Russia and Japan, set out in 1904 in his usual adventurous manner to Japan, in the expectation of becoming an official British observer with the Japanese Army. Jean could not accompany him; he wrote to her: " . . . **Tokyo . . . is a very asthmatic place. . . .** " [**May 30th 1904**]

When the expected cable confirming his appointment in Japan did not arrive from the War Office Ian found himself on the other side of the world without employment. A job had been promised him by an old friend, Lord Nicholson, whom Jean would come to detest: 'Old Nick', as she referred to him, proved to be Ian's arch-enemy. In desperation Ian appealed to Jean to try and do what she could to secure his appointment. The only means of communication was by letter or cable and he wrote, asking her to exert influence on the power elite of the day within the government, the Liberal opposition and the army high command. Jean willingly obliged, keeping a detailed account of her progress in her diary, a valuable example of the power of Edwardian women to protect and advance the careers of their husbands.

Ian's first letter, dated 7 February 1904, was sent from Marseilles. His main concern at this stage was whether he would get the Southern Command on his return.

Now, darling, a few little memos. This is a most critical period in our fortunes: perhaps *the* most critical and every little helps. I *think* Salisbury should be all right but hostile influences might easily intervene if Lord Bobs went, and if . . . the new Secretary of State would be an unknown factor. I have done one good thing I am sure by asking Ewart, who will run the Military Secretary business, to be my Chief Staff officer if I go. He is the best I could choose on his merits but it will also make him keen to get it for me. I think I also have a friend in Davidson, the King's Equerry and Esher has sworn (but he is not reliable) I shall have it whatever happens.

You should try and see something of the Arnold-Fosters and the Dilkes. One is present Secretary of State; the other is the Secretary of State who might be. It is a curious situation. The Board who should recommend me are French, Sir Evelyn Wood, the Duke of Connaught and Lord Grenfell. My best friend on that board by far is Evelyn Wood who will not want to go at all! As a matter of fact, however, the Secretary for State for War will be the man to do the trick one way or the other. But if I got a little success or notice out

of this Jap business, that would be the best way of all to make
certain of Salisbury.

See that Lord Bobs does not forget to cable to get me on the
Head Quarters Staff. I would have got Arnold-Foster to write to
Lord Lansdowne and would have seen the Jap Ambassador Baron
Hayashi but I was afraid by taking too much pains I might attract
too much notice and raise a hitch in some unexpected quarter ... it
would be well I think for Lord Bobs not to wait too long before
cabling.[21]

The letter concluded with a PS to the effect that once on the HQ staff his
pay should increase. They could always fall back on Jean's wealth but
Ian's concern for well-paid employment shows he was too proud to live
off her money alone.

Social connections were all important and in this Jean made a shaky
start. With experience she would become mistress of her art, fostering
good relations with politicians and army personnel. Her privileged background allowed her automatic access to such an elite; the rest was skill in
finding out information and persuading those with influence to help her
advance her husband's career.

Ian's next letter to her was sent on 8 February, 'from the packet boat':

As regards calls I am rather mad to think I forgot one important
thing in my hurried note from Marseilles. It was to call on, and try
and make friends with, Sir George and Lady Clarke. If you see them
you might say (what is true) that whilst they were deliberating I did
not like to make any social advances but that now the report was out
you hoped they would come and lunch, dine, go to the play or
whatever you like. If Sir George Clarke is made Secretary of the
Defence Committee of the Empire, he will be the most powerful
military person in the Empire, more so in some respects than the
Secretary of State.[2]

The 'report' Ian refers to was on the reorganisation of the War Office,
including the establishment of a Committee of Imperial Defence.

On Friday 9 February 1904 Jean gave a dinner party. Her guest list
included Arnold-Foster and his wife, Leo Amery and Ian's secretary, Nellie
Sellar. Jean decided to bypass Ian's advice and appeal to a different source

to influence his appointment. The Hamiltons had known Leo Amery (affectionately referred to as 'little Amery' or 'little Leo') since Ian's service in
the Boer War, when he was an influential *Times* leader writer.

Later that night, Jean wrote how she dealt with Ian's requests: "**. . . I
did not speak to Arnold-Foster about getting Ian attached officially to
the Headquarters in Japan. I felt it was better not. I consulted little
Amery after dinner and he said so too – he thinks he might be made to
represent India, and have some Indian officers under him, so I will
talk to Lord Roberts about this. . . .**" [9th February 1904]

Jean threw herself into a round of social activity, making visits and
giving luncheons and dinner parties, to which she invited Madeline
Brodrick, wife of St John Brodrick, the Secretary of State for India, Lord
Elphinstone, Gertrude Atherton and Colonel Rhodes. Some very unwelcome news emerged: "**. . . Sir William Nicholson is going out to Japan,
and taking Colonel Haldane with him, he is going as our representative. I don't like it at all – I feel it's taking the wind out of my Ian's
sails, and I am sure the wicked Sir William means to do this. . . .**" A
note was added, much later: "**. . . (Long afterwards Ian told me Rawly
[Sir Henry Rawlinson], after seeing him off at the railway station, came
back and found old Nick and gave him the idea to apply for this).**"
[10th February 1904, 3 Chesterfield St.]

Jean then "**. . . went off to an evening party at the Somersets,
where I wanted to catch Lady Bobs to ask her if it was true Sir
William Nicholson was going to Japan officially, but she said she knew
nothing, which I saw by her face was an excessive fib. Why did she say
this?**" [10th February 1904 contd.]

Colonel Haldane lunched with Jean, following which Lord Roberts
came to see her; "**. . . he was cheering and told me he was on his way to
see Lord Lansdowne, to ask him to get Ian attached to the Japanese
Head Quarters Staff as Commissioner.**" [11th February 1904]

But two days later Lord Roberts was dismissed from the War Office,
diminishing his influence, and Ian's career was left hanging in the balance.
"**. . . I went to see the Roberts family. Lord Roberts had been sent,
with no warning, an order from the Committee that his functions as
C.-in-C. were at an end, and that in future all orders would be signed
by the Secretary to the Committee. Lord Roberts walked up to the
War Office, lifted his hat from the peg there, and walked out in great
indignation; he told me this afternoon he sent to the Foreign Office to**

ask that Ian should be attached to the Japanese Headquarters Staff, and the answer he got was that 'Gen. Sir Ian Hamilton had gone off on leave to Manchuria to attach himself to the Russians'." [14th February 1904] Jean knew this to be completely untrue.

The following Thursday, Jean again went to see Lord and Lady Roberts. Lord Roberts told her: " . . . Arnold-Foster had written to him in reply to a letter, 'that Ian had very specially told him that he did not wish to have anything officially arranged for him in Japan'; this is most maddening and can't be true. I am glad to have Mr. Arnold-Foster coming to dine tonight; I feel very worried about my darling Ian." [18th February 1904]

That afternoon, Jean went to visit a friend, Molly Garstin, who was living with Charles Repington, the military correspondent for *The Times*. Repington, who was currently working on an article about the Boer War, told Jean: " . . . 'I am so delighted with your husband's letters, I have been going through them' . . . he said he had just come to that part of his History of the War, and that he had to be very careful, as he said, 'I suppose you know your husband has a great many enemies?' I said carelessly: 'I suppose all successful men have', but felt excited; I had foolishly imagined that Ian could have none, but the idea of his having enemies rather exhilarated me, and made me long to fight them." [18th February 1904]

The feeling stayed with Jean during her drive to the Grosvenor Club, where she met another friend, Frank Lyon ('little Lyon'), who had served with Ian in the Boer War. He, too, raised the spectre of 'Old Nick': " . . . 'Is Sir William Nicholson General Johnnie's friend?' He said it suggestively, and I said: 'Why?' He evidently very much is not, for Colonel A'Court [Repington] said to me also this afternoon, 'Does your husband like Sir William Nicholson?' I looked surprised, and I said I thought they were very good friends – he gave me the impression of being able to say a great deal to the contrary, if he liked." [18th February 1904]

That evening, Jean's dinner guests included Mr and Mrs Arnold-Foster, Captain Wilson, Henry Butcher, Edith Beaumont and 'little Leo' Amery. Afterwards she " . . . wanted to write a long letter to Ian. I had four letters from him this morning." [19th February 1904] Ian's letters took several days in transit so it is reasonable to assume that the letters she was referring to were those dated 9th, 10th, 11th and 15th February 1904.

9th February 1904 – Straits of Messines.
I like the idea very much of your being there and keeping in touch
with people. Try and see something of the paper men as you may
get news out of them to give me. I mean Spender [John Alfred
Spender, editor of the *Westminster Gazette*] and Amery. But do not
ask them together as they do not like one another, I don't think. I
wonder if any people have noticed my departure – I hope not.[3]

In his 10th February letter from near Port Said, Ian commented on the
various personnel changes during the recent War Office reorganisation
and advised Jean as to whom she could pass on his opinions where
they might be politically useful, particularly to the leaders of the
Liberal opposition who would eventually go on to form the next government in late 1905.

It has just occurred to me that you are sure to be questioned a good
deal regarding the new changes and that I have given you very little
information. Well the first thing is to tell you my true feelings and
then advise you as to how far to tell different categories of people.
    I feel then that the changes are in themselves good – but I feel
that it is always much more a question of *personnel* than of
machinery in such matters . . . it is unfortunate that Nick [Sir
William Nicholson] has been replaced by a man greatly his
intellectual inferior. Lyttelton has neither force of character,
industry or brains for such a billet. His straightness, kindness and
good sense will not make up for this.

Ian then discussed individuals in some detail, particularly deploring the
idea that his adored old chief, Lord Roberts, might be replaced by that
'authority on buttons', the Duke of Connaught. His closing lines show
how carefully he directed Jean's activities back in London.

You might give these as my views to any member of the Opposition
– Dilke – Asquith – Winston Churchill – if it comes naturally. If
you see Mrs Leo [de Rothschild] you might tell her.
    To members of the Government you will be more careful. To
Royal Circle people still more so.[4]

Ian's letter of 11 February, from Port Said, was a charming love letter but in his next he told her the devastating news that he had heard that Sir William Nicholson and Colonel Haldane were appointed as observers to the Japanese army ahead of him.

> *15th February, 1904*
> My own darling little sweetheart – How are you I wonder?
> Surrounded I fear by a sort of Zoological Gardens of snakes and lions! I am exceedingly fit though rather downcast by the Reuter saying Nick and Haldane have been accredited to the Jappy Army. If this is true where do I come in and yet I have taken rather a sporting chance by coming out at my own expense before the declaration of war on the promise of being cabled authority for this very billet?
>   The irony of the situation lies in the fact that when Arnold-Foster offered to help me in any way he could, it was Nick who advised against my first impulse to ask him to write to Lord Lansdowne to get me accredited at once. Nick urged . . . some official hitch might arise and that it was safer I should get right away, when I might rely entirely on him to see that I was duly accredited by cable before I arrived! . . . hardly was my back turned when Nick steps forward and secures the very position he had taken pains to assure me I should get!

After some lines doubting whether their 'luxurious friend', Nicholson, would really go on campaign with the Japanese, he pointed out:

> The only sort of document I have to show is the letter of Lord Knollys' telling me the King 'entirely approved' of my going to the front. I suppose you have left London now. If not and you get a chance of enquiring of Lord Bobs or Arnold-Foster about this you might do so. I have written to Aileen [Roberts] this morning.
>   If they cannot accredit another Lieutenant General to the Japanese, they might to the Russians although it would be recognised an unpleasant billet for an Englishman but I had rather have it than not have any position at all.[5]

From Aden, on 17 February 1904, Ian wrote to Jean of the 'pure bad news' as now even the Second Army Corps at Salisbury, which he was relying on upon his return home, was most uncertain. He supposed, that given a change of government, the Duke of Connaught would certainly give it to Kelly Kenny if he wanted it. 'I shan't fret much . . . I have done my best'.

In one of her letters to Ian, Jean had spoken of renting out the house which would have meant it would not be available for her to hold dinner parties at which she could exert her influence. She had also told him she was going to Rome on holiday.

His letter of 22 February 1904 was sent 'from the Indian Ocean' and forwarded to Jean at the Grand Hotel in Rome.

> By the way it comes suddenly into my head that we never
> congratulated the Reggie Talbots on his being made the Australian
> Governor in place of Sir George Clarke.
>
> I wonder what you will do about the house. Do whatever you
> like best dearest. It would be very nice in some ways if you kept in
> touch with people during the Season . . . if I do get the Army Corps
> we will have money enough next year although certainly it will be
> rather a struggle to exist till October if Nick has really done me out
> of my billet.[6]

Whilst Ian was away, Jean dealt with his mail and acted in any way she could on matters raised in letters addressed to him. "**. . . In opening Ian's letters today to forward to him I came across a notice from the War Office, from the new Army Council, to say they 'noticed in the daily papers, that Ian had left the United Kingdom, and as they could not find he had asked for, or obtained leave, they would like him to notify what country he intended to visit so he could have the necessary permit forwarded to him'. I was quite furious as of course Ian had leave given him by the Commander in Chief, Lord Roberts. . . .** "That evening, Jean dined with the Roberts, putting Lord Roberts in the picture about the inaccurate rumours being circulated. "**. . . While I was telling Lord Roberts this at dinner, General Grierson was listening, or rather observing me, as he was too far off to listen – he irritated me, as I thought of him going out with an Army Order to oust Ian, with his Chief Sir William Nicholson who hates and is jealous of Ian."** [26th February 1904]

Two days later, Jean received two further letters from Ian; "**. . . in one** he told me General Nic had urged him before he left, not to try and get officially attached to the Jappy Staff – he urged it was safer to get away at once, and Ian is very crest fallen about the way it has all worked out. I feel so worried about him and do trust his good luck will not desert him, and that all may turn out for the best – old Nic is the devil indeed, and not to be trusted."

That afternoon, Jean had a "**long talk with Lord Roberts . . . in Portland Place**" and found him to be "**very depressed and hurt about the way he has been treated**" over his removal from his position at the War Office. [**28th February 1904**]

By March, Jean had emerged triumphant from her efforts, contacting Ian with the wonderful news that he now had an appointment. St John Brodrick had made him the official observer of the Indian army. "**. . . I wired to Ian, to Saigon, this morning that it is arranged that he represents India. Lord Roberts told me this was arranged at Mrs. Beaufort's dinner.**" [**2nd March 1904**]

Jean dined with Lady Jeune, whose other guests included Lord and Lady Roberts, Sir George and Lady Clarke, Madeline St John Brodrick, Consuelo Marlborough, Rosie Ridley and Sir John French. There had been a misunderstanding between the Hamiltons and the St John Brodricks, brought about by comments made by Brodrick's wife, Madeline, to Jean, concerning Ian's views on a policy document produced by St John Brodrick, when he was Secretary of State for War and Ian was Quarter Master General of the Army. Jean realised she would have to be more careful how she handled St John Brodrick, who was now at the India Office and a key figure in Ian's career. "**. . . Ian asked me to be sure and show the Clarke's some attention, but I did not think it would be wise with Lady Roberts' and Madeline's eyes upon me, so I merely told her after dinner I was sorry not to have seen her when I called. . . . Sir John French, not looking so cock-a-hoop as I expected, seeing he is to command the First Expeditionary Force . . . very nice to me as usual . . . .**" [**5th March 1904**]

In his acknowledgement on 5 March of Jean's telegram, Ian attributed full credit to her for his success in gaining the commission:

My own darling wife,
Your telegram received here was best news I have heard for a long time – I wonder whom I have to thank for it after my better half?
Anyway it has made me feel very very happy and grateful. For now

I ought to be able to shove along and learn something; write
something, and possibly even do something.[7]

His next letter, dated 7 March, confirmed the good news:

> Have just got an official wire from Mr. Brodrick telling me I am
> appointed as a Representative from India. All now depends on
> myself . . . Anyway you will now have lots of money. Go and see
> Holt & Co and find out how much it is . . . Darling wife my most
> warm love and many kisses.[8]

And again his letter of 10 March, from near Shanghai, forwarded to Jean
in Venice, told her that ' . . . a Lieutenant General on *Indian* employ gets
a devil of a lot of money. Mr. Brodrick's cable says clearly that "the Indian
Government has agreed to employ" me.' He had told Jean that he was down
to his last £150 in his own bank account, and would need that amount to
buy new kit and horses. Jean was to pay half his salary into his bank and
keep the rest for the upkeep of their London house. His brother, Vereker,
could help her with the arrangements. He concluded: 'The drama begins'.[9]

On 24 March Ian was staying at the British Legation in Tokyo as a
guest of Sir Claude and Lady McDonald. He had dined, separately, with
Maxwell of the *Standard* newspaper and Sir Bryan Leighton (Violet
Meakin's brother-in-law). He had written to Lord Knollys, Arnold-Foster
and St John Brodrick, and on 26 March sent Jean a summary of the letters
with instructions as to how she should use it:

> After you have read it I would like you to send it to Lord Percy for
> his personal use (Lord Percy, M.P., India Office) and early return.
> After him send it to L. Amery, Esq., 2 Temple Gdns, EC. In doing
> so tell him that it is a précis of official letters and that any 'use' of
> my opinions or expressions would be recognisable. I only send it
> him therefore for his personal information and guidance . . . I think
> Sir Charles and Lady Dilke might like to see it, and failing them to
> Mrs Leo Rothschild or Margaret Warrender . . . [10]

Jean wrote to Ian that she had visited Charles Repington, who as a military
journalist was writing an account of battles in the Boer War, in which Ian
was prominently involved. He replied on 4 April 1904:

. . . your visit can have done nothing but good for evidently in this century it is not enough to win battles but you have afterwards to vanquish the liars and intriguers and jealous ones who say that you didn't. [Rawlinson, an old friend from their time in India, whom Ian now calls 'faithless', encouraged Sir William Nicholson to accept the job of British observer in Manchuria, which Ian had expected to get.] You should chaff Rawley about this next time you see him!

Tell any opposition people you like any little stories I give you. I mean people like the Dilkes, Asquiths or Spenders. It serves to keep me alive. The other side will get my news fully from my letters to Brodrick, Lord Knollys, Arnold-Foster, etc.

I am sorry indeed from the career point of view you are not going to stay on in London, especially now that it seems to be all right about money. But you have earned a good holiday by making all these calls and I do hope darling you will have a charming time in Italy.

P.S. Like a dear write one of your charming letters to Lady Macdonald . . . and thank her for all her great kindness to me . . . Say you hope they will come and stay with us in England and above all ask to be remembered to Sir Claude whom you remember as the best looking and most fascinating of young men in Cairo in 1882. *He remembers you.*[11]

The letter concludes with a second postscript relating to the future prospect of the Second Army Corps (the Salisbury Command), on which Ian was pinning his hopes for long-term employment when he returned to England. It was for this reason he urged on Jean the importance of maintaining contact with the Secretary of State for War, Mr Arnold-Foster, whom Jean found to be a difficult character. "**. . . Dined with the Arnold-Fosters . . . and was very disagreeably impressed with him – he struck me as being so glaringly not a gentleman, he must be difficult to work with.**

After dinner General Neville Lyttelton, an old friend of mine, had just carried me off into a corner to talk, when Mr. Arnold-Foster came and planted himself on my other side as if he were King, and monopolised me, talking of 'that officer now in China' [Ian], and laying down the law about the Army, saying what a splendid and efficient Army he knew he could provide if he got his way. . . ." Arnold-Foster was keen to progress army reform and it tells us a good deal about Ian's status in the army that Jean should have been the focus of attention of such a senior politician.

" . . . **General Douglas took me in to dinner – he don't like Ian I know, and has tried to harm him . . . felt quite pleased on Ian's account . . . that everyone made such a fuss of me. . . . directly I entered the room Lord Selborne, General Lyttelton and Monsieur Geoffrey, very pleased to see me, surrounded me . . . ."** Later, Jean " . . . **dined with Margaret Warrender to meet Sir Arthur Nicholson and Ronald Ferguson . . . "**, all influential figures in the Liberal Party. [**17th July 1904**]

To read Jean's astute accounts of how she progressed Ian's career, no one would guess how life really was for her, left on her own, her mind in a state of emotional turmoil. When she knew Ian was due to leave for Japan in early February 1904, her premonition of the loneliness his absence would bring had already set in whilst they were staying with the Marie and Leo de Rothschild. " . . . **I have been absorbed all morning in the 'Life of Lady Caroline Lamb' – her letter to William Godwin, 1823, I felt might have been written by me, 'I have nothing to do – I move necessarily. There is no particular reason why I should exist. My experience gives me no satisfaction, all my opinions and beliefs and feelings are shaken as if suffering from fright – little shocks of earthquake – I am in an un-sought for sea, without compass to guide, or even a knowledge whither I am destined'. Well do I know the lonely terror of that uncharted sea! . . . "**

But Jean's down side did not last. Following a drive with Ian to Woburn Abbey, the Duke of Bedford's estate, she could muse to herself about the time in Simla when she thought " . . . **it would be no bad thing to be Duchess of Bedford myself. . . ."** She had stood on " . . . **the dusty Simla hillside, watching him gallop up the road thinking in a vague way 'There goes a possible future husband', an easy – too easy prey and I soon abandoned the idea."** [**17th January 1904 Ascot Wing**]

In later recollections, Jean drew a parallel between how she felt when Ian was at home with her and what it was like when he left for Manchuria. " . . . **I am happy here with Ian. He is being delightful – even seems in love with me, and is a gay loving companion; he was like this just before he went to Manchuria, we were so happy together that winter but he left me without a thought or regret for more than a year, and** came back to me with no pleasure. How can such things be, and they happen again and again, till the poor heart grows wise, grows sad and empty too." [28th February 1906 Tidworth]

Supporting her absent husband in his career was one thing, coping with being alone for many months was another. When Ian was away, Jean's old love, Lord Alwyne Compton, was always eager to keep her company. Ian had no sooner left for Japan than Lord Alwyne was on Jean's mind: " . . . I dreamed of Lord Alwyne." [11th January 1904] The breakdown of the Comptons' marriage left Lord Alwyne free so Jean could see him whenever she pleased, whilst still appreciating that she had made the right choice for a husband. " . . . What luck it was for me Ian arrived just at the moment he did in my life – in the very nick of time for I very nearly married Prince Louis Esterhazy that summer. I did not deserve Prince Charming but I was determined not to return to the Deanston life, to Mary Vyner then having taken my place as I did not think I should ever love again, now besides having the man I love, and who best suits me, I have also a life that is very agreeable to my restless disposition, and whatever Ian does, he *never* bores me." [17th January 1904]

Ian always wrote to Jean faithfully and amongst letters she received from him from Japan was " . . . one darling one – a real love letter, which makes me very happy when I think of it. . . . " His absence made her heart grow fonder and missing him more than she could bear, she felt the need for spiritual counselling. The physician for her soul was the preacher Stopford Brooke. " . . . I feel in need of this man's help, of his religion; I *know* he could help me. . . . he gave me the impression of a fine vigorous vitality, very human, very broad-minded, and with vision. A glass of champagne, a pill of opium, or a flash of emotion would put me in touch with him, but I see I could not *depend* on being able to talk to him with any freedom – I shall not be able to take him as my priest and spiritual advisor. . . . " Nellie Sellar came to call and found Jean " . . . blotted out on the drawing room sofa . . . miserable and dejected. . . . " [19th February 1904]

The old days at Simla were a secret place where Jean could escape to in her mind and Lord Alwyne posed an imaginary figure somewhere between love and friendship. A note or phone call would bring him at a moment's notice to have tea with her in her sitting room, though their relationship remained platonic and there was never an affair. " . . . **Lord**

Alwyne dined tonight. . . . we stayed at home and talked. I never
realised his limitations so clearly before, there seemed few things I
cared to talk about that he could understand. He is simple, sane,
manly and good, and still has for me an aroma of romance and charm
and one can never *quite* forget the romance of one's youth. But I hate
his being friends with second-rate women like Mrs. Germander and
Miss Wilson, and he made me cross tonight by saying he had met
Germander somewhere, and asked him to massage him – he is the
husband of one of the Miss Wilson's; this will be a good excuse for
being a lot with them." [21st February 1904]

Torn between longing for Ian, her friendship with Lord Alwyne and
religious guilt, Jean alternated between infatuation for other men and the
spiritual comfort Stopford Brooke could provide. " . . . How mad and stupid our life is – to feel now as I *do*, there is a man near who could help
me, a physician for my soul not half a mile away, and yet I cannot send
for him and say, 'I need your help', and if he came I should not be able
to tell him of my soul sickness. I begin to understand the *necessity* for
priests and confession.

I fear he would think me hysterical, and class me perhaps in his
mind with neurotic women. He has escaped and got out somehow into
sunshine and peace, but how? for he is a man 'full of affections and
lusts' but he has conquered, and now 'fears no evil through Christ'."
[Sunday 21st February 1904, 3 Chesterfield St.]

The mention of Lord Alwyne's interest in other women fired Jean's
jealousy, reawakening old passions. " . . . How surprising is life – ten
days ago I thought how little any man interested me, and thought that
page in my life turned down – no touch of romance or excitement
about any man except Ian seemed left – they interested me as intellects
only . . . and then suddenly listening to one of Liszt's Rhapsodies in the
Queen's Hall, the desire for excitement – romance, again burst into
flame and has burned ever since within me, bringing with it inevitable
ups and downs, disappointments and restlessness! Was I happier
without it? I have been so peacefully happy with Ian all the winter.
Why did he go away and leave me again?" [22nd February 1904
Crewe House Gardens]

Her interest was aroused in other men and they became attractive
again. " . . . I have such a wild sense of life in me just now I can hardly
sleep – feel all alight, every nerve and vein tingling and longing for

enjoyment – I think the shock of Ian's departure woke me up. I felt rather stunned at first, but the shock excited me, and shook me out of the peaceful happy lethargy I have been in, all the winter." [23rd February 1904] " . . . Dined with Mrs. Beaumont tonight and sat next Mr. Rufus Isaacs, an exciting personality – he has brilliant, magnetic eyes, and great vitality – had several stimulating moments with him . . . . " [24th February 1904]

When Jean returned home, word from Mr Stopford Brooke awaited her and she tried again to turn to religion for solace rather than to male company. " . . . I was enchanted . . . as there was the book and the charming letter that I had been waiting for, asking me to come and have tea with him Saturday or Sunday. The book was 'The Kingship of Love', and I have been reading it tonight – 'From the Sea to the City' – the first sermon is so beautiful, much in it is the same as the first sermon I heard him preach which I so loved. . . . I think everyone is nicer than I am, I am imperious and too exacting – however shall I bear life when I grow old? ugly. I feel so glad in my heart that I shall see Mr. Brooke again, if religion is ever any help to me again, it will be through him, by his help." [24th February 1904]

Jean admired Charlotte Brontë, in whose autobiographical novel, *Villette*, the central character, Lucy Snowe, in desperation and spiritual turmoil, turns to a Roman Catholic priest in the confessional. " . . . Tea with Mr. Stopford Brooke in his lamp-lit study was nice, but more like an ordinary conversation than I had hoped for. I cannot talk religion with him – I wonder if I ever will? . . . I told him how Nan and I had gone to hear Father Maturin preach in the Catholic Chapel this morning, and that his subject had been the offerings of Cain and Abel, Cain's offerings being the lovely flowers and fruits of the earth, Abel's the offering of blood as atonement for sin – the slain lamb – with Abel's sacrifice God was most pleased. He took the sacrifices as symbols – Cain's of the broad happy natural religion which believes in the perfecting of mankind, and in the natural God, and Abel's of the recognition that the World is all wrong, has been wrenched away from God by our disobedience, and that only by sacrificial blood and sacrifice, a broken and contrite heart, can be made our peace with God. . . . " [Sun. 28th February 1904]

Jean was being rather melodramatic in her guilt over her infatuation with other men as Ian never objected to any of her men friends, though he called Lord Alwyne 'the snake'. However, there was religious guilt for which she should make atonement. But Mr Stopford Brooke's sermon fell on deaf ears and neither guilt nor the religious fervour of the preacher could quell her jealousy at the thought of Lord Alwyne taking an interest in another woman. **" . . . Lord Alwyne dined with Nan and me last night. I am certain he is preoccupied, interested in some new woman, and I don't know whether it is Mrs. Germander or Miss Wilson – he is uneasy if I mention skating." [Sunday 28th February 1904]**

Still desirous of male company, Jean delayed her holiday to Rome with her sister, Nan, for a fortnight, and invited to lunch Lord Howe, George Beckett, Mrs Craigie and Lady Elphinstone, after which she set off to a concert where she expected Lord Howe to be her escort. **" . . . I had thought Lord Howe was going to take me to the concert, and had got two seats just behind his for Nan and Mab Beckett, and thought I had been clever, however I had made a mistake and he had arranged to take someone else . . . and Nan and I found ourselves sitting behind Lord Howe and his lady, which he *hated*, I know, poor little man, so he also was rather cross." [Sunday 28th February 1904]**

Feeling somewhat unlucky with her male admirers, Jean decided it was time to go on holiday to Rome. **" . . . Dined with Mrs. Beaumont tonight. Sir Rennell Rodd was to have taken me in to dinner, but alas! he sprained his ankle bicycling, and could not come; very annoying, as when I gave myself this extra week in London I hoped to see as much as possible of Sir Rennell Rodd and Mr. Henry Butcher, but all my efforts have been unavailing. I have showered invitations on them both lately . . . but what does it matter? We are but a dance of gnats in the sunshine – smoke, that vanishes away. . . . Lulu Harcourt took me into dinner tonight instead. . . . his father resigned today. . . . We discussed diaries, and he promised me an introduction to a friend of his called Leach in Rome." [1st March 1904]**

Ian was due to return from Japan on 23 April 1905. From past experiences Jean anticipated what might lie ahead. **" . . . How little one ever knows another fellow creature. My . . . man comes back on Sunday . . . . I try to expect from him complete indifference; I hope untinged with dislike, but when I look back on his first return from South Africa, after Ladysmith, I feel the indifference then must have been slightly tinged with dislike, even now I can never think of it with** calmness . . . and I had been ill and had so looked forward to this return, no wonder I wept, but what a stupid thing to do – I was ill, but I am stronger now!" [20th April 1905 Woodstock Ascot]

The despair Jean felt when Ian deserted her for Japan remained with her for many years. Once when she lost her temper and set upon him he responded by laughing and saying " . . . I had a pet snake I was always playing with . . . ", and she found he was " . . . surprised, and rather interested in my outburst, and asked me if I had been cherishing this bitterness against him in my heart all these years, and I said: 'Yes, I have,'. . . ." During that desolate time, she had gone to visit friends and found herself alone on a railway station at night. " . . . I remember being shaken to the very depths of my being. . . . I stood at the railway station, in the dark, and held on to the railings while this storm of feeling swept over me – I was shaking so I could scarcely stand – I felt furiously bitter, lonely and deserted, feeling my youth, my womanhood was all passing away – and why? When I was still young and loveable should I wait and wait and wait for Ian, when we were always 'strangers yet', and he could so easily desert me and go away." [16th Sep. 1919]

'Strangers yet', one of Jean's oft repeated phrases, was both the name of an old song she greatly liked and the title of a chapter of Ian's book, *The Soul and Body of an Army*,[12] in which he discussed the lack of understanding of the people of the nation for their own army. Jean seized upon the phrase as an example of his lack of understanding of her needs as a wife.

CHAPTER 5

Tidworth (1905–08)

"Capt. Maitland has a terrible power of silence and he and Capt. Vincent sat like two enclosed wooden dummies at lunch yesterday, shooting out quite ineffectual missiles of remarks every now and then." [4th December 1905]

As the months passed by in Japan, Ian's attentions turned more towards his return and the prospect of gaining the Southern Command (Second Army Corps) at Salisbury. In a third postscript to his letter to Jean of 4 April 1904, he had already anticipated the fall of the Tory Government and its possible effect on his appointment:

> One thing I think it well to make a note of now. If the Government
> goes out, go to Mr. (or Mrs.) Arnold-Foster at once. Remind them
> of the promise of the 2nd Army Corps. Tell them I have played the
> game fair and square and that to all my sympathising friends, many
> of them very powerful, I have always said I had been well and
> properly treated by the War Office and had no complaint. Ask him
> in view of this at any rate to *tell* his successor of his promise.[22]

Jean prepared to secure the real prize for Ian, not least because it would bring him back to her. The present holder of the post was Sir Evelyn Wood, and when Jean returned from holiday in Rome, she began entertaining immediately. **" . . . Sir Evelyn Wood came to lunch to-day . . . . He says they are going to put in Knox temporarily to keep it for Ian. I think that Arnold Foster ought to let me know. Sir Evelyn says the King says Ian must stay out till the end of the war . . . whenever will that be I wonder? . . .**

. . . Ian told me Tidworth House is where we shall live in this command . . . .

. . . I had two really nice letters from Ian this week, letters that

could not be addressed to [Leo] **Amery, the Archbishop of Canterbury or the Queen." [6th November 1904]**

Ian's ambition was still some way from being fulfilled and the next few months were an anxious time. Despite his apprehensions about journalists, Leo Amery gave Jean good advice, and she also built up a friendship with Arnold-Foster, who was in a position to secure the Southern Command. **"... Mr. Arnold Foster dashed up to lunch with me to-day. ... he asked me if Ian was happy and well in Manchuria, and I said, 'If you ask me straight, I must honestly say he is'. Mr. A.F. had come to see if it would be all right not to offer Ian Salisbury. He is evidently in a hole about it – probably the King is bothering him to give it to Kelly Kenny. He was nice and seemed honestly to wish to play fair to Ian, to whom, he said, he was in honour bound to give Salisbury, if he wished it.**

I felt so worried, fearing my own strong wish to have Ian brought home might influence me – had influenced me to emphasise *his* wish to stay out. I wrote Mr. Arnold Foster a letter afterwards and sent it to his house by special messenger." [29th November 1904]

The following day, Jean saw Mrs Arnold-Foster, who **"... told me to wire or write to Ian to find out his real wishes, but of course that he, Mr. Arnold-Foster, was to know nothing of it. Mr. Arnold-Foster was nervous in case I should broach the subject of my letter to him but of course I did not. I had seen Mr. Amery and consulted him in the afternoon and he thought it best for Ian's career to stay where he was.**

Sir Evelyn Wood also came to see me. He advised me to wire Ian, telling him to wire home at once about appointment but I feel Mr. Amery's advice is best probably for *Ian*, as he is keen about Ian and is his friend." [30th November 1904]

At the Carlton Club, Jean lunched with Lady Salisbury, whom she knew from their time at Hythe. She was **"charming"** and they had an interesting talk about Japan, Jean recalling that **" ... When Ian was Commandant at Hythe ... "**, in 1898, **"... Lord Salisbury was taking a course of Musketry and lived in a cottage at our gates and we saw a lot of him and liked him so much." [2nd December 1904]**

The New Year 1905 began with finer fortunes. Jean was elated when she received a telegram from Lady Salisbury inviting her to Hatfield to view what she dearly wished would soon be hers and Ian's, Tidworth House, which went with the Southern Command. **[2nd January 1905]**

Lord Roberts was also trying to further Ian's chances of getting the Southern Command. When Jean received a letter from his youngest daughter, she realised she would have to apply the same tactful approach to Lord Bobs as she had done with St John Brodrick if she was to succeed in her attempts to secure the post for Ian. " **. . . Edwina wrote me last night, saying Lord Roberts was going to Ireland and did not wish me to see Mr. Arnold-Foster till he saw him, as it would only complicate matters. He does not say why it would, though I had written to ask him if there was anything I ought to know before seeing Mr. Arnold-Foster, and I have promised Mrs. Arnold-Foster to go there on Wednesday. I am very much bothered about it, but my strong feeling is that Lord Bobs is fussing and wishes to keep even the knowledge of Ian's affairs entirely to himself – he has always felt jealous of me with Ian, and would like to keep me from having anything to do with his career, he has never thought much of me – this does not in any way lower my estimation of myself!"** [26th January 1905 Deanston]

In early February Ian was on his way back to England, in response to a telegram from Mr Arnold-Foster. The situation with Lord Roberts concluded with Jean having to swallow hard and allow him to take all the credit for Ian's appointment. " **. . . Lord Bobs was so odd insisting I should not see Mr. Arnold-Foster, 'in case I should complicate matters' he said. Felt annoyed but am quite willing to humour the little man and allow him to feel Ian owes everything to him, felt however it was impossible in Ian's interests to refuse to see Mr. Arnold-Foster as it might have been important for Ian's career that I should see him, so I did, and understood then that having arranged matters with the King, Lord Bobs wished to get the full credit with Ian for what he had done, and he wished to tell me I could wire and tell Ian myself, which was very sweet of him."** [9th February 1905, 3 Chesterfield St.]

When Ian returned from Japan, they were again like two strangers, Ian struggling with semi-civilian life, Jean with having her man about the house again. But she had the consolation that he now had a home command and the future looked optimistic. In June 1905, Ian took up his appointment of the Southern Command at Salisbury. The Hamiltons removed from London to Tidworth House, the Government mansion that would be their home for the next four years.

The move from London to Tidworth meant that Jean would lose her servants and would have to recruit new ones. Industrialisation had meant that servants had fled the basements and garrets for better paid jobs in the factories. Those remaining in service had become a scarce commodity and to some degree had the advantage of their employers. It was only when something unusual happened in the servants' domain that Jean ever referred to them at all and then only by their surnames. There were regrets at leaving London and she had mixed feelings about parting with her servants who, although not perfect, had provided a routine she had grown accustomed to and could work within. " . . . **We left Chesterfield Street yesterday and I said good-bye to Simpson and Mrs. Wagner my cook with regret. A great show of cheerfulness on their part. I was hurt with Simpson who has been with us ten years but showed no regret in parting with me. It would amuse me to see them in their new places. I fancy they will be surprised, they have forgotten, what it feels like to be kept in their places, they have kept me in mine so long, but they have been excellent, good servants and I really hate parting with them, and dread the struggle to settle down with new servants at Tidworth, but I am well for the moment and feel as if I had a heart for any fate as long as Ian and I are happy together; he came here with me last night and is very happy and cheery." [11th June 1905 Weyhill]**

On the way to their new home, Jean and Ian spent some time with Lady Salisbury. After a trying day at a Royal Garden Party at Windsor the Hamiltons returned to Tidworth, " . . . **very tired through the lovely moonlit night to the vast, empty, echoing halls at our new home. It was thrilling entering in together." [14th June 1905 Tidworth]**

Jean was looking forward to their being together again, and to the prospect of a normal family life and the possibility of having a child, though she had just passed her forty-fourth birthday. But her hopes were soon dashed as one set of problems followed hard upon another. " . . . **Oh, new servants! they are the devil. I like Fox and the cook looks like an angel out of 'The Sunday Magazine', but can she cook?" [15th June 1905]** Ian was invited to Blenheim Palace to inspect the Yeomanry encamped in the Park and Jean went with him to escape from the servants. " . . . **I am glad to be out of Tidworth for two days. I can't help getting worried with the enormous place to furnish and new servants to teach and every moment remembering something which has been forgotten." [17th June 1905 Blenheim Palace]**

McAdie, Jean's personal maid, whom she had come to rely on and valued very highly, was the only servant who accompanied her to

Tidworth. Ian was taken ill and Jean had to nurse him herself both day and night. "... **McAdie has hurt me terribly, the only one I knew amongst all these new servants and her obvious terror in case she should be called on to do anything that was not her work is dis-heartening; she has been so nice lately, and I had grown fond of her. I thought she was really changing and growing more sympathetic and kinder when she was appreciated and liked, but she has been hard and unsympathetic now, just when I was feeling lonely and helpless, no, not helpless, I can't say I feel that, I am surprised to find myself so very capable, but of course it's a very difficult position, this huge empty house to furnish and all new servants, and then to have my Ian ill; just a little common sympathy makes such a difference, and of course McAdie is the only one of them all I can turn to for help or talk to at all.**

On Tuesday night when Ian was *so ill* she just went to bed without asking if she could do anything to help me, though she knew I had had a very bad night on Monday, as not only Ian but Puppy was ill all night, then I had a long trying day, nursing Ian and doing a hundred other things as well, which she must have seen, she never once offered or asked to help in any way, and yesterday morning she came in without a word, never asking how Ian was, or if I had slept or seemed to care at all, it is *incredible* – any new housemaid in a hotel would have had more common sympathy, it is very disheartening and I have always so wanted to have a nice comfortable maid, who would be one's friend and kind when one was lonely." [22nd June 1905 Tidworth]

The element of competition was always present in the Hamiltons' marriage, both perhaps fearing Oscar Wilde's claim that 'familiarity breeds contempt'. But Ian seems to have taken it to extremes at times and was unable to relate to Jean as a friend at all and they were on tenterhooks with each other. Jean as wife and lover was distinctly not acceptable as Jean the nurse. "... **Ian, poor darling, *so* ill. I seem to worry him when I do anything for him, though he is quite good about taking medicine, but I feel as I always do when he is ill that I am no pleasure or comfort to him and he hates the sight of me. Any nurse would do better and he would prefer it, of course about sponging him I am not so capable as a hospital nurse would be. I got through yesterday without breaking down, I wonder if I shall get through to-day."** [22nd June 1905]

Ian's health improved but Jean called in a doctor, "... **Ian's temper-**

ature is going down but he is very weak and low. . . . " The doctor brought in a nurse to look after him, who lived in. Those trained in the medical profession can take control of a difficult situation in a way in which the average person cannot. " . . . **Ian . . . likes his nurse; she is a little darling, pretty and attractive, with a nice calm soothing voice, and Ian is charming with her and delighted to have her do everything for him . . . with me he was fractious and impatient, obviously almost unable to bear my presence in the room – that is the sorrow, and what has broken me down, it hurts deeply, it is impossible to believe that he can really love me and feel so hostile to me when he is ill, I feel it is unbearable." [27th June 1905]**

The next ordeal was the arrival of Ian's new staff. " . . . **Col. Bethune arrived unexpectedly this morning and I had to ask him to lunch. I sent word to Mrs. Hudson, the cook, Ian and I when alone eat so little, but she sent a ridiculous lunch for a hungry man like Col. Bethune, and Ian was vexed and we both felt humiliated which I saw pleased our guest. He is inclined to be jealous of Ian. They were young together in the Gordons and now he is to be Ian's Chief of Staff. I had to go and harangue Mrs. Hudson through the dinner slide before we could extract some hot beef out of the kitchen; she resented this and I left her in floods of tears." [1st July 1905 Caworth,** home of the Eddy Stanleys]

The problems with the servants persisted and Jean got out of the house at every opportunity. " . . . **My household is again going to be convulsed as I wrote yesterday to tell Mrs. Hudson, the cook, to go – that I was getting a new housekeeper cook . . . I have to pay her enormous wages, also her kitchen maid – £80 a year . . . and £26 to the kitchen maid, and my present cook gets £45 and the kitchen maid £18." [30th July 1905 Bramley Park,** home of Mrs Beaumont]

Tidworth was an enormous house and for months Jean felt " . . . **like a flea in this vast place. . . . "** Ian, too, admitted that he had " . . . **not yet been really happy here. . . ."** The furniture, which was slow in coming from London, finally arrived, bringing with it memories of the old romance with Lord Alwyne Compton and her friendship with Major Frank Lyon. " . . . **All the things came here today – the West African wooden stool which little Lyon gave me where I have so often sat in the fire-light and waited for Lord Alwyne – my writing table, my great comfy sofa." [August 1st and 24th; November 2nd 1905]**

The servants had improved but the service was not quite perfect when the Duke of Connaught, brother of King Edward VII, came to tea. "**We had a splendid Tattoo in the evening here for the Duke of Connaught, and asked all the Military people and all the near neighbours. . . . There were over 200 people poured in.**
My new housekeeper Mrs. Wheelband is a treasure and gave us an excellent dinner, and the dreamy Fox did wonders, but there were one or two unpleasant surprises, such as when H.R.H. said he would have some hot cakes for tea, just after he arrived, took the cover off the dish and hastily replaced it, saying he would have something else, and when Betty looked under the cover directly after, it was discovered to be empty." [17th August 1905 Tidworth]

When the Hamiltons dined with Lord and Lady Portsmouth they found Lord Portsmouth had adopted a more modern approach to his man servants. "**. . . Dined to-night with the Portsmouths. Just before dinner an interesting looking man entered the room in evening dress, his hair was long, brushed back and fell on his shoulders. I thought he was a poet and turned to ask who 'this interesting stranger could be' when he announced 'Dinner is served, my Lord!'. Lord Portsmouth, pays his butler extra wages to grow his hair to the same length as his own, and his chauffeurs too, arrived at Tidworth the other day with locks flowing in the wind.**" [9th March 1906, 35 Grosvenor Square]

The irritation of getting used to Ian's new staff continued. "**. . . Captain Vincent I can't get on with at all. If left to talk alone with him for two seconds, have a restless longing to escape. Feel he thoroughly misunderstands me, and I shall never be able to get on with** *him* **– never like him, he is simple minded and stupid. When I talk to him he keeps on apologising to me for the things I am saying to him, trying to put a better complexion on my opinions for my sake, and it irritates me to madness, I long to keep on saying outrageous things.**" [5th Nov. 1905 Tidworth] But Jean could make allowances for those who were loyal to Ian. "**. . . Captain Vincent I like now. I don't get on with him, but feel he's thoroughly for us and happy here which is nice. He is awfully devoted to Ian and will be loyal to him.**" [20th Nov. 1905 Tidworth]

Some of the younger officers, whose entire careers had been spent in the male arena of the army, had little experience of the company of women or how to converse with them. "**. . . The new ADC Capt. Crichton**

Maitland, arrived. . . . he is nice looking in a very heavy way but my
heart sank with every fresh look at him, he is very frightened and shy
. . . I don't feel as if I would have much use for him. I miss Standish a
good deal – he was always there and ready to look after people and try
to make them happy and comfortable – now we will have no one about
with nice sociable monkey tricks. Capt. Vincent has no ease of manner, and I want a man badly to entertain our guests, take the men off
to the billiard room, and to make the women's stay pleasant to them
by mild flirtation. I suspect Capt. Vincent would be too serious – this
boy also looks of a very heavy turn of mind." [2nd December 1905
Tidworth] They all eventually got used to each other's ways, Vincent and
Maitland soon came out of their shells where the ladies were concerned,
but neither would ever become ideal staff in Jean's eyes.

Although Jean and Ian were living under the same roof, Ian was so
preoccupied with his new job he had little time to spend with her. "I only
see him for two minutes in the morning every day, if it is three he is
bored." [Friday September 1st 1905] Jean summed up her mood: "I feel
depressed, everything's a bore – living seems an intolerable nui-
sance." [Monday October 9th 1905 Blagdon, home of Rosie Ridley]
Establishing a home and normal married life at Tidworth turned out to be
more arduous than she ever anticipated and sexual relations were slow to
resume, though she admitted: " . . . Once he did love me to be more in
his life, it was I who withdrew then – when I insisted on having separate bedrooms. . . . " [5th September 1906 Cairnoch] Jean sometimes
suffered night attacks of asthma which would have been disruptive of
Ian's sleep so separate bedrooms were preferable. McAdie had to come
into the bedroom to attend to her and, if necessary, give her an injection.
Ian, too, was prone to recurring bouts of illness, common amongst soldiers
who had spent many years serving in the tropics. The change from the
warmer climate of Japan and China to the winds and cold of Salisbury
Plain was rather bracing and he suffered from colds and chills, felt feverish and couldn't stand drafts.

Ian was still recovering from flu but they could get away for weekends
and holidays together to friends and to Jean's beloved Deanston, where, in
the peace and tranquillity of Doune, Ian might begin again to appreciate
his wife's talents. " . . . An enchanting day of sunshine, full of silver
mists and frosty sparkling grass. I feel full of gladness to match the
day. Ian has come back to me quite suddenly. He came this morning

talked and listened and was happy with me. He called me Natasha. He has been reading 'War And Peace' and I feel grateful to Natasha. He is very pleased and excited over my pastels, and I must say they sometimes quite please and surprise me too – they are unexpected. When something beautiful enters into me, and I want immediately to reproduce it and summon my clumsy fingers to my aid, it does surprise me afterwards to find I have actually captured something of the beauty – this is always magical to me." [26th September 1905 Deanston]

But instant kindling of love was too much to hope for and frustration was taking its toll. Whilst staying with Lord and Lady Albemarle, Jean's anger boiled over into a fit of rage. Throughout their relationship there is no indication of Ian ever having lost his temper with her. But his reaction was sometimes one of indifference to her grievances, which distressed her all the more. Jean experienced much deeper feelings of emotional upset to the point of distress. Ian, preoccupied with his army career, equipped with the tremendous self-control of generalship and immersed in his almost ceaseless writing, excluded himself from Jean's seemingly quite ordinary, though necessary wants, desires, needs in a wife. His way of getting her out of a tantrum was to humour her with some witty remark which may have made her smile, laugh at herself for the moment but did not solve the problem. **" . . . I rushed into Ian's room just before dinner in my dressing gown to ease my soul with an outburst, and said all sorts of horrid things – that life with him was an intolerable loneliness, that I dreaded to go to Tidworth and be there alone with him, that he was not a comfortable friendly husband at all, etc. etc. and I wept and fumed and fluttered and it did me good, but he took it as the outburst of a spoilt child, and was gentle and sweet and kissed and soothed me, and said it was luckily not true that we were nothing to one another. He said he saw clearly that he was only palatable with a thick *Muir* sauce, and I said that was quite true." [12th October 1905 Quidenham Park]**

Jean's loneliness did not subside and she no longer had the company of Lord Alwyne Compton to fall back on. He had been too romantic during one of their tête-à-têtes when Ian was in Japan and she put him in his place. **" . . . I have been looking up my diary, and see it was this time last year Lord Alwyne began to hurt and disappoint me. What a petulant, impatient creature I am, but I don't regret it and am glad I put him out and shut the door. I never hear of him now, the only thing I have heard since last March is (Nellie [Sellar] told me the other day)** that he had been had up for too fast motoring." [2nd Nov., 1905 Tidworth] Five months on in their new home, Ian was " . . . being delightful, trying and succeeding in being more companionable." [Sun. Nov. 12th 1905] But she began to realise how reliant she had become on Lord Alwyne and that she had been rather rash in depriving herself of his friendship. " . . . I have a telephone here by my bed and the thought rather tempts me that I could ring Alwyne up and talk to him now this moment if I like – London really is a wonderful place." [15th Nov. 1905 Coburg Hotel London] Ian does seem to have been trying to find time to spend with her and make her happy, whilst coping with the demands of his job. "Last night Ian read me out some of 'Flowers, Fruit and Thorn Pieces' by Jean Paul Richter. . . . " [Friday Nov. 24th 1905]

Captain Peter Pollen (who had recently married Jean's sister, Heather), little Janet Hamilton (later Mrs Leeper), and Colonel Babbington (Babbie), Jean's old admirer who had been in love with her in India, were staying. Lord Alwyne was still on Jean's mind. "Dreamt of Lord Alwyne last night. Can't quite remember what but it was not satisfactory. I wonder if I am ever going to run across him again. Capt. Peter was talking of him at tea last night and said he never appeared at Prince's this year and that he was constantly there last year, skating with the youngest Miss Wilson. The thought of him has almost faded out of my life, but this morning came the memory of his dark head, against my crimson cushion and his caressing voice as he talked French to little Janet, this time last year when he came to tea with me . . . his presence used to make a stillness, for when he was there I know I did not wish for anything else. . . . It seems strange now when I think back that I should have treated him as I did. As I would not have him for my lover it was unreasonable of me to refuse to have him as a friend on *his* own terms. I wanted absurdly to be Beatrice to his Dante – 'The desire of the moth for the star' sort of thing as I was to Colonel Babbie. I shall always feel grateful to him for many happy hours – he has made many rooms and places pleasant to me – they used to look at me with different faces after he had been there. Yet I don't regret having let him go out of my life – the moment had sounded and he was only spoiling memories." Jean seems to have had second thoughts and the words "out of my life" are crossed through. [30th November 1905]

Jean went to tea with Lord and Lady Roberts, and Lord George Curzon of Kedleston was there. His wife, Mary, an American heiress, was the daughter of Levi Leiter, a Chicago millionaire. The Curzons had been at the height of their power as Viceroy and Vicereine of India (1889–1905), but Mary was ill,[2] suffering from a mysterious virus from which she would never recover. Lord Curzon, having resigned as Viceroy of India following a disagreement with Lord Kitchener, had returned to England the previous day. Lord Curzon was " . . . **very nice to me, and chaffed me about Ian's remarks about the Geishas. I told him we had had the same nurse for Ian Lady Curzon had had, and he was interested to hear about her, and asked if it was the pretty one with the whining voice. He told me he had twice seen Lady Curzon die and her recovery was a miracle. Sitting on the Peacock Throne at Delhi seemed to have brought them bad luck."** Ian had brought back with him from Japan photographs of Geisha girls. Jean joked about his 'Geisha wife' and it did not go down well with Roberts or Curzon. There was always apprehension in army circles about any whiff of scandal involving women. Colonel Charles à Court, now known as Repington, had been thrown out of the army just a short time before, over a scandal with a friend of Jean's, Mary, Lady Garstin, the estranged wife of Sir William Garstin, now living with him and calling herself Molly Repington. Doubtless, this scandal was still uppermost in the minds of Roberts and Curzon. **" . . . In talking about Ian's remarks about Geishas, I stupidly said to Lady Bobs, had I ever told her about showing Nellie Sellar the photo of Ian and his Japanese wife, and how horrified she was? Everyone laughed rather uneasily at this, and my explanation that she was the Hotel-keeper's respectable daughter passed unheeded as Lord Curzon suddenly flourished a long official looking paper in Lord Roberts' face and proceeded solemnly to the study."** [10th December 1905 Tidworth]

The year 1906 began better, Jean was playing the piano again and Ian was singing. **"Found an old book and played Ian all sorts of old pieces I used to play as a girl, last night, and he was quite delighted."** [Wednesday February 7th 1906] They were now both growing to like Tidworth. **" . . . a lovely sunny early spring day has just broken. All the snow is gone. It is like a fairy tale to think of the white, white world in which we lived last Friday, when Ian and I walked in the crystal woods, with elfland glittering round us – everything shining blue-**

white, the outlining of stems and leaves showing only a faint yellow, not black. Oh it was lovely – we felt like Hansel and Gretel and Ian was an ideal companion. I am not half grateful enough for Ian. He is just the companion I want, and it is wonderful to have found him." [Tuesday February 27th 1906]

Inspired by the spring beauty of the wild flowers in the woods, Jean settled to painting pastels. They bought a new car and Jean joined the Automobile Club, which met at Claridge's. But she felt Ian still did not spend enough time with her. "**At moments if I look charming and am pleasant he likes to kiss and pet me, play with me for exactly a minute and a half, but if I claim another half minute, intolerable impatience overcomes him. I . . . feel overcome with bitterness . . . to live beside him excluded from everything – his work, his thoughts, his ambitions, his love – his love he gives to no one else as far as I know, thank goodness, but has he any to give?!**

Later

Sitting beside Ian in the Albert Hall to-night while thousands and thousands of people cheered him he looked splendid, I felt *proud* of him and wondered why I had written with such bitterness this morning. . . . His speech was very good and he delivered it well, and then I gave the prizes for drill and we both stood up while all those thousands of voices cheered us both – it was a delightful moment, and Mrs. McKinnon, who was on the platform came up and said, enthusiastically to me, 'I hope you will forgive me telling you how beautiful you both looked, and how much alike – it was a real pleasure to see such a good looking couple.' I felt pleased and though it was dear of her, not just flattering, as she does not know us, or want to." [Thursday May 10th 1906]

A woman confided a secret of a sexual nature to Jean which made her count her blessings that she was married to a gentleman. In the privacy of the bedroom a friend told "**. . . me something about herself and her husband . . . that made me wretched. I could not sleep thinking of it. I can't bear her to be treated so – oh, what animals, what horrid animals men are, it seems a desecrated unclean world to me often because of them – really it is wonderful I should have married the man I did, it would *kill* me to be treated as [she] has been. I said to [her] 'It is *impossible*, a man could not treat me like that, he would feel it *impossible*,' . . . "** The victim's powerless reply placed the blame on her-

self rather than her abuser. "... she laughed and said, 'You are so lady-
like – a Princess in a tight silk gown, and I am a slut.' At this moment
Ian called loudly at the door 'Where are you Jean' and she rolled over
in bed like a frightened child with large dark eyes, and said, 'Oh, it is
the ghost, I know this house is haunted, the ghost is a soldier with a
heavy tread, I have heard him,' and as I kissed her good-night she
said, 'Promise me to be less of a Princess, I'll promise to be less of a
slut.' She is a darling." [Saturday August 11th 1906 Tidworth] "The
thought of [her] is a fragrance in my life, fairy creature with wings of
fire and dew! I don't want to have her husband here with her. I hate
to think of the way he treats her, and she was so young when they
married and submitted to every degradation, she said, 'And now I can
never change, or get back what might have been his attitude to me,'
but it has not touched her soul. ... " [Tuesday November 20th 1906
Tidworth]

Captain Maitland and Captain Vincent had a house of their own but
their meals were provided by Jean at Tidworth and part of their duties
were to help her. Captain Maitland moved about the house in a familiar
way as though he were family, entering her boudoir, lighting the candles
at meal times, accompanying her on occasion to the theatre, buying her
presents and giving her flowers. Along with Captain Vincent, he also
helped look after the guests, taking them out riding on the downs. Jean had
taken up riding again and owned a black pony. "My birthday – Ian forgot it as usual. ... Col. Repington escorted them, riding Major Lyon's
horse ... Katharine Horner looked lovely on Capt. Maitland's large
Kenyon ... Captain Maitland [rode] Captain Vincent's Paddy. ... "
[Friday 8th June 1906 Tidworth] Jean went out driving with Miss
Robins, "... over the downs, to see the Field Day." She spied "... Ian,
standing on a tumulus, and got out and walked up to it with Miss
Robins, thinking myself clever to have found my way to his Head
Quarters, but we were greeted so coldly that I flew off the tumulus at
once, furious and crest fallen we made our way back in silence.

To-night before I went to bed I taxed him with it, and said the only
present he had given me for my birthday was tears. He said he was
sorry, but could not help showing his feelings always, and he was *not*
pleased to see me as he thought a General's wife should not be there
while he was judging a battle – so we parted for the night in peace, but
I don't agree." [Friday June 6th 1906]

Jean and Ian preferred the ADCs to be single men. If they were engaged or married their attention tended to be divided between their work and their partner, and their work was apt to suffer. During Ascot week, a romance developed between Captain Vincent and Kitty Ogilvy, the daughter of Lady Mabell Airlie, whose house, Cranborne, was nearby. On 23 July they became engaged to be married and already Captain Vincent was neglecting his job. On that day a wire came from *The Times* asking Ian to write an appreciation of Kodama, Chief of the Staff of the Japanese Army, who had just died. Ian was away and Captain Vincent went to play tennis without checking Ian's mail. The correspondence was not answered and Ian and Jean were furious. [**23rd July 1906**]

Captain Vincent and Kitty were married in Scotland in September and Jean and Ian went to Cortachy for the wedding. Jean was rather fond of Kitty and the following January, when the young couple were staying with her, Kitty was taken ill and Jean called in the army doctor, Colonel Farmer. Major Simpson Baikie, Ian's newly arrived Military Secretary, had to fly off and fetch him in his motor. Kitty lay upstairs in pain, having a miscarriage, her shrieks could be heard downstairs. " **'Oh God I am going to die, I know I am. Oh, what have I done that I should suffer so? Oh, God, I have not been so wicked, I have never done anything so very wrong – God! God! God. I am a soldier's daughter and a soldier's wife but I can't bear this.'** " Captain Vincent stood in the passage gazing at what was taking place through the crack of the door as Colonel Farmer would not allow him into the bedroom. He gave her morphia to quiet her but another doctor had to be sent for who gave her chloroform and she went to sleep. An elderly nurse also had to be sent for to attend to her. Whilst Kitty slept, Jean went for a walk in the garden with Major Simpson Baikie. She had set her mind against having another married man working for Ian but he told her he was already engaged to be married. **"I had wanted to tell him how badly we wanted a really competent man to look after us, but he was only bent on talking about the girl he was going to marry. . . . his thoughts are evidently crammed full of her."** Already he wanted time off to go and spend a week with his fiancée. [**11th January, 1907**] Having herself been the victim of prejudice against married staff by Sir Fred and Lady Roberts when Ian wanted to marry her, Jean now seems to have taken a leaf out of their book.

Jean's mood swings were unpredictable and she could change from being quite happy one day to the depths of depression the next. Lord and

Lady Salisbury were staying and she **"had a long discussion"** with them
"about suicide, which I think shocked them both deeply. I maintain,
surely one thing you may take is your own life." [Thursday August 9th
1906] But by the end of 1906, she had **" . . . grown fond of Tidworth –**
growing to love it even: my own sitting room is so cosy, a dear little
bright room . . . " [Sunday December 2nd 1906] **"Heavy snow storm**
all day. . . . Ian dragged me out to ski on the pond. . . . he and I skated
alone, singing and doing outside edge together. We were very merry,
and he looked too pretty with his frosty pow and snow on his mous-
tache, eyebrows and eyelashes, I had to kiss him. It has been a happy
year. . . . " [Monday – last day of 1906 Deanston]

The relationship between Jean and Ian was inhibited by their having to
entertain on a large scale. There was almost always people staying with
them and they were seldom able to be on their own or have the house to
themselves. As part of Ian's job, large parties and dances were given,
members of the Royal Family were there and hundreds of people would
attend. **"The Prince and Princess of Wales arrived this afternoon. We**
went to the station – soldiers on one side, sailors the other – . . . .
Dined at the Admiralty tonight to meet Prince and Princess. I wish
our future King would hold himself more erect, and look more of a
man.

She looks very sweet and has a nice gracious manner, but she
ought not to have such a lovely Lady in Waiting, it is unbecoming for
her – Mabell Airlie looked the Queen as she sailed in after them – a
vision of loveliness, with her beautifully poised little head, and lovely
white shoulders.

Ian wore his kilt and looked a darling – everyone was talking of
his good looks – he was by far the most attractive and the smartest
looking man in the room." [Wed. February 20th 1907 Government
House]

"Prince Arthur of Connaught dined and we had a nice dinner
party. . . . I think about 150 came . . . I got tired inducing unlikely men
to dance with the most awful frumps. Lots of good-looking young
Cameronians about.
I enjoyed dancing Lancers with Prince Arthur, and having a tiny turn
of a waltz with Captain Maitland, and one with Ian . . . " [Fri.
November 29th 1907 Tidworth]

It was at this time Jean first made the acquaintance of Norah Lindsay, who would become a lifelong friend, and later achieve renown as a garden designer. Norah lived with her husband Harry in "**. . . an old Elizabethan Manor House, full of old oak panelling, and beauty, the garden a fairyland of colours, but it was the love and good-fellowship which struck me with her husband and two children – Nancy a pretty blue eyed girl and Peter a dark eyed little boy – a beautiful life . . . .**" [Sunday April 22nd 1906 Lockinge Wantage] The 'Manor House', which was at Sutton Courtenay, had been given to the Lindsays by Harry's aunt, Harriet, Lady Wantage. Whilst Jean was staying at Lockinge with Lady Wantage, she felt "**Quite captivated by Mrs. Lindsay – determined to talk to her last night and waited for her after dinner in the hall when she went to her room, she told me Cousin Harriet (Lady W.) would expect her to play the piano and was pleased I waited and we sat in a corner of the great drawing room and had a delightful talk. Afterwards she played divinely. I hope I have made a friend and will see much of her. I love her already.**" [Monday April 23rd Lockinge 1906] But when Jean went to stay with Norah at the Manor House, she discovered it was haunted. "**I was frightened in this grim room as Winnie Portland said it was haunted, and I made Ian come and sleep in my vast bed, and then I could not sleep at all. . . .**" [Monday July 9th 1906 Manor House Sutton Courtenay]

Jean and Norah went on holiday to Italy. Lord and Lady Manners and their children and Katharine Horner joined the party. "**. . . we have all been for a long expedition into the mountains today on donkeys. It was lovely and reminded me of Simla . . . the evening is better, the colour then is so rich, and the olives against the sky and sea give me feeling of rapture.**" [Wednesday March 13th 1907 Hotel Pension Bristol, Bordighera] "**We have been doing lovely expeditions every day amongst the mountains, all of us; most of us go on donkeys which scramble up wonderful places . . . exquisite beauty of the olives against the sky, the blue purple seas, and my milk white Norah with her dewy eyes . . . .**" [Sunday March 17th 1907]

When the others left, Jean and Norah drove to the village of Coldirodi and Jean experienced something of Norah's bohemian ways. "**. . . we stopped for lunch at a horrid Trattoria in the smelly street. An omelette, which we had to wait for while it was cooked, some bread and butter and cheese. . . . All wish to eat left me at the disgusting place . . . .**

... a vicious white cat, obviously about to provide the world with kittens seated herself on the chair beside me, and an obscene dog, obviously already a mother, took her stand beside Norah, and an awful mongrel, belonging to the barber in the village, marauded round, he looked like a lion and a monkey in one, with eyes like the Duchess of Marlborough, and Norah fed him hugely, and gave *him* a golden day at any rate.

She looked like a fairy princess out of a fairy tale, in these surroundings ... and ... loving it all – she is a true Bohemian. I felt ashamed of my fastidiousness and tried not to think of smells, and filthy knives and forks." [Saturday March 23rd 1907]

In April, on the return journey, Jean was joined by her brother Kay in France. They went to see the stage dramatisation of Tolstoy's novel *Anna Karenina* at the Théatre Antoine, Versailles. When Jean returned she went to stay with the Robertses; they lived near a railway line, and it reminded her of Anna's suicidal plunge in front of a train. "I heard the cry of the train at the foot of the garden, as I walked through it alone to-night after leaving Ian at the gate; it reminded me of the level crossing in the play Anna Karenina, where you hear the train whistle and see the smoke, and it was all over for her – it was sinister and solemn, and I thought after all how easy it is to make an end – the bridge here would haunt and tempt me if I lived here." [Tuesday June 18th 1907 Englemere]

Jean and Ian stayed with Frances (later Lady) Horner, her husband Jack and two daughters, Katharine and Cecily, at historic Mells Manor. "We both had a happy day after all yesterday. We went to Wells Cathedral with Mrs. Horner and Cecily. I took the book Mrs. Horner had given me to read last night. . . . it is Burne-Jones' beautiful letters to her – 'From mere me to beautiful you,' is the dedication.

I read the book in the Cathedral listening to the organ pealing the anthem, Ian sitting with Mrs. Horner. I gazed at her in amazement – how could she mean so much to this beautiful soul? . . . These are fine letters, strong and beautiful, making life seem worth living. What a gift from life to have had the friendship and love of such a man, and she seems to me so unlovely, with her ravaged, haunted face. Sometimes I see there the shadow of the sweetness that must have been . . . . [Monday July 30th Tidworth, 1906]

A Field Day was held for Mr Haldane, the Secretary of State for War, who was a friend of Frances Horner's. "**Mr. Haldane is here, Mrs. Horner, Cecily Horner, Norah Lindsay, Lord and Lady Salisbury, Major George Morris, Lord Lucas. . . .**" The Field Day was "**wonderful**" but Haldane seemed more interested in Frances and Jean thought he was in love with her. "**Mr. Haldane wandered about with Mrs. Horner – (as soon as her motor appeared he wanted to get in it). General Bethune was in charge of him and was much disgusted by this as he said the whole Field Day had been carefully got up for him, and now he was not at all interested in it and was 'pothousing about with fairies all the time'.**" [August 9th 1906]

When Jean spent time with Frances in London, she came to appreciate her. "**I like Frances Horner, and see lots of delightful qualities in her and have enjoyed my visit here.**" She was "**. . . wonderful in her home life – such tact and temper. . . .**" [June 13th and 14th 1907, 9 Buckingham Gate] The Horner family became frequent visitors to Tidworth, and when Katharine married Raymond Asquith, Jean was invited to the wedding. "**Katharine Horner's wedding day – she looked lovely. She was married in the veil of Mary Queen of Scots – the one she wore for her execution. I should have been afraid. I hope the lovely pair will have nothing but good luck; they looked such darlings.**" [July 25th 1907 6 Upper Grosvenor Street, home of Muriel Beckett] Winston Churchill had an amusing view of Cecily: "**Winston says Cecily is like a macaroon filled with Vanilla cream, and when I talk to her we go round and round in the macaroon and are choked with the tasteless cream, never got out.**" [Sunday August 11th 1907 Tidworth]

Jean's sister, Edie, younger by eleven years and still single, stayed a lot. Jean thought her gentlemen friends were more taken with Edie than herself and was jealous. Lying in bed one night she raged to herself over "**Edie's long, slow glances**" at the men, and recalled that "**With Lord Alwyne she once nearly did succeed at the theatre. . . .**" In India, Colonel Babbington had been in love with Jean for years but Edie "**. . . ruined and blasted all my friendship with Col. Babbie and now Polly has seceded . . .**" [26th July 1906 Tidworth] Jean thought Captain Maitland and Major Frank Lyon were both in love with Edie. "**Edie is rather in love with little Lyon, I see, I believe she will marry him!.**" [Nov. 24th 1907] Frank Lyon, whom Edie nicknamed Major Polly, proposed but she turned him down. He asked Jean if he could be considered for the job of Military Secretary to Ian but Jean told him it was out of the question; she knew he only wanted to be near Edie, in the hope she might change her mind.

Ian's brother, Vereker, and his wife Lily and their children, 'little Ian', Betty, Marjorie and Janet came to stay for Christmas and the New Year. The children called Jean their fairy godmother and Jean and Ian bought the girls dresses for Christmas. They skated to gramophone records and Jean played tennis with Vereker and 'little Ian'. **"We all dressed up for dinner to-night, as the children wished it so much . . . . The children are so clever at dressing up; little Ian and Margery dressed in Freddy's [Maitland's] kilt and looked delicious; Freddy was much excited helping her to dress.**

We all danced to the gramophone after dinner. I wore my scarlet dinner dress, my white wig and a white paper hat, and got giddy and exhausted dancing.

Ian was sweet this morning. He said he heard 12 strike last night and got up and came to my door, and listened, as he wanted to come in and kiss me, and wish me a happy New Year, but as he did not hear me move, he wished it me in his heart and went quietly away. He seems really fond of me just now, and happy to be with me. I think he likes me gay." [New Year's Day 1908 Tidworth]

The experience of having such a happy family about her made Jean long again for a child. **"Ian ought to have a son of his own, I do feel it is too bad, and quite all wrong. I often wonder if Ian is not dreadfully disappointed about this. I am."** [Jan. 15th 1908] Each blamed the other for their not having children. **"Wednesday night I walked up to the woods with Ian, to look at the primroses, and coming back had a curious talk with him . . . I told him what I feel – that it does not shock me so much that a woman should give herself to her lover when she loves him, as that a woman should live habitually with her husband when she is indifferent to him, and said various things which I feel strongly about, and he was not shocked, he is so understanding.**

The talk depressed me a little and depressed him, and going down to dinner he stopped me suddenly at the top of the stairs going down to the boudoir, to say that if I had not had these ideas we would have children, to which I replied scornfully if I had been married to another man I would have had a large family. He said, 'Yes, because

he wouldn't have been so influenced by you,' so I laughed and ran away, saying what I said did not apply in this case.

He came to my room and lay on my bed when I was going to bed, a long time thinking, and I might have said many things to him which I have had locked in my heart for long, but I did not say them, and I was frightened and hurried him away. I fear the spoken word." [Friday April 10th 1908 Tidworth]

They were returning by train from a visit to Norah Lindsay, one of the few opportunities to be alone together. "**Travelling back with Ian this morning my cushions and book were not put into the carriage. I bemoaned this greatly and Ian said, 'Never mind, I am going to kiss you and make love to you, and you'll never miss them.' Till the next station I listened in a somewhat distrait manner, and when he was kissing me, said in a practical voice, 'Please shut the window, I am cold,' upon which he dropped me like a hot potatoe, and shut the window, saying, 'Who could make love to you?' 'I love you,' I adore you says the man. 'Please give me some of that Pork Pie with plenty of mustard,' says she, etc. etc.**" [Monday July 13th 1908 Tidworth] They seemed to have eventually resolved their problems and some love making took place. It was obviously too late to have children but Jean could record with joy, "**... Another happy night with Ian in the boudoir....**" [22nd Jan. 1908] And again, on 17th July 1908, she wrote in her diary with evident delight that Ian had taken to calling himself the "**daily male**"!

Ian's job at Salisbury was soon coming to a close and it was with some trepidation Jean anticipated their leaving Tidworth, once again to face the unknown. "**I have been thinking sadly – will it be London this time next year – . . . and I have been thinking of my poor Ian there, overworked, tired, fagged out, it's delicious for him here, flying out from his office work to be rested amongst the whispering woods. I wish we could be alone a little – I see so little of him these days, but he likes homeopathic doses of me.**" [Sunday June 28th 1908 Tidworth] The previous year, Repington had caused some alarm, making premature predictions of where Ian might be sent. "**Walking in the poppy field, which was strewn with ragged Robin, he [Ian] told me Col. Repington told him we were certainly going to be sent to India. The unrest there is terrifying just now, and Ian thinks it will increase till there is bloodshed, and I had visions of fearsome scenes of horrors, and of how we, or I rather, would long for safe, green England, and Ian was never**

well there. I would hate to go even if Ian went as C. in C. as Col. Repington declares he will." [July 9th 1907 Tidworth] The possibility of Ian being offered and feeling obliged to accept India was still a possibility; as ever, life for Jean was uncertain and the future never secure or settled.

Ian's good looks, charismatic personality and successful career earned him the admiration of women *and* men. " **. . . A huge Liberal dinner at the Ivor Guests' to-night – fifty-three people – it was great fun. I sat between Mr. Lulu Harcourt, who took me in, and Summy Somerset, whom I much liked, on my other side. We discussed if he were a woman who would he fall in love with in the room, and he said, 'Certainly with Ian'. He said he touched his imagination, and was so good-looking and splendid, and had the love of adventure, which attracted him. He said, 'Look around here now, who has a sense of adventure in this room: Not one, except him.'** [15th May 1908 50 Wilton Crescent] Even the Queen found Ian attractive. When the Hamiltons dined with the King Edward VII and Queen Alexandra on the Royal Yacht, " **. . . the Queen told Ian he must remember to send her his photo, that she had asked for it before and he had forgotten."** [8th July 1908]

Whilst the Hamiltons were staying at Blenheim Palace, the system of national insurance tax, being introduced by David Lloyd George, Liberal MP and Chancellor of the Exchequer in the Liberal Government, was the topic for discussion. Picture Winston Churchill, lying on a rug on the drawing room floor, in front of the fire, at Jean's feet. " **. . . Winston Churchill and Lloyd George are very hand-in-glove – they are plotting all kinds of mischief. I was talking to them both, when Winston quoted something from 'Romeo and Juliet' about fighting or overcoming the inauspicious stars. I said he'd have to be a god to do that; he said, 'Anyway, I *could* fight them' and Mr. Lloyd George laughed, but did not believe it".** [19th July 1908 Blenheim Palace] Winston was, at this time, a Liberal MP and in the Cabinet as President of the Board of Trade. The debate over the system of national insurance tax raged between the House of Commons and the House of Lords for several years. When it was eventually introduced, Jean supported it. " **. . . Have been discussing with Ian whether to pay it or not – McAdie is filled with mischievous glee over it all. . . . I am all for the benefit of the poor at the expense of the rich."** [21st July 1912]

No great house would be complete without a ghost and Tidworth was haunted, so legend had it, by a drummer boy. His ghost stalked the rooms, beating kettle drums and frightening Jean and Ian and the servants and alarming the guests. **"We heard the Drummer last night, Ian and I, and we were frightened, and I could scarcely sleep alone and longed to go to ask Ian to come and sleep with me, but did not, I felt afraid."** [August 6th 1908] Lady Jekyll and her daughter, Barbara, were staying and the drummer came in broad daylight. **"Heard the drummer again this afternoon. McAdie almost dropped what she was carrying in astonishment, it was so loud, just behind the curtain in the recess. Lady Jekyll and Barbara who came in heard it too – it was about 7-15 and I was lying down before dinner – they were astonished they so distinctly heard the roll of kettle drums – the ghost who plays the kettle drum is of a little drummer boy murdered at Tidworth."** [Monday August 10th 1908 Tidworth]

Perhaps the ghost of the drummer was an omen. Edie was often unwell and was more ill than anyone realised, suffering from a fever. 'Little Ian' noted that the drummer was 'particularly active' during the time Edie was ill at Tidworth.[3]

CHAPTER 6

Malta (1910–14)

"Our Silver Wedding day. I awoke thinking of my wedding twenty-five years ago. . . . " [22nd February 1912]

The year 1909 did not begin well for Jean and her family. Her beloved sister, Edie, died in Brighton, where she had gone for her health. **" . . . I sat for long this morning with my darling in her coffin in that joyous little flower filled room by the sea, with all her dear things round me that she loved – Nettie looking at me from her silver frame – Kay on her dressing table, and my funny photo beside her bed, with Major Lyon's poor faded red roses, which had given her pleasure Heather said. . . . " [29th April 1909 Brighton]**

Ian was once again about to accept a command that would take him overseas. The Duke of Connaught resigned the Malta-based Mediterranean Command in 1909. The position was then offered to Lord Kitchener, who refused because he thought it not good enough for him and because he wanted the Viceroyalty of India. Ian was then offered the post.

Before any decision could be confirmed, King Edward VII died suddenly, on 6 May 1910. The following day, Jean could write with intimate knowledge of his death and the predicament of his lover, Alice Keppel. **" . . . The King is dead – and I look from my window and see people riding about talking of it, everything going on as usual – the summer wind is waving the happy young trees in the park. Yesterday morning Nellie came in and told me how ill he was, the first I had heard of it. We were to have dined last night with the Renshawes, to meet Lord Kitchener . . . Lady Wenifred wired 'Dinner put off till 25th' as Lord Kitchener had been commanded to dine with the King. He died at 11.45 last night. . . . splendid man, King Edward, he got up yesterday, and insisted he must be doing something, and if he was not enjoying himself he must be working – I like that – it's exactly how I feel. . . .**

Poor Alice Keppel, how she will miss her King – and all that lot – Julia [Maguire], Lady Saville etc. . . .

The King dead . . . how changed London will be – the meaning of everything seems gone for the moment – the pivot round which the Empire has revolved gone out: I feel more reconciled to the thought of Malta. The court will not be very amusing now – it has been gay and brilliant with King Edward." [7th May 1910, 6 Seamore Pl.]

There was always tremendous interest in the King and Court life and Jean got into an argument on the subject with a friend and admirer of Ian's. " . . . Nearly quarrelled with Margaret Warrender over Alice Keppel today. Margaret arrived, her eyes belching forth spite, and seated herself with an air on my sofa, and said, 'Don't you call it disgraceful Mrs. Keppel being in the Palace when the King died?' I said 'The Queen sent for her, and took her to see the King herself at 4 o'clock'. 'No, she did not take her in to see him' said Margaret. 'Well', I said 'Why did the Queen send for her?' Upon which she had to confess it was because of a pencil note of the poor dying King, who asked to see her. So I said, I could not see, granted the circumstances, that any woman could have acted otherwise than have stayed on as the King was unconscious when she reached him, but at any moment before he died, might have become conscious and wished to see her'. Then she abused her for fainting when she heard that the King was dead, and I just hated her, sitting there so spiteful and nasty, in her black clothes." [11th May 1910, 6 Seamore Place]

The widowed Queen Alexandra wrote a letter to the people that was made public to the nation in the newspapers. " . . . I feared to hear the criticisms of the Queen's letter, and heard echoes of it tonight for the first time from Lord Basil Blackwood, who came to see me here.

Luckily there are many ways of loving. Love is often no less real from being emotional, and every cottage will treasure the Queen's letter. I hear after the King died, Queen Alexandra standing with Alice Keppel beside the bed and looking at him said 'We both loved him' ". [12th May 1910, 6 Seamore Place]

The issue of whether Ian would accept the Mediterranean Command at Malta was being resolved. Jean was initially opposed to the idea, questioning the wisdom of moving so far away from the King and influential political circles. Winston Churchill, who had become Home Secretary in February 1909, heartily approved of the command. Sir Leslie Rundle was already in place as the Governor of Malta. **". . . Winston upset Ian's mind about Malta by telling him he ought to take up his position firmly there from the first, take the Governor's house (which is a lovely place) and do the entertaining. I don't want to do the boring entertaining there – have to entertain the Kaiser and any Royalties who come to the Island . . . and quickly pulled Ian's mind back again (I'd much rather live amongst the orange groves in retirement) to its delights, and the wisdom of leaving the palace and the burden of entertainment to the Rundles who would not at all like to be displaced. . . . Winston turned at the end of dinner and said to me àpropos of Major Bannes, 'Oh you will see him at Malta. . . .' " [12th June 1910 Stoke Court]**

Jean had no say in the matter and Winston got his way – Ian accepted the Mediterranean Command. The only other choice of a post at that time was in India, to which Jean was even more opposed. The memory of the effect of the climate on her asthma was only too vivid. India had been blamed, rightly or wrongly, for the death of Lady Mary Curzon. Thankful for small mercies, Jean prepared to move to Malta.

Once Ian accepted Malta the Hamiltons' popularity evaporated overnight. Kitchener's friends, who were Conservatives, were furious at Ian for upstaging him and helping out the Liberal Government. To make matters worse, Kitchener did not get the Viceroyalty of India. In revenge, his circle of supporters ostracised the Hamiltons socially and Jean in particular bore the brunt of it, being shunned by those society women who supported Kitchener. At almost every house party they attended they were made to feel unwanted. Lord Kitchener took his disappointment badly and when the Hamiltons stayed with Lord and Lady Roberts, he refused to join the party there, remaining at Broome, his country home. **" . . . Lord Kitchener ought to have been here, but he is sulking, shut up in Broome because he is not to get the Viceroyaltyship . . . I looked into a hansom three or four days ago as I crossed from Edgware Road to Marble Arch and felt as though I had looked into hell as I found myself staring into the open face of Lord K. in his worst mood. He has been engaged for ages to come here for Ascot but on hearing about India simply sent a curt wire saying he could not come. . . .**

Everyone greeted me today with a very long flat face about this Malta appointment; Lord Kitchener's leaving is the feeling, but Ian is very gay over it, and intends to make it a great appointment – he sees many opportunities in it." [15th June 1910 Englemere Ascot]

Only the Henry Bentincks threw a **"Brilliant delightful party"** where everyone was **"excited about Ian's new appointment. The Conservatives furious the Liberals triumphant Ian has got them out of a tight place. . . . "** [16th June 1910] At Sunderland House, Lady Londonderry showed her fury by walking away when she saw Ian and Jean coming and later asked: **" 'Is it a matter for congratulation or con- dolence?' And I said: 'Congratulation, of course.' "** [23rd June 1910]

Jean's close friend Ettie Desborough was apparently not aware of the situation and invited Jean and Ian to stay at Taplow Court, her country home in Buckinghamshire, where there was a large party of other guests. Hostilities there reached fever pitch and Jean sat upstairs scribbling in her diary of her fear of coming down to face them. The only one who would associate with her was the Desboroughs' child, Imogen: **" . . . when I arrived last night she took me for a long walk, to see the chickens. . . . "** During the day, they **" . . . played in the hay in the sunshine . . . "** and **" . . . built houses of hay and pretended we were mistress and servant. . . .**

7 P.M. – No wonder I was frightened but it was much worse than anything I expected. I feel as if I had the plague – everyone flies at my approach and all conversation immediately stops. I have now flown to take refuge in my own room. . . . All those people are so political and are furious with Ian for helping the Liberal Government out of a hole by taking Malta when Lord Kitchener had refused it. Ettie tried to arrange tennis for me with Kitty Somerset, but she obviously did not want to play with me. . . . " Ettie asked Jean to **" . . . amuse Lord Curzon after dinner to-night as he does not play Bridge. I said: 'I don't think he likes me,' and she replied, 'Oh, he does, he told me he particularly liked you last night,' and I said 'Oh, Ettie, *how you can.*' – and with such an air of candid truth too.**

Norah Lindsay gave me a lot of messages for Lord Milner which I delivered but they were coldly received. . . . really I feel vexed because of Ettie's disappointment in me but I am hurt with Summy Somerset, I thought he was my friend, but when I sug- gested the river this afternoon he did not seem very keen about it, so I did not give him the chance, but went off at once with Imogen. . . . " [11th July 1910]

" . . . Lady Ulrica Baring is much taken with Ian . . . and took him for a long walk. I was glad of that for Ian feels out of this party also. . . " [10th July 1910] Jean wondered why Ettie wanted them at all. **" . . . I**

would not have believed it possible, with so many intimate friends here, one could feel so out of it. I had almost forgotten how it felt to be a woman of no importance,[1] **and not to have the courage to assert oneself." [11th July 1910** contd.]

Two weeks later Jean was still reeling from the blows: "**... the most crushing experience I have almost ever had was at Taplow. I have been thinking this morning that it's odd the Manners, Hylda Grenfell, the Rutlands, Lady Cunard, none of them asked us to their dances. ... we are being regularly boycotted. Ian is the villain of the piece – a regular Society cabal. It has put the Liberal Government in a hat. The Duke of Connaught had thrown up the Malta Command hoping to be President of the Selection Board which Mr. Asquith** [the Prime Minister] **was determined he should not have, and the Conservatives were anxious no one of any standing should accept the command in the Duke's place so as to show he had been right to throw it up, so are furious with Ian." [23rd July 1910, 6 Seamore Place]**

On Saturday 8 October 1910, Ian left for Malta, ahead of Jean. "**... I awoke so glad it was to be Malta, not India – I don't think I want go back to India. The new wine there could never sparkle like the old." [10th October 1910 Avon Tyrell]** Sometime during that year Jean had written 'Justice', a review of John Galsworthy's play, *Justice – a tragedy in four acts*, which must have seemed somewhat appropriate to her situation.

Richard Haldane (later Viscount Haldane of Cloan), who was a Liberal MP and Secretary of State for War (1905–12), was a friend of Ian's, whom he called his 'Paldy'. Haldane asked Ian to write a book entitled *Compulsory Service*,[2] against conscription and in favour of volunteer service to fill the ranks of the army; Haldane had written a lengthy introduction to the book. If the Hamiltons had remained in London this would have been the next battle they would have had to fight in society. Jean went to visit the Robertses but Lord Roberts was greatly in favour of conscription and a distance inevitably developed between Ian and Roberts over this issue. "**... A very nice party here and I feel unhappy that the dear Bobs are nourishing vipers in their bosom, as Ian and Mr. Haldane's article, which Ian wanted to call 'Delhi or Dorking', comes out in pamphlet form this week, and is a blow to Lord Bob's pet scheme, and is written against conscription." [23rd October 1910 Englemere]**

Jean was now looking forward to going to live in Malta to escape from all the intriguing going on against them in London, and left on Sunday 6 November. By the time she arrived, Ian was already very happy with his new post.

The beginning of the New Year 1911 saw the Hamiltons settled in their latest new temporary home, San Antonio Palace. **"... Ian ... is so well and happy and his book goes on creating wild excitement in London – the First Sea Lord, Admiral Wilson is now going to add a letter to his book, and Ian is vexed with me for telling Sir Edmund Poe this the other night at dinner."** [6th January 1911, San Antonio, Valetta]

Violet Asquith, the Prime Minister's daughter by his first wife, came to stay, bringing praise from Asquith's second wife, Margot. Herbert Asquith had been Prime Minister since 1908 and Margot moved in glittering circles in London society. The Liberal Government were very pleased with Ian's face-saving measure over Malta and the Asquiths flattered Jean. **"... Violet told me Margot Asquith told her last summer that I interested her so much, as I was the only woman who had succeeded in overcoming the determination of the Smart Set (I must use that term for want of a better) to keep the wives of the men they select to honour out of it, but that now they liked me almost better than Ian."** [2nd March 1911]

Whilst in Malta, the Hamiltons retained their house, 6 Seamore Place. Ian went to London on business and wrote to Jean of the atmosphere there. Even intimate old friends like General Sir Reginald Pole-Carew (Polly), who had been Ian's best man at their wedding, had seemingly turned against them. Jean must have felt relieved to be able to view it all from afar. **" ... Ian's book is creating a fearful row and excitement in London – he writes me he is the man of the moment, and Julia Maguire and Margaret Warrender as assiduous as ever. Polly Carew has made a ridiculous speech about Ian but has only done himself harm, poor man. Mr. Haldane evidently officially, has made a mistake in publishing what ought to have been a private opinion for himself alone, but he cares more for his ideas than for the temporal infringement of procedure."** [26th March 1911]

The town of Valetta was 'fascinating' with its 'magnificent Lodges of the Knights of Malta and its many baroque churches ... ' In her luxurious surroundings, Jean painted pastels of the beautiful gardens of San Antonio

Palace, 'set amidst orange groves . . . with fountains and pools and cascades of bougainvillaea on the stone terraces.'³

In London Ian's unpopularity continued. During the constitutional crisis of 1910–11, originally caused by the House of Lords blocking the 1909 budget, the Liberal Government threatened to create enough new peers to force through their legislation, the Parliament Bill, which would curb the Lords' powers. Ian was the only general whose name was on the Prime Minister's list, with a view to the submission of names to the King. This was one more source of annoyance to the anti-Liberal sections of society, already incensed by Ian's book against conscription. **" . . . Ian is, I fear, very unpopular because of his book on Compulsory Service, murmurs of it reach me. . . . Everyone is saying he is about to be made a peer – it would be terribly unpopular if that happened now. . . . "** [7th May 1911 Deanston]

In early April 1911 the Hamiltons returned to England for the Coronation of the new King, George V. The hostilities towards them continued, over Ian's book. **" . . . I see we shall have our battles to fight, there is a strong feeling against him at present. From what I hear Ian will not be on the winning side, but I do not mind that as he has a more ideal vein of patriotism than the more practical and material Lord Bobs and his school. Mr. Haldane has also this ideal. . . . What does infuriate me is when people insinuate, as Ronnie Brooke did the other day – that Ian had changed round and altered his point of view to suit Mr. Haldane's views, which is quite untrue."** [15th May 1911, 6 Seamore Place]

If Ian had been made a peer in the circumstances of a political crisis, it would have identified him so closely with the Liberal Government as to leave his supposed neutrality as a soldier open to question. **" . . . Ian has been congratulated on getting a peerage several times lately, and wrote a letter to Mr. Haldane yesterday to say he hoped it was not true, as it would really do for him entirely if he were given a peerage now. I said I thought so, too, but he'd better wait till he was offered it, I thought. However, he said it would be more difficult to refuse it then as it would have the King's sanction."** [16th June 1911 Englemere]

The Coronation of King George V took place on 22nd June. **" . . . My Ian headed the procession. . . . "** [23rd June 1911 London]

The back-biting in London continued and Norah Lindsay told her that Colonel Babbington said **" . . . Ian need not refuse India on account of** my health as he could very well go without me as he had done already." [25th September 1911] Such a comment must have been hurtful to Jean, coming from Babbington, her old friend from their days in India.

Ian returned to Malta and Jean remained behind, dividing her time between London and Deanston. When Ian was expected back, Jean, accompanied by Freddy Stanley, went to the railway station to meet him. Freddy was always over-attentive to Jean, running errands for her and following her around like a lap dog, getting on her nerves. " . . . **beautifully dressed in my serge gown and blue veil. . . . I was joyously excited and stood in the very forefront of the little expectant crowd, thinking Ian would be eagerly looking out for me, and would be proud and pleased to see me there, but carriage after carriage rattled past, with many expectant husbands' heads, but no Ian. . . . "** The guard " . . . **reluctantly conducted me to a sealed up compartment, where the General was soundly sleeping, having given orders he was not to be called till 7.30. However, I insisted on entering and waking him up. He was delighted to see me, I saw in his gay blue eyes, and very gratified in a way, said it was delightful and romantic of me to come, and we laughed over my tight harem skirt, and kissed one another many times, but he stoutly refused to get up. I was full of dismay when I realised he really did not mean to get up and come back with me, I could not believe it, and yet in a curious way I loved him for it too; most men, however reluctant they were, would have felt compelled to get up, and hurriedly dress, could not have let their wife in a flaunting blue veil go sadly off with only a ridiculous wild bird in a big cage to take home with her; I felt abashed before the Guard and all the porters, who had stared at me a good deal."** [12th November 1911]

London was not a happy place for the Hamiltons at that time, and for Jean, worse was yet to come. " . . . **Lord Alwyne died last Saturday night . . . All day I have felt dazed and now I am alone here to-night with my memories – Ian has gone off to a ball – all London speaks to me of him; to think he has only once been in this drawing-room, but all my old familiar furniture knows him well, this sofa where we have had happy comfy intimate talks, the cushions where he laid back his beautiful dark head, and oh, my little boudoir full of the Malta pastels I so looked forward to showing him, of the orange groves he told me of last year and he has never seen them, and never can now. I know** the hope was always there that I could help him perhaps in the end, and now nothingness; to die all alone in the Bath Club! and I so near him on Saturday afternoon, almost passed the door, and he dying then. . . . oh, how I wish I had sent this letter I wrote him not long ago to let him know I thought of him with gratitude, that his memory was always a happy one to me, but I had not the courage to send it. . . . so large a part of my youth dies with him." [18th December 1911 London]

Jean held many memories of Lord Alwyne in her heart, some happy, some sad.

" 'His eyes be like the starry lights,
His voice like sounds of summer nights,
In all his lowly mien let pierce
The magic of the universe.'

I remember reading these lines of Matthew Arnold in his copy of the poems he gave me in exchange for mine. I wonder where it will go now, my little marked book? I do *hate* cold strangers reading lovely things I have loved and marked. These lines expressed what he seemed to me *then*. I found them and read them again this morning. . . .

What memories crowd on me out of the past – happy radiant girlish hours, they come back fresh as ever. Lord Alwyne standing on the Government House staircase at Calcutta in the middle of a Ball, smiling, dark, graceful, watching me while I kissed Father good-night, as if we were at home instead of in a Calcutta ballroom – how amused he was! . . . and my frivolous life has to go on now and he lying dead. I long to see him. . . . " [19th December 1911, 6 Seamore Place]

Lord Alwyne was buried on 21 December, which would have been his silver wedding anniversary. " . . . His burial to-day – twenty-five years ago it was his wedding day; the night he was married I dreamed of him there, in my small girlish room in Simla. I dreamed I lost the precious little riding whip he gave me with the badge of his regiment – a silver grenade – on it, the happy whip that went always with me on all our enchanting morning rides. . . .

Years later came our lovely Sunday walks down Piccadilly with all the lights twinkling through the evening mist in St. James's Park;

how full of magic London was then, every Sunday the lovely Queen's
Hall Concert, then this same walk because I loved that way, a cosy tea
in my little Curzon Street drawing-room; but he said his boys later on
claimed all his Sundays. How *good* he was then, how high principled –
almost stern – giving a night up every week to go and teach the boys
in the slums. . . .

I longed to see his face again and sent Freddy to the Bath Club
early Tuesday to see if it would be possible, but he had already been
taken away to Castle Ashby.

. . . I sent a wreath of lovely shimmering blue cinerarias with a
bunch of white roses and lilies of the valley to Castle Ashby yesterday
and wrote on a card 'Lord Alwyne Compton. In most grateful remembrance always.' . . . " [21st Dec. 1911]

Jean had not been able to attend his burial but she went to the funeral
service. His loss left a void in her life. " . . . Such a beautiful service yesterday. As I entered St. Margaret's [Westminster] and felt its beauty I
remembered Alwyne had been married there and pictured it to myself
– he glad, confident, happy – she inwardly reluctant, hating it all –
what a shame! His wedding day . . . and now his funeral day – all his
unhappy married life ended.

I felt it strange it was *I* who was listening to this service for him, I
had so often wondered lately if *he* would regret *me* when I died? but I
never thought of death in connection with him – he was so keen about
life – I thought of him there had he been listening to these words for
me. . . . In St. Margaret's I was with him again – the gay charming
friend of my youth – as I listened to the wonderful words of the Burial
Service – 'Sown in corruption, raised in incorruption, sown in dishon-
our, raised in glory,' I realised how little we understand here, 'we see
as in a glass darkly,' our values wrong and worthless. . . . " [22nd
December 1911]

Ian, exceedingly happy with his Malta appointment, shopped in
London at the Royal jewellers for a present for Clementine Churchill, the
wife of his beloved Winston, who had helped him obtain the commission.
Winston had been newly promoted to First Lord of the Admiralty. Ian was
greatly enjoying himself, taking dancing lessons with his niece, the ballet
dancer, Margot Hamilton. " . . . Yesterday evening he told me he had
been to Asprey's to buy a blue enamelled brooch and mirror for
Clemmie Churchill – he never can be bothered choosing anything for

a present or entering a shop, I don't know what has come over him, it seems as though some other soul has come to inhabit his body for a time, such a rage for life and pleasure possesses him! ... he ... danced till 3.30 on Wednesday night and flew off to Margery to have dancing lessons for the Boston. ... " [22nd December 1911]

The end of the old year always provoked in Jean anticipation of the new. " ... I wonder if I shall see another last day of the year come up and where? Is Lord Alwyne out of the diurnal course where we revolve ceaselessly with leaves and stones and beasts and flowers, a perpetual wheel, or is it a spiral staircase leading back to God? Is Lord Alwyne too quite, quite gone out of my life for ever? I remember writing these lines out for him:–

'Remember me when I am gone away into the silent land
And you no more can hold me by the hand,
Nor I half turn to go, yet turning stay.'

How often have I seen him do that at Chesterfield Street and at Curzon Street. When I think back I see how he turned to me in the crisis of his life, but when he asked for bread I could only give him a stone; when he confessed to me the emptiness of his life I showed him the fulness of mine; when he told me his wife did not love him and he got no sympathy at home, I told him I loved my husband and had promised him never to let another man kiss me. He was very darling after that to me, but looking back of course I realise he put me definitely out of his life then, the moonlight night we drove back from the river together, and I was so cold, so chilled, and wrote him afterwards 'We'll go no more a "roving by the light o' the moon." ' " [31st December 1911 Carnell Ayrshire]

The Hamiltons returned to Malta but Ian was often away inspecting troops elsewhere, and there was a great deal of entertaining to be done during the Malta years. " ... Ian arrived Tuesday, the 13th, in time to dine at a great formal boring banquet on the 14th, at the Palace. I wore my white satin with fur. Friday, the 16th, we had a huge dance about four or five hundred people here, which much depressed me, but went well, except that there was a scarcity of food, and Monday, the 19th, there was a huge Carnival ball at the Palace about 1300 people. Ian wore his soldier's dress of 1830, and I wore an early Victorian dress of brilliant pink crinoline and a little black coat, and poke bonnet trimmed with pink roses; it was a darling dress and I hated to take it off, it suited me so well. ... " [21st Feb. 1912]

However, in Malta, they were away from the gossip and hostilities of London. Jean still suffered from asthma and Ian was enjoying life to the full, continuing his dancing.

They awoke to a momentous occasion: " . . . **Our Silver Wedding day. I awoke thinking of my wedding twenty-five years ago in that large low room in 15 Store Road. . . . I remember how frightened I was when I thought 'the day is actually here', I had felt it was so impossible it should arrive – my wedding day, and now I have been married twenty-five happy years, and Ian looks younger, gayer, happier than when I married him. I remember at Darjeeling on our honeymoon, riding on ponies somewhere, and seeing him riding in front of me and thinking I have the happiness of this charming man now in my keeping, and resolving firmly to guard it."** [22nd February 1912 San Antonio]

In the evening they had a large party and danced to a silver band. ". . . **Two tables of ten each – Sir Leslie and Lady Rundle, the Stapleton Cottons, and Gores . . . the nicest people on the Island, and about 20 people after dinner, and we danced till 12 with Lambolton's band – it was a delightful party, and I very much enjoyed it."** It was a day that Ian, too, would always treasure. 'Our Silver Wedding Day passed in a silver dream. . . .' The pastels Jean painted at Malta always reminded him of that day, possessing 'a very special charm for me.'4

Jean and Ian remained in the party spirit and Malta was a very happy time for them and successful from Ian's career point of view. " . . . **Last night we had an after dinner dance again and I actually danced every dance. . . . Ian simply loves these dances and dances like a school-boy or rather like** *l'age dangereux* [that dangerous age] **for men, as no school-boy would** *so* **know how to enjoy the fleeting moment. I love to see him in his kilt gaily footing the one-step which he actually went and learnt in London so he really does dance it properly . . . he enjoys himself gloriously and doesn't care a hang for his dignity, he is quite frankly happy dancing with all these girls and I would quite enjoy slipping about with some of these nice boys if I did not feel I must hold on to my dignity as it's the only becoming garment for my years."** [3rd March 1912 San Antonio]

The Hamiltons were decidedly more popular in Malta and the rumpus with Kitchener soon blew over. Many visitors from England would find their way to Malta, Kitchener and Churchill amongst them.

CHAPTER 7

The Beginning of World War I (1914–15)

"I . . . thought of . . . Ian, and how wonderful it must be to be a man absorbed in fighting, leading a free wild life . . . real things for which you will die. . . . " [4th September 1916]

When the Hamiltons returned from Malta in 1914, they bought a large house, 1 Hyde Park Gardens, which was Jean's choice. No. 1 HPG, as it was referred to in the family, would become their most prestigious home in London. Jean personally took charge of the redesigning. The walls, including the drawing room and ballroom, were painted jade green. Gothic columns, painted to look like lapis lazuli, an idea brought from Deanston, were installed at the foot of the stairs, next to the balustrade that led to the ballroom on the first floor. The black Buddha Ian had acquired in Burma **" . . . sits and dreams . . ."** at the foot of the stairs. A magnificent full-length portrait of Jean, wearing a cloak designed by Worth of Paris, which was painted by her friend Charles Furse, and stood nine feet high, faced the top of the main staircase. The drawing room, furnished by Roger Fry from his Omega workshops, drew particular praise. Throughout the house the walls were hung with paintings by her artist friends, two of which were the portraits of Jean and Ian painted by Singer Sargent. Others were by Sir John Lavery, Charles Furse, Walter Sickert, and young, undiscovered artists. The setting provoked appropriate conversation, Lord Ribblesdale discussed **"sin"** with Jean in the **"black drawing-room. I maintained what the world considered sin was often the best activity of one's life."** The dining room was on the south side, panelled in oak linen-fold with a frieze of family portraits above. The house was highly acclaimed in articles published in the fashionable ladies' magazines of the day. 'Lady Hamilton knows the importance of the fireplace in a room and she has made all hers interesting; the one in the big drawing room is an enormous mediaeval affair for which specially large logs have to be cut, and it looks really magnificent with a bright fire burning.'[1] *The Queen* dedicated a centre-page spread with photographs of the elegant Gothic columns and the balustrade, sweeping upstairs to the ballroom. Rosa Stuart in *Every Women's* said it was 'a beautiful British home . . . furnished on modified Futurist lines, but it is a futurism devoid of any kind of gloom. Lady Hamilton's own boudoir . . . is a study in cream and gold . . . £30,000 is by no means an unusual sum for an especially valuable picture.'[2] **[25th Feb. 1915; 9th May; 10th and 15th Oct. 1919]** Jean's bedroom, which she completed herself, overlooked Hyde Park. **" . . . I love my green bedroom high above the trees in the Park, where I wake every morning before the dawn, and watch it come stealing up over the sky touching the spire of the Catholic Cathedral and the top of the Albert Memorial with gold. . . . I have painted the fireplace green myself and stood over the workmen while they painted the wood like malachite." [20th January 1916 London]**

Jean and Ian had only just settled into their new house when World War I broke out, but Ian had a commission at home, at least for the moment. **" . . . attired in my blue velvet dressing gown I dine with Ian in my sitting-room next door."** On Sundays they drove in the open motor, Jean accompanied by Musta, her latest dog, to Harewood Downs. Arriving at noon they ate lunch at the Club House and then played golf. **" . . . Ian, I and Musta all happy together in that *lovely* place – we play very evenly together and have quite exciting games – then home to tea in the black drawing-room."** Ian sang to Jean playing the piano. In the evening they dined at **"the old Troc."** and listened **"to lovely music – they know us well there now and always have our special table ready. He is always loving and sweet to me *now*, and I love the way he calls me 'Judy.'"** [New Year's Eve; 7th March 1915]

Ian's term as Inspector General of Home and Overseas Forces was coming to an end and was up for review. Jean feared that he would lose out to Sir John French, who was without a posting since his resignation as a result of that unhappy and divisive incident in the history of the British army known as the Curragh mutiny, in Ireland.

The Hamiltons' house-warming party was a star-studded occasion. Their guests included Lady Diana Manners, Nancy Cunard (daughter of Maud, Lady Cunard), the Duchess of Rutland, Lord Birkenhead (formerly Sir F. E. Smith, the Attorney General), Ann, Lady Islington, and the Hamiltons' close friends, Viscount Haldane of Cloan (now the Lord Chancellor), and his sister, Anne. **" . . . I think the house looked lovely,** and . . . everyone very excited over it. Lord Birkenhead was especially excited . . . 'what a house' he called to me as he bounded up the stairs . . . . Ruby Peto said it was the most wonderful house she had ever seen, and the most beautiful." [24th July 1914 London]

Ian called Haldane his 'Paldy', to which Jean seems to have prefixed 'Haldy'. " . . . I wanted to talk to Lord Haldane about Ian's appointment, as yesterday at the Asquith's garden party, I had told Frances [Charteris] that Ian would refuse Ireland if it was offered to him, and that the only appointment he wanted was that of Inspector General of Home and Overseas Forces, which he has made into a really wonderful appointment and we fear may be given to General French, as there does not seem much else the Government can give him. Ian has been promised this appointment for a year as Jack Seely promised he should have it before he left, and he is very keen to get it, as at his suggestion, it has been made into a very important combined one.

Haldy Paldy was very preoccupied and slippery and I could not get anything out of him tonight, but I had told Miss Haldane yesterday exactly what we thought and felt as I drove her home from the Royal garden party, and I know she told him as I asked her to. . . .

Ian, I think, is really enchanted with the house. . . . " [24th July 1914 contd.]

Margot Hamilton, having appeared with Diaghilev's Ballets Russes, danced for them at the party, admired by Felix Warre, who would become her husband. " . . . Margery danced beautifully for us – her Russian dance was most successful. Felix Warre was much taken with her – she looked enchanting." [24th July 1914 contd.]

A few days later, Jean's ambitions for Ian's future were dashed. " . . . The blow has fallen. Sir John French came to tea with us yesterday . . . Ian said to him: 'My appointment is up on August 1st', and Sir John said: 'You know I am to succeed you in this appointment?' Ian said: 'No, I did not know it,' but took it very well, and did not show at all what he felt. I felt sick with rage, no wonder that wicked Lord Haldane tried to avoid talking to me 24th! . . . Ian told General French . . . he had wished for this appointment himself, but wished him the best of luck, and in the evening wrote him a charming letter, and said he wished him well in his appointment and if there was a war he hoped he would take him with him.

It is a shame and I think Ian wonderful the way he takes these

San Antonio Palace, Malta, pastel by Jean, Lady Hamilton.
(By kind permission of Elizabeth, Lady Muir)

Major Ian Hamilton, circa 1887
(By kind permission of Mr Alexander Hamilton)

Miss Jean Muir in her wedding finery 1887
(By kind permission of Elizabeth, Lady Muir)

The Muir family on the Golden Wedding Anniversary of Sir John
and Elizabeth, Lady Muir, at Blair Drummond, October 1986.
(*By kind permission of Mrs Fiona Goetz, daughter of Sir John and Lady Muir*)

Back row left to right: Sebastian Goetz, Dominic Goetz, Rebecca Aird,
Fiona Muir, Lisa Muir, Tony Shapiro, Sophie Muir, Alexandra Muir;
Louisa Muir, The Lady Linda, wife of Sir Richard Muir, 4th Baronet,
Philip Muir, Belinda Aird, Primrose Muir, Sir John Aird, Walter Goetz.

Second row: Griselda Muir, Andrew Muir, Ian Muir, Sir Richard Muir,
4th Baronet, Elizabeth, Lady Muir, Sir John Muir, 3rd Baronet, Lady Aird,
Jamie Muir, Fiona Goetz, Robert Muir.

First row: Hector Muir, Willy Muir, Juliet Muir, Anna Muir, Daisy Muir,
Jamie Aird.

The Hamilton family on the Wedding Day of Mr & Mrs Ian Hamilton,
January 1987, Jamaica.
(By kind permission of Mr Alexander Hamilton)

Left to right: Miss Helen Hamilton, Mr William Hamilton (best man),
Mrs Barbara Kaczmarowska Hamilton (bride), Mr Ian Hamilton (groom),
Miss Laura Hamilton (bridesmaid), Mrs Sarah Hamilton,
Mr Alexander Hamilton.

Maurice Greiffenhagen's painting of Mary Queen of Scots'
last battle, Langside.
(By kind permission of Mr Alexander Hamilton)

Sheep at Cap Martin, pastel by Jean, Lady Hamilton.
(By kind permission of Elizabeth, Lady Muir)

Valetta Harbour, Malta, pastel by Jean, Lady Hamilton.
(By kind permission of Elizabeth, Lady Muir)

The Garden at San Antonio Palace, Valetta, Malta,
pastel by Jean, Lady Hamilton.
(By kind permission of Elizabeth, Lady Muir)

blows of fortune, he manages, somehow, to turn them to advantage."
[29th July 1914 London]

Jean's hopes for a cosy home and normal family life were short lived.
By the end of July the threat of war filled the newspapers. Archduke Franz
Ferdinand and his wife had been assassinated at Sarajevo. "... A delight-
ful day for me socially, but heavy war clouds are in the air. The
Sarajevo murder crime may have fearful results. Ian had to leave us
and rush off to the War Office at 4 o'clock. . . . " [30th July 1914]

Ironically, with Sir John French now needed to command the British
Expeditionary Force, Ian was quickly promoted to take command of the
Home Army. "... Ian was so near to me two days ago, now I find him
so far away, the war absorbs him and his mind roams with Army
Corps – Divisions, where I am not at home and never will be – nothing but war is now talked of or thought of. Ian told me yesterday to lay
in stores and provisions, it sounded like a siege – one can't believe it,
it has all come with such surprising rapidity.

Ian is to command the Home Army – Sir John French in the Field,
and all our little plans are tumbling about us like a pack of cards. Is
this really war? War – how terrible. . . . " [1st August 1914 London]

An announcement of Britain's decision to go to war was imminent.
"... Wildest excitement; at last Lord Grey [Sir Edward Grey, the Foreign
Secretary] has decided to join in the war. Aileen Roberts has been staying with us for the last three days in a state of tense exasperation at his
hesitation – poor Lord Grey, it's a fearful decision to have to take.

He is staying with Lord Haldane in Queen's Gate and passed
sleepless nights. Anyway the die is cast now and we are in for it and
the decision seems popular with the people; as Ian and I walked home
tonight crowds surged past us singing by the Marble Arch – I looked
down the long, straight, lighted way to our house and quoted to Ian:

'News of battle: news of battle,

Hard tis ringing down the street'.

Our servants went to Buckingham Palace where there was a multitude cheering, singing and calling for the King. He and the Queen
appeared several times on the balcony and were tremendously
cheered." [3rd August 1914 London]

On Wednesday 5 August 1914, Herbert Asquith, the Prime Minister,
held a war council attended by Lord Haldane, Kitchener, Lord Roberts, Sir
John French, General Sir Henry Wilson, Earl Haig, General Grierson and

General Sir Ian Hamilton. Haldane proposed a plan, agreed with Sir John
French, that five cavalry brigades and six divisions of the Expeditionary
Force be sent at once to France. The war council opposed his suggestion
of sending all six divisions, preferring to keep two back in case of a
German descent on the coast of Britain, thereby causing a delay in the
smooth organisation of mobilisation.[3]

John Seely, who resigned over the Curragh mutiny, had held the post
of Secretary of State for War. The Prime Minister had taken it over in the
meanwhile and it now had to be filled. The Hamiltons favoured the
Liberal, Lord Haldane, who they knew to be a good administrator, he having previously held the post. The Conservatives supported Kitchener, who
was a Conservative, though Kitchener himself would have viewed his
political situation as neutral. The people too, preferred Kitchener, known
through the newspapers as the great war hero who had conquered the
Sudan. "**. . . The terrible war depression is everywhere – a heavy cloud
of doom over all. Ian is full of hope and good cheer; he had a letter this
morning from Lord Haldane, saying he had taken over the Office of
Secretary of State for War and wanted to see Ian tomorrow; the people clamour for Kitchener, who has been stopped and dragged off his
steamer on his way to Egypt. Lord Haldane said: 'Rather than he
should be Secretary of State for War, I will take it on myself', and so
the P.M. sent a note of apology to Lord K. for having detained him
unnecessarily and K. is raging and fuming." [5th August 1914]**

Haldane may have been undertaking duties normally assigned to the
Secretary of State for War but he was not in fact appointed. The Hon. Julia
Maguire, wife of James Maguire, a former Nationalist Irish MP, and
daughter of Arthur, Viscount Peel, formerly Speaker of the House of
Commons, was a friend of both Lord Kitchener and Count Mensdorf and
was obviously supporting Kitchener for the post. "**. . . Lord Haldane . . .
asked Ian to go and see him at 6. I motored him to Mr. Ralli's house
next to the Austrian Embassy.**

**Julia Maguire came out of the Embassy, very important, in a
bustling hurry, shaking all over like a jelly, in her foulard gown.
At first she pushed past me into the Austrian Embassy to see her
friend Count Mensdorf – Lord K. is staying there with Pendeli
Ralli – then she flew down the steps and gave a note scribbled in
pencil on her card to her chauffeur, then back to the Austrian
Embassy – I wonder what stupid mischief she thought she was up**

to. Ian said she was very busy talking to Lord Kitchener when he went in. . . . " [5th August 1914]

The government of the day was Liberal. The Conservatives, who supported conscription, now demanded it. Vying for power, and supported by the Tory press, they made Lord Haldane the target of their venom. Dubbing him pro-German, the press raised in adverse terms a visit he had made to Berlin in 1912, suggesting he had proposed a bargain against Britain's interests then, and now accusing him of delays in the war effort.[4] The real issue may have been that Haldane, as a Liberal MP, promoted Home Rule for Ireland, which the Tories vehemently opposed. The Hamiltons had some key figures to dine: Major-General Henry Rawlinson, who would command 4th Corps throughout 1915; Brigadier Gerald Ellison, a close friend of Ian's, who had been his Chief of Staff during his time in Malta; and John Alfred Spender, Editor of the *Westminster Gazette*. **" . . . Ian said after dinner they had a thrilling talk, and Spender told them how the Harmsworth Press were going to attack Lord Haldane in the morning. Rawly was going to see Lord K. this morning and Ian, Lord Haldane, to try and arrange they should work together; if it could only be done it would be an excellent combine. . . . "** [5th August 1914] Viscount Harmsworth was Lord Northcliffe, the newspaper baron, who controlled the *Daily Mirror*, *Daily Mail* and *The Times*.

Jean was optimistic Haldane would be the next Secretary of State for War and that he and Ian could work together, as they were in complete agreement on the role of the Territorial Force and on voluntary service as opposed to conscription. Haldane had instituted a policy of voluntary recruitment for the TF to support the Regular Army as an alternative to conscription. Haldane's biographer, Major-General Sir Frederick Maurice, explains that Kitchener, whilst being in support of voluntary recruitment for the regular army, 'distrusted the Territorial Associations in the belief that the influence of county magnates would be used to secure military appointments for their friends'.[5] The Conservatives believed that in the event of the outbreak of war, these volunteers would refuse to fight abroad, since the TF was recruited primarily for home defence. While the great majority of the Territorials did volunteer for overseas service, enough of them chose not to do so immediately to confirm Lord Kitchener in his initial doubts about using them as Britain's first reserve.

The press attacks on Lord Haldane achieved their goal. The appointment of Secretary of State for War was given to the great and distin-

guished Earl Kitchener of Khartoum, satisfying the Tories and the nation
that was clamouring for him. Kitchener was a military general and his natural arena was the battlefield. Without previous experience of government,
he was unsuited to political life. If Lord Haldane had been retained as
Secretary of State for War, with Lord Kitchener acting as his military
adviser, and Winston Churchill performing the equivalent role for the
Navy, Britain might have stood a much greater chance of early success in
the war. " . . . **Lord K. is War Minister and has ousted Lord Haldane,
I am sorry for Ian's sake as he could have worked so well with Lord
Haldane, but I do feel it best for the Empire that it should be K.**

**Ian came in straight from the great Cabinet Committee Meeting,
where it was decided about Lord K. Ian spoke at it and suggested that
our Expeditionary Force should go straight to Amiens, and afterwards when Lord K. spoke he said the same." [5th August 1914]**

Haldane would have expanded the army by increasing the number of
Territorial formations. Instead, Kitchener created the 'new armies', known
as the 'Kitchener armies', from extra battalions of the regular army under
his direct control. Maurice says he decided to 'improvise', in the manner
to which he had been accustomed in Egypt, and 'improvisation was the
very thing which Haldane's scheme was designed to avoid'.[6] Kitchener's
strength, however, was that from the beginning he envisaged a lengthy
war, lasting some three years, and the plans he laid were within this con-
text. But from the outset, Haldane's carefully laid mobilisation plans,
agreed with the army commanders as appropriate for the type of campaign
they were all expecting, were on a complete collision course with those of
Kitchener, who was in full control.

Kitchener's limitations as an administrator were already known to the
Hamiltons, from when Ian served with him in the Boer War in South
Africa. Ian said of him: 'He was a Master of Expedients. I say that in all
confidence . . . because I have, for a space, gone as near as any human
being could go to sharing his arctic loneliness'.[7] " . . . **Ian has gone to
York, sent there and all sorts of other places by Lord K. who is playing hell at the War Office – what the papers call 'standing no non-
sense' but which seems to mean listening to no sense." [12th August
1914 Deanston]**

Peter Simkins explains in his award-winning study *Kitchener's
Army* the difficulties under which Kitchener laboured. In a government
more concerned with Irish Home Rule than the supposed threat from

Germany, the function of Secretary of State for War had been neglected. Britain was clearly unprepared for the sort of long struggle that Kitchener himself predicted and he was able to dominate the Cabinet from the outset. He failed to 'adapt to the concept of collective responsibility' and routinely failed to keep Cabinet members informed of his decisions. He was distrustful of politicians, fearing that they and their wives leaked sensitive information. 'If they will only divorce their wives', he said, 'I will tell them everything'.[8] He had an autocratic manner, accentuated by his large, physical stature; his critics said he behaved like a 'bull in a china shop'.

As soon as Kitchener was appointed his administrative shortcomings became apparent but, to be fair to him, he had been out of the country for some time and could not be expected to know about localised army matters. "... **Ian writes he has seen Winston several times as there seems to be trouble and struggle going on over his appointment – whether he is Commander in Chief of the entire Home Army or only the Central Striking Force. Lord K. when he saw him on Tuesday thought Ian was in command of the whole Home Army; Ian said his ignorance of even where the various places were he was speaking about was extraordinary. He is creating great storms at the War Office – one man rushed out and said it was 'hell with the lid off' in there. . . . he is very popular with the people but amongst people who know, he is called the Great Disorganiser." [16th August 1914 Deanston]**

Soldiers held a fascination for Jean and she admired their daring and bravery. "... **I am reading 'Men Around the Kaiser' – the men are so wildly interesting and so much of the forecast is coming true." [17th August 1914 Deanston]**

The Hamiltons dined with Haldane, who continued in his post of Lord Chancellor (1912–1915). Other guests were Sir Edward Grey (Foreign Secretary 1905–16); Sir Charles Douglas, Inspector-General, Home Forces (1911–1914); Frances Charteris, who was married to Guy Charteris, the son of Lord Wemyss; and Lord Esher, a permanent member of the Committee of Imperial Defence (1905–18). "... **nothing of course but war was talked of. All Sunday our troops were fighting and the 9th Lancers have been cut up, caught on wire entanglements. Lord Esher told me they were tripped by the ruse of pointing the guns the other way. Grey believes that these horrible German atrocities are true – Ian does not, as he says the same stories were told about our soldiers in the Boer War." [26th August 1914 London]**

The newspapers reported the retreat from Mons, during which Vereker Hamilton's son, 'little Ian', who was serving with the Gordon Highlanders, went missing, having been captured by the Germans. " . . . **Our gallant Army . . . is being all cut up and decimated according to a Special Edition edited by 'The Times' and published early today. Ian says it's the first time the truth has been allowed to leak through.**" [30th August 1914 London] Vereker Hamilton's grandson, also Ian Hamilton, says that when he was twelve years old, his father told him that during his captivity, every time there was popular press coverage of 'big Ian' in the newspapers, the Germans threw him into solitary confinement and put him on bread and water. 'I said, in that case dad, when "big Ian" lost at Gallipoli the Germans must have had a banquet for you'.[9]

Two German warships, the *Goeben* and the *Breslau*, evaded a hunt by the Royal Navy in the Mediterranean and escaped to safety through the Dardanelles to Constantinople. The gift of these ships to Turkey went a long way towards bringing Turkey into the war on the side of Germany and Austria-Hungary. It would eventually be Ian Hamilton's destiny to fight them at Gallipoli in 1915. Admiral Troubridge was Rear Admiral – Commander of the First Cruiser Squadron in the Mediterranean and had been a guest of the Hamiltons during their time in Malta. Sir Berkeley Milne was Commander in Chief of the Navy in the Mediterranean.

The Winston Churchills dined with the Hamiltons, Winston bringing: " . . . a terrible list of casualties . . . ." John Manners, son of the third Baron Sutton, was missing, he was killed in action serving with the Grenadier Guards. Lord Castlerosse was also missing. There was " . . . **No news of little Ian, he was sent back to escort guns put out of action by Major Allen, a dreadfully dangerous job, Ian says.**

Winston was very interesting about everything, very outspoken. He says Admiral Troubridge is a ruined man, and will probably be court-martialled and shot – like Admiral Byng. . . . he is mad with fury about him allowing the escape of the 'Goeben' and 'Breslau' which is terribly serious for us. . . . but I feel there must be much to be said on Admiral Troubridge's side – I can't believe him to be lacking enterprise and courage. Sir Berkeley Milne has exonerated himself and seems to have given the proper orders alright which Admiral Troubridge took on himself to disobey. I asked Winston what he was going to fight the Zeppelins with, and he said: 'With aeroplanes – set

fire to them,' he seemed very confident about winning in the long run, even if this great battle going on now, goes against us. He has always been in favour of compulsory training for men, but now he is enthusiastic about the spirit of the nation. I hope this is going to be a complete vindication of voluntary service – of course all the women purse their lips, and say with bitter looks at me; 'Oh, if we only had Lord Roberts' National Army now', and I retort: 'Then we would not have our Navy' and a violent discussion begins, for we would not have had our Wonderful Expeditionary Force either and that is thanks to Lord Haldane." [8th Sept. 1914]

The casualty list mounted and Jean became active in the war effort, helping the soldiers who were short of every kind of military supplies, the rush to volunteer in 1914 having overwhelmed the army's system of recruitment and provisioning. " . . . Our tragic armies still locked in the grim struggle, and searing, burning drops fall one by one on the anguished hearts of the women of England as the Casualty List is slowly, slowly wrung out of the War Office.

. . . I had promised palliasses made and sent down when I motored to Didcot Camp, it looked so desolate and wretched for men sleeping on the cold ground, and Ian had told me the War Office would pay for anything just now, and that any officer could go to Harrods, and order any necessity for his troops, but not a bit of it – when it comes to pinning Ian down to that, he says now only through the Ordnance Officer – I know what that means, the men doing without their palliasses for weeks and weeks, probably months, so I am glad I ordered them at once, even though now I must pay for them, and the pillows at once myself, and it will cost me £60." [20th September 1914 London]

Jean's opinion of Lord Kitchener improved, at least temporarily: " . . . it is indeed a blessing Lord K. and not he [Haldane] is at the War Office! I feel Lord H. is played out, the wheels run down somehow.

Lord K. is rather splendid. I feel jealous about him, but I love his reckless Imperial way, he is the only match for the Kaiser we have." [4th October 1914]

Over dinner " . . . Ian was discussing with Lord H. the fortifications and measures to be taken against German invasion of England which Lord Kitchener thinks imminent, and Winston thinks Count Zeppelin also nightly meditates a raid." [21st October 1914 London]

Lord Roberts and his daughter Aileen dined with the Hamiltons. " . . .

**He talked most sensibly at dinner saying Ian ought now to have the
full command he is to have, if there is an invasion. He wants to bring
up this question at the next meeting for Imperial Defence, but I saw
Ian was not for this, fearing to put Kitchener's back up." [10th
November 1914 London]** But on Sunday 15 November, whilst Jean and
Ian were staying with Mary Hunter, news reached them that Lord Roberts
had died of pneumonia in France. Ian had lost a lifelong ally.

A committee had been set up on prisoners of war and a lecture was
planned to take place at No. 1 HPG. Jean was on the committee and went
to Aldershot with Haller and Ronnie Brook to see the German prisoners of
war. **" . . . We visited the poor German prisoners after lunch – such a
dreary scene their old flimsy tents, ankle deep in mud, we were
ploughing through the mire to get to them. I could hardly bear to look
at them through the wire entanglement which surrounds their cruelly
wind-swept area. Some of them stared at us with deep-seated resentment and bitterness, some with heavy sadness – it must be awful –
there was a lovely sunset, and in the squalid canteen tent where they
were all massed, buying what comfort they could, poor wretches, they
seemed brighter and healthy enough – the Adjutant told me they had
four blankets each, which I was glad to hear.**

**We talked to two Red Cross German prisoners, such nice men, in
the camp tent. Haller speaks good German – I wish I could – it seemed
strange to hear it spoken again. . . . " [5th December 1914 Peper
Harow]**

The lecture was given by Mr Page Gaston, on the plight of the British
prisoners of war in Germany. About 150 people attended, including Lady
Wynne, who addressed the audience, Lady Johnson, Norah Lindsay, Una
Troubridge, Mr and Mrs Walter Sickert, Julia Maguire, Lady Brassey and
Campbell Swinton. **" . . . It was pathetic all that crowd asking pitiful
questions about the fortresses and prisons in Germany in which their
dear ones are locked up. . . . " [9th December 1914]**

Jean's admiration of Kitchener evaporated when she realised that his
competence had not improved from the Boer War days. There was a shortage of ammunition, and quite by accident Ian discovered Sir John French,
back from the Western Front to see Kitchener. Though the visit was unex-
plained, it is probable Sir John was trying, in desperation, to wring out of
Kitchener urgently needed ammunition and supplies from London.
" . . . Ian was away inspecting last night with Peter [Pollen] **and Major**

Bell; as they passed Broome, Lord K's place, Ian had the idea to go in and see him. As he got in he saw Lord K. walking up and down the lawn, talking to a soldier, and he nearly fainted when the soldier turned round . . . he saw it was General French, whom he thought in France. . . . that French is here is a profound secret. I am sure Ian was the last man Sir John wanted to meet." [21st December 1914]

The war raged in Europe but the well to do still dined sumptuously and supped champagne whilst the rest of the country faced the prospect of food shortages. Jean and Ian went to a dinner where it was already known amongst at least some of those present that Ian was being considered as the general to command the Dardanelles Expedition. " . . . Dined with Ava Astor – an embarrassingly smart dinner – I have not been to such a smart party, nor has Ian, since the beginning of the War.
Ian sat between Lady Cunard and Fox McDonald, and I between Col. Fitzgerald, Lord K's man [Kitchener's military secretary] and a friend of Freddy's [Stanley], and . . . Lady Johnson's brother, an American. Violet Asquith . . . said to me 'I have been hearing so much of your husband.' I said: 'Nice things, I hope,' and she said: 'Plans,' – so I suppose she means the Dardanelles!! . . . " Since Violet Asquith made these remarks to Jean some days before Ian's actual appointment took place, it is small wonder that Kitchener was wary of 'chattering wives', or in this case, daughters, posing a security threat! Violet " . . . then set to work on my man and Lady Johnson on Fitz. I did not have much of a show. . . . Maud Cunard was amusing . . . declaring she was going to start a new lot of middle class friends, she was so sick of the talking of all her present lot. . . . " [8th March 1915]

Jean was once again about to be left alone whilst Ian went to war. Within a few days he would be given command of the Mediterranean Expeditionary Force that would take him to Gallipoli, where he would become engaged in a battle that would alter their lives for ever.

CHAPTER 8

Gallipoli – The Battle that Would Never End

"His want of fresh troops – want of ammunition is appalling . . . after that magnificent landing, if he had had one fresh Brigade it would have made just all the difference." [18th May 1915]

The suggestion for an attack elsewhere than on the Western Front was first mooted by Maurice Hankey, a Lieutenant-Colonel in the Royal Marines who, as Secretary to the War Council in 1914, produced the Boxing Day Memorandum,[1] in which he favoured an attack on Turkey through the Dardanelles as an alternative to the trench stalemate in France and Flanders. Winston Churchill took up the idea, in response to an appeal from the Russians early in January 1915, to divert Turkish forces from their offensive in the Caucasus, and suggested the attack should take place at Gallipoli.[2]

The attack was initially made by the Royal Navy alone, but from the forts guarding the Dardanelles (the sea passage between the Gallipoli peninsula and Asia Minor), Turkish guns proved too much for the fleet. The warships were unable to suppress their fire long enough for the minesweepers to clear the minefields in the straits. As the Navy got into increasing difficulty it was finally realised that troops would be needed to complete the operation.

Kitchener approved the release of troops from England and Egypt and placed General Sir Ian Hamilton in command of the Constantinople Expeditionary Force (later renamed the Mediterranean Expeditionary Force), then gathering in the eastern Mediterranean.

Initially Hamilton's orders were only to support the Navy in its operations. The major naval attack on 18 March 1915 ran into an undetected new minefield and was broken off after heavy loss of ships. At a meeting between Hamilton and the commander of the fleet, Vice-Admiral de Robeck, it was decided that the army would attack the Gallipoli peninsula and clear it of Turkish guns and forts before the navy would renew its efforts. Together they would clear the way for the expeditionary force to reach and capture Constantinople and put Turkey out of the war. However, the Dardanelles campaign – the joint naval and military operation – soon became the Gallipoli campaign, Hamilton's purely military effort to clear the way before the fleet would renew its attack.

The main theme of Jean's diaries throughout the Gallipoli campaign is her complete faith in her husband and her total conviction that he could have won at Gallipoli and gone on to take Constantinople, which would have gone some way towards winning the war for Britain.

Initially it would seem that Ian was not, in fact, destined for the Dardanelles and might have been sent to Serbia. Jean and Ian dined with Sir John (Jack) and Frances, Lady Horner at Mells Manor, Somerset. Lord Haldane, Lord Crewe, the George Lambtons and Raymond Asquith, the Prime Minister's son, were there. "**. . . When we got home Peter** [Pollen] **rang up from Horse Guards to say Colchester was destroyed by German air bombs, and the Zeppelins or aeroplanes were now on their way to London.**

Lord Haldane told me last night he had spoken to Mr. Asquith about Ian commanding the expedition to Serbia, and that Mr. Asquith had already spoken to Lord Kitchener about it. I said: 'Ian knows all that country well.' I wonder if he will go? I know French does not approve of K's Generals for the new armies except in the case of Ian.

Ian spoke to the King the other day about Kitchener's new army, and the King, annoyed, said: 'Don't call it that – Kitchener does not do so,' and ten minutes afterwards Ian forgot and did it again." [22nd February 1915]

For Jean, the Gallipoli campaign opened with her 'darling Ian' taking with him high hopes for victory for Britain in the war against Germany and its allies. "**. . . Ian came home in great glee, this evening and told me there was great news – he is to be the General to go to the Dardanelles in Command. He is fearfully pleased and excited, but it's bad news for me, though I can't help rejoicing with him too, he has been so surprised and disgusted at being given a home command and not one at the Front. . . . .** " Jean gave a large dinner party; the guests included Sir Neville Lyttelton, Lord Nicholson and Lord Haldane. "**. . . Lord Haldane told me that Kitchener had himself proposed that Ian should go to the Dardanelles but the date is not yet settled."** [10th March 1915]

The Hamiltons were being treated like celebrities as it became known in certain circles that Ian had been given what was considered to be a prestigious appointment. Winston Churchill's idea of an attack at Gallipoli had been taken up by the Government and a great celebratory dinner took place at the Prime Minister's house. Guests included Ettie Desborough, Ava Astor, Muriel Beckett, Clementine Churchill, Gwendoline Churchill, Lady Ripon, Nellie Londonderry, Lord Kitchener, and Winston Churchill, First Lord of the Admiralty. Their party was hosted by the Prime Minister's wife, Margot Asquith. It would be Jean's last outing with Ian for some time. "... **We dined with the Prime Minister to-night – wonderful party – all the loveliest women and nicest men London can, at present, produce"**. Margot " **. . . wore the oddest dress, just slung across her shoulders reminiscent of Montmartre. . . .** " Winston was "**beaming**" with delight, no doubt that Kitchener had adopted his pet plan for the Dardanelles. " **. . . Sir Edgar Vincent took me in and I sat next Lulu Harcourt.**" The Hamiltons left the party early and Jean " **. . . drove Ian to the Admiralty at 10.30 to consult with Winston about the Dardanelles Expedition."** [11th March 1915 London]

The day of Ian's departure for Gallipoli dawned and the way in which Ian confided in Jean of his fears before leaving shows how well aware he was of the risks involved. He was sufficiently experienced in war to know that the Turks under German command would be a formidable enemy. " **. . . As Ian wrote '13th' this morning on a letter in my bedroom . . . I said quickly: 'The 13th is always a lucky day for me. . . . I fetched him in the motor from Horse Guards before luncheon, and we walked back together through the Park – from Grosvenor Gate he talked of many difficulties, and said: 'This is the biggest adventure I have ever embarked on. It may be a terrible disaster, or the turning point in the war if we can win through and take Constantinople, but no one knows the strength of the enemy, or what we will have to face'. . . . "** [Saturday 13th March 1915 Reigate Priory]

Just prior to Ian's departure, Jean received a letter from Philip Sassoon, a newspaper journalist, " **. . . begging me to ask Ian to take him with him on his staff, saying he will black his boots if he only will and that this is going to be far the most magnificent thing of the War, and placing all his places at my disposal – Trant and his place at Folkestone if I will do this for him.**" Ian's reply was that his " **. . . staff was all fixed up. . . .** " [13th March 1915 Reigate Priory contd.]

In the afternoon Jean drove Ian to Charing Cross railway station in London, where a great crowd of well-wishers had gathered to see him and his staff off to Gallipoli. All the Hamilton family were there, together with Winston and Clemmie Churchill, the Midletons and Frances Horner and Jean's sister, Heather Pollen. Ian's staff included Jack Churchill (Winston's brother), going out as a special service officer, George Brodrick as Ian's ADC, Captain Peter Pollen as his Military Secretary, and Major-General Walter Braithwaite as his Chief of Staff. " . . . **At the last moment I went up to Ian . . . and he turned hastily and kissed me through my veil, and I pulled it up and said: 'Not through my veil, darling, it is unlucky.' He kissed me again, but it had vexed and put him out, and he said impatiently: 'Why do you say that – too bad to say unlucky.' I felt awful and put my head in at the carriage door to say: 'I only did not want you to kiss me through my veil,' and he said rather crossly: 'Well, if it is unlucky you should not have said it.' This saddened me terribly. . . . Frances Horner seized me, and said: 'Don't watch him out of sight, it's not lucky.' " [13th March 1915 Reigate Priory** contd.]

And so it was that on Saturday 13 March 1915 General Sir Ian Hamilton set forth to Gallipoli. The assault landings there would be the first ever attempted against a defended enemy coast in the history of modern warfare.

On Saturday 27 March, Jean received a telegram from Ian, " . . . **'Going strong', bless him – I do, do trust he will make a success of this and refute all his enemies – everyone seems jealous of his having this Command." [28th March 1915]**

Lady Randolph Churchill lived at Brook Street, London, and she dropped in on Jean who was lonely. " . . . **Lady Randolph came to see me to-night . . . she amused me, sitting there, hard and black and concrete in my lovely green room. She tells me Ian is in Egypt and that there will be no concerted action between the troops and the fleet for another three weeks. She was very funny about her footwoman – she has had to send two beauties away – Winston gazing at one said: 'Does that *glorious* creature bring in the beef?' – everyone has to have parlour-maids now as all the footmen are off to the war." [Holy Thursday 1st April 1915 London]**

On 25 April, six weeks after they left England, Ian Hamilton and his forces, the 29th Division, the Australian and New Zealand Army Corps (famous ever after as the Anzacs), the Royal Naval Division and a French corps landed on the Gallipoli peninsula. In the darkness and due to a navigational error, the Anzacs missed the intended landing place near Gaba Tepe and came in at Anzac Cove, where in any event the Turks were less well prepared to meet them. After a day of desperate fighting the Anzacs held on to a perilously small beachhead. The landings at Cape Helles were fiercely opposed and the exhausted 29th Division clung to their landing places and slowly expanded their foothold on the peninsula.

From the day Ian left for Gallipoli, Jean became almost completely preoccupied with his progress and remained fully supportive of him in the task that lay ahead. Ian kept in as close touch with her as the circumstances of battle allowed. " **. . . Lunched with Heather to meet Lady Birdwood** [wife of the commander of the Anzacs]**, Col. Dick (King's Messenger), who had just seen Ian, was there . . . – it was splendid hearing firsthand news of Ian who is well and in good heart but I nearly quarrelled outright with Col. Dick, as he was violent against the Christmas feeling of good will between our troops and the Germans – he said he'd shoot any man he saw having any friendly feeling towards the enemy, and hate was the only incentive to trust to in the war . . . I strongly disagreed with all he said.**" [8th May 1915 Deanston]

Jean would often go to very great lengths to find out how the campaign was advancing and worried constantly for Ian's safety. One source of information was Lord Haldane. " **. . . Motored over to Cloan to see Lord Haldane this afternoon, and had tea with him . . .**

I had a few minutes' private talk with him, and he showed me a letter from Ian, saying that his task was a heavy one, and that the Turks were being reinforced by batteries from Europe and Asia. Lord Haldane said the landing at Gallipoli was magnificent, and that everyone thought so – he was impassive and impenetrable as usual . . . he thinks Italy will come in with us probably. I hope so to, but Ian felt she hardly could, with honour, I know." [16th May 1915 Deanston]

The early reports by the journalist Ellis Ashmead-Bartlett were favourable to progress at Gallipoli. " **. . . Ashmead-Bartlett's splendid account of the fighting for Achi Baba – the heroism and the hopelessness of it is more than I can bear. Gallipoli seems beyond human power – that great Achi Baba grim like a Chinese god, still untaken in spite of all the blood that has been shed. . . . "** [18th May 1915 Deanston]

The initial euphoria over the landing came into perspective in the days ahead when the heavy casualty list became known.[3]

As the battle for Gallipoli become more and more difficult to win due to the Kitchener's continuing failure to send reinforcements and ammunition, new fears were aroused in Jean for the security of Winston Churchill's position as Ian's main supporter within the Cabinet. Within three weeks of Ian and his troops landing at Gallipoli, Asquith had to concede a coalition government to the Conservatives. The crisis was engendered by the resignation of Admiral 'Jacky' Fisher, the First Sea Lord, who loudly declared that he could no longer work with Winston Churchill at the Admiralty. **" . . . The Cabinet has crashed! brought down I fear by Winston's mistake in bombarding the Dardanelles Front by the Fleet before they were supported by the troops, and that old rat, Lord Fisher, has ground a hole in the sinking ship, and left it, jumped into the Scotch Express, pulling down his blinds, and off to nestle in the bosom of the Duchess of Hamilton – he has resigned, now I believe a Coalition Government will be formed." [18th May 1915** contd.]

There were other factors which were forcing Asquith's hand. Trevor Wilson attributes Asquith's decline to several factors. Firstly, there was his public image of leisurely activities during a wartime crisis. He played bridge two hours each day – Maurice Hankey, Secretary to the War Council, wrote that 'Bridge is the vice of the PM and most of the Cabinet members'. Hankey had difficulty in getting Asquith to set aside time so he could meet with the War Council. Rather than spend his weekends on the nation's business he could be found at Garsington, Lady Ottoline Morrell's country home.[4] At a time when the country was fighting for its very survival and when he could have found better things to do, Asquith's attitude was construed as insensitive and his activities as frivolous. Secondly, he tended to mingle with an anti-conscription, even anti-war, section of society. Thirdly, the Conservatives craved power and, along with the press, criticised the way in which the war was being conducted. Bonar Law, leader of the Conservatives, informed Lloyd George that his members were demanding a parliamentary inquiry into aspects of the conduct of the war, which would undoubtedly include Gallipoli. Three months earlier, Lloyd George had spoken to Bonar Law about his own memorandum of 1910 suggesting the possibility of a Coalition between the Liberals and Conservatives.[5] A threatening liaison was thereby emerging from these two politicians. Asquith's gradual decline was creating a political vacuum which Lloyd George would be able, eventually, to fill.

Lord Kitchener's competence was long under fire because of Britain's inability to win a war that everyone thought would be 'over by Christmas'. His lack of organisation had resulted in failure to send ammunition to sustain the fighting in both France and Gallipoli. There was adverse press coverage. Repington was Military Correspondent for *The Times*: "... **Colonel Repington has *nearly* smashed Lord Kitchener too, by his saying our failure to get on in France is due to the fact that we are using shrapnel instead of high explosive shells. . . . "** [18th May 1915 contd.]

Ian clearly understood the terrible difficulties he faced as the Turks poured reinforcements into Gallipoli and his own formations withered away for want of them. Perhaps unknowingly he conveyed some of his anxiety to Jean. To add to their troubles Winston had felt obligated to resign from the Cabinet over Fisher's resignation. " **. . . I got three, no four darling letters from Ian, such precious ones, but they added to my terrible anxiety as they were very grave, and much more than usually loving; it was as if he was looking back to appreciate what our life had been together – they have made my heart ache and stand still with dread. Then to feel that the Dardanelles has caused Winston's downfall will be very bitter to him – conscription is *certain* now for the war.**

His [Ian's] want of fresh troops – want of ammunition is appalling – he says after that magnificent landing, if he had had one fresh Brigade it would have made just all the difference." [18th May 1915 contd.]

Jean, who was in Scotland, staying with her sister, Nan, knew that some reinforcements were being sent to Gallipoli: " **. . . the Lowland Division under General Egerton is going to the Dardanelles."** Jean was horrified as Egerton had told her this as a secret and she had told no one, not even her sister. Nan had dismissed her German maid, whom she was sending back to Germany and Jean was concerned she might be a security risk. Jean and Nan went to the railway station to see off Major-General Egerton and his troops. Egerton had spent time with Ian at Malta and accompanied him on the manoeuvres at Gibraltar. Ian's work with the Territorial Force made him a very popular figure with the soldiers. " **. . . I told the men they were going to Ian, and they were all *so* pleased, and said they would serve him well – some of them cheered loudly for Lady Hamilton. The first train load, with General Egerton, left at**

9.30. G. E. told me 4,000 of them go in the 'Mauritania' – he is very anxious and worried – so many maddening things have happened to detain them. . . . " [21st May 1915 Deanston]

Jean went to tea with Miss Haldane, Lord Haldane's sister, where she heard: " . . . all Winston's own party are furious with him, and apparently want to get rid of him – except Mr. Asquith. I am very sorry to hear this as Winston is Ian's best friend in the Cabinet and the Dardanelles is his pet plan. Lord Fisher's behaviour is disastrous – the last time I met him lunching with the MacKennas . . . he said looking menacingly at me: 'Ah yes, your husband – I have a great many things I am going to say about him in my Memoirs.'

It is true that Lord Kitchener has never told the Cabinet that high explosives were being demanded from the Front.

Lord Northcliffe has been at the Front in General French's camp as well as Col. Repington. Miss Haldane says Lord Haldane keeps quite calm in face of the disagreeable way he is being treated by everyone, and does not mind at all not being included in the Cabinet. . . . people all abuse him now as a pro German which is utterly untrue." [24th May 1915 Murrayshall]

On Tuesday 25 May, Jean received three letters and copies of despatches from Ian from which she discovered that German submarines had got to the eastern Mediterranean and posed a major threat to the Royal Navy there. The task which lay before Ian " . . . was almost beyond human power. . . . The 'Triumph' and the 'Majestic' have both been sunk by submarines and Ian writes they are being shadowed by one of those monsters – bogies by day – bogies by night – it is horrible – I am haunted – haunted everywhere in this lovely Spring by the thought of his danger. . . . " Ian's letters took about two days in transit and by the time Jean received them the situation had altered and the War Office was not cooperative toward her. " . . . I feel very down-hearted and as if things were not going well at the Dardanelles – yet now we have a footing on Gallipoli if only Lord K. will send reinforcements all should go well. I am terribly in the dark but know it is useless for me to bother them at the War Office." [29 May 1915 Deanston]

Jean's suspicions over Ian's difficult situation at Gallipoli spurred her on to another burst of activity. She went personally to the War Office but was unable to find out anything and fell back on Lord Haldane for help. " . . . I am going to see Lord Haldane this afternoon. . . . it must be

**maddening to be suddenly out of office now when he has done so much
and worked so hard for the Army – it's all due to him and not Lord K.
we could send our Expeditionary Force off so quickly. . . . "** [30th May
1915] Haldane had lost his seat in the Cabinet and did not support
Gallipoli. **". . . I don't like what Lord Haldane tells me of Gallipoli at
all – he says Lord K. was very hopeful till ten days ago – the submarines are deadly and Lord H. says the Staff work of the Turks is
wonderful."** [31st May 1915 Deanston]

Ian was still confident of success at Gallipoli but all depended on
Kitchener keeping his word to send out reinforcements and ammunition.
**". . . There is *terrible* fighting going on in Gallipoli – had two letters
from Ian on Friday night . . . Ian says we *must* win *if* ammunition and
men don't fail to reach him."** [6th June 1915] A major blow against the
Gallipoli campaign was the removal of Winston Churchill from the
Admiralty. His powerful, persuasive oratory was therefore absent from the
War Council. **". . . Winston being out of the Cabinet makes it all much
more difficult – no one now there to fight for Gallipoli and get the
sorely needed reinforcements."** The shell shortage continued to pose
problems for the conduct of operations, both at Gallipoli and on the
Western Front. **". . . Col. R. [Repington] says he has seen the signed
despatch from Sir John French, asking Lord K. for those high explosive shells, which Lord K. never asked the Government for at all."**
[7th June 1915]

In Asquith's newly formed coalition government of Liberals,
Conservatives and Labour, a Ministry of Munitions was created with
Lloyd George as its Minister. It was a promotion that enabled him to take
control of munitions from Kitchener who, in his innocence, failed to
recognise him as a political threat and wrote to Lloyd George of his delight
in hearing that 'you are coming to help me'.[6] It was not Lloyd George's
intention, Grigg says, to be 'a mere supplier of requirements laid down by
the War Office, because he had no confidence in the generals' capacity to
assess the army's needs in the matter of weaponry. His aim was to control
the ordering as well as the production of arms. But he had to be content
with achieving this aim by stages'.[7] Lloyd George's gradual ascent to
political power would proceed along parallel lines with Kitchener's down-
ward slide. Kitchener was losing the confidence of the Cabinet, yet his
popularity with the people was so great the Prime Minister could not sack
him and replace him with someone more competent.

Northcliffe, the newspaper proprietor, was of the opinion that through his newspapers he had elevated Kitchener to his position as the great hero in the minds of the British public. He now believed that Kitchener had betrayed him, by his 'ban on press reporters at the front and by his ill-usage of Sir John French', with whom Northcliffe was said to have a 'special friendship'. Sir John French embarked upon an attack on Aubers Ridge that failed and French attributed it to Kitchener's failure to send him munitions. French made his views known to the Northcliffe press and to 'Kitchener's most devoted adversary in the Cabinet, Lloyd George', along with Bonar Law, the Conservative leader and ex-leader Balfour. On 14 May *The Times* ran a leading article on the shortage of munitions and though it did not name Kitchener, it placed the blame on the War Office. However, Kitchener survived the changes of the Coalition Government, though with diminished powers. Northcliffe's attacks on him over the munitions scandal had backfired, resulting in a public backlash in his favour. Since Kitchener proved immovable, Asquith embarked upon a course of action that would eventually undermine him, allowing his posi-tion to be usurped by Lloyd George. In his new position as Minister of Munitions, Lloyd George proceeded in his usual boisterous manner to make known his 'distinctive views on strategy', voicing 'his differences with most of his Liberal and Labour colleagues over conscription'. Now in a position to threaten the government, he claimed in a speech to Parliament that 'general prosecution of the war was always "Too late" '.[8]

Jean, agonising over Ian's painful situation, attempted sometimes with success, sometimes in vain, to find out information on how matters were proceeding at Gallipoli and whether Kitchener and the government were going to support Ian and send him the reinforcements and ammunition he needed. In desperation she waited for any sign of hope for her husband. **" . . . my poor Ian is clinging on with his eyelashes to the utmost edges of Gallipoli, with only his forlorn handful of men – what relief to write the bare truth, to the world. I have to smile and smile, and say how cheerfully he writes – 'Are we downhearted? NO.'**

Nothing comes through to me – no news – a veil of silence – Ian does not want me to wire, or to bother anyone at the War Office, but the waiting and being able to do nothing about reinforcements is awful.

I lunched at Lady Maud Warrender's [the famous opera singer] **with all those horrors seething in my heart. . . . "** [18th June 1915]

In his letter dated 3rd June, 1915, Ian wrote:

Sweetheart mine. I got another delicious letter from my darling yesterday, – 12th May it was dated – bless you. The guns are making a great noise as I write but that is nothing serious. Tomorrow we expect a big battle. How I wish we could have them without casualties. I hate to think of the number we shall have. . . . I'm going to try and call you tomorrow morning but it is *really* very difficult darling and is not allowed to others. Our generals – Birdwood and Hunter Weston – have now for 5 weeks been living, eating, trying to sleep under fire – sometimes 2000 shells an hour and countless bullets. Of course they are dug in but still their life is very different from that of Rawly for instance in his castle. The men are wonderful. For 3 weeks they did not even have a blanket, just what they stood up in; and they are still cheery, and more than cheery, enthusiastic. How is the money lasting? Let me know. I am spending much more than in other campaigns and if you could manage I might want later on to cut down your £3000 to £2500. Besides mess etc. I am going to entertain constantly one selected officer from each Division; that means 8 officers always my guests and perhaps one or two more odd ones. But if the big house eats it all up, why then I shall manage.

I have heaps to go on with and there is no *urgency*. But just let me know anyway for curiosity's sake how you are getting on. How tragic the falls of Haldie Paldie and Winston. I've written them both. I am sincerely sorry, for them and for the weakness and ineptitude of the Govt. in giving way to Times, Daily Mail, Globe and Morning Post. Alas they've made me pull down your little flag. They say it is a positive cert for the German aeroplanes who would make a bull's eye of my tent at once – Love my darling

Your ever so much devoted hub. Ian.[9]

Other correspondence followed, telling Jean of the mounting difficulties at Gallipoli. " . . . I got letters from Ian tonight – the mosquito net I sent him is just what he wanted and has secured him some rest and sleep . . . but the copy of the letter he enclosed, to Lord K., depressed me profoundly, showing plainly the fearful difficulties hemming him in on every side – he fears the water supply will soon run short, and all supplies are a difficulty – it's so unlike Ian ever to see difficulties ahead." [24th June 1915 London]

Jean did not know who to ask for up-to-date information on the situation at Gallipoli and could not get any response from either Kitchener or his Military Secretary, Fitzgerald (Fitz). Others, it seemed, were being told more than the wife of the general in charge of the campaign. " . . . **Lady Sarah [Wilson] told me Mr. Balfour had shown her two telegrams from Ian the night before, in which he said there had been an advance on the left, hundreds of yards of Turkish trenches taken, but they were expecting a severe counter attack – the second telegram said that the counter attack had taken place, and we had more than held our own, and inflicted considerable loss on the enemy. It was rather bitter hearing of these telegrams from Ian, from Lady Sarah. . . . Lord K. is impenetrable, and I feel furious with that tiresome squit, Fitz . . . whom he adores.**" [30th June 1915 London]

Jean saw Molly Repington. " . . . **Molly tells me Col. R. has written her that Mr. Balfour, Lord K. and Mr. Asquith are going now to France to confer with the French Authorities about the best war policy to be pursued, and there is an idea of making the Dardanelles the principal centre of the war now – how mad that would make General French! and how splendid that would be.**" [7th July 1915]

News, which Jean heard from various sources, was mixed and hopes were raised one moment and dashed the next. " . . . **Lord Dalhousie . . . told me that our troops in Flanders were now to be put under General Joffre and General French recalled. He said we had not nearly enough trenches in Flanders, that the campaign there had not been well conducted, and the idea was now to make the Dardanelles the principal initiative. This was splendid news, if it proves true.**" [12th July 1915]

Jean visited the Winston Churchills on 19 July and Winston was still confident of success at the Dardanelles and planned to go out there. " . . . **Yesterday, Monday, I lunched with the Winston Churchills, and Winston told me all sorts of things. He still maintains the Fleet** could **have got through the Narrows unassisted by the troops.**" He was " . . . **full of confidence that a great victory is coming at the Dardanelles, and wants to be there to see it – he is off early tomorrow, he said, and would take anything I like to Ian, so I sent him a parcel and letters . . . .** " On the night of 20 July, Jean wrote " . . . **to my astonishment they**

were returned to me without a word – what can have happened? . . . I
asked Mr. Balfour tonight why he [Winston] had not gone? He said he
could not think, as he had given his consent to his going, and thought
it was alright and that he had gone." [20th July 1915] Several days
later, on 25 July, Jean learned from Lady Randolph Churchill that: " . . .
the Government stopped Winston going to the Dardanelles at the last
moment – she is furious about his being prevented from going there –
so am I! . . . Winston is Gallipoli's best friend and I fear some devilry
is afoot." [25th July 1915]

" . . . Today's *the day* for the new advance at Gallipoli, and I feel
frightened and anxious – what is taking place there now – where is my
Ian . . . ?

Sir John Cowans told me yesterday that the Turks attacked on
Friday, he had seen a telegram from Ian saying it was without success.
Ian hoped they would attack before his great advance . . . .

Poor General Egerton – Ian is angry because he said three times
of different regiments: "The remnants of the —th," the remnants of
the —th", "the remnants of the —th", – Ian then sternly told him he
must *never* repeat such a remark, especially as it was not justified on
the last occasion.

I fear alas! it was only too true of the first two, but such things
must not be said in war." [8th August 1915 Avon Tyrel]

Reinforcements were needed as badly on the Western Front as at
Gallipoli. " . . . I hope Gallipoli's fate was not decided when the
Government took the fatal decision of making the push at Loos and
sent the reinforcements there that my poor Ian was clamouring for at
Gallipoli – if they had only sent them to Ian we would be within sight
now, I feel sure, of the end of this awful war. Betty Balfour came to tell
me about this decision; Col. Repington also sent me word of it and
alas! the reinforcements were of no use at Loos and the push there a
dead failure".[10] [12th August 1915 London]

The August offensive at Gallipoli had failed and the inaction of
Lieutenant-General Stopford's 9th Army Corps at Suvla was a most sig-
nificant factor. Hamilton had originally requested a younger and more vig-
orous general to command at Suvla Bay but his request was denied by Lord
Kitchener. Instead the post of commander of the 9th Corps went to Sir
Frederick Stopford because of his seniority. He had been a competent Staff
Officer but had never commanded troops in battle at any stage of his career.[11]

" . . . The post brought me wonderful, thrilling letters from Ian, dated 11th and 12th of that wonderful August week, telling of the landing at Anzac and Suvla Bay – how near they were to victory – and of the terrible disappointment that the 9th Army Corps did not make more headway – it makes me *mad* to think of it. I know if Ian had been in command there, the victory would be ours *now* instead of having to wait for it still. He says he found when he got to Suvla at 5 o'clock, General Stopford's troops strolling about as if they were having a holiday, feeling they had done wonders, would rest now and wait till tomorrow, when every moment was priceless. Ian is going to lead them himself to take Spion Kop – Hill 60 – etc. I feel terrified about this, but thank goodness, had a wire from him on Thursday." [21st August l915 Deanston]

" . . . The papers have just come in – no Gallipoli news except from a Turkish source, which says: 'Enemy attacked by sea and land on 27th, and were repulsed with severe loss'." [30th August 1915]

Jean had a disagreement with Nettie Henderson, whose husband, Lieutenant-General Sir David Henderson, was Director-General of Military Aeronautics from 1913 to 1918 and was General Officer Commanding RFC from 1914 to 1917. " . . . I had a fight with her over the Dardanelles, as she said the Government ought now just to face it, and recall the Expedition – cut their losses and acknowledge they had made a mistake. I maintained success had very nearly been achieved – two or three already, and that if we could only win there, it would alter the whole situation – that it was not a mistake to have sent the Expedition and more reinforcements ought to have been sent there, though I thought Winston had blundered in not having *concerted* action when the Fleet first went to bombard the Dardanelles as the element of surprise was so important – that there was a completely other view to those she had been hearing. I knew she would naturally only hear French's view and the Flanders side from David and others. I said Ian wrote quite calmly and confidently – had never once grumbled, or said it was impossible, though he perfectly realised the difficulties of his task." [3rd September 1915 London]

" . . . Ian is wonderful and keeps his spirits up – his letters this week are full of good cheer . . . he says they have 13 miles now to consolidate their position at Anzac and Anafarta. They had only 2_ before the Suvla Bay landing." [1st October 1915]

When Bulgaria declared war as an ally of the Central Powers, and posed a grave and immediate threat to Serbia, the Balkans crisis was to prove fatal to the Gallipoli campaign. " . . . **Bulgaria has tricked and hood winked us all this time; Greece has failed us, and the situation in the Dardanelles looks very serious indeed.**

Behind these black war clouds Ian is still shining at Gallipoli – *so* **extraordinary it is to think of that little home party at Head Quarters Camp at Imbros – Ian, Freddy, Peter** [Pollen] **who is now Ian's ADC; Alick, Lipscombe, Coles and Duke." [10th October 1915 Deanston]**

The main threat to the Gallipoli operation was now Lloyd George's plan for an attack at Salonica, though it would be some months before his part in its downfall would become known. " **. . . The landing of the Allies at Salonica was a dramatic stroke . . . only to be followed by the dire news of the resignation of Venizelos. . . . Blunder** *seems* **to have followed blunder in our Balkan policy." [10th Oct. 1915]**

Lloyd George stepped up his efforts to get the Gallipoli campaign shut down and the resources transferred to Salonica to support Serbia. On 12 October 1915 he circulated a memorandum round the War Cabinet arguing that Allied drafts on their way to the Dardanelles should be immediately diverted to Salonica. Of Gallipoli he said the idea of making another attack there was 'an insane one'. Bonar Law also issued a memorandum arguing that troops should be sent at once from Gallipoli to Salonica and that any further reinforcement of Gallipoli would be 'quite indefensible'. Troops were moved from Gallipoli to Greece. Asquith, Balfour, Curzon and Churchill supported a further effort at Gallipoli; Lloyd George, Bonar Law, Chamberlain, Long and Carson supported the Salonica option.[12]

Reinforcements and ammunition were not sent to aid the completion of the Gallipoli campaign and hopes for victory started to slip away, though Ian still hoped they would be sent. " **. . . my heart felt a little lighter as I had had happier letters from Ian . . . he seemed to think fresh reinforcements might be sent, and to think they might hold on.**

His letter last week was discouraging, for the first time his high courage and hope about ultimate victory in Gallipoli had failed; he said he had always hoped to get the Turks to attack, but now he hoped they would not, the troops were so depleted and so weakened by illness of various kinds.

This afternoon . . . I went to Cloan to see Lord Haldane – he and Miss Haldane met us at the door. I went for a walk with him and to my

horror he told me he felt certain the Government meant now to recall the Dardanelles Expedition and that he, Lord Haldane, had always been against it." [16th October 1915 Deanston]

On 15 October Kitchener recalled Hamilton from Gallipoli, sending General Sir Charles Monro out to replace him and carry out an assessment of the situation there. Along with her sister, Heather, Jean set off in the motor to the railway station to meet Ian, wearing " . . . my smart black and white clothes, with white boots." She had wired Vereker and Lilian Hamilton with the news. Driving along they saw May Spender and gave her a ride to the dentist, " . . . while she discoursed most dramatically to us about the plots and counter plots against Ian, and how *they* – the Government, Kitchener and Winston – required a scapegoat to sacrifice in order to appease the populace, and Ian was the one selected. She had known of this going on for some time, and three weeks ago had written Ian an unsigned letter, saying 'We are standing by' and had thought of writing to Kay to warn him. . . . " [22nd Oct. 1915]

May Spender was the wife of John Alfred Spender, editor of the *Westminster Gazette*, and she undoubtedly obtained her information from her husband. The names of those accused of plotting to use Ian as a scapegoat are not reliable. Winston was Ian's friend but his boisterous oratory could have been misconstrued when talking in company with Spender. Unfortunately, in essence what May said was a chillingly accurate prediction of what lay ahead, and all before Ian had actually returned from Gallipoli. Asquith, the Prime Minister, members of the government and possibly Kitchener were guilty. But it would be some months before who was *actually* behind Ian's recall from Gallipoli would emerge. Jean was dismissive of May Spender: " . . . She is a wild woman, and I can't credit her tale, which is that K. has recalled Ian to give Birdwood, who is very disloyal to Ian, *she* says, his chance. I said: 'Then why has he not now given it to Gen. Birdwood? Why send out Sir Charles Monro?' She begged me to ask Ian to go and see Alfred to-night, as he must at once take a strong line with K. . . .

May also said Winston was trembling with terror in case it would come out that K. wanted the troops to go out first to the Dardanelles before the Fleet, which by their bombardment, had eliminated the element of surprise; it certainly would have been far wiser for the Fleet and Army to have acted together at the beginning of the campaign in May." [October 22nd 1915 contd.]

May Spender was quite wrong about Kitchener wanting to send troops
out before the Fleet but her point about the importance of joint action was
valid. John Alfred Spender was hostile to the continuance of the Gallipoli
campaign, so he may have embellished whatever information he found
out. Winston Churchill was at that time trying to influence Spender, sending him a memorandum urging support for Gallipoli, but Spender did not
comply with his request.

> Churchill's instinct remained in favour of continuing the attack at
> Gallipoli. He was concerned about the effect of withdrawal upon
> Russian morale, and Russia's ability to continue the war. 'The one
> great prize and reward which Russia can gain . . . is Constantinople. .
> . . The surest means of re-equipping her, the one way of encouraging
> her efforts, is the opening of the Dardanelles and Bosphorus. With
> the evacuation of the Gallipoli Peninsula that hope dies'.[13]

The problems that hampered the Gallipoli operation existed on at least
three levels. The first, referred to in several of Jean's diary entries, was the
failure to send sufficient troop reinforcements, ammunition and supplies.
The second was that the Dardanelles campaign was one of several campaigns being conducted simultaneously. Scarce resources, human and
material, had to be shared out amongst them. There were acute shortages
and the munitions factories in Britain were having difficulty meeting the
spiralling demand. Transport from the coast of Britain to far-away theatres
of war was slow and hazardous. The third was the administrative failure
by the British Cabinet to coordinate the war effort efficiently. The
Liberals, who were in power, and the Conservatives, who were fighting to
obtain power, did not pull together. It was not until well into the war, when
Britain was struggling to cope with new demands on all sides, that they
were compelled to form a Coalition Government and put the defence of
the country before personal and political ambition. This third reason may
have been greatly, if not entirely, responsible for the failure of the
Dardanelles campaign. An additional factor, not known about at the time,
was the role of sections of the British press. Two players in particular are
worthy of note: Ellis Ashmead-Bartlett and Keith Murdoch. Their key role
in bringing down the Gallipoli campaign will unfold in Chapter 10.

On the night of Friday 22 October, General Sir Ian Hamilton arrived
home from Gallipoli. As Ian stepped from the train, Jean felt " . . . **proud**

of my man, as we drove away together through the moonlight in the open motor. It was lovely and I said: 'Let's go for a walk,' so we walked home through the Park – the shining Park, and talked and talked, or rather Ian talked and I listened. It was the happiest home-coming for Ian *I* ever had. It was sweet to feel he needed me, and the shelter of his own home – and the comfort and beauty of it, and his attitude is wonderful – finer even than I hoped – not a word of grudge or bitterness or anger, at this *monstrous* act of *frightful* injustice, which makes me boil with rage and fury. However, Mrs. Spender's dark tales are not true I am sure, as K. wired Ian in secret code *three* days before the recall cable, asking him to change Braithwaite for Kiggell. Ian had given the secret code cable to Braithwaite, and so they deciphered this *together*; it was a *fearful* blow for Braithwaite who turned pale and Ian generously promised to stick to him, as he considers he has done excellent work for him, though he is very unpopular, I know, so he has dragged his Chief down for the moment. . . . " [22nd October 1915 contd.]

Braithwaite was a very experienced staff officer, though his manner was brusque, and to silence the press, perhaps Ashmead-Bartlett in partic-ular, Kitchener was prepared to sacrifice him as the scapegoat. Hence his request to Hamilton 'to change Braithwaite for Kiggell'. Jean held this to be the fatal blow to Ian's standing and her bitterness towards Kitchener grew. " . . . But! in the morning light Ian looks haggard – worn – does not sleep. He seems staggered by this dastardly blow – amazed and wondering what it means. . . .

Kitchener evidently feels his own position tottering – Ian is to be offered up, as the populace demand a human sacrifice. He thought Braithwaite *might* be enough, but when Ian refused to sacrifice Braithwaite, the ruthless monster threw him over, well knowing he had been unable to send him reinforcements and ammunition – had kept him without them, and then even taken away some of the few troops for Salonika; even then Ian held bravely on, hoping when the terrible useless move in France was over, his chance would come." [23rd Oct. 1915]

The 'terrible useless move in France' refers to the costly and unsuc-cessful battles around Loos in September 1915. The men and munitions expended there would have been decisive if used at Gallipoli.

Years later, Ian wrote of Jean's loyalty to him: 'When her close friend

Lady Horner wrote a letter of condolence on my being relieved of the command at Gallipoli she replied that she was delighted to get me back. When Lady Horner went on to point out, very kindly, that she feared Jean did not quite understand that my supersession by General Charles Monro must leave a blot upon my military career, she replied that the blot would be left, not on me, but on the Government, and would grow larger and larger with the passing years'.[14]

In November, Lloyd George was pressing Lord Curzon, Lord Privy Seal, to support his demand for the complete abandonment of the Gallipoli operation, which Curzon refused to do, to Lloyd George's great annoyance. Bonar Law also forcefully demanded withdrawal from Gallipoli, which information Jean learnt much later from Winston Churchill, high on champagne at dinner. Ian, as the Commander-in-Chief of the Gallipoli campaign, Winston Churchill and Lord Kitchener were greatly criticised in both the press and society for the failure of Britain's effort there. A Dardanelles Commission of Inquiry was set up by Prime Minister Asquith in 1916. The Commission was to look into what took place at Gallipoli and its cloud would hang over the Hamiltons for nearly two years.

Ian was without employment and Winston Churchill, who was out of the government, was being blamed for causing the resignation of Lord Fisher (First Sea Lord) through carrying out negotiations relating to the fleet one night after Fisher had retired to bed. Jean and Ian had taken Postlip Hall in Gloucestershire, the home of Jean's brother Will and his wife Clara Muir, for a holiday and Ian invited Winston to stay. Secret and sensitive topics were often discussed amongst friends at the Hamiltons' gatherings.

"... We had a very exciting dinner. Winston after two large goblets of iced champagne, became very communicative and told us all about the Fisher episode of this time last year, and of his determination to get Fisher back into the Admiralty. I said: 'But he is far too old and gaga now'. Winston admitted 'Yes, he is rather', so I said: 'Well why do you want him? The public did believe in him, but they have lost their faith in him altogether'. So he said he wanted him back because he was his tool there and did everything that he wanted, and admitted that every single thing that was done at the Admiralty after Prince Louis of Battenberg went was initiated by him (Winston); also Lord Fisher was far easier to work with than Battenberg: Lord Fisher always rose at 4, and Winston worked late, so they carried on between them all the time.

Winston said what caused Lord Fisher finally to resign was just two words from him – '*After Action*'. He decided to send out something to the Dardanelles, or to take some instant action about Gallipoli – and wrote out a letter before leaving the office, adding 'Communicate to First Lord *after action*', and this was put by mistake on Lord Fisher's table, where he found it on entering his office as usual at 4 a.m. He flew into a sudden rage, and at once resigned, refusing to speak or to hold any communication with Winston again – so the tragedy of the Dardanelles possibly turned on these two words '*after action*'. . . .

. . . a large bunch of gay little Columbine flowers stared out of the darkness at the end of the table: the candles lighting up Winston's ugly excited face, gleaming on his white eye lashes, and falling on Ian's beautiful quiet face – it was very thrilling, and we sat there till 10.45 much to the servants' disgust. I wonder what will come of all these plots and counter plots.

Winston seems unbalanced and excitable just now, but he has go, and vision, and is the enemy of caution and 'wait and see'.

Afterwards in the drawing-room, he walked about the room, declaiming, shouting, trying his oratory on me, as Ian says. He was terribly excited talking about Lord Kitchener, said he had a spitting toad inside his head, he pressed his hands hard over his own head and eyes to show the baffled weariness of trying to deal with such a fool. . . ." [29th May 1916 Postlip Hall]

As the government and the War Cabinet struggled to reduce the powers of Lord Kitchener, with the ultimate aim of removing him from office, the conduct of the Gallipoli campaign became a political battleground. Ian Hamilton's perceived failure there was to be used as a weapon against Kitchener.

At the end of October, Lloyd George and Bonar Law jointly threatened to resign unless Kitchener was removed, at which point Prime Minister Asquith sent him on a tour of inspection of the situation at Gallipoli. While he was away, Asquith transferred final control over the supply of war material to Lloyd George. Kitchener also ceased to be the Government's adviser on strategy, which role was taken over by the new Chief of the Imperial General Staff, Lieutenant-General Sir William

Robertson. Kitchener offered to resign but he was still so popular in the country that the government could not risk the outcry that might ensue. With Kitchener stripped of his power and remaining only as a figurehead in the Asquith government, decisions could then be taken by others in his name. If they later proved wrong, as might be the case in calling off the Gallipoli campaign, then in the eyes of the country, the press, indeed in the eyes of history itself, Kitchener, as Secretary of State for War, could be blamed. Kitchener's later tragic death by drowning when the *Hampshire* sank en route to Russia meant he was unable to challenge allegations against him.

The Allies had suffered a serious reverse in a campaign that began with such high hopes. There was a need to understand what had gone wrong but the immediate response was to seek a scapegoat and to protect the reputations of the real culprits – the politicians in London.

Failure at the strategic level in the war may have been brought about greatly by weakness at the political and administrative level, due to lack of organisation and coordination. The War Council (later the War Cabinet) failed in two aspects in particular: firstly, to work out a plan to target an enemy area favourable to their own success, in this case the Dardanelles, and see it through; secondly, to concentrate their efforts (backed up by fresh troops, ammunition and supplies) at Gallipoli, in order to make way for the British Fleet to pass through the Straits to conquer Constantinople, with the chance of knocking Turkey out of the war. It remains speculative whether such a success would have won the war but it would have seriously weakened the German war effort and provided a much-needed moral boost to Britain and her allies. The best of the Turkish troops were concentrated at Gallipoli under German command. Pinning them there in battle prevented their being deployed elsewhere, thus seriously weakening the whole impact of German strategy. As it turned out, all the other attacks on the Western Front and at Salonica failed, and Gallipoli, Jean believed, had been needlessly sacrificed.

Fragmentation at several levels appears to have been one of Britain's greatest handicaps. The ultimate casualty was Gallipoli, the one campaign, as Jean said, that might have reached a decisive conclusion. The mistake Lloyd George and Bonar Law made in demanding its abandonment in favour of Salonica (as part of their efforts to further weaken Kitchener's power) was that they failed totally to recognise either the possibilities or the progress that was being made at Gallipoli. But then neither Lloyd

George nor Bonar Law had any military experience, they were merely politicians. In his *War Memoirs* Lloyd George says of Ian Hamilton 'He was perhaps better fitted for a Staff post than for a Commander in the field', but goes on to praise him as 'the only leading soldier who had actually seen and made careful study of modern warfare.'[15] The Germans knew Hamilton somewhat better than Lloyd George. In 1911 an article in the journal of their Great General Staff described Hamilton as 'the most experienced soldier in the world'; praise indeed from the most professional army in the world.

As criticism of the Gallipoli campaign mounted, Asquith's government was forced to institute a Dardanelles Commission of Inquiry to examine the preparation and conduct of the campaign. From that time Hamilton was never again given a commission or command in the field, his career was ruined and the press sought to tarnish his name. Jean passionately believed Ian's version of events; that it was Kitchener's failure to send reinforcements and ammunition to Gallipoli that jeopardised the whole operation. She considered Ian's treatment to be a great injustice both to him and to the nation. Gallipoli preoccupied her more than any other subject. It is hardly surprising, therefore, that a somewhat different version of the events unfolds through the pages of her diary.

From Jean's diary we know how well three of the main protagonists knew each other. Winston Churchill was a close friend of Ian's and was a frequent guest at the Hamiltons' dinner parties, and vice versa. The Hamiltons and Churchills were like family to each other. Winston was always about the Hamiltons' houses and Jean wrote in her diary: **"Ian adores Winston". [9th November 1916 London]** Several of the Hamiltons' circle lived within close proximity of No. 1 HPG: the Winston Churchills had a house at Eccleston Square and Sir John French lived at Lancaster Gate.

If the Hamiltons saw less of Kitchener socially, Ian knew him particularly well from their service together in the Boer War. Shortly after the South African War, the Hamiltons entertained Kitchener, Rawlinson and Jean's widowed sister, Betty; Jean possibly hoping for a romance between Kitchener and Betty. **" ... We took Lord Kitchener to see 'The Country Girl.' He was pleasant and happy and enjoyed it thoroughly, so did Ian and Rawly. I made the Rawlinsons ask Betty to dinner as it was our box, and we had a combined party. Rutland Barrington sang some topical verses about Lord K. who sat behind the curtain of the** box, but Mr. Barrington looked up as he sang them; and someone called out 'Three cheers for Lord Kitchener' at the end of the play. Lord K. was furious and hid more than ever behind the curtain muttering angrily 'The fools.' At dinner I told him the most dangerous age for a man, if he wanted to avoid matrimony, was between 60 and 80. He looked alarmed. Evidently he has been congratulating himself that he was now quite safe. He is simple and primitive, and I like his lack of adroitness in trivial conversation. He reminds me of Mr. Sargent. I was glad I carried my point about having Betty included in our little party as Lord K. used to be a friend of hers. . . . " [21st July 1902]

Politicians knew little, if anything, of command in the field; to men like Hamilton, Kitchener and Churchill it was second nature. When Hamilton organised a series of amphibious exercises at Malta in 1912 and 1913, they were attended by Kitchener and Churchill who were out there at that time on an official visit. These generals knew each other well and understood there was no room for dissent on the field of battle; they had practical experience of working around each other's idiosyncrasies.

Churchill and Hamilton worked particularly well together. Hamilton defined 'genius' in relation to battle as 'the faculty; the intuitive perception; the piercing power of comprehension; the innate originality and, above all, the intrepidity which takes all these and uses them; the intrepidity without which they would merely amount to imagination. That genius about which I write is made up of four parts: one part imagination, one part energy, one part enthusiasm, and one part courage'.[16]

To Churchill, Hamilton attributes three strokes of genius. The first was at Antwerp, when in 1914, as First Lord of the Admiralty, he made a military decision to insert the Royal Naval Division into the port of Antwerp to deny it to a rapidly approaching German force. Such a decision, a calculated military risk by a Navy man, Hamilton considered to have been 'prompted by an imperative impulse to threaten the enemy's right, and to hold up his advance on the Channel Ports, if only for two or three days'. The second was the allocation of Navy funds to develop the tank as a means of safely crossing no-man's-land between the trenches on the Western Front and crushing the German barbed wire. The third was the Dardanelles campaign, which 'move was calculated to save Russia by piercing a deep-sea, warm-sea passage to her heart, clean through the enemy's left.'

Hamilton described the Dardanelles campaign as the effort 'to get outside of an overcrowded area'; a move 'inspired by genius' and 'worked out from start to finish', in the 'face of an outcry from France'.[17]

Through the writings of historians like Alan Clark, the British war effort has been caricatured as the work of 'lions led by donkeys'. The Gallipoli expedition has been considered for many years to have been an ill-thought-out plan in which Hamilton set off with his troops to Gallipoli with no idea how to land there. Heavy losses were incurred and no one is disputing that that was a tragedy. But Jean's diary reveals that the actual achievement of the landings was considered 'magnificent' at the time, and Hamilton was more prepared for the task than any other general of his day.

From 1910 to 1914 Hamilton was Inspector General of Overseas Forces and General Officer Commanding, Mediterranean. Hidden away in the archives at King's College, London, are Hamilton's official reports to the War Office of amphibious exercises he carried out, the most successful of which took place at Malta, and a less successful exercise at Gibraltar, in 1912 and 1913. The reports are marked 'secret', so only a handful of people would have seen them at the War Office. There had been a continuing effort to get the Army and the Navy to cooperate more fully in developing plans for amphibious warfare, as the requirement to convey troops overseas to battle was a regular feature of British warfare. The actual assault upon an enemy held coast was very rare and extremely hazardous. Hamilton, through his work as commander of the Mediterranean region, had more experience of this type of problematic operation than almost any other general in the army.

As part of these exercises harbour defences were tested against the event of an attack from the sea. In his Memorandum to the War Office dated 1912, he detailed the benefits and drawbacks of test mobilisations in Malta and Gibraltar:

> . . . the mobilisations of the naval and military fortress defences were carried out simultaneously whilst two cruisers and four destroyers represented a hostile fleet. During the test operations that ensued, 500 officers and men of the Gloucestershire Regiment were landed from one of these two cruisers under cover of darkness. Lessons of the highest value have been gained as a result of these joint naval and military operations. . . . on a dark night all the advantages rest with the invaders.[18]

During that time, key personnel were in Malta. " . . . **The Prime Minister, Winston Churchill, Lord K. descend upon our peaceful island. . . .** " [26th May 1912] Winston at that time had even more power, having been promoted at the end of 1911 to First Lord of the Admiralty. On Monday 27 May Brigadier-General Egerton stayed. Egerton would later command the Lowland Division that left Scotland in May 1915 to serve with Hamilton at Gallipoli.

Combined naval and military operations took place on Thursday 17 and Friday 18 April 1913[19] and greatly impinged on Jean's domestic arrangements: **"Mrs Trowbridge [sic] stayed with us last Thursday night for my dinner party which was a failure as all the men in the island were out at manoeuvres, naval and military. . . ."** [20th April 1913 San Antonio Malta] Others who are mentioned in Jean's diary as having stayed with the Hamiltons at Malta in 1913 include Captain Darnell and Admiral Troubridge, who commanded the blockading Fleet in the Dardanelles in 1914.

We can assume that Hamilton's theoretical experience of amphibious operations helped Kitchener select him, and Churchill to support him, as the general to command the Gallipoli campaign. However, Hamilton's experience was with the British army and navy during peacetime. As yet, no one in the modern era had ever attempted assault landings in war.

Not to be underestimated was the contribution of Major-General Braithwaite, Hamilton's Chief of Staff. He had entered the army in 1886, and after nearly thirty years of service was Director of Staff Duties at the War Office in 1914–15. Kitchener personally selected Braithwaite to serve with Hamilton at Gallipoli, probably on the basis of his time as an instructor at the Staff College, Camberley, where he had worked closely with General Aston, Royal Marines, who was particularly keen to develop joint operations between the Army and the Navy.

Further discussion of the technical merits of the Gallipoli campaign are outside of the remit of this book and readers may wish to pursue the subject through the accompanying biography of General Sir Ian Hamilton, *A Soldier's Life*, by John Lee. What we do have is evidence from Jean's diary that she was well acquainted with her husband's work, and had a good understanding of the problems and the possibilities of a vigorous allied offensive through the Dardanelles. Her opinion on the matter is a valuable one.

CHAPTER 9

Lady Hamilton's Gallipoli Fund

" . . . we have our parties for wounded soldiers every Thursday and they grow more enormous every week and it's difficult to seat and feed them. . . . " [28th October 1915]

Jean was an active member of the Red Cross throughout the war. On certain days throughout the year, the Hamiltons' house would be 'thrown open and a good tea given to meetings of every sort of good work.'[1] Jean set up a Gallipoli Fund to raise cash to buy supplies that were sent to the troops at the Dardanelles.[2] The appeal was published in the newspapers on 12 July 1915 and 'brought an immediate and most gratifying response.' The Committee consisted of Mr Henry Fenwick Reeve (a senior executive officer of Queen Alexandra's Field Force Fund); Mrs Charlotte Sclater, Hon. Secretary; Mr W. L. Sclater, Hon. Treasurer; Mrs Braithwaite, wife of Major-General Braithwaite; and Jean's sister, Heather Pollen.

Hundreds of bales of comforts and medical stores were packed at Jean's house, 1 Hyde Park Gardens, under her supervision, and at the depots of Queen Alexandra's Field Force Fund. The supplies were then shipped to the troops at Gallipoli and to the base hospitals at Mudros (on the island of Lemnos), Alexandria and Malta. Jean wrote in her diary on her birthday: **" . . . No rest or peace all day, telephoning and worry from dawn to midnight. . . . Heather and I were so busy with Red Cross work. . . . much agitated all day getting ten huge bales of Red Cross things off to Alexandria – they had to be off at 2.30 – Miss Batt, my new war secretary, quite lost her head, but Heather's chauffeur came to the rescue and took them off in her motor and they were in time." [8th June 1915]**

Items sent to the troops included: 17,000 shirts; over 7,500 vests; socks, mufflers, shorts and sweaters; 14,000 mosquito nets; 37,000 towels and 20,000 cakes of soap; nearly 1½ million cigarettes; 1,648lb of tobacco and over 13,000 pipes; 1,500lb sweets; 359 barrels of apples; boracic and carbolic ointments and vaseline; 360 mouth organs, 20 gramophones with records, 6 sets of boxing gloves; pocket mirrors, scissors, and soldiers' housewives (sewing kits). Supplies for the hospitals included 100 pillows and pillow-cases, bandages and dressings, slippers and bed jackets.[3] At Mudros a recreation tent was erected capable of holding 500 men, and was equipped with a piano, gramophones and several refrigerators.[4]

Many of the supplies were urgently needed. The *Observer* published an interview with Jean in which she said that Ian had written to her 'that the men were finding the food monotonous, so a consignment of apples, bloater paste, curry powder, Worcester Sauce, pickles . . . have been sent to each Division'.[5] Jean decided to send the greater part of the comforts in bulk to the base camps at Lemnos and the rest camp at Imbros. By the end of September of 1915, thirty-five regiments had benefited. The distributors at Mudros were Mrs Van Agnew and Mr Arthur Baker, the latter having lived in Constantinople for many years and gained much local experience of the Near East. The Acting Secretary was Phyllis Keyes. Clothing sent out later included 3,000 khaki shirts for the Indian Brigade, 3,000 pairs of shorts for the Gurkhas and 1,000 'Kache Ras' for the Sikhs.[6]

Ian, always attentive to the well-being of his soldiers, told Jean what to send. In a cable dated 24 July 1915, he advised: 'Officer to whom goods should be despatched is Captain Rebsch, 29th Indian Brigade Transport Officer. Increase tin milk to 1,000; reduce cigarettes to 50,000.' [7]

Jean was given a great deal of help by her sisters Betty and Heather. Heather helped Jean pack the bales at No. 1 HPG; Betty was an experienced organiser and was running Peel House, an overseas club for Australian and New Zealand servicemen. **[20th October 1915]**

Amongst the subscribers to the Fund were such notables as Sir Ernest Cassel, £200; Countess Roberts, the wife of Lord Roberts, £40; Viscount Haldane of Cloan, £25; Lady Airlie, £10. Amongst the institutional donors were the 2/8th Battalion, Lancashire Fusiliers, NCOs and men £12, officers £10; Tinsley Park Colliery £10 10s; the Mill Workers of Robert Ashworth, £10. The Muir family gave generously, Margaret, Lady Muir (Jean's mother), Clara Muir (Will's wife), and Heather Pollen donating among them nearly £500. The name of every contributor was recorded, covering all those small sums of a few shillings which often represented the better part of a week's wages for working-class families. By the end of September 1915, £12,608 had been raised.[8] The Hamiltons received vast quantities of letters acknowledging their work. The following is one touching tribute:

Kathleen Sanderson,
Lyne Villa,
Ferry Road,
Edinburgh.
13/7/1915

Our Daddy went out to fight at the Dardanelles and was killed on 28th June. Roy, Eileen, baby and I wish to send you 10/- of our own money for comforts for the soldiers out there.

With love from Kathleen Sanderson.[9]

When Ian returned from the failed Gallipoli expedition in late October 1915, Jean did not abandon her fund-raising efforts for the Dardanelles but rather intensified her work. Courageously, the Hamiltons faced their demise together in public and amidst adverse press reports about Ian. They continued to do everything they could to help the soldiers at the Dardanelles and showed no animosity towards Sir Charles Monro when he was sent out to Gallipoli to replace Ian. At a committee meeting of the Near East branch of the Red Cross of St John, Jean told Princess Christian that Ian was **" . . . still determined to do all he could to get reinforcements and ammunition for Sir Charles Monro, if he decided to go on with the campaign . . . "** and she suggested that they ask **"Lady Monro to join this Committee."** Princess Christian proposed Lady Monro and Jean seconded her. **" . . . Lord Plymouth . . . said: 'But Sir Charles Monro has only gone out to report, I understand?' so Princess C. said with her German accent: 'Oh, I don't know anything at all about that,' and looked at me; upon which I said, in a calm voice: 'Not at all, Sir Charles Monro has gone out to report, and to back his report by staying out and carrying it through.' . . ."** There was an uncomfortable atmosphere but Jean **" . . . felt perfectly mistress of the situation." [29th October 1915 London]**

Jean had turned round what could have been an embarrassing situation by bringing Lady Monro onto the Committee. Lord Rosebury helped Jean organise a flag day to raise funds. " . . . **Went to Croydon to-day, to Thornton Heath, to receive gifts for my Gallipoli Fund, and had a splendid reception. I read out a little speech Ian helped me write saying Ian wished all success to his successor at Gallipoli as it was vitally important it should not be abandoned now – enjoyed hearing the touching and grateful speeches made by the men there – in fact it has made me wish to go on with the Fund in my own name, as it may be the means of making some demonstration in favour of Ian."** [6th November 1915 Bowood]

Jean was still full of confidence in her ability to run her Gallipoli Fund separately from Queen Alexandra's Field Force Fund. " . . . **I am thinking of keeping on my Fund now, under my own name, as I see a way of helping Ian with it, and will get Lady Birdwood to join with me.**" There was favourable press coverage of her work: " . . . **'The Wife of Gallipoli Hamilton', so some of the newspaper portraits of me are headed! . . .** " [7th November 1915] Jean had addressed a fund-raising meeting and " . . . **was rather startled to see in 'The Observer' 'Lady Ian Hamilton and Gallipoli' and the sentence quoted from my little Croydon speech in which I said 'we could win right through there now, and if new changes meant reinforcements and that the gallant troops there would be helped to do so more rapidly no one would rejoice more than myself.' I wanted to say how gallantly these men were holding 250,000 Turks there now, but Ian would not let me.**" [9th November 1915]

To the next meeting of the Red Cross, in Pall Mall, Jean drove up with Lady Monro in her car and introduced her to Princess Christian. " . . . **I sat by Princess Christian, who was most gushing to me again, kissing me and patting me, and I lifted my voice at the end of the meeting to insist on recreation huts being at once sent over to Mudros from Alexandria, and Lord Plymouth had a telegram sent to Sir Courtauld Thomson to that effect. I think Sir Frederick Treves returned to try and stop this when my back was turned, as there is some hanky-panky about these wooden huts going on, which I don't quite understand. Sir Courtauld Thomson was rather nervous having ordered very expensive ones, thinking the Government was going to pay for them, and wanted me to stand by him, which I did.**" [12th November 1915]

A week later Jean rose at 4.30 in the morning to deal with Mr Sclater's accounts on the balance of the Gallipoli Fund and in the afternoon " . . .

went to a grim and funereal meeting – *huge* it was – of Queen Alexandra Field Force Fund – both Lady Monro and Lady Murray were there.

Lady Haig and Lady Murray were elected and . . . Lady Murray . . . is to be President of the new Fund, as my Gallipoli Fund is now to be affiliated to Queen Alexandra's, but I won't merge it till the accounts are all finally closed and audited, and I have a good surplus to start well." [19th January 1916 London]

Jean's fund closed on 22 January 1916 with a total of £17,746 donated, and between October and December a further 21,136 parcels were sent out to the troops.[10]

At No. 1 HPG, Jean gave parties for wounded soldiers and sailors every week, helped by Ian when he returned from Gallipoli. It was this type of event that was eating up the Hamiltons' money. Between 150 and 250 soldiers and sailors would attend. Rodacanachi, a Greek millionaire, brought a busload at his own expense every week. 'The passports to entry were the bright blue kit and bright red ties of the genuine article – or for those who were convalescent, an Anzac hat.'[11] Women volunteers served tea and celebrities gave their services at half price. Lady Maud Warrender, the famous opera singer, gave renditions of 'Annie Laurie', Helen Marr told funny stories, Miss Hoare sang ragtime and Percy Kahn played the piano and danced up and down across the keys.[12]

" . . . Thursdays are always full of feverish bustle, as we have our parties for wounded soldiers every Thursday and they grow more enormous every week and it's difficult to seat and feed them – we got an extra allowance of *butter* for them! To-day Ian and I snatched a quiet lunch in the drawing-room together . . . .

I felt happier and more in touch with Ian. I told him how little I cared, if it were not for him, for position here in the world – that I was quite ready to cut the whole thing at his bidding, with a heart for any fate, and that I hoped if Lord K. treated him badly and threw him to the dogs, he would cut the whole show, and go off and join the Russian Army and waive his rank.

The Bosphorus, Constantinople, Gallipoli – there our hearts lie, not in this dull stale Flanders, where both sides will sit for ever in the trenches.

We are Adventurers here, no children – no claims on us – as free as possible, and we don't care:–

'We don't want to fight –
But, by jingo, if we do
We've got the men, the money –
And the big guns too.'

... Our Soldiers' Party was a success to-day. Maud Warrender sang 'Annie Laurie' divinely for our soldiers this afternoon . . . May Spender – Lady Robinson – General Neville Lyttelton and the usual lot of helpers came. I feel immensely interested in everyone's attitude just now. Most of our real friends stand the test well." [28th October 1915 London]

" . . . Last Thursday we had a very successful Soldiers' Party . . . 140 men – Mr. Ryan, the Prime Minister from Queensland, came to tea and made them a charming speech, in which he praised Ian and what had been accomplished in Gallipoli. . . . the way the Cabinet try to wipe out Gallipoli and Ian from mention and remembrance makes one mad." [28th May 1916 Postlip Hall]

The soldiers' parties continued long after the war was over. Jean had an adopted child, Harry Knight. The three-year-old, with his sweet blonde curls and loving way, dressed in a blue and white sailor suit, charmed the sick and wounded men. " . . . Soldiers' party day, very hot, all the soldiers sat about under the trees in the garden, and our usual lot sang to them afterwards – Lilian Hoare, Della (a great artist he is), Major MacLean, Helen Marr. Harry was delicious with them in the garden. Diana Grove . . . danced in a lovely Classic dress afterwards . . . Harry sitting on a soldier's knee, was thrilled by this spectacle." [29th May 1919 London]

CHAPTER 10

The Dardanelles Commission of Inquiry

"His country does not know it yet, but some day they will and meantime I am satisfied with the heroic part he has played." [27th September 1918]

As one nightmare was ending for the Hamiltons, another was just beginning. The eventual outcome of the failure at Gallipoli was the setting up of a Dardanelles Commission of Inquiry, which lasted many months, with the Final Report not published until after the war was over. Elements of the press, baying for a sacrifice, wanted General Sir Ian Hamilton court-martialled. Considering the enormity of his struggle to win at Gallipoli and the traumatic effect on both his wife and himself of being recalled to face humiliation, the suggestion can only be viewed as outrageous. Kitchener had originally meant to use General Braithwaite as a scapegoat, by suggesting they 'change Braithwaite for Kiggell' in an attempt to spare Hamilton. Being the man of honour that he was, Hamilton refused, leaving himself open to blame and to accepting full responsibility.

Not until his return to England did Hamilton fully realise the damage done to him by the journalists Ashmead-Bartlett and Murdoch. On 13 October 1915, whilst still in command at Gallipoli, Hamilton had received a memorandum from his trusted friend, Major-General Callwell, Director of Military Operations and Intelligence at the War Office (1914–16) enclosing a copy and asking for his comments on Keith Murdoch's letter, dated 23 September 1915, to Andrew Fisher, Prime Minister of Australia.[1] On 25 September, Murdoch had sent the same letter to Herbert Asquith, the British Prime Minister, with a covering letter stating that he did so at the request of Lloyd George:

Arundel Hotel, Victoria Embankment, September 25, 1915.

The Right Honourable
H. H. Asquith, P.C., M.P.,
Prime Minister.

Dear Sir

MR LLOYD GEORGE has suggested to me that I should place at
your disposal whatever knowledge I gained of the Dardanelles
operations while an Australian civilian representative there.

I therefore take the liberty of sending to you a copy of a private
letter I have addressed to Mr. Fisher, in conformance with his
request that I should write him fully on the subject.

This letter was, of course, intended only for Commonwealth
Ministers, and contains references which will have no interest to
you. But I feel justified in sending it to you, because if it adds one
iota to your information, or presents the Australian point of view, it
will be of service in this most critical moment.

I write with diffidence, and only at Mr. Lloyd George's request.
In any case, you will know that my motive is one of affectionate
regard for our soldiers' interests.

I have the honour to be,
    Your obedient Servant,
        K.A.M.

On 28 September, Murdoch's letter was circulated as a State Paper at
the Committee of Imperial Defence and the Dardanelles Committee (as
the War Council was now known). What is uncertain is whether Kitchener
knew that Lloyd George had been instrumental in directing Murdoch's
actions, who otherwise would have been unlikely to have taken such a
step. That action was to be taken influencing the possible direction of a
military operation on the word of a mere newspaper reporter was unprece-
dented. Lloyd George's reasons could only have been to bring pressure to
bear on the Dardanelles Committee to recall Hamilton and wind up the
Gallipoli operation. The Dardanelles campaign was Kitchener's and
Churchill's plan and potential success story, and bringing it to an end
would ensure that, in the eyes of the cabinet, Kitchener was a failure. If the

operation had succeeded, the story would have resounded through the press, further elevating Kitchener's position in the eyes of his adoring public and making it even more difficult for Lloyd George to get rid of him. The careers of Hamilton and Churchill may have been sacrificed as the incidental casualties of the attempts of Lloyd George and his circle to inflict a fatal blow against Kitchener. But since no blame was attributed to Kitchener in the press, the image of his role in the war effort remained intact in the minds of the British public. The demise of the Prime Minister himself would be one unforeseen outcome.

Lloyd George, Ashmead-Bartlett and Murdoch needed each other. Lloyd George needed support for his proposed operations through Salonica to further his own ambitions in politics. Ashmead-Bartlett and Murdoch needed sensationalist stories to sell Northcliffe's newspapers to obtain increased advertising revenue. When Ashmead-Bartlett returned to Gallipoli as a reporter, he had his own marquee and a butler.[2] While he supped champagne, wearing a silk dressing gown, the fighting men were enduring the most difficult conditions on the peninsula. As Ian had described it to Jean, 'For 3 weeks they did not even have a blanket, just what they stood up in.'[3]

Later, Jean would receive valuable first-hand evidence of the opinion of at least one young serving officer about Ashmead-Bartlett and his pernicious effect at Gallipoli. Jack Cowans, the Quarter Master General and friend of the Hamiltons, wrote to Jean on War Office notepaper on 25 January 1917, sending her a letter which Lord Ribblesdale had sent him, written by his son, the Hon. Charles Lister. Lister's letter was dated 3 June 1915 and was sent from the Blue Sisters hospital, where he was recovering from an injury received whilst fighting at Gallipoli.

> Ashmead-Bartlett has been here, home bound. He was blown up on
> the *Majestic* and escaped . . . I hope he will get us more men sent
> out; but his tone is pessimistic and his statements exaggerations . . .
> so perhaps they will take no notice of him. The Turks are
> exhausting themselves by these attacks on our trenches and losing
> great numbers, and with a few more men we could do the trick soon
> enough. . . . My only fear is Ashmead may paint in such gloomy
> colours that the Harmsworth Press may plump for a complete bunk.
> . . . Our hold is *very* firm now, and it's simply a question of more
> men to effect our advance.[4]

In another letter from Charles Lister to his father, dated 1 August 1915, he spoke well of his commanding general: 'Sir Ian was most kind and affectionate in his enquiries after you . . . He lives very simply . . . ' and ' . . . chatted pleasantly on the demoralized state of the Turks . . . .'[5] Sadly Charles Lister, an officer of the Household Cavalry, serving with the County of London Yeomanry, died of his injury on the 26th.

Murdoch's letter had laid sweeping charges against Hamilton's conduct of the Gallipoli campaign and made allegations about the conditions at Gallipoli that reflected equally badly on the government. 'We have abandoned our intentions of taking Achi Baba by frontal assault. This was always a hopeless scheme after early May, and no one can understand why Hamilton persisted with it. Achi Baba is a gradual, bare slope, a mass of trenches and gun emplacements, but so little did the General Staff know of its task that it expected to storm it with ease.' Murdoch spoke of 'heavy loss of men' and '*morale* severely shaken'; 'inadequate clothing supplies . . . London . . . still sending out . . . shorts'; 'lack of water'; 'monotony of a salt beef and rice diet'. 'Hamilton . . . as a strategist has completely failed. Undoubtedly the essential and first step to restore the *morale* of the shaken forces is to recall him . . . and his Chief of Staff [Braithwaite], a man more cordially detested in our forces than Enver Pasha'. 'Cabinet Ministers here [London] impress me with the fact that a failure in the Dardanelles would have most serious results in India. Persia is giving endless trouble and there seems to be little doubt that India is ripe for trouble.' 'Nor do I know whether the appalling outlay in money on the Dardanelles expedition, with its huge and costly line of communications, can be allowed to continue without endangering those financial resources on which we rely to so great an extent in the wearing down of Germany's strength. Nor do I know whether any offensive next year against Constantinople can succeed. On that point I can only say that the best military advice is that we can get through, that we would be through now if we had thrown in sufficient forces. Whyte, whom we both admire as an able soldier and an inspiring Australian leader, assures me that another 150,000 men would do the job. I presume that would mean a landing on a large scale somewhere in Thrace, or north of Bulair.' ' . . . whereas our 3rd Australian General Hospital on shore we had 134 fever cases, including typhus, with only a few mosquito nets, and no ice, and few medical comforts, the "Aragon" staff was wallowing in ice.' 'Do for Heaven's sake, make every effort to secure the recall of Sir James Porter, the Englishman in charge of the medical services. . . . He lives on a luxurious yacht in Mudros.'[6]

When Ian was recalled, Ashmead-Bartlett's attacks on him in the press increased. In the following diary entry Jean is implying that Murdoch smuggled into England a letter that was really the work of Ashmead-Bartlett, whose most critical despatch was intercepted by military censors and, in all probability, was subsequently destroyed at the War Office. Jean was making a reasonable assumption as Murdoch could scarcely have produced such a detailed analysis of the situation at Gallipoli since he was there for only two days and had no particular military training or knowledge. Ashmead-Bartlett on the other hand considered himself a great expert on strategy and tactics, based on his experiences as a war correspondent.

" . . . Ashmead-Bartlett . . . is going about lecturing, advising the withdrawal of the troops from the Dardanelles – a real snake in the grass he has been. Ian told me the night he returned (as we walked about in the moonlight) of his treachery, and of how he had been warned again and again, and given his word of honour as a gentleman not to send any despatches home uncensored but he did this again and again, and conspired with Murdoch. . . . He had come and most humbly begged to be allowed to see Anzac and Ian had let him go there for two days with Ashmead-Bartlett. . . . Mr. Murdoch had then written a long account. . . . This despatch was full of abuse of Ian's management of the campaign and these two managed to smuggle this through to Australia. Ashmead-Bartlett also wrote a terrible damaging article on the Gallipoli situation blaming Ian which was to be smuggled through to England by Murdoch and given to the Prime Minister. It was, and circulated round the Dardanelles Committee. Ian had never seen the cad, as it was Braithwaite who dealt with him in his usual harsh uncompromising way, and as he left his tent, dismissed and sent home for spreading despondency and defeatism amongst the troops, A.B. said: 'I will do for him,' (meaning Braithwaite), and he has – quite regardless of the fact he has dragged Ian down with him. . . . " [24th October 1915 London]

Years later, Jean attributed the failure at Gallipoli greatly to adverse press reporting and believed that things would have been different if the journalist Philip Sassoon had been given the chance to provide press coverage there. " . . . I shall never cease to regret that Ian did not have him

[Philip Sassoon] **with him at the Dardanelles. I am convinced if he had had the war would have been over two years earlier and many young lives saved. Murdoch and Ashmead-Bartlett would have found their wrecking plans outwitted. . . . " [4th June 1939]**

Jean decided to use her own influence, contacting two journalists, Harrison and Garvin, the latter a correspondent for the *Observer*. **" . . . I feel spoiling for a good fight, and mean to make friends with the Mammon of unrighteousness – the Press. I have written to Austin Harrison, and had a long talk with him, and I mean to get Mr. Garvin to my aid too, he is a friend of mine – and the Spenders are longing to plunge into the fray." [28th October 1915]**

But Ashmead-Bartlett's tirade against Ian continued through newspaper articles and lectures in Britain. **" . . . Ashmead-Bartlett is doing Ian terrible harm – he lectured last night and told many harmful lies – said *no* preparation for water for the troops at Suvla made, etc., and his whole lecture was against the Gallipoli policy and management – why he is allowed to do this passes my comprehension.**
I hear he goes about making violent personal attacks on Ian." [29th October 1915] Ashmead-Bartlett then visited Australia, New Zealand and America with the same stories, supported by the press barons; he was, for the time being, unstoppable. **" . . . Ashmead-Bartlett . . . is touring round America now and goes on to Australia and New Zealand preaching a crusade against Ian, and all our papers are publishing his interviews with gusto." [13th February 1916]**

Kitchener had allowed Murdoch's letter to be passed round the Committee of Imperial Defence, of which Ian was a member. In early November, the War Committee was reduced to a new inner council of four, Asquith, Lloyd George, Balfour and Sir Edward Grey. Ian had no special friends or direct influence on the new council, or any means of knowing what was being decided there. **[3rd and 5th November 1915]**

The Hamiltons at this stage were still unaware of Lloyd George's full part in bringing about Ian's recall from Gallipoli by encouraging Murdoch to send his letter to both the Australian and British Prime Ministers. They were still under the impression, as was Winston Churchill, that Kitchener was to blame for all that had gone wrong. For once there was a gap in Jean's intelligence! Although a copy of Murdoch's letter was sent to Ian at Gallipoli, the covering letter, showing Lloyd George's direct intervention, seems to have been omitted, otherwise Ian and Jean would have been alerted to Lloyd George's role much sooner and Jean would have written about it in her diary.

Jean relied greatly for information on Winston Churchill, who blamed the demise of the Gallipoli campaign on Bonar Law. It would be some seven months from Ian's recall in October 1915, until May 1916, before Jean began to suspect Lloyd George's part in Ian's downfall. In the meantime, Lloyd George was trying to deceive Ian and turn him against Kitchener. "... **Ian lunched with Lloyd George today, and he told him what had damaged him with the Cabinet was that they were told he chose Stopford, as he was a personal friend of his, and the Cabinet thought a man who could do such a thing, was not to be depended on. Ian explained, and Lloyd George told him Lord K. had been there, and had stood by silent while Ian was censured for this; he said it was a dirty trick, and he never could feel the same to K. again." [9th November 1915 Bowood]**

Clearly Kitchener had failed to inform the Cabinet of Hamilton's request for younger, battle-tried generals, or that his choice of Stopford was the only one left open to him. Lord Curzon was equally to blame in this regard. On Lord Roberts' anniversary, after their attendance at the service, Jean and Ian set off to see both Winston Churchill and Lord Curzon. "... **Winston has resigned! and written an excellent letter – I envy him being able to do it. I wish Ian could, and state he was off to serve in another land – Russia – and flick the dust of the Government of England off his wings. ...**" Winston's house was the first stop: "... **Winston himself opened the door, and was delighted to see Ian. ...**" **[13th November 1915]** Jean sat outside in the motor, talking to Clementine and Eddie Marsh, who had been Winston's Private Secretary from 1905 until November 1915, when he became Assistant Private Secretary to Herbert Asquith, the Prime Minister.

The Hamiltons then travelled by train to Hackwood, to see Lord Curzon, who was not apparently suffering any shortages, either in terms of food or staff. "... **lovely arriving here ... such light, colour and comfort, the gorgeous array of good-looking footmen again is surprising in these stern recruiting days – why ... are they not stretched on beds of anguish, these good-looking young men? I am glad indeed they are not, they are a refreshing sight in their knee breeches. ...**" The rest of the party staying were Julia Maguire (Kitchener's friend), Tommy Maguire, Harry Chaplin, the

Walter Lawrences, Sir John Jewitt and Lady Herbert. Curzon's eldest daughter, Irene, gave them tea. At dinner Jean " . . . **sat between Sir John Jewitt and Sir Walter Lawrence, and drank exquisite champagne; Ian sat between Julia and Lady Herbert. . . . "** [**13th November 1915** contd.]

The following day, Jean sat next to Lord Curzon at lunch; he discussed the inadequacies of his nanny, the demands of American women, and soldiers' wives being too exacting. In the afternoon they played tennis. " . . . **After tea, Lord Curzon took me all through his beautiful rooms to show me his pictures. He certainly has a lovely lot in the blue room – Hoppner – Gainsborough – Reynolds – Raeburn – all of lovely women.**

In the large tapestry room is the wonderful silver chandelier he has had made out of all his silver presentation cups – it is copied from the one now belonging to Ettie Desborough at Panshanger.

Wore my lovely tarnished silver dress, that I bought at Jay's sale, to-night, and Ian thought it lovely. Lord Curzon took me in to dinner, and we had a delightful talk about Shelley, Byron, Trelawney etc., started by Julia on his other side. . . . Lord C. had been reading all his favourite modern poets to them. . . .

After dinner . . . presently on the subject of Lord K. we joined forces, Julia held forth on his strength a magnificence, he had only to lift his little finger to crush any member of the Cabinet; finally she said: '*When* he returns to England—' stopped suddenly and there was a dead silence, which I broke by looking quizzically at her, and saying: '*Is* he returning to England, Julia?' 'He will the moment he wants to,' she said in an aggressive way. . . . I continued: 'I thought he'd be of much more use in Gallipoli, and that Ian had written quite plainly telling him this' and I added 'I did not think the Cabinet wanted him back' which made Julia furious and there was a long silence, difficult to break – Lord K. is Julia's God at present. . . .

. . . Ian had a long interesting walk with Lord Curzon to-day. Lord Curzon is keen there should be no evacuation of Gallipoli, which he considers would be a ghastly disaster. Ian sees clearly now that Lord Curzon stood by and said no word when Ian's *supposed choice* of Stopford was used to damn him, though he must have seen Ian's first cable and knew he had no choice, though Ian had to wire afterwards accepting Stopford in the end and this is the only cable that has been shown and his first has been suppressed.

All this I told Tommy Maguire last night, which may account for Julia's antagonistic attitude to-night. Julia is the kind of Tabby that loves a primitive fighting man like Lord K. – how well I remember him as Major Kitchener, going out to Somaliland, on my way to India to stay with Betty; Addie Goodrich, Mrs. Charlie Muir – all those Anglo-Indian women running after this celebrated woman-hater, with his flaming red beard, and I, (with my romantic Greek god type of hero firmly enthroned in my heart,) marvelled at their curious taste.

Ian lunched with Arthur Balfour to-day, and A.B. was bored at the idea of having to go and listen to Winston's long speech in the House of Commons this afternoon. I can't understand that – how I should have loved to hear him, this young ardent spirit at last being able to breathe and speak out freely; however, I well understand the Government will hate it." [14th November 1915 Hackwood]

Jean put the entire blame for the withdrawal from Gallipoli on Kitchener, based on a letter Ian received from General Callwell. " . . . **Lord K's treacheries are being unmasked one by one. General Callwell has now written and told Ian clearly and fully how K. made Carson, Balfour etc. believe Ian was getting all the reinforcements and ammunition he wanted. Ian put all his eggs in a leaky basket when he put all his faith in Lord K."** [21st November 1915 London] It would emerge many years later that Kitchener might have had reasonable grounds for thinking that Ian was receiving more reinforcements from Egypt than was the case. It is also known that Britain's supply of ammunition in 1915 was simply inadequate for the many demands upon it.

The decision to evacuate Gallipoli was taken without any real attempt to fight it out to a successful conclusion. Jean later took tea with General Birdwood, nicknamed Birdie, who told her that when Monro went out to Gallipoli to assess the situation he " . . . **had never studied any position in Gallipoli at all, and not only did he sprain his ankle but Lynden Bell sprained his foot, so they were** *both* **laid up . . . they spent about two hours on Gallipoli altogether. Birdie said he had at first thought he could get through, but afterwards . . . was convinced of its impossibility."** [23rd April 1916]

Ian chaffed at his enforced idleness while his country was at war with the most dangerous enemy coalition it had ever faced. " . . . **Ian thinks**

probably Lloyd George, having adopted Murdoch's (the Australian journalist) point of view of him (Ian), does not now want his vile lies refuted, and will be determined not to allow him to raise his head again till the war is over." [24th May 1916]

Once Churchill, himself the subject of tremendous personal attacks in the press, began to demand that the state papers relating to the campaign be published, the government could see that its own weakness in supporting the effort would be exposed and moved to head off this event by calling for a commission of inquiry.

Meanwhile Winston was manoeuvring politically and was prepared to enlist the aid of Lloyd George, which Jean viewed with some alarm: " . . . **I asked him** [Winston] **about Lloyd George, and after looking appealingly at me, and saying: 'This is all very *private* and *confidential*, just between us as our interests are in the same boat more or less', he told us his plans for forcing the Cabinet to produce the Dardanelles papers: spoke of Lloyd George turning Asquith out, and he (Winston) being able to recall Fisher and put him again at the Admiralty. . . . I listened in disapproving silence to the Lloyd George idea, which I have known for long, but applauded the idea of forcing the Cabinet to produce the Dardanelles papers. I do hope he will manage that. . . .**

. . . McKenna he hates, says he was hide-bound about the Dardanelles, and Bonar Law was always dead against it – that it was *he* who wrecked it." [29th May 1916 Postlip Hall]

A few days later, Winston had gained some measure of success. " . . . **Winston dined with us tonight. He was much excited over his speech, and having induced the Government to promise to lay the papers about Gallipoli on the table . . . . He said to me at once: 'Well I've done it'. He was divided between that performance and his paintings of Postlip, which I had brought up with me. . . . " [5th June 1916]**

On that day events took another dramatic turn and fate again entered the equation in the story of the Dardanelles. Lord Kitchener had set forth to Russia aboard the ship, the *Hampshire*, when it struck a mine off the Orkney coast and sank. Together with the Easter uprising in Ireland and the Battle of Jutland, where the Royal Navy lost more ships than the enemy, the British public now had to face another shock, the horror of the death of their great hero, Lord Kitchener of Khartoum. At the time Kitchener drowned the Cabinet was busily trying to cut his salary as a mark of censure. Jean now began to doubt Kitchener's part in Ian's downfall. " . . . Lord Kitchener is dead – drowned – while we were dining last night, and Winston busily engaged talking of his imminent downfall, he must have been then in his death agony, or already dead . . . .

I could not help admiring his silence and dignity in never attempting to answer the criticisms and insults being launched at his head on every side now. I also, for the first time, wondered if he could not help himself in regard to Ian – that his hands were and had been politically tied. . . . " [6th June 1916 London]

Later that day Jean and Ian lunched with the Churchills. " . . . It was a terrible lunch. I sat next Winston, Milly Sutherland was on his other side; he was incapable of any connected conversation. It did not seem a possible thing to happen and one could not realise the great Lord Kitchener was *gone*. 'Fortunate is he in death', quoted Winston when we were seated. . . . Ian told us Lord Kitchener had a great dread of cold water, and would die at once he felt sure in the sea. Lord K. has escaped just in time to save his great name." [6th June 1916 London contd.]

The nation was plunged into mourning and a memorial service was held for Kitchener. " . . . All London has been mourning Lord K. today. We went to the Memorial Service at St. Paul's. It was very beautiful.

When the 'Last Post' sounded, dying away on its last tragic note, I had a vision of Lord Kitchener, tossing about in the dark waters, battered and torn, and almost immediately the sun touched a statue of Victory in a distant aisle. Victory crowning a hero – the Victory of Death! It was like a sudden vision as the crowd closed up and I never saw it again, but it was glorious and comforting.
The last glimpse I had of him alive was on Anzac Day, trying to bolt out of the Cathedral, and suddenly standing back because he had nearly rushed into Queen Mary, who was leaving. . . . "

Jean had an unpleasant encounter with Lord Nicholson, who hated both Kitchener and Hamilton. " . . . As I was going out I saw Lord Nicholson, standing off cynically watching the crowd leaving the Cathedral. I said: 'How do you do?' to him. He seemed delighted to see me, as if he had been watching for us, and said at once: 'Do you find this a very pleasant service?' I looked at him in surprise, and he went on mockingly: 'Does it move you to tears and all that sort of thing?' 'It does', I replied shortly and turned my back on him. . . . What a mocking old wretch he is – he hated Lord K. and was there rejoicing at the death of his life-long enemy." [13th June 1916 London]

With Kitchener dead, Lloyd George became the new Secretary of State for War. Viscount Haldane took tea with Jean. " . . . **I had a nice long talk with Haldy Paldy – he was amused at Lloyd George's success in thrusting himself into the S. of S. for Warship.**" Haldane had asked Lloyd George " . . . **what he was going to do for Winston, and he screwed up his face enigmatically and said: 'Well, we must see – he has not had a good press lately'. L.G.'s own press has not been too satisfactory either!**" [2nd July 1916]

So eager was Jean to promote Ian's career that she left a General Assembly at the Covent Garden opera, which had been specially arranged for the Women's Tribute in the presence of the Royal Family, to keep an engagement with Lord French, whom she had invited to tea. " . . . **He** [Lord French] **had been kept by Lloyd George he told me when he arrived – Lloyd George, at last seated in the Secretary of State's office.**

I told Lord F. about the Gallipoli papers and General Callwell's amazing letter to Ian, stating that the Government dare not publish any papers after Ian's landing, as it would so completely give them away and exonerate Ian.

Lord F. says they will never publish them, at any rate till after the war, so I suggested in that case something must be found for Ian, and said he had always been interested in the Grand Duke and Russia, and that a Mission there might be a good thing, so Lord F. said he would mention it to Lloyd George, but although he promised that he would see to it, it by no means meant that it would be done, I know.

I told him also I felt nervous about Winston, as I thought him over-strained and not well balanced – I felt nervous – I don't feel his judgement at all sound at this moment, nor can he gauge accurately the strong feeling there is against him, and I fear he may ruin Ian instead of pulling him out of the ditch. I just hinted all this to Lord F. who asked if I would like him to see and speak with Winston. I said yes, I would like him to see him, but not to say I had spoken to him about this.

Ian has seen Winston several times, and shown him Callwell's letter, which Winston says would pull down the Government if it were used.

After Lord French went I flew back to Covent Garden, but it was

empty, and I felt rude as I had been invited to tea with the Royalties in the box.

At dinner tonight, talking about the execution of Sir Roger Casement, I said to Ian: 'After all what does it matter when a man dies, if he has lived to his very fullest extent of living?' Ian said he was glad he had not died after his first taste of fighting, and of that full life he had enjoyed so much and that he had been so happy since then, and I said: 'Well, I certainly am glad as I should never have known you, darling', which pleased him – we have such happy comfy little dinners together in my sitting-room every night." [6th July 1916]

" . . . Lunch for Lord French today, – Ava Astor looking lovely sat next him, and all went well. Just before lunch my Ian rushed up the stairs after me to tell me he had seen Winston, who told him that the Gallipoli papers were not to be produced publicly, but in secret, which made me *furious*, and Ian sad. I said: 'Let's *fight* now for all we are worth – if you sit down under this you may knit to the end of the war'. I told Lord French at lunch, and he said he had arranged for Mr. Lloyd George to go with him to dine with Lord Haldane on Tuesday night, and he intended to tell L.G. it was impossible to keep men like Ian unemployed." [11th July 1916 London]

In a letter dated 12 July 1916, to General Braithwaite, Ian expressed his opinion of the Government's decision to have an inquiry:

> . . . yesterday the Government at a Cabinet Meeting decided that
> they could not face the music by laying the Gallipoli papers on the
> table. . . . in view of the tragedy on the "Hampshire", it would be
> impossible to reveal miscalculations which are now comfortably
> resting on your shoulders and mine, but which would then have to
> be shifted onto those of the national hero. Actually it is their own
> skins and not poor old K. which they have in view. They are going
> to have a secret enquiry. The Government will appoint their own
> agents, and naturally, whoever may be blamed, they will come out
> with flying colours.[7]

Asquith set up the Dardanelles Commission of Inquiry on 20 July 1916. Ian, helped by General Braithwaite, Winston Churchill, Jean and other well-wishers, prepared a statement to present to the Commission, to answer the allegations made against him, largely the outcome of Keith

Murdoch's letter. Weeks followed, during which Jean tried to find out as much information as possible to further Ian's defence.

Jean dined with Mary Hunter, where she had an interesting conversation with Mr Detmar Blow, the architect who had worked on Lord Kitchener's house Broome, and the private chapel there, another cause for criticism of Lord Kitchener's extravagant taste and divided attention during wartime. " . . . **Mr. Blow, the architect, is here, and sat next me at dinner tonight. He talked to me of Lord K. He loved him – loves him still, says he was Christ-like, and hated hurting anyone's feelings. He talked so enchantingly of him I felt all my rancour and rage against K. melting out of my heart. Mr. Blow declares he never heard him say one hard or ungenerous word about anyone, and never blamed a subordinate. I think it is true that he did not gossip about his soldiers, or attribute blame, as I feel sure he never blamed Ian in any way to Julia** [Maguire] **whom he knew well, or to Ettie** [Desborough], **or Mr. Blow. Alice Salisbury, who was his great friend, is alas! now a closed book to me. I wonder if Winston is all wrong about K.. . . . "** [30th July 1916 **Hill House]**

A major problem was that Lord Nicholson, Ian's old enemy from the Russo-Japanese War days, was on the Dardanelles Commission, with the very important advantage of being the only member with military experience. Andrew Fisher, Prime Minister of Australia, was also on the Commission. Jean spoke with Lord French about " . . . **the Dardanelles Commission, and he said he 'wondered how Lord Nicholson would behave – no one could depend on what he would do or say – Right or Wrong will have nothing to do with his decisions, he is always out for pure mischief'. It is indeed a shame he is on the Commission at all as he is an enemy of Ian, but Ian feels he cannot object as he has already objected to Fisher, the Australian Minister, being there as he supports the snake Murdoch."** [4th August 1916]

The Dardanelles Commission of Inquiry began interviewing witnesses in September 1916, but Ian was not called until January 1917. " . . . **Ian went back to London tonight as the Commission begins its sitting tomorrow, 12th. It had had preliminary meetings; Sir Charles Monro's evidence was taken before he left for India."** [11th **September 1916]**

It is held by some historians that Ian Hamilton did not keep a diary at Gallipoli and that the one he published was an artificial construct. Proof comes from Jean's diary that the daily diary Ian kept at that time was in existence and was being typed by his secretary, Mrs Mary Shield.[8] **" ... I have just finished reading Ian's Gallipoli diary, with tears – it is all too sad, what a history – I hope some day this record of it will be given to the world – the cruelty and the folly of it. . . . "** [26th September 1916]

At the Dardanelles Commission Lord Nicholson was putting the blame for failure of the fleet to get through on Vice-Admiral de Robeck, who commanded the Allied naval forces at the Dardanelles between March 1915 and January 1916. **" ... Winston had been up before the Commission. He said he liked them all, and had walked back with Lord Nic, who had seemed to think the Navy could have got through the Narrows at any moment, de Robeck was like the man who sat in a cellar for years before a closed door, because he had never given the door a good kick – it had really been open all the time."** [29th September 1916 contd.]

Ian raised with General Braithwaite the question of Murdoch breaching the rules of censorship, to which Braithwaite replied: '. . . Murdoch, by writing the letter he did to Fisher, broke every rule of honour and gentlemanly feeling. . . . Not only did he break his word – for he had pledged himself to observe the censorship rules in force . . . he broke it again by trying to smuggle through, without it being censored, the letter he took home for Ashmead-Bartlett.'[9]

The coordination of evidence did not always go smoothly. Ian sent a copy of his statement to Winston but he **" . . . would not let him say 'The Naval Division was not up to its *supposed* strength', which worries me as of course everyone whose business it was to see that his units were up to strength naturally will object and find good reasons why this should not be mentioned, but I thought Winston had the courage of his opinions – but Winston and Ian must stand together in this and Ian is always most loyal to Winston."** [2nd November 1916 London]

Winston was understandably eager that Kitchener's negligence should be made known and advised Ian to engage a lawyer to represent him at the Commission and sent him to see Sir F. E. Smith, the Attorney General. **" . . . I am feeling very uneasy and uncertain about Winston at this moment. I don't like his trying to persuade Ian to engage a lawyer for his case and then turning him over to F.E. Smith, whom I don't like or trust . . . I said at once: 'On no account do it – don't employ or consult**

a lawyer if it means F.E. Smith has to defend Kitchener – I would not touch it'. [9th and 14th November 1916 London]

Ian's account of the meeting with Sir F. E. Smith was that Smith had recommended his brother to represent him and that he, Sir F. E., would be representing Kitchener. Ian says it was agreed when: ' . . . I had opened the door to go home . . . wishing I could have asked my wife's advice first, when F.E. called out, "Of course you understand that when you attack K. I shall defend him". . . . "Attack K.!" I repeated, "I'm not going to attack K.!" "Oh yes," he said, "so far as I can size up the lay of your case – you *must!*" "I'm sorry," I replied, "but I'm damned if I do! If that was your assumption our deal is off!" "Yes," he agreed, "the deal is off but you'll be sorry some day, I more than suspect." '[10]

Hamilton's protective stance towards Kitchener may have been taken more with the country's reputation in mind. To engage a legal defence team which would attack Kitchener would have escalated an internal inquiry into matters between the armed services and government to the status of a trial and caused major political upheavals. Hamilton undertook the Gallipoli operation at the behest of Kitchener, whom he viewed more as a commanding officer (he was still on the active list) than as a political office holder. Betrayal of one's chief was alien to Ian. Sir F. E. Smith would have defended Kitchener stoutly, the case would have become headline news and the dead hero's adoring public would not have believed any ill of him.

Jean had already witnessed at first hand Sir F. E. Smith's methods in the courtroom, in June 1916, when she attended the trial of Roger Casement, the Irish patriot who was sent to the gallows.[11] In 1917 there had been a supposed attempt on Lloyd George's life by someone throwing a poisoned dart at him. In the subsequent 'Wheeldon Trial' Jean saw the accused, Winnie Mason, **" . . . bullied and baited by F.E. Smith and the Judge. . . . The judge occasionally seemed to pity her – F.E., never – he was ruthless and unfair."** [6th and 9th Mar. 1917] The thought of Sir F. E. Smith exercising his interrogative powers over the sensitive disposition of her 'darling Ian' was enough to make Jean shake in her shoes.

In death Kitchener became an even greater hero. All the War Cabinet's efforts to bring him down had failed and their only other recourse was to use someone else to destroy him. By setting up the Dardanelles Commission and attacking Hamilton, forces in the government who were hostile to Kitchener may have thought to put Hamilton in the position that he would have to expose Kitchener's failings, to save his own reputation. What they did not foresee was that Hamilton would not attack a fellow soldier and one who had actually given him the command.

Hamilton's career was destroyed because the government would not employ him again until the Report of the Dardanelles Commission was complete and he was exonerated. Hanging over the government was the constant threat of further press attacks so it was in their interests to place the outcome of the Commission 'on hold'. The Report did not appear until 1918, the year the war ended.

Neither Lloyd George nor Asquith could stand up to too much scrutiny by the Northcliffe press, considering the scandals in their own lives. The skeleton in Asquith's cupboard was his mistress, Venetia Stanley, and in Lloyd George's his mistress, Frances Stevenson. Always in the background was a dread of a revival of the Marconi scandal of 1912. In that episode the Liberal Party, and Lloyd George in particular, had got involved in what would today be called 'insider dealing', concerning thousands of shares in the American Marconi company at a time when huge imperial telegraph contracts were being awarded.[12] If the press chose to rake all this up again in 1916, they could possibly have brought down Lloyd George, and more seriously Prime Minister Asquith, and damaged the Liberal Party, in whose name shares had also been purchased.

The press may have possessed incriminating evidence against Lloyd George. **" . . . Mrs. Spender, whom I had an interesting hour with yesterday, in her flat, was amazing on the subject of Lloyd George, whom she says is intriguing still against the P.M., and that he is entirely in Northcliffe's power as Northcliffe holds Marconi telegrams of his, also several very disloyal letters of his about his colleagues – letters too about his private life – so can blackmail him at any moment, and he (Northcliffe) intends to be S. of S. for War when Lloyd George is Prime Minister." [24th May 1916 London]**

" . . . Ian is going for Lloyd George about Murdoch in his statement for the Commission, backed up in this by General Braithwaite – he has been to Salisbury to see him today. There is no doubt the Murdoch letter reached L.G. just at the psychological moment to be used as a lever to decide the fate of the Dardanelles Expedition and was unscrupulously used by him to influence the War Council and political opinion against Gallipoli and in favour of *Salonika*, the base he had wished for from the beginning." [20th November 1916]

Jean and Ian attended a large dinner party at Mary Hunter's house. Other guests included Colonel Clive Wigram, Sir F. E. and Lady Smith, Lady Randolph Churchill and the Duchess of Sutherland. " . . . **Sir F.E. was enthusiastic about our house – said it was the most beautiful house in London – he looked very blank when he was told to take Lady Randolph in to dinner, and so did she! I wonder why? It was naughty Eddy Marsh's fault, as I told him I was going to put F.E. next Milly Sutherland, and he said: 'Oh, what a waste of Milly – F.E. admires Winston so you'd better give him to Lady Randolph.'**

Sir F.E. did not know that Clive [Wigram] was the King's favourite equerry and was talking . . . about teetotalism, and said: "The King was now the only mug left in it", which was a little awkward. . . .

Lady Randolph told me . . . Winston . . . is in despair and feels convinced this Government will never employ him." [2nd December 1916 Hill Hall]

If Ian had decided to clear his name and expose the truth about Gallipoli, and that was always an implied threat, he was in a position not only to expose Kitchener but the whole Cabinet and do much to de-stabilise the government. The government managed to keep him at bay by allowing him to *think* he might be re-employed and given a command any day, when in fact they dare not antagonise the newspapers, most of which were baying for his blood.

The next drama was Asquith's resignation. He had been driven to nervous exhaustion and collapse by Lloyd George's relentless quest for power, and the reduction of the higher direction of the war to a four-man committee was the breaking point. He resigned, affirming he would not serve under Lloyd George in his new Coalition Government. " . . . **The impossible has happened, and Asquith, the immovable, has resigned – not induced thereto by the Angel Gabriel, as Margot foretold, but shoved off by the bumptious cuckoo, Lloyd George. . . .**

It is more than a year ago that Mrs. Spender told me of the letter Lloyd George wrote to Mr. Bonar Law urging him to join him, and promising him that with the aid of Northcliffe they would be strong enough to turn out Asquith. He put this letter by mistake into Mr. McKenna's despatch box. Mr. McKenna promptly read it – showed it to the Prime Minister and told Mr. L.G. that he had done so, upon which he wrote and said: 'There is only one cad in the Cabinet

capable of such actions, he is the man who listens at keyholes, and repeats what he hears.' " [6th December 1916]

Frances Horner told Jean that Asquith " . . . **believed in Lloyd George's loyalty to him to the last, and that on Sunday L.G. had embraced him, with tears in his eyes, professed his undying loyalty, and on Monday had betrayed him.**" [7th Dec. 1916]

Jean tried to be fair to Lloyd George and gave him credit where it was due. " . . . **Jack Islington came to tea with me to-night. . . . He was sensible in what he said, he really did me good, for although he acknowledged the treachery of Lloyd George, he was full of immense relief of feeling there was someone at the helm who would act promptly.**" [10th December 1916 London]

A joke at the Secretary of State's expense was too much to resist: " . . . **John Morley's mot, which is going the round, now, of Lloyd George is that:–**

'**He has the fidelity of Brutus**
The veracity of Ananias
And the rest I leave to Marconi'
Hilaire Belloc said he would say: 'the fidelity of *Judas!*' " [12th December 1916]

Ian appeared before the Dardanelles Commission for the first time, a year and three months after his recall from Gallipoli. " . . . **Ian is at this moment, 11 o'clock, appearing before the Dardanelles Commission – how I wish I could see him – the darling.**" [8th January 1917 Deanston]

The day before Ian had written to Jean saying he had heard from Brigadier-General Winter, who had been his Quarter Master General at Gallipoli: 'he had come back from the Commission where he "certainly did not distinguish himself" so he said. Also that he had "a most unpleasant afternoon". He came along afterwards and told me Fisher had attacked him throughout as if he was a criminal and had evidently been posted up against the Staff by Murdoch. If Fisher goes on this way with me I shall read out my letter written to the P.M. *before* he was appointed: saying he could hardly be considered unprejudiced.

I am to spend the whole day from 11 a.m. to 5 p.m. with the Commission tomorrow.'[13]

On 8 and 9 January 1917, Ian wrote long and detailed letters to Jean, telling her what took place at the Commission. His letter of 8 January

ends: 'I wish I had you here to advise me'. Jean wired back: " . . .
**Certainly state your points to President about Murdoch and A.B., but
without animus."**

Mr Roch was Secretary to the Commission, and he published a minority report that Jean eventually read. " . . . **Mr. Murdoch has been had up
before the Commission. He did not want to go, and cautiously
inquired whether Ian would be there and to most of the questions he
was asked, he answered, 'Oh, that was hearsay'! What can be thought
of that by the Commission? His letter is full of only hearsay, and yet
was made into a state paper! . . . Ian . . . dined last week with Barbara
McLaren to meet the Asquiths, McKenna and Alice Keppel. . . . Mr.
McKenna (after whispering for some time to Mr. Asquith turned to
Ian just before he (Mr. A.) left, and said 'Don't you think it would be
a monstrous injustice to publish the report of the Dardanelles
Commission without the evidence, as the report is not based on the
evidence – the only correct and fair report based on evidence is Roch's
Minority Report, and that** *can't* **be published as in it he says the three
Divisions promised by the Greeks could not be sent as the Russians
would not hear of a single Greek landing in Gallipoli – for these reasons it would be impossible to publish Roch's report'. Mr. Asquith
looked at Ian for his opinion, and Ian said, 'but Mr. Asquith, in that
case why on earth did you appoint the Commission?' and Mr. Asquith
turned away with a despairing gesture as much as to say, '***Why*** on
earth did I?' " [7th February 1917 London]**

Jean and Ian had to lunch Sir John Cowans, Colonel and Molly
Repington, Colonel Freyberg and Lady Scott. After lunch, Jean took the
women away so that the men could talk. " . . . **Ian had an interesting talk
with the men, and that was the object of the lunch party.**

**We talked of the Dardanelles Report, Lady Scott had actually
seen it, but she was frightened to say so, when she found Ian had not
. . . .**

**I had a chance to say to Colonel Repington I thought it a great pity
that Ian had not got his Generals all to sign against evacuation before
he left Gallipoli, as of course, as they did all sign for evacuation it was
impossible for them now to go back on this before the Commission.**

**I long for Ian to make a wonderful statement at end of
Commission, summing up situation, proving we ought to have stayed
on in Gallipoli, and confound the knavish tricks of his enemies. I read**

all the evidence as we go along and already I think Mr. Fisher must feel ashamed of his champion, Mr. Keith Murdoch. When he was summoned to the Commission he did not want to come and asked if Ian would be there, and was much relieved to hear he would not be confronted with the man he had attempted to murder, by handing Lloyd George the knife to stab him in the dark.

The Interim Report comes out on Wednesday." [18th February 1917 London]

Ian appeared before the Commission for the last time in March 1917, but: "... **The Report hangs fire though we must know many who have already seen it.**" [26th February 1917] The Report was not made public until mid-November 1919.

Winston Churchill regained some political power and in July 1917 became Secretary of State for Munitions. "... **Winston had been thinking about protesting about Lord Nicholson's hostile attitude – Asquith & Co. appointed Lord Nic to smash Lord K. as he is his great enemy and the Dardanelles Inquiry was promised in the first instance to try and get rid of Lord K., but they may now smash Ian incidentally – L.G.** [Lloyd George] **is** *capable de tout* [capable of anything]." [5th March 1917]

"... **Adéle Essex, Norah, Eddy Marsh and Mr. Nevinson lunched today.**

We discussed the Dardanelles Report of course, and I said indignantly that if 'The Daily Mail' had a heading 'Murder will out', the name of the murderer of the Expedition ought to be printed below, as no one ever surely murdered a glorious Expedition more surely than General Monro – rendering vain all that had been achieved.

Ian scolded me for this, both publicly and privately, but I stoutly affirmed that I hoped to live to hear the Evacuation of Gallipoli condemned as the *greatest blunder* **of the war. 'The Daily Mail' is so furiously vicious I think they must be afraid the new Government is tottering, which it is, and the 'Push and go' has been a little rapid and may lead to destruction. Margot** [Asquith], **I hear, says they will be back again by Easter, but I think the Dardanelles Report will prevent any danger of that, and rightly. Mr. Asquith was criminally wrong to neglect it, as he did, and allow himself to be misled. If he had been more loyal to his friends and kept Winston in the Cabinet, Winston would have seen to the**

life of the Expedition and had it properly fed and nourished."
[11th March 1917]

Here Jean would seem to have her finger on the pulse, given that Asquith
had already expressed his regret at ever setting up the Commission in the
first place. " . . . Ian has gone before the Commission today, at 2 o'clock
– probably for the final time. Asquith had been just before him, and
won the hearts of the Commission by his excellent temper and manner, though he must be feeling perfectly mad with them – it gave me a
feeling of the profoundest mistrust when Ian told me this, for he can
smile and be a villain, and have Ian to lunch in a friendly way, all the
time sheltering himself behind him in the most treacherous manner.
Ian was quite pleased with my phrase the other day, apropos of his
defence of Lord K. I said: 'Asquith has sheltered himself behind a live
soldier since the Dardanelles, and now he was going to shelter himself
behind a dead one [Kitchener].' " [29th March 1917]

On 27 August 1917, the *Daily News and Leader* published an article
by the journalist J. C. Sergrue Berne, based on his translation of a book
published in Switzerland by a German journalist, which must have lifted
the spirits of the Hamiltons. Harry Stuermer was the special correspondent
of the *Kölnische Zeitung* in Constantinople during 1915–16 and the spring
of 1917, the equivalent of Ashmead-Bartlett on the German side. The
newspaper cutting was retained by Jean:

In the article, 'NEW LIGHT ON THE DARDANELLES', Berne gives an
account from Stuermer's book, *Two Years of War in Constantinople*, in
which he says 'Shamed and disgusted by the Turkish massacres of the
Armenians . . . Herr Stuermer and his wife fled from Constantinople
into Switzerland . . . to Geneva'. Stuermer's description of the struggle
for the Dardanelles, based on the observation of an eye witness who
was in the confidence of the German Ambassador and the German and
Turkish commanders, shows how near success the great Gallipoli thrust
reached. He says that the fate of Constantinople hung upon a hair, and
proceeds: 'The risking of several more warships on March 18 would
have settled the fate of Constantinople. The courageous fellows who
were serving the coast forts were amazed when they saw that the attack
had ceased. Dozens of German gunners who worked the
Tschanokkoleh batteries on that memorable day told me later that they
had reached the limit of endurance, and regarded the breakthrough as
inevitable. In Constantinople itself people waited from hour to hour for

the break-through, and, as I knew from the highest sources, the archives and the funds had already been removed to Konia.

. . . on a later occasion – the first days of September – the fate of Constantinople hung upon a hair. On this second occasion the English, after considerable reinforcements of troops had reached them, extended their attack from Ariburnu northwards to Anafarta, and after a most heroic assault the Anzacs had in fact occupied the summit of Kodjadjemen-Dagh, which absolutely commanded the whole Gallipoli Peninsula and the comparatively unprotected back Dardanelles forts. Even today in Constantinople people do not know why the British troops could not follow up this achievement to final success. . . . archives and gold were speedily transported into Asia . . . Whilst the Turks defended the City of Caliphs at the door of the Dardanelles, the remaining half of the capital, the cosmopolitan Galatea-Perea, trembled at the weal and woe of the struggling Allies, and lived hours of tremendous anxiety right through till the final solution was reached. The Turkish stand on Gallipoli threatened to collapse through lack of ammunition . . . ' Stuermer described German methods of 'corruption at Constantinople' where 'huge chests filled with gold' which were to be 'distributed for propaganda purposes' were 'constantly arriving at Constantinople from Berlin'.[14]

By the beginning of 1918, the tide was turning in Hamilton's favour. Two events in particular took place that placed him in a more advantageous position where the Government and the press were concerned. Firstly, offers were being made to him from the press where, if he wished, he could fight the politicians and journalists like Murdoch and Ashmead-Bartlett by publishing his own account of Gallipoli. Secondly, there was the gradual increase in power of his friend, Winston Churchill, who had secured a new Cabinet post. In addition, Sydney Moseley, a war correspondent at Gallipoli, working for Central News and Exchange Telegraph, published a book entitled *The Truth About the Dardanelles*, in which he put his account of the campaign, vigorously supporting Hamilton and attacking Ashmead-Bartlett's newspaper articles, saying 'It is regrettable . . . that the whole of the London Press should have been fed from this jaundiced source.'[15] As the year advanced, there were newspaper reports that were favourable to Hamilton and the Dardanelles campaign.

Ian was eagerly sought after by a number of newspapers as a possible commentator, based on his highly acclaimed writings and his unrivalled experience of war. This must have struck terror into the hearts of the government, who were desperately trying to exonerate their own poor showing over the Dardanelles through the Commission. The first offer to Ian to state his views publicly came as early as February 1917: **"... Colonel Repington ... proposed to Ian that he should write a criticism of the Dardanelles Report, putting his own views strongly as *he* (Repington) would have to write an article for 'The Times'."** Jean advised Ian against this and he wisely did not do it, as the Commission was still in session and such a move could have prejudiced the outcome against him. **[26th February 1917]**

A year later Repington again made an offer to Ian and though he did not accept, the Commission was now over and he was still without a job. **" . . . Col. Repington is thinking of going to America – accepting £5,000 a year and giving up the 'Morning Post'. He proposed that Ian become Military Correspondent in his place to the 'Morning Post'. Ian abhors the 'Morning Post' and all its works, but I can't help feeling what fun it would be to give some of them hell through its pages – he has offers from 'The Times', 'The Pall Mall', 'The National News' – they all want to get hold of him. . . . " [2nd February 1918]**

Ian's change of fortune and newly found support may have encouraged him to write the letter which must now dispel any notion that he was prepared to accept blame to protect Kitchener over the failure at Gallipoli and sacrifice his career. The letter was addressed to the Secretary of State at the War Office and dated 17 January 1918:

> In today's "Times" the Chancellor of the Exchequer is reported to have said in Parliament that the Dardanelles Report would not be published for the present.
>
> Two years and three months have passed away since I was relieved of my command in the field upon grounds which have never been made clear to me. During all that time my military reputation has been subjected to ill-informed and ill-natured criticism whilst my hands have been tied, at first by the belief that I was about to be re-employed, afterwards by the fact that the question was sub judice.
>
> Now it seems I am threatened with an indefinite extension of this period of sitting under a cloud – for that is how the decision of H.M.'s Government bears upon me – and I have hopes that the Army Council may feel some sympathy with me in my suspense and that they will answer me the following question:–

Does the Report of the Dardanelles Commission reflect upon my conduct of the operations in terms indicating that I am ineligible for military command?[16]

On 1 February 1918, Hamilton received a terse reply from the War Office. 'In reply I am to inform you that without entering into the Report of the Dardanelles Commission the Secretary of State is not at the moment prepared to give you further employment'.[17] It was signed by the Military Secretary, Lieutenant-General Sir Francis Davies. The Secretary of State at the time was Lord Derby.

Ian discussed the letter with Winston Churchill, who had asked him to do nothing about it. The Hamiltons were able to pursue the matter at a tea party at Mrs Dudley's, where they met Francis Davies. **" . . . He [Davies] felt worried when he saw us. . . .**

(I had felt certain Winston would try and keep him [Ian] quiet). He told Ian that the War Council were furious at his foreword to his new Despatches, and there had been a suggestion, to Court Martial him, but Lloyd George had laughed heartily at the suggestion, and said he quite agreed with what Ian had said.

Sir Francis told Ian as we were leaving that he had had the letter dictated to him, so it must have been Lord Derby, *a nice friend he is* – writes to Ian always still as 'Dear Johnnie', and in old days was always so friendly and jolly – *is* so still if one meets him, but positions are somehow changed since South Africa." [2nd February 1918]

Winston Churchill had regained considerable power, having been made Secretary of State for War and Air at the beginning of 1918, and Ian was able to call in a favour from his old friend. **" . . . 'Great developments', Ian said . . . 'Winston has just been on the telephone to me, and he says he has had it out with Derby, who professed himself distressed that a letter should have been sent to Ian in such a form, and conveyed the impression that it had been a blunder'. 'This seems odd', I said 'as Joey Davies distinctly told you that it was dictated to him'. 'Not exactly dictated', he said, "I took it down verbatim" but he did not say *from whom'. . . . "**

There was still the possibility of getting Ian into the soon to be vacant command of the Home Force, and Winston told him **" . . . 'that Lord Derby said: "If Mr. Lloyd George would make some sort of public pronouncement in Ian's favour now the Dardanelles Commission was**

not to be published, Ian could have that". Ian said: 'Of course if Lloyd George would make this pronouncement it would be almost a public apology. I do trust he and Lord Derby will be forced to do that, though I am not very keen about *this* **appointment. It is the same one, shorn of its glory, that he had before he went to the Dardanelles.' "** [4th Feb. 1918]

Hamilton was not prepared to let the matter of his reputation wait any longer and wrote again to the War Office: 'With reference to War Office letter 64202/58. (M.S.1.a), dated 1st February, I have the honour to point out that my letter of the 17th ultimate, to which it is purported to be a reply, made no application for further employment but was an appeal to the Army Council for information. I still hope, therefore, that I may get an answer to the question I asked in my letter aforesaid.'[18]

Sir William Robertson **" . . . telephoned . . . he wanted to know what happened about the letter Ian sent to the War Office, he could not think why it had not come up before the War Council."**

Following dinner at the Hamiltons' home, **" . . . Ian was depressed I saw, after they left, the reason was that Sir William told him that Lloyd George had said he must personally read the Report, and Ian knows from Grimwood Mears that Lloyd George has already read it, so it looks as if he were up to mischief again." [6th February 1918]**

The Eastern Command was available, which Ian could have undertaken. Lord French told Jean that he had been asked to give it to Sir William Robertson. **" . . . Lord French has been trying to give it to Ian for a year. . . . " [19th February 1918]**

Jean got Maud Cunard to arrange for her to meet Walter Roch, Secretary to the Dardanelles Commission, at her dinner party on 12 March. Jean learnt that Mr Roch **" . . . had detested Lord Nicholson." [10th and 12th March, 1918]** Jean then invited Mr and Mrs Roch to No. 1 HPG. **" . . . My Roch effort so far has been quite successful. I asked him and his wife to lunch yesterday, and they both came. . . . As Mr. Roch went out he said to Ian it was very hard lines on him the Dardanelles Report being suppressed, as he came out of it well – 'It's hard on you,' he said, 'but perhaps lucky for some others'. This greatly pleased Ian, bless him! His astonishing lack of all bitterness is a perpetual surprise to me – he seems so pleased with** *any* **small tribute." [14th March 1918]** A few days later Ian received a letter from Lord Derby telling him he could come and see the Dardanelles Report, as General Stopford had seen it. [6th April 1918]

Another stroke of fate entered the Dardanelles equation. Sir William Nicholson, Ian's principal critic on the Dardanelles Commission and arch-enemy from the days of Japan, died suddenly. " . . . **Lord Nic died last week – I wonder to what limbo he has gone – if he had to go, why did not he die a year and a half ago? It would have saved a lot of worry and injustice, but perhaps he's a blessing in disguise, he fought tooth and nail to keep Ian out of the war and he has succeeded. . . . His country does not know about it yet, but some day they will and meantime I am satisfied with the heroic part he** [Ian] **has played. . . . he managed very nearly to do for Ian's reputation on the Commission sitting on the Dardanelles, being as he was, the only member with military knowledge."** [27th September 1918]

Whether a coincidence or not, soon after the death of Nicholson, Hamilton was given a new position, which might only have been a pre-retirement sinecure but was a form of official recognition which pleased him. " . . . **Ian is off to London tonight, to find out his duties as Lieutenant of the Tower of London."** [1st October 1918]

Henry Nevinson, a journalist who had written about the Dardanelles campaign and who was a friend of Jean's, was writing a book about Gallipoli. " . . . **Mr. Nevinson came to tea with me, very disgusted because his Gallipoli book was not out one month ago, as it ought to have been. It is a pity it is not out now and also Ian's on the Millennium. . . . All the papers now are veering round about Gallipoli, saying the flower of the Turkish Army was destroyed there – for nothing, as it was evacuated – and are busy climbing down about the side shows, and the Eastern Front. The fatal mistake there was sending Monro, nothing could be done** *after* **that, as he went with evacuation in his pocket and was only two hours** *on* **Gallipoli himself. Before that, with proper reinforcements, Ian could have taken the peninsular at any time, gained Constantinople, and ended the war. Garvin handsomely says so in 'The Observer' this morning, and 'The Times' yesterday."** [4th November 1918]

"The Walter Roches, Major Wedgewood, General Aspinall lunched with us today. . . .

Mr. Roch wanted to talk to General Aspinall about the Dardanelles, he is writing a book – 'The Life of Mr. Lloyd George'. I

told him I could give him some details that would be interesting and
told him about the Murdoch letter, and how Mr. Lloyd George urged
him to send it at once to Mr. Asquith, so as to stab the whole expedition in the back.

I took the women away as quickly as I could, so as to leave the men
to have a good talk. . . .

General Aspinall told Mr. Roch about General Monro and
General Birdwood, and of how General Lynden Bell said General
Aspinall must be most careful of General Monro as his nerve had gone
since he was knocked senseless by a bomb bursting close to him near
Ypres, and General Aspinall took charge of General Monro when he
landed at Gallipoli, as General Lynden Bell had sprained his foot and
could not go. The first day he got to the Dardanelles, before landing on
Gallipoli, General Monro told General Aspinall that he intended to
advise evacuation, and only required backing, and after he landed
and spent not three hours altogether on the Peninsular Colonel Reid
spread the news of evacuation, though it was supposed to be a dead
secret. He (Col. Reid) was always for evacuation, the horrible fellow,
and he now commands a Division." [8th Jan. 1919]

In 1918 and 1919 Winston Churchill, who had done everything in his
power to help Ian, offered him a choice of several jobs: the Governorship
of Malta, GOC Scotland, and Maxwell's Northern Command. Jean says
Ian refused all of them because the only one he really wanted was the
Governorship of Constantinople, which was not on offer. [March 15 1919
London]

" . . . Ian has been sent for, to go and see Winston at the War
Office. . . .
Ian went on to the War Office, and when I sat down to dinner to
wait for him, he met McAdie at the door and made her announce
him as 'His Excellency the Governor of Malta'. I was afraid for a
moment it was really so, as he said for the sake of the Dardanelles
he would take it for a few months though he would not want it.
However, he told me he had as a matter of fact refused it –
Winston had offered it to him, and had also offered him Scotland
and Maxwell's Command – which would mean York and be quite
horrid. However, Ian does not want any of them and prefers to
stick to his writing if Winston will publish the offer of Maxwell's
Command and his refusal of it, which he has undertaken to do.

Plumer wants Malta. It was a pity Ian was not offered Scotland a year ago, when he would have accepted it, now he really does not want any appointment, unless it was the Governorship of Constantinople, which is not likely to happen, as the French seem likely to seize that." [15th March 1919 London]

Jean gave a large party for Ettie Desborough who was staying with them, all their loyal friends at last able to breathe a sigh of relief: Lord Desborough, Harry and Merrie Rawlinson, Sir Ronald Graham, Rosie Ridley, Herbert Trench, Sybil Graham, Hugh Walpole, Sir William and Lady Robertson, Brenda, Lady Dufferin, Alice Keppel, Singer Sargent, Anne Islington, and General Brancker. It was cold March weather, and Jean was very susceptible to cold. When she got all the guests settled, she slipped downstairs to the hall fire to warm herself. **" . . . At last some statement has been made about Ian in the newspapers and everyone is talking about it. Winston has done his best and Sir William Robertson told me tonight that the letter he wrote the Chief of the Staff or to Winston I think he said, was much stronger than what they published – he said he would show it one day to Ian. He told me he had looked back over the correspondence with Joey Davies and was furious at the insolence with which Ian had been treated – Joey Davies has now given himself the Scotch Command which ought to have been given to Ian when McCracken got it." [31st March 1919 London]**

A report appeared in the *Pall Mall Gazette* dated 31 March 1919, entitled, 'General Sir Ian Hamilton – Echo of Gallipoli Campaign – Post Declined'. A letter from Winston Churchill to General Sir Ian Hamilton was published:

> The Chief of the Imperial General Staff having advised me that he
> concurs in the opinion officially recorded by his predecessor, Sir
> William Robertson, that there is nothing in your command of the
> Allied Forces in the Gallipoli Campaign which ought to preclude
> you from being considered for further employment, and Sir Henry
> Wilson having further recommended that you be re-employed
> before your service on the Active List terminates in January next, I
> desire to know whether I should submit your name to the King for
> the Northern Command, which will become vacant on June 1.
> (Sgn.) Winston S. Churchill 19th March, 1919.[19]

Hamilton's reply was published, saying he was declining the offer, preferring to stand aside and give a younger man a chance. " . . . **Peace Thanksgiving services everywhere to-day. . . . Ian got a command through Sir Reginald Brade . . . and two tickets for us for St. Paul's to-day and we sallied forth. I was very glad we did go, it was wonderful and exciting. . . . I would have liked to have waited outside and heard the crowd sing "Old Hundredth" with the King and Queen on the steps, but we had to go inside where we had wonderful places, which pleased us both – we were in the front seat – on one side all the sailors with Admiral Beatty, and on the other side all the soldiers with Rawly in Douglas Haig's place. . . . Ian sat next . . . Betty Henderson and then came Sir John Maxwell, then me. . . . all the Cabinet Ministers were sitting in a row close to us and we were just behind the Royalties.**

Rawly presently came for Ian, saying: 'Johnnie, you're wanted,' and off they went to meet the King, and we heard the Old Hundredth Psalm peeling up to the sky in the distance.

After the Royalties had all paraded in . . . the service began and was wonderful. . . . The Archbishop of Canterbury was very pompous – it all seemed a gorgeous mockery to me, and I had a mad impulse that I'd like to jump up, stand on my seat and condemn this false peace, having lost all we fought for, if we fought for 'the right and to end war, as we boasted – Right against might!' 'Does material victory mean spiritual defeat' – on this text I reflected while the Archbishop complacently enumerated all our advantages of pomp and circum-stances – to the principalities and powers here assembled. If the Allies have *their way* the next great assemblage will be the trial of the Kaiser . . . . I wondered how great enemies felt in the old days, when they were allowed such a good show before their heads were cut off in the Tower." [6th July 1919 London]

Jean shared Ian's opinion that in seeking a harsh and vindictive peace settlement with Germany, the Allies were losing the chance to secure the undying friendship of the German people and were about to begin storing up that hatred and resentment that would lay the foundations for another war. It was the attitude towards beaten adversaries that Ian had held since the Boer War. Charles Repington, when writing about the 1914–18 war, was the first to refer to it as 'the First World War', with the shocking implication that there would be a second.

" . . . **The Dardanelles Report came out a week ago and 'The**

Times' was very nasty, trying to twist it against Ian – the article was probably written by that horrible Murdoch. 'The Express' (Daily) too was nasty – Beaverbrook's paper, but as Ian has been making speeches against 'the *Hate* Propaganda' that Northcliffe boasts has won the war, that is not surprising." [23rd November 1919]

In fact the Final Report of the Dardanelles Commission went a long way to restoring Hamilton's reputation as it fully explained the extraordinary difficulties he had to contend with at Gallipoli.

In a final twist to the Gallipoli story, in the 1920s, when Hamilton was asked to read drafts of the official history of the campaign then in preparation, he made an incredible discovery – a cable dated 6 April 1915, from Lord Kitchener to Lieutenant-General Sir John Maxwell, commanding the troops in Egypt, that would have utterly transformed his chances of success at Gallipoli. The cable read:

> You should supply any troops in Egypt that can be spared, or even selected officers or men, that Sir Ian Hamilton may want for Gallipoli. You know that Peyton's Mounted Division is leaving for Egypt. This telegram should be communicated by you to Sir Ian Hamilton.[20]

This vital cable was not passed to General Hamilton, who had been in Egypt since 1 April. Maxwell had always been reluctant to supply reinforcements to Hamilton at Gallipoli. Why it did not reach Hamilton is open to speculation but it must certainly have been seen by Maxwell. The cable message was crystal clear and was from Kitchener, personally. If Kitchener had given the instruction as a commander in the field, Maxwell's failure to carry it out would have left him open to a court-martial. Maxwell's failure to contact Hamilton or send troops may harp back to Malta, in 1910, when Hamilton accepted the Mediterranean Command over Kitchener's head. Maxwell was Chief of Staff to the Duke of Connaught, who had thrown it up in the first instance. Hamilton had earned a good deal of bad feeling for taking up the post and rescuing the Liberal government from a dilemma. Was there some residual ill feeling still in 1915? Kitchener did not follow up this important cable to Maxwell but, as a field marshal, he was accustomed to having his every word obeyed, his message was quite clear and the failure rested with Maxwell.

Jean's diaries have shown repeatedly that the want of fresh reinforcement early in the campaign frustrated Ian's plans time and again. If he had only known that he could have called on the garrison of Egypt at any time it might have been the decisive chance for victory. As Jean wrote: " . . . **after that magnificent landing, if he had had one fresh Brigade it would have made just all the difference.**" [18th May 1915]

When, years later, the *Tatler* published a full-page portrait of Lloyd George, accompanied by a wonderful adulation of his heroic part in winning the war, Jean wrote across the top of the picture: **"except at Gallipoli"**.

And Now the War is Over

" . . . the fireworks were wonderful last night in spite of the rain. Winston said he had wanted to spend £50,000 on them – it was certainly worth anything to give the people pleasure." [20th July 1919]

The Hamiltons' relationship was much better when Ian returned from the Dardanelles. Jean still felt Ian could treat her with indifference, but she was always demanding of his attention and sometimes jealous in a petty sort of way. Ian had received a letter from Theodore Roosevelt in America, and at a dinner party at Lord Curzon's was talking to Lady Herbert (who was placed next him), which was good manners on his part. " . . . I saw him show her the wonderful letter full of understanding and sympathy Roosevelt has written him, and my heart contracted with annoyance and jealousy: how easily he makes friends with, and confides in women." [13th November 1915 Hackwood] She even admitted she could be jealous of her aunt, Nora Anderson, to whom she was very close: " . . . I like being pampered and petted for a change. I have always loved Nora and being with her: she does not get on with Ian, it has often worried me, but in a way I am glad as she likes men so much, and if she got on with Ian, she would prefer to talk to him when we were together and that would vex me." [10th September 1928 Braco Castle, Perthshire]

When they stayed at Deanston, Jean vacated her favourite bedroom to Ian, probably because it was larger and he had more space to write books. She slept in " . . . the blue room near Mother . . . I miss it – the bed is more comfy, and I hear the birds there." [30th January 1916 Deanston] On one occasion, her aunt Nora Anderson " . . . came in early to see me before she left, she wanted to see why my bed creaked and made noises that frightened me at nights. She found Ian in pink pyjamas snuggling in my bed, and was much embarrassed – he was not at all. . . . " [1st February 1916 Deanston]

Jean could take much comfort from Ian being back by her side but she realised fully that a battle would have to be fought to restore his previously lustrous reputation, not least amongst the press. " . . . I love my dainty dinners with Ian in my sitting-room, it always looks so cosy and dainty, the pretty table laid for two with its shaded candles and coloured fruit. I think often when I look at it, 'What is all the honour and glory in the world to me in comparison to having him with me in such loving, happy companionship?' I don't think we have ever been so happy together before as we have been ever since his return." [26th Sept. 1916 London]

A Doll Show and Sale was organised at Sunderland House to raise money for charity and Jean shared a section with Adéle Essex. " . . . I have dressed twenty-four dolls. . . . Diana Manners and Hazel Lavery have such lovely dolls in the Section opposite ours. I have been dressing up 'little Willies' all day. Mr. Haselden, the cartoonist, has modelled me two Kaiser heads, and two heads of 'little Willie' (the Crown Prince), – he has been having an amusing series of these in the 'Daily Mirror' – and I have made a scarlet throne, and seated the two, clothed in shining armour and ermine as Autocracy, and down below on the wooden seats, the two are seated as Democracy, clothed in fustian and rags. It is really a successful group, but I hated clothing the poor Kaiser and the Crown Prince in rags even as I did it. . . . My other smart dollies are rather lovely, but *who* will buy them all? . . ." [8th December 1918 London]

Betty helped Jean at the Doll Sale. " . . . I put Mr. Nevinson's four pictures of the Seasons as a background, and posed my dolls against them and made a sort of little skating scene. Adéle was delighted. I used my lovely Indian scarf that Kapurthala gave me, as a decoration.

The Queen came for a private view at 3 o'clock. . . . She was shocked and amused by my group of 'the Willies', as 'Monarchy and Democracy' and asked who had done it, and said: 'Oh,' putting her hand over her mouth. She could not really like it, and I felt half sorry. I do feel for our Royal Family and all Royalties just now, they must feel uncomfy and afraid. I got the prize for originality for my Willies, and Lady Reading wanted at once to buy the group, they all said I must charge 20 guineas for it, and she thought that too much.

Lady Werner and Minnie Paget had an awful row over Lady Werner's General Botha and General Smuts, they were on too big a scale, so Minnie Paget rejected them, and Lady W. declared it was because she was jealous. . . . Lady W. has paid hundreds of pounds getting all her South African contingent dressed by good teachers. I am so thankful I declined to dress the Scotch Regiments for Lady Paget. She has arranged a wonderful scene of the trenches and Red Cross, and the entry to Jerusalem – all the Generals modelled from life – Kitchener, French, Allenby, Smith-Dorrian, only my Ian, I think, unrepresented – it seems odd to me . . . Smuts and Botha represented, and not to have Ian.

We dined to-night with Mrs. Colefax – quite an amusing dinner – Alice Keppel, Léonie [Leslie] Maud Cunard, Diana Manners. . . . It was a very noisy dinner. Maud was very silent after dinner, but burst out with a terrible indictment of religion just as the men came into the room after dinner. [9th December 1918]

Alice Keppel, Adéle Essex and Hazel Lavery lunched with Jean. " . . . There was nothing but *doll* talk, and Alice Keppel, standing in the window before lunch with me said: she 'had been profoundly shocked last night by Maud's outburst against religion,' being a friend of Nellie Sellar's she thought, I suppose, I would be also, but I said, to her surprise 'I thought there was something in what she said, and the clergy seemed curiously ineffective at this moment and that they did not practice what they preached or hold to their religion when they run counter to public opinion, and I quoted Dr. Fleming laughingly, and said it had been a relief to hear him declare that God had made this war." [10th December 1918]

The war ended on 11 November 1918, and the blackouts were over. Life was returning to normal and dinner parties could take place in a more relaxed atmosphere. Ian became Lieutenant-Governor of the Tower of London and a house was placed at the Hamiltons' disposal but they continued to live at No. 1 HPG. " . . . Alice Keppel has just been here with her sister, Mrs. Hope – Alice K. very vital and attractive with her grey hair and beautifully shod feet, and quite frankly middle aged. She says we have a delightful house of our own in the Tower and ought to live there." [3rd October 1918, 3 Rosebury Crescent Edinburgh]

There was always great interest in stories about Alice Keppel, as King Edward VII's lover of many years. " . . . I talked rather too much to Major Griscom about Muriel Beckett, who is a friend of his. I told him about the time when Muriel was sitting on Alice Keppel's bed and

King Edward came in, in his dressing gown, just as any husband would. Muriel was also in her dressing gown and didn't know whether to get up and drop him a sweeping courtesy, or sit tight – the King signed to her not to move and after consulting Alice about some State papers he carried in his hand, he departed like an ordinary husband by the door wherein he came." [22nd January 1919 London]

Alice Keppel had a house in Grosvenor Street, about a ten-minute drive from No. 1 HPG. "A wonderful dinner at Alice Keppel's last night – about 34 dined; I thought they would never stop pouring into her lovely comfy warm house. She wore the same blue and gold sort of tea gown she has worn every time I have seen her lately, and I don't think it suits her – it is one of the Wilson gowns, and Nan McGrigor got one and wore it at Deanston when she stayed, but she had fur on hers instead of gold fringes Alice Keppel and Phyllis Williamson have on theirs – they wore theirs the same night they were at Hill House, and the gown suited neither of them. Adéle Essex tripped in, in black with bright red shoes and stockings, and a very short skirt – how she had the audacity I can't think, she looked like a flamingo, but very pretty, but she is too old for these 'flageries' as McAdie calls them. I wore an old Jay dress done up by Mrs. Reeves, and it looked lovely – Ian loved it and praised it a lot. I sat next George Keppel and Roderick Jones. George Keppel told me a lot of ridiculous gossip about Bertie Capel and her wedding night, which amused me, and also told me about the adopted son of Susan Townley, and how they got him, and it made me sad to hear of tears pouring down the real father's cheeks as he watched her sailing off in the steamer with his boy.

Violet Bonham Carter looked very well – the Willingdons were there and Muriel Wilson with poppies in her dark hair and her new husband (whom everyone praised) with her. Ian sat next her.

I feel happier and more interested in life since going to this party – everyone was so nice, but Alice Keppel rather alarmed us by leaning over the table and asking Sir Roderick Jones if it was true that Germany and Poland were having a great battle, that the Peace Conference had broken down, and Foch been summoned." [16th February 1919 London]

Now the war was over and the Dardanelles Commission successfully concluded, Ian was very relaxed, continuing his dancing, which Jean should have enjoyed. But she could not help reflecting on a time in India when he was a great deal more severe, particularly with her, though his workload then for Roberts was so great he had little time for leisure. " . . . **The evening dance for Beauchamp Lodge was a great success last night . . . looking down on the madly dancing couples to this new gay jazz music, Ian the maddest of the throng, he is always begging and entreating me to dance, and I reminded him of the days when we were** [newly] **married and he used to spoil my dancing fun by standing sulking in the doorways and taking me home at the eighth dance (how I hated that number 8), he used to lecture me solemnly by telling me women always danced too long and forgot their age, 32 was the age we fixed for me to stop dancing, and in fact I never** *went* **to dances after that age expecting partners . . . " [9th May 1919]**

Several of Jean's friends, also great society hostesses, some renowned for their beauty, got married during or soon after the First World War. Violet Asquith married Sir Maurice Bonham Carter, 'Bongey', as the Asquiths nicknamed him. Jean was staying with her brother Will and his wife Clara Muir at Postlip Hall, near Winchcombe, in Gloucestershire. **" . . . In the evening we had a dinner for the David Hendersons – Bongey (Mr. Asquith's private secretary) sat next me, and Ian took in Violet Bonham Carter. She at last married Bongey after refusing Hugh Godley many times, and lives near us now. Violet looked very remarkable in one of the new short white chiffon frocks – like an overgrown child coming in to dessert. Ian gazed at her in astonished disapproval, but she is certainly fascinating, and anxious to please."** [28th May 1916]

The beautiful Jennie Churchill had divorced George Cornwallis-West in 1914 and reverted to her former title of Lady Randolph Churchill. She was now about to be married for the third time, to Mr Montagu Porch, who had served in the Colonial Service in Nigeria and was three years younger than Winston. Jean and Jennie went to the opera together. **" . . . Jennie was at the top of her form, her Porchy returning on Sunday. She was looking so handsome, quite twenty years younger – she said Léonie** [Leslie, her younger sister] **had written and told her 'To associate with her contemporaries', but on the contrary she meant to continue to fly at their approach as they depressed her to the last degree, they were all blind or deaf or lame. . . . "** The opera was *Romeo and Juliet* and they sat in Maud Cunard's box, **" . . . named aptly 'The play box of the**

Western world' and it was crowded and fun as usual. I felt well, happy and excited. Jennie told me as I drove her home she 'was 65, and was going to marry the handsomest man in London whom all the girls envied, felt quite young, and had just bought herself three lovely gowns'. I quite understood his infatuation last night, her joy was infectious." [26th April 1918]

Elizabeth Asquith, the Prime Minister's youngest daughter, married Prince Antoine Bibesco, a Romanian diplomat. The newspapers reported the guests arriving for the wedding: Lady Diana Manners, wrapped in sable, accompanied by her mother, the Duchess of Rutland; Mrs Cavendish Bentinck, wearing a coat of striped velvet and brocade ribbons of gold; Lady Ian Hamilton, gorgeous in blue velvet and gold braiding. " . . . Elizabeth looked well . . . her train was lovely . . . ", borne by a little boy who " . . . looked very like Puffin. . . . " [8th May 1919 London] The Bibescos lived at 13 Hyde Park Gardens, a few doors along from Jean and Ian. In years to come, their daughter, Princess Priscilla Bibesco, would become a friend of Jean's adopted daughter, Rosaleen James.

Lady Diana Manners, 'hair like honey, complexion pure orchard-blossom, throat like an arum lily',[1] married Alfred Duff Cooper, later Lord Norwich. On her wedding day " . . . she looked radiantly happy . . ." but the groom was " . . . a poor little man . . . the last of Diana's group of friends, the others were all killed in the war, and he is nice and quite clever." [2nd June 1919]

Lord Ribblesdale, whose first wife, Charlotte Tennant, died in 1911, confided to Jean: " . . . 'I'm seriously thinking of committing matrimony.' I said severely: 'You would never be so foolish, you have tried it once and it was not a success,' meaning his brief engagement to Miss Verschoyle, at the beginning of the war. He said: 'Oh, I think I could make it a success – I'd like to marry a woman of the world like you, who would be understanding – a companion.' 'Oh, no,' I answered laughing 'you'd hate to be married to *me*, and *you* would be simply impossible as a husband!' . . . " [29th May 1919] A few days later, on a train, Jean read in *The Times* " . . . an announcement of Lord Ribblesdale's marriage last Saturday to Ava Astor I was horror-struck when I remembered all I had said to him Thursday night – no wonder, poor man, he could not tell me! I wish now I had not been *so* unsympathetic, but *Ava*

Astor! **She is the very last woman in London I would have though Lord Rib would want to marry." [2nd June 1919]**

Although the Dardanelles Commission was over and Ian had been cleared, the smear would remain and, on important occasions when he would normally have taken a prominent position, he would be sidelined, probably because he was considered a failure and an embarrassment to the government. It was Peace Day and Jean, lying in bed, could see from her window the celebrations in Hyde Park. **" . . . As I lie here I am listening to the multitude in the Park singing 'Land of Hope and Glory' and the guns are firing dismally – it is pouring with rain . . . .**

Norah Lindsay . . . says: 'Of course Winston ought to have had Gallipoli represented in the Procession – now was the moment', but Ian says such an idea never entered his head. . . . I think it would only have irritated me to see him riding behind Haig when he ought to have been in Haig's place." [19th July 1919]

The return to peace meant that the aristocracy and gentry (though much reduced in terms of wealth), and the moneyed classes, whose investments were safe and had survived, returned to as near normal life as circumstances allowed. Many famous families had lost their loved ones; mothers had lost husbands and sons; sisters had lost brothers; officer casualties had fallen heavily on that section of society. Gala Night at the Covent Garden Opera House, 1919, was a great public show of the British Empire re-establishing itself, in an attempt to put the events of 1914–18 to rest. Jean carried out a dress rehearsal beforehand, two dresses at the ready, one pink and silver, the other black. Always artistic and innovative, she made a Russian-style tiara from diamonds and pearls taken from other headdresses. The pink dress, she thought, **" . . . did not look well with the tiara and** [she] **hastily changed to the black. . . . "**

In the press reports of the gala it was made clear that it was the King's special wish no money should be spent on decorations for the Opera House. A succession of ladies paraded in floor-length gowns of silk, satin, velvet, their heads adorned in diamond crowns and tiaras, each looking like a queen. The scene was dazzling, resplendent – the faded backdrop paling into insignificance against the splendour.

King George V, Queen Mary, the Royal Princes and Princess Mary arrived at half-past eight to an ovation. The King wore evening dress with his favourite white carnation and the Order of the Garter. The Queen was in mist-grey, shimmering with mother of pearl and crystal embroideries, a tall diamond crown on her head. Princess Mary wore a frock of light sky-blue and a small wreath of diamonds. The Prince of Wales received an ovation all for himself. The National Anthem was played.

In the box next to the royals were the Queen's ladies, the Duchess of Sutherland, in bright sapphire-blue, with a very wide diamond tiara on her brow, and her hair pulled out full over the ears. In the box opposite the royals were the Corps Diplomatique, the Marchesa Imperiali, Mme Merry del Val in white lace, wearing her diamond tiara low on her brow. Maud, Lady Cunard, all in white, " . . . **was a great sight, seated in the midst of the Corps Diplomatique . . .** ", her hair drawn off her forehead, leaving it bare, " . . . **her diamond crown well back on her head – she looked exactly like Queen Victoria. . . .** " Jean gave Mr and Mrs Lloyd George a mention, grudgingly, she looked " . . . **homely and pleasant! . . .** "

Lord George Curzon's new wife, Grace, an American and the widow of Alfred Duggan, wore a dress of white tulle and a tiara of diamonds low on her hair; she was, in Jean's opinion, " . . . **the loveliest woman there. . . .** " In a large box was Mrs Brinton, founder of the Society for Housing Officers' Families, the American Ambassador and Field Marshal Sir Henry Wilson. The women wore tiaras, and the men their full decorations.

The grand tier, just below the royal box, the omnibus box, contained Lady Randolph Churchill, her niece, Clare Sheridan, who wore a Benetian red dress, and a wreath of red leaves in her hair and General Sir Ian and Lady Hamilton. Jean was glad she decided to wear her black dress rather than pink, as Clare Sheridan and Hazel, Lady Lavery (wife of the artist Sir John Lavery) were both wearing the same shade of deep pink. " . . . **Hazel whispered to me 'I don't mind telling you it has entirely spoilt my evening.'** " Hazel had a small wreath of pink flowers in her hair " . . . **and looked lovely.**" Lady Randolph Churchill sat next Jean; " . . . **Jennie regretted the old days when the Opera House was smothered in paper roses on Command Night. . . .** "

The performance began but the early selections " . . . **were bad – 'Nail' being the worst by Isidore de Lara, it was slightly hissed and only the King and Queen being there prevented it being so openly – everyone was bored. . . . We had one scene from 'Boheme' – my favourite Opera, one from 'Romeo and Juliet' and the last act of 'Louise' . . .** " It was supposed by the press that the disruption caused by the war had affected the performances of the singers. [31st July 1919]

Jean was always very happy at her old home, Deanston. During the autumn she spent several days there with her mother, who, in her later diaries she affectionately called 'little Mother'. Heather Pollen, her sister and children, May Moncreiffe, Chattie Muir, Jim's wife, were also staying. Each night little Harry Knight, aged three, whom Jean was fostering, was tucked up in bed with the other children. It was one big happy family and Jean found it "... **very peaceful here....** " The place was alive with people and they played tennis. Jean's only complaint was that when her maid ran her bath it was too cold. She missed Edie, and reminisced about the early death of her beloved sister, " ... **so much more lovelier than any of us**". The family went to church on Sunday: Jean, her mother, Kay and his wife Grace. Nan opened a new Welfare Centre in Stirling: "... **it looked a veritable paradise on earth ... and Nan, who has worked and arranged, and made it all lovely, quite humbly took a back seat and the Duchess of Montrose opened it with much éclat – little Nan is wonderful – and does so much with quiet tenderness to brighten and help all around her....** " [17th and 21st September; 9th October 1919]

It was always a wrench for Jean to leave her beloved Deanston. "... **This is our last day at Deanston ... these golden Autumn days, they have been so lovely, so exquisite, Deanston at her very best – the glory of the trees is indescribable, and all about the gauzy blue haze, which gives it the unreal beauty of a dream – it is almost too lovely and gives me an impatient pain that I cannot seize it and enjoy it all enough – one wants to soar to heights of emotion unknown, but has only five senses.**" Leaving the " ... **Autumn birds singing** ... ", Jean drove to Stirling Station with " ... **darling little Harry** ... **it was lovely moonlight, and the stars twinkling all around us, and he was enchanted with 'the ickle stars', and wanted to 'have one in Haway's own hand to give to Joy'. Joy is Mr. Scott's (the clergyman's) little girl, and Harry loves her....** " [21st September; 9th and 10th October 1919]

The train journey to London was long and arduous in the cold and Jean suffered an asthma attack. When she arrived home she was in for further upset: she found the house transformed by an enormous painting she had commissioned as a present for Ian and which had been installed in her absence. " ... **Nearly all the servants have gone to Lullenden ... and on entering the hall I got a terrible shock – the sight of the new fresco in our hall, of 'Mary at Langside' on a great white cart horse and all the picture in crude startling colour, reducing our hall to the size of a cell, nearly knocked me down. I felt quite faint with the shock of it. Ian came springing down the staircase at that moment, and supported me**

in his arms, very distressed I was ill [but] he cannot bear to go up in
the lift with me.

Whatever will I do with 'Mary'? It's too appalling – I wonder if
Kay would have her in his 'Memorial Hall' for Doune. I feel I'd gladly
pay a thousand to get rid of her this moment, and I was looking forward so much to this wonderful fresco by Grieffenhagen which I . . .
paid £500 for. . . . " [10th October 1919]

However, tomorrow was another day. " . . . I am becoming more reconciled to her. I have covered the picture with smoke coloured chiffon
which has made it all look much better. . . . " The opinions of others
gave her encouragement; Peter Pollen and Norah Lindsay liked it. Jean
decided a change of colour scheme in the hall would help the picture blend
in and was " . . . inclined to make it all blue, leaving the pillars whitish
– onyx perhaps. . . . " [15th October 1919] The fresco of Mary, Queen of
Scots at Langside today elegantly graces almost an entire wall of the
library of the home of Alexander Hamilton, the eldest son of 'little Ian',
and his wife Sarah.

Jean had taken little interest in politics, which she hated, but as Ian's
career progressed she became more involved, particularly during his time
at Gallipoli and throughout the aftermath. She wrote a booklet of poems
and religious thought, *The Magic Child 1919 – salvator mundi natus est*,
dedicated to 'the lonely women of 1919', which was published.[2] Initially
she could not envisage women making a success of politics, believing the
female electorate would be swayed by handsome men rather than political
views. " . . . I hope women will not get the vote, they would be too passionate and with little judgement – what can they know of the men
they select – the worst cads, the most unscrupulous, as long as they
were orators, would most likely to be their choice especially if good-
lookers. I wonder if Lloyd George will be the end of the Party system?
At present his reign promises fairly well – he has made such good
appointments, and Mr. Balfour and Lord Robert Cecil have taken
office under him." [29th December 1916 Deanston] When, in
November 1919, Nancy Astor became the first woman to take her seat in
the House of Commons, Jean thought it an "historic day". But at Julia
Maguire's dinner, Julia, Kitty Somerset, Mrs Greville and the other
women did not agree. " . . . Lady Lowther fulminated against Nancy
Astor . . . said the dignity of the House of Commons was lowered, and
that she had said to Lady Astor: 'Nancy, I just *hate* your being in the

House' – and says she has attracted all the worst elements in the House about her – the Bottomley lot . . . all the other women joined in and were as venomous as they could be, except Alice Keppel, who is always good-natured." [5th December 1919]

CHAPTER 12

Love, Sex and Children

'Sweet Harry' – 'Dark Rosaleen'

"I dreamed last night that my beloved Puppy turned into a darling little baby boy, with delicious soft baby arms. . . . " [Jan. 11th 1904]

Jean's early diary (1886–87) concludes at the point where the newly weds retreat to their love nest, Stirling Castle, in the hills above Simla. Surely, such a blissfully happy love match between the beautiful Jean and handsome Ian must bring forth babies? Jean provided no clear explanation why she did not have children. 'Little Ian' says she 'had not wished to have children' in the early years.[1] Jean seems to have changed her mind after their return to England and some admission is made during the time Ian was at the South African war of what had taken place in their marriage whilst they were in India. **" . . . I often suffer these days realising what Ian must have gone through during the early years of our married life when he loved me, before he had shut the door of his inner self between us. Knowing his intuitive and critical character I realise now what must have been his surprise and disillusionment at finding he had married *me* and *all* that *that* means! Can any human creature, I wonder, live in perpetual close intimacy daily and hourly with another and not suffer disillusionment? It is terrific to live so near, so close to another soul, that one sees the springs of action and the untruth or at least only partial truth of what they utter. . . . " [March 28th 1902, Riviera Palace Hotel, Monte Carlo]**

The first mention in her diary of Jean wanting a child was made when Ian was in the South Africa and she was staying with Melise Thorburn, who had an eight-year-old son, Keith, whom Jean was much taken with. The child affectionately **" . . . brought me a pink rose . . . this morning, the darling. . . . "** On the morning of her departure, Keith **" . . . brought me 25 red roses from his own garden, bless him. How I wish I had a child! . . . " [25th and 30th June 1902 Bracknell House]** The following month, Ian returned from the war for good. They went to Scotland and visited Skene together, where Jean thought their romance was new-born. " . . . **I thought at last the birthday of my life has come! New vistas seemed opening out before me of home life together. . . .** " Their lives were always rather crowded and a large group of people visited. " **. . . I hugged my secret and at last we got away alone together and went for a walk; it was a radiant evening, but almost at once impenetrable walls of silence were about me again – tongue-tied, baffled! defeated! my dream faded away and I realised we were as far away from one another as though a whole Continent divided us though we walked arm in arm through the sunset field. . . . perhaps he does not want that in his life – and love? Love!** *that* **would hamper** *him* **terribly, but I can't be content with a pleasant playmate. I want more than that. . . .** " [September 2nd 1902 Wynyard Park]

Soon after, Ian left for Germany with St John Brodrick, Lord Roberts and Lord Kitchener. When he returned he had been given the order of the Crown of Prussia by the German Kaiser. Later that month, he went by royal command of the King to Balmoral for two days. Jean wrote of their relationship: " **. . . I have been married to this charming man for years and years now, and still I know very little about him, and he even less about me – we are strangers yet; more and more so as the years go by. I feel caught back again now into the flat of married life, and inclined to resent it, but after all, we have been and are good friends; very happy and comfy together all these years and I dread reactions, especially with temperaments like ours. We are so different, and yet in some way so subtly alike. . . .** " [September 23rd 1902 Deanston]

Jean even admitted she didn't like babies. Whilst holidaying in Verona with Edie, they came upon the contadini people: " **. . . neither Edie or I much like babies, and one old woman would plant her dirty little baby as near Edie's dainty skirts as possible in the hope we would play with it, till we gave her some money to take her most unattractive child away. . . .** " [May 26th 1904 Hotel de Londre Verona]

The sexual side of the Hamiltons' marriage seems to have grown cold in India and Jean's attempts to revive it after their return to England were because she wanted a child.

When Ian left for Japan in early 1904, Jean still had not conceived and Ian was gone eighteen months. It seems they were trying to have a child whilst he was at home. " **. . . I dreamed last night that my beloved Puppy turned into a darling little baby boy, with delicious soft baby**

**arms – I was being photographed with him, and Nan said how per-
fectly lovely he was, and I felt so proud and pleased, and kissed him
again and again on his fine white and rosy skin – then I awoke, and my
arms felt empty indeed."** [January 11th 1904]

They were together at Tidworth for four years, Jean still hoping for a
child. **"... I dreamed of a child again ... I wonder if I had had a child
five years ago, when I so longed to have one, if life would have opened
up before me. ... "** Ian had wanted children in the early years of their
marriage. **"... Ian is a mystery, I thought he wanted a child, but since
I summoned up my courage to tell him I wanted it so much it seems to
have created an impassable barrier between us.
My little son would have been four years old now had he come when I
longed for him and there is no reason why he should not. ... "** [2nd
October 1906 Deanston]

It is difficult to differentiate between Jean's written views on sex and
what her true relationship was with her husband. Victorian morality prevented young girls knowing anything about sex until their wedding night,
but women had now entered an era of more public expression of their need
for liberation. Between 1904 and 1906, Jean wrote of her deepest thoughts
on sexual relations. **"... More and more clearly do I see that the feeling of love is something quite apart from brutal sexual passion which
is the sacrilege and desecration of love; that love should survive marriage seems wonderful to me, has always seemed wonderful to me, yet
it is not that I am sexless – men are a great excitement to me, and a
man can thrill me with emotion just because he's a man and I, a
woman; but it is in a way which I have no words to express – when I
think of this my thoughts become entangled, I seem to get into a maze
and see no way out – the physical facts of marriage darkens the world
for me. How well I remember when I first married, and I thought if
this is so, never again shall I be happy, and feel as I did with men –
never again will the admiration and love in a man's eyes thrill me and
fill me with pleasure if this is what it leads to; the life force! how per-
plexing! ... "** [June 8th 1904 Deanston]

When Heather, her sister, was about to be married to Peter Pollen,
Jean worried that she would be put through the same ordeal, and that she
was standing by letting it happen. It did not occur to Jean that Heather
already knew what took place on the wedding night. Jean's worst fears
were not realised and when she next saw Heather and Peter, they were a

perfectly happily married couple. " . . . **Came here yesterday to stay with Heather Pollen – it still seems too wonderful to me when I see them together, utterly happy and he utterly devoted, and this time a year ago – 6 months now – he seemed far off, utterly unattainable. She stands radiant in 'fields of dewless asphodel' and Peter too, he seems to wish for nothing more. I always used to feel he was a man it would be impossible to content, to satisfy.**" [April 20th 1905 Woodstock Ascot] Jean's puritanical views, nearly twenty years on, were rather old fashioned.

" **. . . I read this morning in Otto Weininger's book, 'Sex and Character' –**
'**All love as such, without going into aesthetic principles of love, is antagonistic to those elements (of the relationship) which press towards sexual union, in fact** *such elements tend to negate love.*

'**Love and desire are two unlike and mutually exclusive opposing conditions, and during the time a man really loves, the thought of physical union with the object of his love is insupportable. Because there is no hope which is entirely free from fear does not alter the fact that hope and fear are utterly opposite principles, and it is true that a love entirely free of sexuality has never been known. However high a man may stand he is still a being with senses.'**

I read this to Ian this morning, but he will have none of it, and retains his opinion through thick and thin that the instinct for the continuance of the race is at the back of all love. It grieves me he should think so. . . . " [September 22nd 1906]

When a young girl Jean knew got married, the next day Jean wondered how she " **. . . feels to-day? I hope for her own sake not so outraged in every atom of her being as I was by discovering the meaning of conjugal rites (or is it** *rights?*) **I still feel horrified at the thought of how such things can be, and am thankful I have no daughter – I should shiver to see her wed – but I suppose I am not properly adjusted to life.**

It is no use telling me sexual passion is a beautiful thing, even if I had not been carefully trained from childhood to feel as I still do about such things any man's face under the influence of that impulse they share with the animals is enough to show what it is – the most beautiful and refined face is disfigured by that look of wild beast desire – it *terrifies* **me when I see the glimmer of it. Once I was startled in Simla, after I was engaged to Ian, by seeing him look at me in that**

hungry way – it gave me such a sense of indignity. My wonderful refined Ian to look at me so! . . . I tried to explain my point of view to Charlie Furse once and to Alwyne Compton, and felt their instant hostility – it makes one laugh now to think of it how I would dare.

. . . the girls of to-day are so different. . . . Companionship is what I want, and *love*, that most rare and lovely thing, if I can get it – but never lust. . . . " [23rd Feb. 1914]

Jean seems to have viewed love, sex and children as three separate and perhaps unrelated concepts. Love was a kind of **"Companionship"**, sex was **"brutal sexual passion"** and she wanted a child but not necessarily a baby or any of the trappings that went along with having one, and it had to be a boy. If Jean's experience of **"conjugal rights"** was such that she was **"outraged in every atom of her being"**, she did not write about it in her early diary. On the contrary, three days after the wedding day, she gave the impression of perfect bliss: **" . . . I felt all day in a dream, rather like the old woman in the nursery rhyme: 'This surely can't be I'. . . . " [25th February 1887 Barrackpore]** There is the possibility that at the time of writing, the marriage had not yet been consummated but with no further explanation from Jean, it is pointless to speculate.

The Hamiltons had only just returned from Malta and set up home in London when the First World War broke out in August 1914. By the first week of March 1915, Ian was on his way to Gallipoli. After his return, Jean was weary of war and its terrible consequences for Ian. Whilst the Dardanelles Commission hung over them her mind turned once again to having a child. **" . . . Ian . . . rushes off to London tonight to see General Braithwaite before he goes off to France – how I wish we had a little son of our own." [August 17th 1916]** Braithwaite's son, Val, had been killed on the first day of the Battle of the Somme.

When Jean had all but given up the prospect of ever having a child, the chance abandonment in 1918 of a sixteen-month-old boy made her dream come true. He had been left outside the door of the Paddington Crèche of which Jean was president, with a note pinned to his clothing that read 'Harry'. The crèche had been set up so that women could leave their babies there if they were ill or had to go into hospital and could not look after them. No one claimed the little boy and after three months a standing order threatened to send him to the workhouse. Jean agreed to foster him and drove him in her motor to a draper's shop where she dressed him in a blue linen suit with yellow buttons and red shoes. Bringing him home to 1

Hyde Park Gardens, she introduced him to Ian, who must have been sur-prised if not greatly shocked. Jean put Annie Woodger, one of her maids, in charge of nursing and feeding him on crumbled biscuits and cream.[2] Harry settled into his new surroundings very happily and McAdie and the servants doted on him. For Jean, after twenty years of waiting, it was almost beyond belief – she had a son at last!

London, like other large cities, had a high crime rate. Down among the masses, slums screamed of child poverty and neglect. The term 'child sex abuse' had not yet entered the English language, although it occurred regardless of wealth or class. From a discussion with Winston Churchill over dinner some years earlier, it is apparent Jean knew of such abuse amongst the privileged classes, going undetected and unpunished. " . . . **Winston . . . has just been made Home Secretary and about the mid-dle of the feast he suddenly turned to me and said: 'After all we make too much of death.' 'Yes,' I said 'I think we do – but why do you say so now?' 'Because I have had to sign a death warrant for the first time to-day and it weighed on me.' 'Whose?' I said 'For what?' 'A man who took a little child up a side street and brutally cut her throat.' I was relieved and said cheerfully: 'That would not weigh on my mind.' 'Think' he said rather savagely 'of a Society that forces a man to do that.' 'I can't', I said 'If that man lived in our society his crime would be much worse – not brutal like that but some horrible, unnatural, decadent crime.' He was not satisfied and we discussed whether the man was of unsound mind. I argued that criminal lunatics were just the people who ought to be put away, as if a man was in his senses he might repent but a criminal lunatic was a danger always to all. I was *very* interested in all he said – he was sensitive and in an excitable mood – alive." [21st February 1910, 6 Seamore Place]**

Harry's true identity never became known. Many years later, Ian related a story which contained a clue to his background:

In one of the picture books Jean had bought him was a page showing an old lady of dignified appearance sitting in an armchair and wear-ing a black poke bonnet. The first time he saw it he was driving with Annie in the motor. The moment his eyes lit upon this picture he became greatly agitated; 'No! No!!' – he cried. 'No! No!' throwing the book away. He seemed to imagine he was being taken to that old lady. When Annie told Jean she thought she would see for herself. So

next time she took him out driving she pulled out the picture book
and all went well until he saw the old lady in the black poke bonnet.
There was no doubt about it; he was terrified – again he cried out
'No! No!' and flung the book away – at the same time clasping Jean
in his arms.[3]

Jean was very eager for Harry to grow up into a handsome young man
but was very conscious of his dubious background. " . . . **I wish he had a
more distinguished look, he has a sweet face and is a darling little fellow – he has something very attracting about him, everyone loves him
who comes in contact with him, all my servants adore him, and the
soldiers, he always comes down here for Soldiers' day. Last Thursday
when I looked into McAdie's room I saw him dressed in a sweet little
blue and white suit of clothes Matron had brought down to put on
him, and he was enchanted with his importance in this, and was running around, first to Matron, then to Annie our second housemaid
who adores him, and then to McAdie, flinging his arms round their
necks with joy. As soon as he saw me and Heather he stumbled over
and flung his little fat arms round my neck."** [16th June 1918]

Harry was big for his age and strongly built with a strong set of lungs.
He ran around the sitting rooms and halls of the various houses the
Hamiltons frequented and at Deanston cried and bawled and shouted. Ian
would have nothing to do with Harry, and the child, not being able to call
him 'Dardie' (guardian) or 'papa', mimicked what he heard the grown
men say, 'old boy', or at least that part which his infant speech could pro-
nounce and which came out as **"boyeee"**, and Jean saw that Harry was
" . . . rather frightened of Boy. . . . " [7th January 1919] Harry's blonde
hair and blue eyes, and loving and kind nature endeared him to the other
members of Jean's family, and her mother and brother Kay were particularly kind to him.

Winston and Clementine Churchill came to stay with the Hamiltons at
No. 1 HPG in June 1918, when Clementine was expecting her fourth child.
Jean arranged a dinner for Clementine on the 18th. Afterwards, in private,
the two women discussed children. " **. . . Clemmie . . . urged me on no
account to adopt Harry . . . she asked if I'd like to have her baby; of
course I said I would, and asked her when she expected it. She said:
'In November', and I offered to have her here for it, as she had been
telling me how expensive a Nursing Home would be – £25 a week for**

**room alone, and she said she could not possibly afford it. She said if
she had twins I would have one. . . . " [21st June 1918]**

Clementine's suggestion to give Jean her baby was made at a particularly difficult time in her life. The outcome of the Dardanelles campaign
was taking its toll. The Churchill and Hamilton families were subjected to
a barrage of abuse, daily, in the newspapers. Although Winston was now
back in government he had been unemployed for some months. As we
have seen in Chapters 8 and 10, a shocking time had preceded these
events, from the spring of 1915 when the Dardanelles campaign was under
way. Lord Fisher was First Sea Lord and Winston, as his boss, was very
reliant on his support. Fisher had resigned in a fit of rage, saying he was
opposed to the Dardanelles campaign and Clementine was very upset over
this incident. Fisher's resignation had ultimately forced Winston to
resign.[4] Soon after the Prime Minister also resigned. Clementine's daughter, Mary, The Lady Soames, wrote: 'Many years later, looking back over
her life with Winston, Clementine was to say that, of all the events they
had lived through together, none had been so agonising as the drama of the
Dardanelles.' During that time, 'she shared with Winston every anxiety,
every brief hope, every twist and turn of the devious course of the crisis.'
When Winston's biography was being written, Clementine told Martin
Gilbert: 'I thought he would die of grief'.[5] Edwin Montagu, the fiancé of
Venetia Stanley (Asquith's former mistress), wrote of how he found
Clementine: 'She was so sweet but so miserable and crying all the time. .
. . how I feel for her and him.'[6] The night before Clementine offered to
give her baby away, Jean wrote in her diary that they had been to dinner
with friends and **" . . . Clemmie was tired . . . "** and she had to **" . . . take
her home. . . . " [20th June 1918]** Jean, too, had had her moments of
despair after the failed Gallipoli campaign and felt she wanted to flee the
country and go to Russia to escape from it all.

The lease on the Churchills' London house, 33 Eccleston Square, was
about to expire.[7] Through shortage of money, they later let their country
house, Lullenden, to the Hamiltons, who eventually bought it. Clementine
was now over four months into her pregnancy with the spectre of no settled home for her confinement looming ahead. In that moment, when
Clementine offered to give the baby to Jean, she may have felt she was
putting the welfare of her child first, in trying to secure a place for it to be
born. It is a very human story. Clementine was a devoted wife and mother.
Two years previously, when the Hamiltons were staying at Postlip Hall

and Ian invited the Churchills, only Winston came; **" . . . Clemmie is not coming – she has waited at home to be with her boy Randolph, as tomorrow is his birthday."** [**27th May 1916**] All references to the Churchills in Jean's diary are to a very happy family with Clementine and Winston totally devoted to their children and to each other. The new baby was the adorable Marigold, the 'Duckadilly' as the family called her, a treasured child tragically destined to die before her third birthday.

Jean was so desperate for a child she had accepted Harry, who had been abandoned on a doorstep. Clementine had wisely warned her of the risks of taking on such a child. People who had knowledge of Harry would eventually appear.

The Hamiltons were looking for a country home and the Churchills obliged. On a Sunday afternoon, Jean and Ian arrived at Lullenden, 'a half-timbered Elizabethan house with a Great Hall and solar room'.[8] Jean's first impression of the place was that it **" . . . looked messy . . . clay and mud all about, and rather untidy garage and outhouses, but we loved it all the same . . .** *just* **the sort of place we want. I was fascinated by the rocks and little pool at the side of the house and all the possibilities of the place. . . . "** Jean was also somewhat in awe of the beautiful Churchill children. **" . . . The white dining room was happy and delicious, with the lovely boy Randolph, sitting at the head of the table with his governess, and the gentle little maid, Diana – she had white eyelashes. . . . "** [**16th March 1919**] Years later, on Diana Churchill's wedding day, when Jean saw the ninth Duke of Marlborough's sons, now grown up, **" . . . it seemed no time since Ivo sat on my knee at the Christmas pantomime that I took him and Blandford to. He was sensitive, excited and eager, and I longed then for a child like him. . . . "** [**12th December 1932**]

Mary Soames says her father's aunt, Lady Wimborne, came to Clementine's assistance, 'ever kindly Aunt Cornelia lent Winston and Clementine her house: 3 Tenterden Street', thus providing a place for Clementine's confinement.[9] Two days before the baby was due, Jean and Ian **" . . . Dined with Sarah Wilson to-night to meet Winston Churchills. . . .** *Clemmie* **. . . thinks it** [the baby] **may arrive to night . . . . "** [**13th Nov. 1918**] There was no further mention of Clementine wanting to give the baby away; the momentary crisis had passed. The Hamiltons and Churchills were like family and Clementine had confided in Jean as though she was a sister. She had no way of knowing that Jean wrote everything down in her diary. Clementine was a strong character and worked tirelessly, doing war work as well as having a home to run and a family of small children to care for. Her voluntary work continued throughout her pregnancy. After a dinner party at Lord Haldane's, " . . . **Clemmie Churchill and Frances** [Horner] **departed in high dudgeon about 11 o'clock to the night shift of the Hackney Canteen. . . . "** [**14th June 1918**] Clementine was at that time a member of the Munitions Workers' Auxiliary Committee and later took charge of organising nine canteens, each one providing meals for up to 500 munitions workers. In later years, Clementine received several awards: the Order of the Red Banner of Labour from the Russians, in recognition of her work for aid to Russia; the Grand Cross of the Order of the British Empire, bestowed on her at Buckingham Palace for public services; and the Distinguished Red Cross Service Badge.[10]

On 1 July 1918, Jean received a letter from Phyllis Holman, the matron of a clinic for orphan children at 3 Hyde Park Square. A friend of Miss Holman's, the victim of a wartime tragedy, was having a baby out of wedlock that Miss Holman was offering to Jean to foster with a view to adoption. " . . . **I hanker after it but see Ian hates the thought of it.**" [**3rd July 1918**] The baby was born to a lady's maid, living and working close to No. 1 HPG. Jean had attended the trial of Roger Casement, who was hanged in 1916, on a charge of conspiracy. Spiritually and romantically linked to the Irish people through her support for Irish Home Rule and her admiration of Casement, whom she viewed as a patriot who laid down his life for his country, Jean wanted to give the child an Irish name. " . . . **Rosaleen – 'my dark Rosaleen' – I think I would like to call her that – her father is Irish.**" [**8th July 1918**][11] The baby's father was said to be of Irish gentry, and had been on his way back from the war to marry her mother when the train he was travelling in was bombed. He was seriously injured and brain damaged and committed to a mental asylum. Such was the tale told to Jean by Miss Holman. To Jean's dismay, when she saw the baby for the first time on 13 July, she had already been christened Phyllis Ursula, named for Miss Holman who was her godmother. [**14th July 1918**] Jean was not about to give up her choice of a romantic Irish name and called the child Rosaleen. She now had a girl and could dream of her growing up to be a great beauty, having learnt from Miss Holman that her mother had golden hair and her father had violet blue, Irish eyes.

Already Jean's life was transformed, and though still only a foster

parent she was too attached to both children to turn back. Providing new
clothes, a cradle and pram for Rosaleen, she sent her to a wet nurse.
Adoption of both children was now only a formality. "... **I saw her yesterday for the first time at 3 Hyde Park Square in Miss Phyllis
Holman's arms.**

**Joan Poynder lunched yesterday. She has arranged for the baby
to go to nurse White at Calne, and I am to pay 10/- a week for her.**

**Miss Holman said the mother never wished to hear anything more
of the baby at all, and I said: 'But if I bring up the child and she grows
up a lovely girl and she wishes her to know she is her mother, and
influences her, how could I prevent her meeting her, when and how
she wanted, and also the father, *if* he recovers and had intended to
marry the mother, surely his first thought would be to find the girl,
and do what he could for his child, and one cannot keep a child from
her own father and mother'. Miss Holman insisted that a lawyer must
arrange it and the mother sign that she renounced all rights, or claim
on her child.**

**Of course if the mother happens to be nice any lawyer's business
would be useless, as if later on she wanted her own little child I could
not keep her. At present she has a horror of the child and of the father,
and of all connected with it, but will it last? I greatly doubt it. How
could one put being a mother utterly out of one's thoughts, and out of
one's life?" [14th and 17th July 1918 London]**

"... **I love to think when I wake up in the morning now of Harry's
blue eyes waking up, and Rosaleen's dark ones, in their little cottage,
and I often dream of all I would like to do for them to make their path
straight." [8th September 1918]**

For the next two years, Jean went each month to see Rosaleen. Her
friends Lord and Lady Lansdowne, who lived at Bowood, joined in the
adventure. "... **Travelled here this morning to see 'my dark Rosaleen'
at Hill Martin, and after luncheon Lady Lansdowne and I set out on
our expedition. Lord Lansdowne, she and I had been alone at luncheon, they live just in one corner of this great place, most of it is shut
up, and the rest used as a hospital. Hill Martin is the loveliest village
of dignified cottages, and Nurse White's has a lovely yew gateway and
a nice lawn. ..."** Rosaleen was "... **a beautifully made little thing,
with lovely hands and feet, and great blue Irish eyes, and lovely little
mouth. ..."** [August 9th 1918 Bowood]

Becoming a mother began to alter Jean's view of war, having seen the sons of her friends killed and wounded in the First World War. " . . . **Would I have wished to have borne and brought up a son to fight and die in this war: 'Be you a soldier of Life' is a sentence in a book, 'Realms of Day', I am reading and it's a motto I should like to give my little Harry."** [6th October 1918]

Ian's indifference towards Harry complicated the relationship and Jean decided to send him to school until she could find a suitable house in the countryside to which she could take him out from under Ian's feet. **" . . . Last Friday 18th, I took him** [Harry] **to see Miss Kenny at the Montessori School at Campden Hill, McAdie was with me and he was so good and sweet, and loved Miss Kenny at once. . . . "** [20th October 1918] Little Harry was a joy to wake up to, greeting Jean with " **'A "mornin", Dardie' "** and taking his **"tea and bikkie"** (biscuit) with her. **" . . . He calls Ian 'boye' but boy won't look at him, or play with him, unless I make him and little Harry is always trying to engage his attention and ingratiate himself with his 'Look! Look!' he says, taking his hand and pulling him down on the stool in front of the fire, to show him his toy."** [20th November 1918]

Harry, two years and three months old, was placed in a boarding school, whilst Jean tried to settle on a country house with separate accommodation for the children and their nanny. **" . . . After church we went in mother's motor to Tower Cressy to see little Harry – McAdie and I had taken him there on Friday, he fell asleep in the motor going there, so we lifted him, still sleeping, into his little cot and left him, and I felt worried to think of the darling waking up and finding his happy world melted away from him – how he must have wondered, when he woke up, but I have no niche for him here yet and Ian is not reconciled to me adopting him, so Tower Cressy seems meantime a solution till I get something arranged. When we got there today Miss Kenny took us upstairs where all the little girls were having their Sunday dinner round a nicely arranged low table, and there was my little Harry, in the rough brown suit I got him for country wear. I think he had forgotten, and felt puzzled how to fit me into his new life. However, he soon brightened up, and was awfully pleased showing me his bath and that he could get into it himself, and put the taps off and on. . . . Miss Kenny says he plays happily with David."** [24th November 1918 London]

It would be almost another month before Jean brought Harry home again. "... **Little Harry came back today. I took him with me to the Doll Show and he put pennies in the bird cages to make them sing, all afternoon, and was very sweet and good. 'What a darling', Diana Manners said, 'Who is he' but when I said he was mine, and I did not know who his parents were, she looked very dubiously at the determined little man in his pale blue coat and white fur hat."** [13th December 1918]

Jean and her staff then found that Harry had learnt bad habits at school. "... **Harry has been so terribly naughty all day – McAdie and I are in despair....** " In his bath he was "... **playing with his ducks and beating them virulously, saying 'Bab boy', which was ominous, as he never had heard the words 'bad boy' here, or done this before, so obviously that Montessori nurse must have either beaten him, or little David, calling him 'bad boy'.... Mrs. Hussy tried to put on his pyjamas, and then he opened his mouth and howled with rage, all in a moment, wriggling about naked all over the room ... Mrs. Hussy lifted him naked and shouting and clutching at her wildly, into his cot, and I shut the door and left them, but dining with Ian later I could still hear him sobbing and crying...."** [14th December 1918]

Harry was reprieved and was not sent back to boarding school. On Christmas Eve, Jean went to Will and Clara at Postlip Hall "... **for the Children's Christmas Tree Party and was greeted joyously by Harry flinging himself on me, dressed all in white with the little red shoes he is so proud of."** Harry got lots of presents there with Jill and Karen. Jean "... **had give him a Noah's Ark and he was thrilled by that, lying flat on his little fat tummy while I arranged the animals two by two."** Harry's background remained a mystery and Jean could not help wondering "... *where* **he spent his last Christmas."** [Xmas Day 1918 Clere Hill]

Jean and Ian went to Deanston for the New Year to stay with Jean's mother, family and friends. Whilst Harry amused himself and the adults looked on bemused, Jean happily painted a pastel of Doune Castle in the days of Prince Charlie, for her brother, Kay Muir, who doted on Harry. "... **Harry sings ... 'There was a naughty birdie', but he never gets further than the first line, and then we all have to clasp our hands, he leading the chorus, thumping his fat little puds together. 'Tadie'**

[McAdie] **always appears at these orgies – adores the little man, and he really is adorable." [9th February 1919 Deanston]**

" . . . Ian has become a most delightful friend and companion, and I love our little dinners together in my sitting room, it is so comfy being with him now. I want to settle down to a comfy old-age life together with little Harry and Rosaleen for interest and excitement and I hope now that the war is over he will creep back to some sort of interest in Art and Literature." [15th January 1919 London]

" . . . – Had a pitched battle with Harry this evening. I tried to be firm and severe, and fondly imagined I had conquered, but feel some-what dashed by hearing from McAdie that he confided to Annie 'How naughty Dardie had been'! McAdie was rather pleased to tell me this, she adores him and can't bear any discipline being used towards him. . . . " Coming home in the motor, **" . . . he would stand leaning against the door and I was afraid he would fall out so took him on my knee to hold him there and let him look out; . . . but he kicked, struggled, screamed and yelled with passion – his whole body was convulsed with rage as he struck and beat me. I slapped his hands as hard as I could, and held him as tightly as I could – it was quite exciting as he is fearfully strong. He was still howling with rage when we got here, so I made Annie go indoors, and Clark (the chauffeur), and told Harry we should sit there in the dark till he was good, so finally when he saw it was hopeless, he gave in and said he was 'dood now'. So we came up in the lift . . . and we danced to the Musical Box, and all was forgotten till he went to bed. . . . " [20th February 1919 London]**

Jean was about to legally adopt Harry. Such a step was not without dilemmas and misgivings, and her interest was aroused in stories of other adopted children. **" . . . Little Harry fascinates me, he develops character, and is so gay, sweet and naughty, with such a scowl when he is naughty and the sweetest tentative engaging smile when he is good, McAdie can in no wise resist him, and crawls about the floor at his bidding – it is a sight to see her and Harry crawling on all fours like lightning all about my room after his bath, he expects me to do the same in my best gown, but my knees don't permit.**

In the afternoon I went to a large meeting of the Children's National Adoption Scheme – Col. Burgyone had forcibly put me on the Committee; . . . a poor woman sitting beside me broke out at question time with the grievance that she had an adopted son of 13, who

had a bad mother and who had never come near them since he was a baby but now was always molesting him and waylaying him in the streets. The Committee was much bothered by these indiscreet questions, which I kept egging her on to ask, as I can see no way of dealing with this; even if a new law is passed a mother is a mother, and a son *is* a son, bone of her bone and flesh of her flesh 'God and the soul stand *sure*' Browning says, one sometimes wonders about that, but as long as this world lasts, Mother and child must stand sure with links no law can really sever. I prefer the way I have acquired my little family of two. Both utterly deserted by their mothers." [7th March 1919]

Rosaleen was now nine months old and Jean saw she was "... **rather a depressed and heavy looking child with lovely blue eyes."** [31st March 1919]

Jean was very concerned that the children should have a moral perspective on life and considered giving them a Roman Catholic upbringing, but her experience of the Montessori school of Italian origin may have changed her mind and she decided to bring them up in the Anglican faith.

By April 1919, the Hamiltons had moved into their country home, Lullenden, at Dormansland, East Grinstead, Sussex, which they rented from the Winston Churchills. The Churchills' removal was a very public affair, the newspapers printing the story with photographs of Winston's portrait by Sir John Lavery, along with the furniture, being carried out of the house. " ... **Well! Well! Well! Here we are established bag and baggage, servants and Nan, *chez* Winston's quaint old encampment. I love it and want it for my own, and would like to plunge and buy it and set to work at once to fashion one or two things more after my heart's desire, for on the whole it's the sort of romantic place I long to have – it's a snuggy place with rocks, pools, trees and streams such as my childish soul loved, and still loves – unluckily it's clay soil, very damp, cold, chill clay soil all around, though the house is dry and smells dry.**

Poor Clemmie Churchill is ill with 'flu in London; little Sarah has also had it and baby Marigold, and they are here now with Diana and Randolph in the Barn. . . . " [13th April 1919 Lullenden]

The Hamiltons were so enchanted with Lullenden that they bought the house, and the farm for Ian, in September 1919. Jean thought it the ideal location to raise her two children. The Robin Hood Barn was converted as a nursery for Harry and Rosaleen and the oasthouse was converted into a writing room for Ian. " ... **Last night at dinner Ian was quite keen** about buying Lullenden at once for £10,000 *if* Winston would include all the livestock on the farm.

Harry has just been here, too sweet and lovely, but as he stood by the window for one flashing moment I seemed to see the kind of man he might grow into ... he is growing huge and looks like four or five although he is only just learning to talk. I have sometimes terrible misgivings as to his parentage, and what he may grow into. Mrs. Winston warned me: 'He is just at the sweetest age', – he is really more attractive than any other children I know, but I wonder what his father and mother were like, and if they are living now. ... " [16th April 1919]

The move to Lullenden marked a new beginning for the Hamiltons and it was their happiest time. " . . . Went to Communion . . . in the lovely old church here. I wanted to thank God for Harry! he grows in grace daily and is such a joy to me – I never thought he'd grow so lovely." [Sunday 1st June 1919 Trent] " . . . Mother and I took Harry to Loch Lomond, all through the lovely Rob Roy country to have tea with Muriel Beckett. I love to see little Harry, his curls shining in the sun, dancing along the well-known, well-loved paths here – it seems incredible he belongs to me – I often look at him full of wonder that he should actually *be*." [13th June 1919 Deanston] " . . . It is strange and so joyful to see little Golden-locks here, the embodiment of dreams, how I longed for such a little man when Ian was in South Africa, and dreamed of him, and when I played bridge with father . . . I was so pleased if I got a card with a little cherub on it then I believed my dream would come true." [21st June 1919 Deanston]

Only Rosaleen was needed to make their lives complete but her arrival was still some way off. " . . . McAdie and I had a long, somewhat hot drive to-day to see Rosaleen at Hill Martin – she has improved and is looking a real nut-brown maid, she has lovely eyes, large and deep blue, fringed and lovely lashes, and tiny little brown hands, and her legs feel and look better and stronger. I think it will be better to leave Rosaleen there all this winter." [12th August 1919 Mells Manor]

Harry was as yet without a surname and Ian would not allow Jean to call the children Hamilton. Rosaleen had been registered in what was believed to be her mother's maiden name, James. " . . . I am worried as to what to call him ... it was so wonderful the way he came to me, like little Moses out of the bulrushes I don't want to call him Kay, Muir or

Hamilton, though I should prefer Hamilton. . . . " [6th October 1919 Deanston]

Lullenden brought much joy to the Hamiltons but parting with it was a great wrench for Winston, though he had the advantage of still being able to visit there. " **. . . We spent this dripping pouring day at Lullenden – Jack Churchill drove down with us and back also, I was quite glad of his company – he's a comfy creature, and the great Winston was really charming to-day. I feel sorry for him having to give up Lullenden, he loves the place, and does not want to part with it at all, I see, but is forced to do it for want of money.**

Violet and Bongy Bonham Carter motored down to lunch, and Sir Ernest Cassel was staying here – he is a great friend of the Churchills' and seems to know all about breeding pigs." [20th July 1919]

By mid-October, the Hamiltons and their servants were fully in residence at Lullenden and their London house, No. 1 HPG, was let. Jean woke in the mornings to " **. . . sunshine and robins singing at my latticed window, the autumn trees making a pattern on the blue sky . . . my bedroom is most enchanting." [19th October 1919] " . . . Harry arrived with Annie. . . . he wanted to go and see Sarah, the pony. He was delighted with 'Haways own ickle 'ouse'** [Harry's own little house] **in the Barn . . . "** where Jean " **. . . had put Randolph's** [Churchill's] **rocking horse for him, which he at once mounted. . . . " [21st October 1919]**

Ian began breeding a herd of belted galloway cattle and kept pigs. " **. . . Ian . . . loves the place and is so excited over the farming. . . . "** [3rd Nov. 1919] He could continue his writing in peace, and to be fair to him, he was now looking forward to enjoying his impending retirement. It must have been something of a shock to his system to have two strange children foisted upon him. The following January, 1920, he retired from the army, aged sixty-seven.

Jean adopted Harry and Rosaleen, and her ideal of a normal family life began at last. In the early days, Ian took nothing to do with the children but, being the softhearted individual he was, he came round eventually. The newspapers reported in November 1919 that General Sir Ian and Lady Hamilton had adopted two children, a little overstated as Ian would not become guardian to the children for some years. Jean gave Harry the romantic surname of Knight, seeing him as her 'knight in shining armour'. Harry charmed her and completely won her heart, preparing " . . .

Dardie's bath, and put in the scent, and arranged the hot and cold water with McAdie, then brings me my slippers and takes my hand and leads me to the bath." [23rd November 1919]

Lullenden was popular with family and friends. "Alice Keppel . . . told me she had nearly bought Lullenden." [5th December 1919] Christmas Day 1919 was a day of " . . . furious rush and bustle, with Harry running like a golden thread through it." They had a " . . . huge Christmas Tree." 'Little Ian', father of the present generation (Alexander, Helen, Ian and the late Mary Pearce), visited and played mahjong with the Freybergs and Nabokoff. Jean's mother, Lady Muir, despite her advanced years, made the journey all the way from Scotland.

Jean revelled in the fresh country air, and with Harry now aged three and a half by her side in the garden and her dedicated maid, McAdie, taking care of her, her asthma subsided and she experienced fewer attacks. Ian enjoyed country life and gained great satisfaction from the farm. " . . . I go out early mornings now, planting fox gloves and poppies in wild parts of the garden, and rooting up the spreading array of nettles everywhere here – the place is truly like the Irish farm of the McClarty's I used to hear so much about in my childhood – it wants twenty men working hard from morning to night to put the place in any sort of order – just labourers. We are putting up new farm buildings and making a nice garage and putting in electric light – it ought to make a delicious home, and I hope after it has been a home for Ian and me it will be a home for my little Harry. I hope to bring little Rosaleen up here too, and that they will both love it and each other, and perhaps marry. . . . " [New Year's Day 1920 Lullenden]

The servants enjoyed Lullenden with its large grounds and gardens, and in little Harry Jean found a willing helper, planting flowers in the garden. " . . . Harry and Annie came out to help me, and Harry planted his first plant, a fox glove, and put 'the dirt' as he called it round it – 'Harry own icle self' [little self] – he kept calling out eagerly 'Haway can, Haway knows. . . . ' " Jean bought a " . . . boy's cinema, to have parties for the servants and children in the Barn. Harry was thrilled, sitting on my knee, looking at all the wild adventures in the Wild West, and with puffer trains – he loves anything to do with trains or horses.

Last Friday when I went to London for the day, Harry was determined to pay for Dardy's engine with his half penny, he had been looking for it all morning, strutting about the platform with me say-ing: 'Haway paid for Dardie's engine' after he had presented his half penny solemnly to the delighted ticket collector who came to punch my ticket." [7th January 1920]

" . . . I love to see little Harry here, going about the place with his little sturdy figure and golden aureole of curls, he has been running about without his 'tat' [hat] as the thorn bushes snatched it off his head . . . he carries the 'dirt' (earth) for me to plant my flowers in. . . . " [8th January 1920]

Jean and Annie took Harry to a children's party at Claridge's, dressed in a " . . . grey glacé silk suit . . . with fine frilled collar and cuffs. . . . " But he wouldn't dance even though " . . . Jean Baikie dragged him . . . out to the middle of the floor . . . and he got panic-stricken and fled. . . . " [11th January 1920]

Deanston, covered in snow, made a postcard New Year beginning. " . . . Harry at 7.15 comes in, in his little blue dressing gown to say 'Good-night' and his prayers – he was having a tiger ride on my knee. . . . " [17th January 1920]

But Jean's happy family was shattered by the sudden appearance of two women posing as Harry's relations. A telegram from Matron Neal of the Paddington Crèche where Harry was originally abandoned sent shivers down Jean's spine. Whilst Harry innocently built a snowman in front of the house with McAdie, Jean opened the telegram, feeling " . . . a pang of fear go through me when I read it: 'Have you got the child safely with you? A woman has been here asking for him – I told her nothing and have warned your servants in London'. . . . " [28th January 1920] The first woman had turned up at Matron Neal's house in Surrey. Harry's 'real' surname it seemed was Stone. It was a shock that Jean would never really get over and the shadow of Harry's 'relatives' – if that is who they were – would haunt her throughout the rest of both the children's lives.

More news followed: " . . . A note from Matron saying the same woman she thinks who left Harry at the Crèche waylaid her, and asked her where the child going by the name of Harry Stone, who was left at her crèche 18 months ago, was now. Matron replied she could ask the police, and would not tell her, and when Matron asked who she was, she tried to threaten her, but when Matron in turn asked who she was, she ran away. I have written a long letter to Mr. Ducane, my lawyer, to ask how I can get Harry made a ward in Chancery, and also how I can change his name and get him registered. I feel dreadfully worried and anxious about the child and think I shall leave him here till I can secure the position in some way. . . . " [31st January 1920]

Ellen Varney, Jean's head house maid, wrote her a letter describing a second woman who had challenged her in the Mews, just round the corner from No. 1 HPG. " . . . I had hoped I had found something that would stay and be eternally quite mine in little Harry, now dim shapes which fill me with apprehension seem rising on every side – the fair woman Ellen describes with pretty complexion is the most terrifying, for if Harry has a gentle and sweet Mother he can no longer be my little son, as I have felt him to be ever since I got him – something I had rescued from the wreckage and meant to save eternally, if anything I could do would dot it, anyway give him the ways and means of a happy childhood, boyhood and manhood.

I feel so afraid this coarse dark woman Matron Neal describes may have been given little Harry to look after by the fair woman, she may have been given money to look after him and she got rid of him by leaving him at the Paddington Crèche. . . . "

The very landscape seemed threatening. " . . . The morning is now gloriously red along the horizon and the firs of the Tullickin Knowe looking dark against the light and the pencilling of the trees in the Park. . . . " [2nd February 1920 Deanston]

Ellen also wrote to McAdie about the fair-haired woman. " . . . McAdie got a letter from Ellen saying on Saturday night, about 7.00 . . . a woman crossed over from . . . the corner of the Mews, and said to her: 'Little Harry has gone to Scotland with his nurse'. . . . she said she had heard his nurse tell another nurse this in the Park. Ellen says the woman was fair, and had a very pretty complexion, so obviously she is not the same woman, who took Harry to the crèche. I am haunted by the fear that this is his mother. I woke up several times on Friday night – listening to the wind, and thinking it was perhaps Harry's mother's heart wailing for her little lost son. I feel terrified when I think, there must have been a hundred sad reasons why she had to leave him at the Crèche. I feel I must trace this woman now for Harry's sake as well as mine as she might reproach me when he grows up and longs to know who his mother is. . . . I feel so afraid of Harry being kidnapped, and I think Annie will be afraid of going out with the child in London now. . . . " [8th February 1920 Deanston]

Oblivious to the controversy surrounding him, little Harry brought 'Dardie' a bunch of snowdrops he'd picked in the garden at Deanston. Perhaps they melted her heart and the terrors of the night faded away in the daylight. "**. . . Harry is a ray of brilliant sunshine, how thankful I am he is here with his vivid flower-like face and pretty ways; he grows so clever and amusing! He was so pleased to see the snow when he came in this morning and called out 'Haway was going out to make a snow-man' – 'Wif you too,' he said consolingly, as he tried to climb on to the bed. 'But it's *raining*', I said, and he climbed down again and ran to the window: 'It's very *rude* of it,' he said ruefully, and I felt so too. . . . "** [15th February 1920]

Jean could not find the courage to trace Harry's maternal mother and hand him back to her, and she continued with the seasonal festivities. "**. . . Yesterday, I took my little Harry to see 'Puss in Boots' acted and danced by Margaret Morris' children. Harry was terrified of the hor-rid, large, black puss, but very brave, and when the Giant was trans-formed into the Elephant his little heart beat right up in his throat – he was sitting on my knee, but he declared, loudly he was not at all frightened of Jumbo.**" [20th February 1920]

Neither of the women who enquired about Harry ever returned. It is possible they were impostors who knew Harry's sad story and thought to obtain money from Jean. It is also possible that the fair-haired woman was his mother, but why she should wait two years to return to the Paddington Crèche to collect him is difficult to explain.

Jean decided the only way to protect Harry was to hide him at Deanston, and when the time came for her and Ian to return to Lullenden, she left him behind with Annie and her mother, afraid he might be kidnapped. [23rd February 1920 Deanston] Back in Lullenden, she was able to find out more of the two women who came in search of him. Ellen told her the second woman "**. . . was pretty with curly fair hair like his, and had a nice voice and good accent; she said she looked as if she were in business. . . .**" [24th February 1920] Jean met her solicitor, Sir Charles Russell, to discuss making Harry a ward in Chancery but changed her mind, possibly because that might involve press coverage and exposure. Attention may have already been drawn to Harry by the newspaper announcement in November 1919 of the children's adoption. It was not until almost the end of May 1920 that Jean felt it safe to bring Harry back to

Lullenden. Life returned to normal and Jean and Ian began having the stable turned into a garage and a new wing built. [17th **March** 1920]

Travelling between the peace and tranquillity of Lullenden and Deanston, Jean's fear of the threat to Harry faded and she enjoyed family life again. Ian, having retired from his post at the Tower of London, had more time to devote to farming. " . . . **Ian is happy here and loving his pigs, he goes to see them every day. . . .** " [5th September 1920] The belted galloway herd he started there became a famous breed of cattle. In Scotland today, their prize-winning descendants inhabit the farms of his great-niece, Helen Hamilton, and great-nephew, Alexander Hamilton, and his wife Sarah.

The autumn brought further joy. Jean was at last able to bring Rosaleen, now aged two years and two months, home to Lullenden. " . . . **Just awake, and had a lovely dream about little Rosaleen. Yesterday Harry and I drove to 'Three Bridges' to meet her. Molly Repington sent her Nanny to bring the child to me, Nurse White being too upset over her loss to be able to face bringing her herself – little Harry was delicious, hugging himself with the anticipated joy of her arrival, and saying at intervals 'Isn't it 'citing, Dardy.' When the rather dowdy little bundle arrived in Nannie's arms, with very tight little mouth, and large reserved eyes calmly appraising all they looked at, his joy was rather damped, but he affectionately kissed her when she was deposited on two rather unsteady little legs on the platform beside me – she did not respond, and he took one hand while I took the other, and we watched 'the puffer' hissing out steam while Nanny reclaimed her little go-cart from the van. All the way here she never uttered a word, but lay still in my arms, a light little burden, staring at Harry sitting opposite, with her great violet eyes.**

After tea however, when she was left alone with Harry in the little school-room I heard a great burst of merriment and peeping at the window saw Harry with his arm round her instructing her as to how to push the Walrus animals into the Ark. I left them together and when I came back an hour afterwards Harry had made great strides with the small dame, inquiring anxiously: 'Do you like being here with me?' and 'Do you love me, Rosaleen?' He speaks very distinctly now, and is quite a little man. I gave him a bookcase yesterday to keep his stories in, and he was delighted and said: 'I never had a bookcase before', and arranged all his fairy tales in the different shelves.

Rosaleen's birthday is the 30th June, my month – Harry's is the 30th August, so she is nearly two years younger.

She cried a little . . . on being put into the large bath last night. I wish I had told Annie not to give her a bath in the large bath, but just to sponge her, as it was too alarming for the poor mite, but as Nanny was taking charge and has great experience, I did not interfere . . . as the child is shy with me yet." [30th Sept. 1920]

It was at this time, when Rosaleen spoke her first words, that she gave herself the pet name Fodie her pronunciation presumably of Rosaleen or Rosy. " . . . Harry grows jealous of Rosaleen. This morning they both came to my room after I had breakfast; Rosaleen whimpered a little, she is still a little shy and strange with me, and whenever she goes out she thinks she ought to go in the motor car, which she *loves* – 'Make Fodie clean girl go Motor Tar' is her little whine – she is rather a sad little girl, but very sweet when she smiles. Harry wants all my attention and wants me to read him fairy tales – he don't much like this silent little girl sitting somewhat inertly on my knee, and playing with his toys. McAdie gave her his beloved Teddy Bear this morning to play with while I read 'The Blue Belt' to him but he seized both its paws in his great fat puds and said it was his, very decidedly, and after lunch when I asked Annie to bring Rosaleen to see me while he was resting, he ordered Annie to go and bring her back – he was highly displeased she should be with me. . . . " [4th October 1920]

Musta, Jean's pet dog, died and they buried it in the garden at Lullenden. " . . . All afternoon Harry helped me to arrange Musta's grave – Alfred, the hall boy and Jeffrey carried the stone down that I had engraved, to the little cemetery for pets . . . . the wood is enchanting, and little Harry and I planted ivy and rock plants about the stone.

'Is Musta in the grave, Dardie?' Harry asked in his delicious full treble – he was very troubled: 'Is he down there?' He was so sad; I said he would be all right, and we would see him in Heaven coming to meet us, and wagging his tail. He laughed and clasped my hand, reassured at that, and said: 'Won't that be nice?'

Yesterday I took him to church with me, and took Annie too, and he sat between us in his new fawn coat and lovely little golden head; at prayer he kneeled on the high hassock, with his fat little hands folded and his face screwed up in the crumpled way in which he always addresses God, and I heard him whispering:–

'Let my sins be all forgiven.
Bless the friends I love so well.
Take me when I die to Heaven,
Happy there with Thee to "gwell" '.
'My Nanny taught me that', he told me proudly when I came back
from Scotland – it was an important addition to his usual prayer
which is:-
'Jesus, tender Shepherd, hear me
Bless They little lamb to-night.
Through the darkness be Thou near me,
Keep me safe till morning light'.
Then with a tremendous swing comes – 'Bless my *d a a r l i n g D a a r
d i e* and keep her safe and well' and then with great relief and pre-
cipitancy: – 'Amen'." [4th October 1920]

Jean redesigned and replanted the gardens at Lullenden, Harry by her
side. " . . . The heavy stone work I ordered at Crowthers has come. I
am possessed with the idea of creating above the cliff a ruin that will
look like a bit of an old church. I want a romantic stair too, and long
for a cypress tree to put beside it, but I will have to be satisfied with a
yew I fear. The labourers must think me mad, jaunting about in my
corduroy breeches, and yellow and brown smock, and getting them to
cart about massive fragments of old stone." [4th October 1920]

Ian was showing signs of coming round to accepting the children. " . . .
Ian came back from Scotland to-day, and came down to Lullenden to
lunch with me – much to Harry's disappointment. . . .

I think Ian is rather taken with little Rosaleen – she is pretty, I
think, but such a sad whiney little thing, with an immovable set face.
Annie sighs rather impatiently over her sometimes, as she won't cheer
up and be gay. I rather fear it is her nature. She was always like that
at the cottage too. She looks sweet when she gives her rare smile, but
speaks with a most boring drawl at present, and with a vile accent."
[5th October 1920 Lullenden]

" . . . Rosaleen is very quiet, very still beside him [Harry], but has
her own attraction – 'Harry is a vild, vild Booy,' she says with the
neatest and most possessive accent. . . .

. . . I had great fun playing 'Hide and Seek' with them in the large
Barn room. I hid standing up against the high window behind the curtain. I was so high up I could peep at them looking for me everywhere

below, and it was a most dramatic moment when I pulled back the curtain and stood like the Virgin in a picture; they both screamed with delight, dancing about and clapping their hands. . . . " [27th October 1920 Lullenden]

" . . . Ian has just been reading his article to me on the Unknown Soldier and the Cenotaph for Armistice Day next Thursday – it is very beautiful, and I have been lying looking out on the beauty as I listened – a soft early morning sky with rose pink clouds, the sun gleaming through the Autumn leaves and interlacing stems – the fronds of yellow and orange fern on the cliff I see across my orange eiderdown from my window at the end of my long bedroom. . . .

I said to Ian I wondered this morning if we realise how happy we are now to have reached our great age – to be together – to possess all this beauty – it frightens one almost to say it, and added to this, to have my little Harry and Rosaleen.

Another perfect Autumn day with the birds all singing their swan song. . . . " [8th November 1920 Lullenden]

Jean had bought the children fur coats and they set off to Valescure for the winter. Ian had taken to calling Harry **"the young Archduke"**, and Jean had become a doting mother, though neither of the children would ever call her 'mama' or Ian 'papa'. Throughout their lives, the children always called Jean 'Guardie', short for guardian, and Ian 'Boye'. Jean's life was now that of any parent, one endless round of buying clothes and toys, arranging children's parties, looking for Santa Claus at Christmas, settling Harry and Fodie into the right schools for a young gentleman and lady and watching her two children grow up. [17th and 24th November 1920]

By 1924, Harry, now eight and a half years, could go skating with Jean. Fodie was six and a half years and Christmas meant so much more to Jean with the children looking in their stockings on Christmas morning for what Santa Claus had left. " . . . Harry has just rushed down to show me the treasures he found in his stocking. Ellen told me she heard him singing, 'I aren't nobody's darling' in his bed, so I told her to tell him to come down. He is delighted with the railway I gave him, and tells me he woke up at 12 o'clock last night and looked at his stocking –

Here is little Fodie, just awake, bringing her stocking to unpack on my bed – the angel. . . . "

Christmas Day was a lovely day of " . . . soft Spring wind and sunshine . . . " and " . . . **Ian took me out for a little walk on his arm before lunch. . . . "** It was a traditional family Christmas – well, almost: **" . . . Ian lunched at his Club, and Harry and Fodie had their Xmas dinner and plum pudding beside me near the fire, on a cosy little table in my bedroom; they looked sweet and lovely, and it was a great pleasure to lie quietly in bed and watch them there – Harry still with the remnants of his baby grace about him. . . . "**

In the afternoon, they had a Christmas Tree party and the usual quarrels between children over toys. **" . . . We had a sad little scene after lunch. Harry was keen I should see his train run on the new railway I had given him, and when I went out with Ian for a little turn in the Park his eager voice begging me to go and see it came pealing down the lift after me, but Ian would not let me go back, so when I got back and was in bed he had brought it down to my bedroom, and was busy setting it up on the floor behind the foot of my bed. Fodie was evidently interfering with him as I heard terrible sounds of impatience, and presently she was flung on the floor and either her own finger or Harry's went in her eye, and she flew into my arms a silently convulsed weeping little creature, and Harry had to be sternly dismissed up to the nursery, carrying his railway train! terribly sad and humiliated.**

When the servants' Xmas dinner was ready, no Harry came down as arranged, to stay with Fodie and me, and McAdie had to fly up to fetch him and found the poor little fellow weeping heart-brokenly on a chair, everything matters so terribly to Harry. . . . "

However, everyone enjoyed the Christmas Tree party and **" . . . the children adored it, and the tree looked lovely – three trees we had – one large, two small and a mirror on the floor in front of the trees to reflect the lights, with swans and fish floating on it, the trees were lit up with electric light. . . . "** [Xmas Day 1924]

Having a son growing up filled Jean with dread of war and killing. **" . . . I thought of the poor boys shot for desertion in the war, poor young hearts and nerves ruined and shattered by the awful sight they saw. . . . "** [6th January 1925 Deanston]

In 1925, **"sweet little Fodie"**, now aged seven, was sent to board at Miss Griffiths' School. **[15th October 1925]** Christmas became the highlight of the year, when the family were all together. Ian had come round and was now in the role of a doting guardian to the children, who bright-

ened up Christmas for him and he joined in the festivities. **" . . . a jolly
children's party inside – Xmas Tree and dancing – all the children,
Harry and Fodie, love and no smarties and it all went so well that Ian
said it was one of the best we ever had. Harry and Fodie were very
good as host and hostess. Fodie was dressed as a fairy in pink net with
silver wings and rosebuds, and little Barbara Warre to match, stood
on each side of the tree, which we had in the green drawing room. I
quite enjoyed it. Ian was cross at the end because I would not dance
with him.**

**Harry and Fodie are stuffed full of presents – too excited almost to
look at the parcels they were opening so eagerly, as they were always
looking at the next and thanking Boye and me. . . . "** [Xmas Day 1925
London]

The only complaint Jean could make was that Ian now spoilt the children terribly, which undoubtedly brought her great delight. Harry aged ten
and Fodie aged eight were old enough to organise their own parties and
invite their friends to No. 1 HPG. Jean's guests were Dorothy Grosvenor,
Evan Charteris, Lord Hugh Cecil, Alice and George Keppel, and Boggie
Harris. Jean thought the butler announced that lunch was served **" . . . and
down we all trooped. . . ."** But the food wasn't ready **" . . . and nothing
happened for ages. . . . "** To amuse the children, **" . . . Alice Keppel and
I simultaneously began to tell the story of 'Holiday House' from our
childhood's days. Fortunately just at the end of our tale, the Scotch
eggs promised on the Menu appeared. . . . "** [25th February 1927
London] The sight of Alice Keppel telling children's stories would have
surprised Violet, her daughter, who claimed the only 'Once upon a time'
she remembered as a little girl was when she was 'usually exhibited when
coffee was served' to the King, to whom she had to curtsy.[12]

The children were fast growing up and were both at boarding school,
mixing with young people of their own age and finding their independence. When they returned to Jean and Ian there was a generation gap and
Jean could not grasp that the children now related more closely to their
own age group. **" . . . Going back to Deanston . . . today and glad to be
going. . . . I feel like a fish out of water here. I feel terrified by the complete neglect and indifference of the young; I was glad I had arranged
Harry should leave before I came, as I felt afraid. He loves being here
and I am very grateful for their kindness to Harry, but I felt him very
estranged and difficult on Saturday when I sent for him to come and**

play golf with me at Dunblane. I seem to have lost my influence over Harry and Fodie now – I don't think they love me any more – they are getting drawn into the current, and becoming children of the age, and often fear now they will accentuate, and not alleviate, the loneliness of my old age. I am too old for them, and don't find the joy I thought I would find in seeing them happy and giving them pleasure – but then, I don't *see* them – all their joys are away with other children, and they don't even tell me about it. 'Yes, Guardie,' 'No, Guardie,' is all I elicit with questions. I used to adore seeing Harry play with other little children when he was little – used to laugh when Nanny Sedgewick warned me I had undertaken a great responsibility. I thought I should always feel the same tenderness and delight in them – they were so loveable and loving in those happy days. [10th September 1928 Braco]

The fact that Harry and Fodie had maternal parents somewhere always nagged at the back of Jean's mind. The threat remained that the children might be taken from her or be subjected to blackmail. Fodie now attended the prestigious St James's School, West Malvern, and approaching adulthood brought new concerns. Phyllis Holman, Fodie's godmother, was getting married. " . . . Worried greatly over this letter from my little Fodie asking me to let her be bridesmaid to her Godmother, Phyllis Holman, but have now written her to say 'No:' saying it would be a pity to ask a favour of her, her first month at her new school at Malvern. (She wrote me how delighted she was to be there). Also that her Godmother will have now got someone else. I did not give her my other two reasons – one that possibly some of her Mother's friends, or at any rate some who knew her sad story might be at the wedding and her Mother might see a picture of the wedding and Fodie's picture, and also I want to keep Fodie as free as possible from future complications, she might not care for Phyllis Holman, when she grows up, but I *hate* to disappoint the child.

Went to a concert . . . in Stirling yesterday: . . . A miner's daughter, Jean Day sang an exquisite song, 'Like a Lovely Flower' – it was an aspiration as the pure young notes floated upwards, and I thought of my little flower, Fodie, and breathed a prayer that she might be kept 'unspotted from the world'. What a world of license that my two little pets are entering into – all the old restraints gone. The books today are terrifying, and, to me, disgusting. I must take back to Lord Esher to-day 'Mr. Weston's Good Wine' – it revolts, and yet there is

a kind of animal coarse morality and wisdom in it, but I can't read it.
... " [5th October 1928]

At No. 1 HPG jazz bands blared on the wireless from morning till night. Fodie had taken up dancing, no doubt influenced by Ian, and the two of them danced and jazzed about the house together. " . . . **Fodie danced to the gramophone. . . . It was a wonderful performance and I was really delighted with it, such spontaneous grace and inspiration, moving naturally to the music, inventing steps and gesture. She has taught herself and she danced again this evening for Mother, Ian watching her with keen delight appreciating every movement. He adores dancing and is infatuated with the child. . . .**

. . . He spoils her terribly, but she is very sweet and good and charming to me and I love having both children here.

. . . Ian wants to have Fodie trained as a dancer. I wonder? it's not a life I would choose for her, but she evidently adores it and has genius, bless her! . . . she and Harry are so happy together. . . . " [17th August 1929 Deanston]

When Fodie was fifteen it was time for her to be sent to a finishing school. Switzerland was the favoured location of many well-connected families for their daughters. Jean sent Fodie to Germany, partly because that was her choice, to be with her friend Princess Priscilla Bibesco, the daughter of Elizabeth Asquith. But it was also greater assurance for Jean that she would not come into contact with anyone who might know her real parents, a threat which remained all the greater whilst Fodie lived in England. Fodie's ambition was to become an actress and film star, and in September 1933, she sailed to Germany to join Priscilla at Countess Harrack's School in Munich. When at home, Fodie had spent some time at Priscilla's house, where she was influenced by her mother, Elizabeth, who wrote short stories, plays, novels and poetry.

" . . . **I was delighted to get a nice interesting letter from Fodie yesterday morning – she does not mention the sea so it could not have been so very rough.**

Ellen told Ian she seemed a little sad at leaving and said: 'Even if Boye and Guardie are dead I will send you and Annie good seats for the first film I am a success in,' – so her mind is still set on films and it gave me a cold shiver that she could say so lightly: 'if Boye and Guardie are dead' – I could never have contemplated the thought of anyone I loved being dead or even when my darling little Mother was

nearing her end have voiced such a thought and it hurts – I so passionately have hoped to see her first success, if she does go on the
stage, but I have lately ceased to think she will, as I can see no sign in
her of creative art, nor will she try to get her walk right or hold herself straight though I have tried and tried to tell her the importance of
this on the stage. She might be so lovely but her bones are getting set
into these ungraceful lines – but it is the way of the young to be wilful
now and in this she goes with the herd. Her summary to Ellen of the
situation was that 'Boye and Guardie fussed and Nanny sulked' when
she was leaving North Berwick.

Ian says it's the Irish character – to be cold and hard at core,
though emotional on the surface – she has never been emotional to me
even on the surface, though I do remember a sweet saying of hers to
me at Lullenden when she was a child and said: She wanted to marry
me so she never would have to leave me. . . . " [1st October 1933]

Contrary to Jean's instincts about war, Harry, now aged seventeen,
was attending Wellington College (of which Ian was a governor), a
preparatory school for the Royal Military Academy, Sandhurst. Jean was
ambitious for Harry's future but as with Fodie, the spectre of his relations
haunted her. " . . . I want to speak to Lawrence Drummond who is here,
about Harry going into the Scots Guards, which he wants to do. Ian
thinks it shows want of ambition and enterprise on his part but I think
Harry has neither and would be happier in a regiment with good
friends and I think the Scots Guards would be as good as any other
regiment and would keep him near me – I don't want him drafted off
to India as soon as he joins and never to see him again, but when I
woke at 4.30 I was assailed by terrors of his being black-mailed – I
can't forget that awful woman at Dunblane who called out to me so
threateningly and mockingly: 'Harry Knight!' when I was walking in
the street with Nora. Harry had been mentioned in the papers as
shooting on the 12th with Kay and I can't help sometimes feeling terrified for my two children – Harry about his career and Fodie about
her marriage and if she wanted to go to Court. I feel I could deal with
Harry's Mother if I were here to protect him. I would threaten her but
he would be rather helpless if she could prove she was really his
Mother, and she might bleed him white and ruin him – but these were
dismal midnight thoughts and now I want to go on with it and ham-
mer away at Ian to write to General Codrington. It is very difficult to

get him to move in the matter and he wants me, I see, to ask Lawrence Drummond to get his name put down, but I only intend to ask Lawrence to speak up for Harry if he is referred to and to ask his permission to use him as a reference. I feel a certain excitement in living dangerously and love to go for the big thing. Harry might easily get into some less swagger regiment from Sandhurst but I am determined to have a try for him to get into the Scots Guards. I wanted Ian to get him into the Gordons but he would do nothing about it as he said he must have Scotch relations to go into the Gordons." [22nd October 1933]

Harry and Fodie were now teenagers and living away from home permanently, though they would visit frequently. " . . . Fodie is writing me charming letters, they are so very interesting, they make me long to answer her at once, which would bore her. I hope I have done right in sending her to Countess Harrack's so young – she is having too much freedom I fear for 15, but she is old for her age, quite as old now as I was at 17, older in many ways, and she has always had perfect self control and a will of iron." [31st October 1933 London] Harry surprised Jean and Ian by doing rather better at school than they expected, especially in his cadet training. Writing to Jean in January 1934, he told her: " . . . I passed Cert 'A' exam fourth in the school. . . . " It looked as if his army career was assured.

CHAPTER 13

Jean: Artist and Poet

"No prouder name than Anzac will ever warrior bear"
[From Lady Hamilton's poem 'Anzac', 1916]

Whilst Jean was still a bride, the Hamiltons had taken a holiday in London. They spent time with Vereker and Lilian, who lived at St John's Wood, the artistic centre of the day, where they had a studio. Vereker and Lily influenced Jean artistically and along with their artist friends Charles and Bill Furse, Charles Gore, and the young H. G. Wells, they frequented the Eyre Arms pub in Baker Street.

The portraits of Jean by John Swan and Singer Sargent were followed by studies by Sir John Lavery; Charles Furse, who painted Jean wearing a cloak designed by Worth of Paris; the Norwegian, Carlo Schultz, who sketched her in an Indian scarf; and Von Blaas, who sketched her in a crinoline gown. The gleaming white satin of the gown Jean wore in her portrait by Singer Sargent radiated against the jade green walls of her drawing room. There were pictures of Venice by Walter Sickert, a leading member of the Camden School of English painters. Bakst's designs for the Russian Ballet were modified to conform to the colour scheme of the bathroom. In 1915, when Ian went to Gallipoli, the prestigious magazine *The Sketch*, printed a two-page spread dedicated to Jean, the centrepiece of which was her portrait by Singer Sargent (1896), under the heading 'Still the Portrait of the Year'. Jean, 'like her husband, a figure of romance', was seated in a wonderfully painted gilt chair which seemed 'carried into new etherealness by the sitter; and the pearls which she decked, were the most picked row of all in the Sargent paint-box, the oyster he alone opens.' In 'that lovely portrait, the painter achieved more than a personal record – he commemorated a type – and let Scotland listen and rejoice.'[23]

Singer Sargent was one of Jean's earliest friends. **" . . . I had a most interesting talk with Mr. Sargent about his work for the Boston Library, talking about Symbolism in painting; he was more inarticu-**

late than ever, and yet made me understand his meaning in some wonderful way, waving his hands and rolling his eyes in his own special manner; he said his Madonna must not show any personal self-conscious feeling, she must stand for a great idea, that it would be wrong and a lowering of the idea to make her express any ideas of her own: the same with the Christ, who must express nothing beyond the Divine made human – he wishes to paint the Child in the act of being born, with already His little hand outstretched to bless – he does not wish to paint just a Mother and Child, as that would be a mere re-representation of what has been done hundreds and hundreds of times before, but he is nervous about shocking his public. I said Blake had done something like this, I had a copy of it, which Sargent said he'd like to see. He went on to tell me the Early Masters represented a Madonna with seven swords in her heart, the swords represent agony and many terrible things, but it would be wrong to make her face express this, or be contorted in any way: so with the St. Sebastian, he ought to have a serene impassive look though stuck all over with darts. I have often laughed over this, as it seemed absurd to me but I wonder.

I said without having clearly grasped the symbolic idea, 'But lovers? Would you represent them kissing one another, the mere action of the kiss – all the lovers' expression, attitude, feeling – nothing? And he answered, 'Yes – for *symbolic* painting, certainly that would be enough.' 'But it would be dull,' I objected. He smiled slightly and his smile stung me, it seemed to show me how much I missed his thought. He said, 'It is not dull, but of course, you would think it inartistic.' " [December 6th 1903, 3 Chesterfield St.]

Years later, when Jean attended a silver show at Philip Sassoon's house, which also included paintings, the Sargent room brought back memories of the time when he painted her portrait. " . . . it's a vast display of gorgeous silver of every date, laid out on priceless Venetian velvets: the whole house redolent of Eastern splendour . . . the Sargent room . . . is hung with Mr. Sargent's favourite colours, blue and Venetian red – he once pointed them out to me on a sword handle, and must have done to Philip S. as the room is hung with pale blue velvet and the chairs all Venetian red velvet: there are twelve wonderful Sargents there and they are magnificently treated. . . . " [7th March 1929 London]

Jean was influenced by Walter Sickert, whose work she admired and whom she met for the first time in 1904, whilst staying at the home of a friend, Mr Williamson, during a holiday in Venice. Sickert's photographs portray him as modern, youthful and irresistibly good-looking. Influenced by Degas, he was known for his etchings and paintings, having studied at the Slade School and worked with James McNeill Whistler for several years.

" . . . **This enchanting old Palazzo fascinates me as much as ever, and the garden is enchanting – it's delightful to wake up and listen to the spring birds – how I love them, 'All that ever was joyous and fresh and sweet speak to me in their notes.'**

. . . Ian is wildly happy in Japan and I have made the acquaintance of Walter Sickert! he is coming to lunch today! He is a wild Impressionistic artist whose acquaintance I've always wanted to make since I heard he advertised in the 'Morning Post' that 'he had had the honour of having two pictures rejected by the Royal Academy. . . . " [4th May 1904, Palazzo Capello, Rio Marin, Venice]

Whilst riding in a gondola with her sister Edie and friends on the canal at Burano, which Jean was sketching, another gondola had came up carrying Walter Sickert and Blanche, the French artist, and his wife. They stopped and Jean's " . . . **first impression of Walter Sickert with his head thrown back recalled Browning's lines on 'Waring'. He was lazily lounging in the gondola by the side of the brisk, cut-and-dried and very French, Madame Blanche, hatted, veiled and gloved; what a beautiful humorous face has Walter Sickert. . . . "**

Sickert came to visit the following Sunday, where Jean and her party were having tea in the garden. " . . . **turning I saw coming towards us, through the light and shade of the long pergola, the charming figure of Walter Sickert. . . . I got up at once and went to meet him, and felt immediately I had known him a long while. . . . "** The tea was cold and Jean was glad as it gave her an opportunity to have him to herself: " . . . **it gave us the excuse to walk away under the lovely pergola from the tiresome party to the canal, to order tea. . . . "** When the others " . . . **at last departed I took him up to our wonderful Salla and into our little drawing room, and I sat in a favourite chair, opposite the window looking over the red roofs and talked to him. . . . We talked of Ventnor, and of Charlie Furse and the new English Art Club, where I used to see his work . . . . "**

Jean was due to leave soon to return home but extended her holiday, gaining many more happy hours with the charismatic Sickert. " . . . **The Walter Sickert lunch was a great success. I like him much better than anyone else I have met in Venice; he wore the most ridiculous baggy trousers I have ever seen – he wears them in Dieppe, he says. He has a charming way of saying things, and a delightful quizzical face; he tells me none of the brutal facts of life bother him at all – he 'would not mind having to kill and eat raw flesh' this seems to me unlikely with his face, but it interested me; he says nothing in life disgusts him I wonder! He strikes me as refined, even fastidious, with a very distinct quality of distinction in everything he says and does. He says that when one tries life it is all interesting, and that nothing is really ugly, it depends on the point of view.**

We went to see the Tiepolos at the Libini Palazzo . . . – splendid frescoes of Anthony and Cleopatra – I liked them better than any-thing I have seen in Venice; a magnificent courtly Cleopatra and a most grand Anthony – superb gestures – she is quite Venetian. I have been reading 'Anthony and Cleopatra' this morning:-

> **'Of many thousand kisses the poor last**
> **I lay upon thy lips.**
>
> **– – – – – –**
>
> **I am dying, Egypt, dying:'**

It's a wonderful story, I should like to see Sarah [Bernhardt] **act it. . . . "** **[6th May 1904 Palazzo Capello]**

John Alfred Spender of the *Westminster Gazette* dined and the con-versation turned to Ian and the Russo-Japanese War: " . . . **The Japanese have gained a great land victory on the Yalu on May 1st. Mr. Spender speaking of the delight of living in Venice touched on the absence of those one loved. 'That is holy ground,' Walter Sickert said, and would not discuss it. . . . "** **[6th May 1904** contd.]

Jean suffered an asthma attack and had to be carried up and down the stairs by Marco, a servant, and did not see Sickert for a few days. " . . . **Mr. Sickert has come every day to ask for me, and to-day I was moved into the drawing room for tea, and wore Edie's pretty blue tea gown, and he came and had tea with us, and stayed a long time. He brought me a sketch of a church which I liked only passably, I wish he had given me something I really liked. . . . "** **[10th May 1904** contd.]

Jean " . . . went to tea with the Montalbas, and saw Clara Montalba's lovely water colours. There was one of the Campanile and St. Mark's, a most poetical conception of it, in a holy white still light. . . . " Mr Williamson had a library and in one of the books Jean found a " . . . delightful essay on Cleopatra by Anatole France . . . . " [7th May 1904 Palazzo Capello]

" . . . Walter Sickert came yesterday afternoon. . . . He looked charming in a checked blue shirt and old-fashioned tie, like an old print of some delightful author I have never seen – a mixture of Shelley, Keats and Lamb; the teapot handle was hot and when he poured out tea for himself he had to pull out his pocket-handkerchief, which was a common checked one so incongruous with the distinction with which it was used – a distinction which marks all he does – it was a pleasure to see him sit down at the tea table and have tea. He attracts me greatly, he is the only interesting man I have met since coming abroad. I wonder if I really like him and want to go on, or if it is only a passing fancy? However what does it matter, 'Gather ye rosebuds whilst ye may,' and I should like to 'say to the moment, "stay" '. It's wonderful having found him here – a great relief. . . . " [14th May 1904 Palazzo Capello]

Sickert brought her " . . . a charming little sketch . . . of an Italian girl, that reminded me of what Edie used to be. He is an interesting milieu – knew Mallarmi [Mallarmé] a little, was a friend of Whistler's, and has read a great deal, knows Arthur Symons and mixes in Paris with, I imagine, a very Bohemian and interesting set. He *never* comes to London, has not been there for five years. . . . I feel I have so much to say to him and no time to say it.

I arranged my hair rather like his little sketch this afternoon, and it rather suited me. Only to sit in the drawing room was full of attraction – the light there then had a peculiar fascination, and the swallows flew about the old Palazzo with shrill cries – the sadness of parting was there." [14th May 1904 contd.]

Jean's asthma grew worse and she was taking morphine. Still unable to climb the stairs, she was being carried up and down by Marco. The doctor blamed the climate for her asthma and advised her to leave Venice. But Jean was intrigued by Sickert and his visits continued. " . . . **Mr. Sickert said yesterday afternoon . . . that people had a habit of addressing him in a jocular sort of free and easy way, he supposed because he had** been divorced, and because he painted Music Hall pictures, and he particularly objected to it, being a rather sad and serious individual – it was rather a shock to hear he had been divorced. . . .

The other evening he spoke of his wife having written 'Wistons', and George Moore having thought it clever, he said this with evident pleasure, and when I gave him Walt Whitman's 'Out of the Cradle' to read, he shut up the book quickly, with a look of pain, and said 'it came too near' him, and I think he meant the lovely lines of 'The seamew to his mate.' I fancy he has treated her badly, and is now much in love with her, and longs to have her back. I wonder what his story is." [May 16th 1904 Palazzo Capello]

" . . . Yesterday the garden was enchanting, full of exquisite sunshine, shadow, and the colour of flowers. I was happily painting there when I was surprised by Walter Sickert; this agitated me, as I did not want him to see what I was doing, but he insisted as he said he might be able to help me, and he said it was 'not bad', but I could not bear him to look at what I did though I do think I had got *something* as he added 'you can't arrive at anything like that without hard work'.

Clara Montalba came in directly, and we then had tea in the lovely garden – it was enchanting. Walter Sickert looked terribly ragged and forlorn, and wore an *awful* hat, I was glad when he took it off; he is terribly poor, I am afraid. He is 'the beloved vagabond'; he showed me his Music Hall sketches in the Yellow Book; they are full of go and life I can see, but did not please me, and I did not know what to say to them. I long to understand and care for his work, which absorbs him – the one thing he lives for.

After Miss Montalba had gone he insisted on carrying me upstairs as Marco was not there . . . this was exciting, but distressed me as I felt it was too much for him; it was a terrible strain and he would not put me down, and was so pleased because he managed to carry me to the top – three flights of steep stair. . . . " [May 17th 1904 Palazzo Capello]

Jean and Sickert met for the last time when they went to tea with the de Meyers. Jean could see that Sickert " . . . admires the Baroness. . . . " Edie " . . . filled all the rooms with roses . . . ", which were " . . . out in masses everywhere in the garden. . . . " The Baroness de Meyer was a "cool sweet little" woman, " . . . looking like a green lettuce in her delicious green linen dress, she is a poem, accompanied by her funny little Baron. . . . She likes him [Sickert] I saw by the gleam in her mysterious eyes, he has known her since she was sixteen, and knew her Mother well. . . ." Sickert told Jean that King Edward VII and others, including a Polish gentleman, were lovers of the Baroness's mother, and Sickert " . . . thinks **Olga de Meyer is the daughter of this Pole, because she has an intelligence exactly like his; he says King Edward thinks she is his daughter, and is pleased to think he has so clever and intellectual a child!** . . .

. . . Marco carried me up, and I put on my little white wrapper, and then had quite a thrilling talk in the half-dark of the delicious little rose-filled salon with Walter Sickert, who had followed me to have a last talk.

He told me to-night what I had guessed, that his life is absorbed in another's – like myself I could not ask, though I think he wished to tell me. I had asked him if he would like to live again, and he walked about the room, and said 'it sounded sentimental – ridiculous – but as we were talking seriously it was like this, that his life depended on another's, he only lived through her – if she lived again, he would wish to live again, if she died now, he would wish to die', etc., etc. I asked if he felt certain of always feeling like this, and he seemed surprised, and said 'it was no question of feeling – it was his existence – he had no other', etc. etc. A great many extravagant things he said which surprised me. I said I had heard men say these things before – he said 'one could only express what one felt at the moment, and that was how he felt,' he included however 'that although absorbed in love like that, he often fell in love with other people, people he knew little about and saw seldom, and asked nothing from.' From this worshipper of common sense this surprised me, and I said, 'That is your German temperament;' he said, 'Perhaps' and I laughed and said he was like Shelley, who thought 'the more he loved the more love he had to give', and he answered quite seriously, 'Precisely, that is just it.' . . . "

A servant came in and lit the lamp. " . . . the swallows uttered their piercing restless cries as they swept past the open window behind me. . . . and then Edie came in . . . .

He said, 'You see you can't get rid of me,' – he had said a final good-bye to her an hour before, but still he sat on, moving over to the corner by the fire, opposite me and I felt happy conscious of his eyes watching me as I talked to Edie. . . .

. . . After he had gone Edie and I leaned out of the window and looked at the new crescent moon, shining over the roofs and lights of Venice – cool, luminous, dewey, and full of dreams. . . . " [17th and 18th May 1904 Palazzo Capello, Venice]

The cultural holiday of a lifetime was drawing to a close and Jean and Edie were on their return journey, staying at the Grand Hotel, Vittoria. " . . . Talking to Mr. Sickert that last evening in Venice, I told him he had been quite wrong when he said 'there was no such thing possible as un-returned love'. . . . I said the feeling he alluded to as often as not produced antagonism in the other. I was rather struck with his reply; he said, 'Well, if it was so, it was because one made a mistake, as if one should think he was drinking champagne and found suddenly it was *ink*.' He was very expressive when he said this – I should think he soon dashed the ink away. . . . " [May 21st 1904 Grand Hotel, Vittoria]

"Enchanting happy day all through. I awoke with a delicious feeling of health again, though I am very weak. I tried to sketch the thunderstorm last night, which amused me. It was not very successful, but I got a sort of look of it as I remember it. . . .

. . . To-night after diner I walked out into the little Square with Edie, and on into the garden lying round the white statue of Garibaldi – the moon looked very mysterious behind clouds, the mountains black and sinister. Sitting there in the soft darkness I realised I was growing old, that life was passing me by! – I had only to stretch out my hand to love again vividly, but I could not! Why? – *peur de vivre* – loyalty to Ian – dislike to froisé Edie – distrust of my own sensations – what prevented me? I don't know – my guardian angel – perhaps? In plain English I was tempted to write and ask Walter Sickert to join us here but I won't. . . . " [May 22nd 1904 Vittoria]

Jean possessed that ability to view people and scenery with the eye of an artist. " . . . Coming back from our drive to-night the little town of Vittoria was so gay, with the band playing in the Square – 'Lucia de Lammermoor'. . . . " [22nd May 1904]

" . . . The people delight me here, as no people of any place have ever done before, they have such charming ways and clothes – they rush to greet one with such bonhomie, *never* begging, and sure of their welcome – the way they carry water and everything, with a long bent stick over their shoulders and coloured copper vessels balanced on either side is lovely . . . the harmonious blues, browns and greys of their clothes, their happy, good animal faces – all is enchanting – 'no lying awake and crying over their sins', no scheming and pushing to get on – there is no sign of the 'struggle for life' here. . . . " [24th May 1904]

" . . . The times when I have found men and women impressive has always been by something very simple and unexpected – a group of old peasants praying in the fading light in the old Cathedral here the other night impressed me far more than the worshipping crowds in St. Peter's – I was not expecting to be impressed, not crammed with 'reach-me-down' sensations – it is the things one finds out for oneself that are thrilling." [25th May 1904 Vittoria]

Jean and Edie moved on to romantic Verona, setting for Shakespeare's *Romeo and Juliet*, and stayed in the Hotel de Londre. " . . . Edie and I went to see the famous Georgione, Lord Alwyne's favourite picture – he has often told me of it. We were rather disappointed with it, not the rich colouring I expected. I liked the men in armour and the face of the Virgin, and the composition, and am glad to have seen it as Lord Alwyne loves it. We then drove as near to Asolo as we could, and I made a sketch of it from a wheat field, where we had tea; where the contadini much bored us, though they are a delightful people. . . .

It was a lovely tender afternoon of half-lights – soft mauves and pinks and greys, and we were very happy, but both sad thinking it was our last day together. I have loved having Edie. She is an ideal companion – delicious to be with, sweet-tempered and reliable, her beauty is a constant joy." [May 26th 1904]

Jean had seen both the drama and the opera of *Romeo and Juliet*, which was one of her favourite plays, in all the grandeur of the London theatre. It was disappointing to her to find that the 'real' Romeo and Juliet had not enjoyed such splendour and that little had been done to endear the site as a tourist attraction. " . . . To-day we visited Juliet's tomb and looked on her house and Romeo's, which were indeed disillusioning – small and somewhat mean-looking, and they both immediately took a much lower place in my imagination, and I seemed to see quite a squalid love-story; it will take many Operas, with lovely gardens and balconies, to sweep away this impression. Juliette's tomb also was disillusioning; we had to pass through a gigantic stable, like a London barrack-yard, to get to it – a stone canopy was over the tomb, which was filled with dirty visiting cards. . . . " [May 27th 1904 Verona]

When they arrived in Paris there was an exhibition of Sickert's work at Bernheimer's Gallery and Jean bought two of his paintings of St. Mark's, Venice. [**May 31st 1904**]

Back in London, Jean wrote to Sickert, who replied:

> I went to Paris and to Munich thanks for your letter. Since then, Blanche tells me you have bought some of my pictures. I wonder which. Just the thought of their being yours, but if you had asked me I would have told you of better things you might have got in Paris. Did you see my exhibition there? What impression did it make on you? . . . I miss you very much here. You are so kind to me. It was fun to join you regularly at the Rio Maria. . . . You must not take my opinions or half-opinions as having all been confirmed. One sometimes says things, as it were, to please a lady or from a hesitation to come at once to close quarters on every subject. I had with you at once that delightful feeling of being at home in your soul. Now when one is quite at home the contentment is so great that one's *first* instinct is not, as the peasants say in France 'de profiter avec' . . . . But to turn one's face away to the wall and say 'Oh don't ask me to say anything. We have *so* much time, and it is *so* good to be here just now let me sleep. I feel so *safe* and so comfortable. Do I like Shelley? No! As far as I can remember. At least not yet. . . . I . . . saw the Giottos and the Monteverdis again. I have discovered the loveliest picture in Venice, Catena's St. Christina in the church of the Mater Dominici. If I can get a good photograph I will send it to you. . . .[2]

Sickert came to London and Jean dined with him at her club, the Ladies' Athenaeum. "**. . . I liked him and have asked him to Tidworth; he has sent me a huge most wonderful fearsome picture of a vulgar woman in a violet crinoline. . . . I don't know where the devil to hang her – she affronts me and yet there is something I rather like in the colour, despite the brutal treatment. . . .**" [**Sunday July 30th 1905 Bramley Park** home of the Beaumonts] But when she saw Sickert again in 1907 and 1908, the old romance of Venice had faded. He was wearing glasses and, for Jean, that meant he had lost his sex appeal.

The First World War brought them together again. In 1914 Sickert was in London, wanting to become a war artist, and he wrote to Jean, reminding her of their time in Italy, when he carried her up several flights of stairs to her room.

. . . I was wondering whether with all your gondoliers in the trenches you were wanting my arm to carry you upstairs! . . . As to the war it is dark work for anyone who is not in the trenches. If I had only had the sense to be a territorial years ago I might have made a good soldier. I suppose an eye for drawing is an eye for shooting. We were in Dieppe during the mobilisation and cleared out when a German aeroplane flew over Dieppe. We were within a motor-visit of the Germans 'Ils sont à Rombaix' [They are at Rombaix] the Dieppois said. . . .[3]

" . . . Walter Sickert dined to-night, and Lord Haldane – just we four, and we had an interesting evening. Lord Haldane and Ian discussed the war very freely; Walter Sickert was thrilled, and rather relieved, he said to me afterwards over the boudoir fire: 'Well, anyway you don't take me for a German spy.' I really think as he has a foreign name he was feeling nervous. . . . " [21st October 1914]

A newspaper article described Sickert as 'a chronicler of the vanished music-hall, of middle-class and low-life interiors, he has looked with shrewd, amused, but not unkindly eye on aspects of the half-world and under-world. . . .'[4]

Jean's recollection of meeting Sickert was as two subjects in a painting: **" . . . there was a sketch in water colour of the pergola in Mr. Williamson's garden, in Venice, which really was good. I had watched Walter Sickert walk down that pergola into my life. . . . "** [5th October 1926 Lullenden]

By the 1930s Sickert was living in London, having made his name as an artist and become an Associate of the Royal Academy. His etchings were on exhibition. Jean saw everyone with the critical eye of a perfectionist. The personal appearance of artists and how they dressed was often more in keeping with their bohemian lifestyle than the immaculate works of art they produced, which hung on the walls of the art galleries or graced the homes of their patrons. Many years had passed since Jean last saw Sickert. His appearance was positively eccentric though his outlook on life was as optimistic as ever. Now aged sixty-nine, he had married again a few years earlier. **" . . . Went to the nicest party I have been to for years at Burlington House last night, given by Mrs. Chamberlain – everyone there. . . .**

Margot [Asquith] **looked terrific in a bright scarlet gown and**

Walter Sickert, who suddenly accosted me, looked like the old man of the sea with the long strands of beard, puffy cheeks and chuckling eyes, his head looked shaved with the hairs standing up. I gazed at him in horror and he said: 'You don't know me.' I said 'No, I don't. I have never seen you in my life before,' when suddenly a tone in his voice brought a recollection of the beautiful Walter Sickert – was a shock, and I asked: 'Are you Walter Sickert? and why are you here? The first thing that interested me about you was an advertisement in 'The Times' 'Mr. Walter Sickert has had the honour of having two pictures refused by the Royal Academy and here you are an A.R.A. associating with R.A.'s. . . .

I wore my old velvet gown now trimmed with fur – it's dowdy but rather suits me. I rejoiced I had not embarked in a remarkable new dress as Ian wished, when I saw how awful my contemporaries looked." [13th February 1930 London]

In 1938, Eric Newton said in a newspaper article about Sickert that for all his 'clowning' there was nothing in which he was 'more serious' than in his 'craftsmanship'. Describing the influence photography had produced on his art, he wrote: 'If a snapshot of himself emerging from the wine-cellar with a bottle under each arm can be turned into a charming study in green and brown called "Home Life" . . . then the camera has not been invented for nothing. . . . '[5]

When Jean was disenchanted with the problems of managing a large house at Tidworth she sought solace in painting, and she came to appreciate the beauty of the countryside through nature, particularly in flowers and birds. **"The air is full of the scent of the limes and the fields of flowers." [Aug. 1st 1906 Tidworth]** In the spring she would sit in the wood and paint pastels of primroses and daffodils and, in the summer, fields of poppies. Visits to the homes of others also provided the opportunity to paint. When staying with the de Rothschilds she sat **" . . . under the trees this morning, doing a pastel of the lovely daffodils in the sunshine, with the birds all round singing their very sweetest songs, I struggled hard to forget myself and be in the mood." [Sunday April 8th 1906 Ascot Wing]** Having started out hating Tidworth, she came to find it **" . . . so delicious here; I wake up to the joyous singing of birds every morning, and the shadowy beauty of the sunshine." [March 17th 1908 Tidworth]**

During the time the Hamiltons lived at San Antonio Palace, Malta

(1910–1914), Jean painted several fine pastels, including studies of Valetta Harbour, the beautiful Garden at San Antonio Palace, and the romantic San Antonio Palace[6] itself. These comprise a few of the many pastels she painted, copies of which have survived.

Jean and Ian were holidaying at Postlip Hall, in the tranquillity of the Gloucestershire countryside. Jean was hoping to **" . . . practise the piano and do pastels, and wander about in the Spring." [27th May 1916]** The weather was glorious and the garden full of tulips. Winston Churchill was coming to stay, and it was with some trepidation Jean anticipated his arrival. **" . . . Ian is motoring down with _Winston_ to-day, who comes to stay with us till Monday – rather alarming. I wonder how I shall like having him here. . . . " [27th May 1916]** Even when discussing matters of great moment, Winston had his paints and brushes with him. **" . . . Winston has arrived and is walking under my window with Ian, his easel in his hand, on painting bent. He is talking busily, I can hear of 2nd line units, and 3rd line units – now I have just stuck my head out of the window to say good morning to him. . . . He wants to paint the house, which he thinks quite perfect, and says he can do two pictures in a day.**

Ian tells me Winston was frightfully interested in Carlo Norway's pictures, the blue purple sitting-room is hung with the ones I selected and sent down to Will and Clara last year. I have brought my pastels to copy the duck one." [28th May 1916 Postlip Hall]

At last Jean and Winston were brought together by their mutual love of art, and in total harmony they painted pictures together. **" . . . it was great fun having Winston painting here like mad all day. He is rather wonderful, very sincere and direct in his work, and paints like light-ning, he loves being watched and being told how it is going all the time. He painted two pictures – one of the house which I instantly copied in pastel, and one of the view from the front of the house. He would not leave his painting of the glowing pink hawthorn to come in for tea, and we had to get another brew – Ian and I were sitting under the hawthorn, Ian discontented because he wanted to lie in the full sun. . . . " [29th May 1916 Postlip Hall]**

Winston's paintings enthused Jean's efforts with pastels, particularly a picture of the house and a detail of the interior, which she finished in London. **" . . . Got up at 7 a.m. to finish the gaily coloured fighting par-rots – pastel I was doing from a Jap panel hanging in Clara's bath-**

room. . . . " [4th June 1916 London] She also brought Winston's paintings of Postlip Hall with her when she returned to London, presumably for
inspiration, as she thought they were " . . . **ever so good and he is very
excited over them – he helped me too with a pastel I did of Postlip."**
[5th June 1916 London]

France was a favourite holiday destination with the Hamiltons and in
March 1920 Jean was staying in the Cap Martin Hotel. " . . . **It's lovely
here, warm sunshine and brilliant flowers everywhere, the stone pines
and blue sea are an intoxication! I have been longing to see olives,
stone pines, mimosa and cypress trees again. . . . "** [21st March 1920]
At Valescure she explored some ground owned by Lady Amherst and
thought of buying it " . . . **the old, old olive trees fascinated me, a sort of
tender melancholy hangs about the place and touched me. . . . "** [31st
March 1920] A love of olive trees was something Jean shared with
Winston, and she painted a picture of sheep browsing amongst olive trees,
Sheep at Cap Martin (undated). Winston painted an *Olive Grove at La
Dragonnière, Cap Martin*,[7] rather similar in content and style to Jean's
picture, though Winston's use of colour is much stronger.

In April, Jean and Ian were staying with Ettie and Willie Desborough
at Panshanger, their country home in Hertfordshire. The Desboroughs' two
eldest sons had died tragically. Julian Grenfell, heir to the title and the estate,
died of his wounds during the First World War; William was killed in action.
Only Ivo, their youngest son, remained, having been too young to serve. "
. . . **Ettie is as adorable as ever – wherever she comes she brings sunshine, and her Ivo is like her – a most delightful and charming boy. . .
. "** There was a large party staying, including the American Ambassador
and Mrs Davis, Mr Montagu, Venetia Montagu, Diana Duff Cooper and
Winston Churchill. Ian and Winston teamed up for bowls,
" . . . **they won which pleased him. Winston painted dull pictures all
day, and was quite happy; he said to Ian quite sentimentally: 'To think
Julian would have had all this!' He was painting 'The Orangery' at the
moment. . . . he works in a long smock, and looks too funny. . . . "** [18th
and 19th April 1920] Ivo died tragically in a car accident in 1926.

Over dinner with Gwendoline Churchill, Winston's sister-in-law, " . . .
**Winston was almost affectionate to me . . . inviting me to lunch with
them on Wednesday to see his pictures – I could not lunch, but
promised to go afterwards, as he insisted. . . . "** [16th November 1920
London] That night, Jean dined with Sibyl Colefax. Winston's talent for

Jean Hamilton 1900.
(By kind permission of Mr Ian Hamilton)

Lord Alwyne Compton, DSO 1900, Lt.-Col Beds Yeomanry.
(By kind permission of The Marquess of Northampton)

Stirling Castle drawing room, Simla, India.
(By kind permission of Mr Ian Hamilton)

No. 1 Hyde Park Gardens, London.
(By kind permission of Mr Ian Hamilton)

Winston and Clementine Churchill on their engagement day August 1908,
taken by Mrs F.E. Smith, wife of the Attorney General.
(By kind permission of The Lady Soames, DBE)

Deanston, near Doune, Perthshire, former family home of Jean, Lady Hamilton. *(By kind permission of Mr Ian Stirling)*

Blair Drummond Castle, Perthshire, Home of Sir Alexander Kay Muir, (1868-1951); 2nd Baronet 1903.
(By kind permission of Sir Richard Muir 4th Baronet)

Miss Janet Hamilton 1920 aged 22 on her engagement to Mr Allen Leeper.
(By kind permission of her daughter, Mrs Katharine Cobbett)

Mrs Katharine Cobbett, daughter of the late Allen and Janet Leeper.

Left to right: sons Roly and Brother Hugh Cobbett (S.S.F.), daughter Susanna, Mrs Avery.

Children of Susanna and James, *(left to right)*, Gideon, Rachael, and Chloe Avery.

The staff at the Liddell Hart Centre for Military Archives,
King's College, London.

Left to right: Robert Baxter, Archivist, Kate O'Brien, Asst. Director
of Archive Services, Patricia Methven, Director of Archive Services.

painting had greatly developed and he was receiving notice from Sir John Lavery, who joined them for dinner. " . . . **Sir John Lavery advised me to buy one of Winston's pictures. . . .**

. . . Winston never got back to show me his pictures, he was lunching with Lloyd George, but Clemmie was there, and I thought them really lovely, and would have *loved* **to buy one at once. . . . "** [17th November 1920]

Jean was on holiday from the end of November until the beginning of May 1921, at Lou Casteon, a large villa at Valescure, near Cannes, which she rented from Lord William Cecil. " . . . **I have been absorbed doing pastels the last few days, and have done ten sketches of Fréjus and St. Raphael – not bad – they are reminiscent of some of their moods and phases anyway. . . . "** [22nd March 1921]

When Jean returned, Winston wrote to her on 25 June 1921:

You expressed a wish to buy one of my pictures the other day. I have been doubtful about selling any of them because I don't think they are good enough and also because I am steadily improving.

Nevertheless as several people have been asking to buy, I have said that I will sell them at £50 a piece this year. If therefore you'd like to come in and choose one I shall be delighted to have it framed and sent to you.

A certain number of those you saw have to go away for about a month in order to be reproduced in colour for the Christmas Number of the Strand Magazine. But the delay is not long and the pyramid one which you liked was not among these.

Mind you do exactly what you like, for I am genuinely reluctant to sell these daubs – particularly to a friend.[8]

Winston and his daughters, Diana and Sarah and their French governess and woman chauffeur visited the Hamiltons at Lullenden and Jean got her painting. " . . . **Winston approves of all we have done to the house – he has been painting a lovely picture of the Barn, with brilliant sunshine and shade effects all day. . . .**

. . . Winston brought his picture of 'Ightam Moat' . . . I paid him £50 for it. . . . " [16th October 1921 Lullenden]

There was the outstanding matter of where to leave the portraits Singer Sargent painted of Jean and Ian. Lawrence Binyon was in the habit

of sending his Odes to Jean for her opinion before he completed and published them. In October 1926, Jean consulted him for advice about the portraits, which were eventually bequeathed to the Tate Gallery.

Jean was widely read and authors whose works could be found on her
bookshelves included the philosopher Immanuel Kant and the dramatists
and novelists William Shakespeare, George Bernard Shaw, Matthew
Arnold, Charlotte Brontë and Virginia Woolf. Poetry was an abiding passion and gave Jean most joy. Walter de la Mare, Byron, Browning, Keats,
Tennyson, William Blake, W. B. Yeats and Emily Brontë were among her
favourite poets. In discussion with Winston Churchill and George Keppel,
Jean had maintained that " **. . . a poem was as necessary as a knife, and
a poet as necessary as a manufacturer. . . .** " Winston supported her
point of view but George Keppel " **. . . seemed to think it obvious that a
knife must be the more important. . . .** " [**New Year's Eve 1903
Gopsall**]

Poets, writers and artists were often entertained at the Hamiltons'
houses. Yeats dined with them at both No. 1 HPG and Lullenden. In
London, Jean invited a **"flamboyant"** Maori chief, **"clad in crimson and
gold"** to sing for Yeats and her other guests, which turned into something
of a sensation. She nearly " **. . . burst into wild laughter . . . when he
uttered wild curses over our heads with shaking fingers. . . .** " [**7th and
8th July 1910**] Conversation at the dinner table could range over diverse
intellectual and spiritual subjects. Eddy Marsh, Rosie Ridley, Jack Leslie
and Norah Lindsay were dining one day when séances were topical in
fashionable society. **"Mr Yeats came in . . . and said he had just come
from the British Museum, where he had proved beyond all possibility
of doubt the immortality of the soul, as by Planchette his Indian spirit
medium had given messages from the spirits with their names and
how one died in poverty and distress – he had been and looked them
up and found them all correct. Jack suggests the Indian had looked up
the suggestions before him; the same thought struck me whilst Mr
Yeats talked to me about it. . . .** " But Yeats' eccentric ways did not deter
her and she found him to be **"delightful"** and was **"quite drawn to him
again."** [**19th July 1913**]

At No. 1 HPG, Jean's room was to the back of the house, several floors
up, overlooking Hyde Park. When she awoke in the mornings she would
lie in bed and read her favourite poems. " **. . . I love the quiet then, and
read – mostly poetry. Yesterday I read Bottomley's 'King Lear' in**

Edie Marsh's new Georgian book and we talked it over at dinner last night." [20th January 1916]

John Masefield, famous author of 'The Wanderer', was loyal to the Hamiltons during the Gallipoli crisis and was another whose poetry Jean admired. Whilst staying with her friend Mary Hunter at Hill Hall, Jean was reading Masefield's work. **" . . . I have just read:-**

'And soon men looked upon a glittering earth,
    intensely sparkling – like a world new-born.
Only to look was spiritual birth -
    So bright the raindrops ran along the thorn.

So bright they were that one could almost pass
    Beyond their twinkling to the source and know
The glory pushing in the blade of grass –
    That hidden soul which makes the flower grow.' "

Jean often used poetic language to describe her surroundings. **" . . . On such a morning I look out now – the sun, newly uprisen and very low, prints the window on my shutter – his gold now steals along the frosty grass. The delicate lemon and pink dawn was a spiritual birth. I have been awake very long." [23rd January 1916]**

Autumn at Blair Drummond took on an almost human dimension, with capital letters personifying sky and landscape. **" . . . The most perfectly beautiful day of the year. Intense blue Cloudless Sky above, gorgeous Autumn Colour below . . . "** and in the midst of such beauty, another war visited Scotland, which Jean faced alone (Ian was in London) in jaunty style: **" . . . this afternoon, the German attack is launched in Scotland: Quite a chic Air Raid round about Edinburgh, the Forth Bridge and the Pentlands. . . . " [16th October 1939]**

Percy Bysshe Shelley was one of Jean's favourite poets. The rebellious son of a baronet, Shelley was considered one of the great English romantic poets. In 1811, he had eloped to Scotland with a sixteen-year-old girl, Harriet Westbrook, whom he married. He later separated from Harriet and eloped again with Mary Wollstonecraft, whom he married after Harriet committed suicide. Shelley died in 1822, in a storm, whilst sailing in the Mediterranean and was cremated on a beach in Italy. At the time of his death he had left Mary for a lover named Jane. Jean had been reading a newspaper article about Shelley. " . . . I have read this morning of the drowning of Shelley – I could scarcely bear to read it. . . . poor Mary's journey for news, the finding of the bodies and the burning – that is worst of all – too horrible. . . . to be given the ashes of his heart, which whilst dying . . . belonged to Jane." [21st September 1903]

In 1913, whilst on holiday in Italy with Betty, Jean went on what to her must have seemed like a pilgrimage to Shelley's house. " . . . We reached Lerici about 5.50 after a wonderful rush of 40 miles through enchanting country, past Carrara with it's huge blocks of marble, its trellis straight down from the Carrara Mountains, they looked like the glass mountains of our fairy story – long yokes of grey and white oxen 10 and 12 pairs to bring the marble away along these winding roads, those great blocks, with their still silent sleeping souls – will there ever be another Michael Angelo to call them forth – still Rodin makes them speak audibly enough. I find in Michael Angelo something of Rodin – he must have taken him for his ideal: Sargent's picture of Carrara marble brought the mountains nearer and gave them keener edges for me. At last a smell of the sea and sweeping round a point all the enchanting coast lay below us – a winding road amongst olives led down to the shore, an old and grand looking Castle juts out to sea guarding Shelley's Bay of Lerici – the place where he wrote 'Lines written in Dejection' and 'She left me at the Silent Hour" and now alas covered with band, bathing boxes and machinery, but on going on farther we came to an old pier and we had tea there looking down on the Mediterranean which drowned that lovely soul and stopped his singing here, and looking out at the Bay from there, in the misty evening light, it had a mysterious spectral look. We looked in vain for Villa Magna and asked several Italians but they had never heard of it. As a last chance of finding it after scanning all the country in vain we turned a point and found ourselves in another village 'Sertica' or some name like that, so in despair I said 'turn, we must go back' as it was after 6 o'clock – just after we turned I was looking at a house embedded in the village and thinking that might be the verandah described by Mary where the fishing tackle was stored, and looking up I caught the name 'Shelley' on a tablet, and there was the darling house. We sent a little boy off for the keys and went in to find, to our joy, Shelley had been far more beautifully housed than one had imagined – a nice hall quaintly shaped with jolly Italian floor – beautiful marble balcony with a balustrade hanging right over the sea, the long, slow waves rippling underneath, it was there he wrote 'Ariel to Miranda' – how happy he must have been that last summer there with his Miranda – lucky Shelley to die at the end of it. I stood in his little bedroom too and looked out to sea – a pretty domed Italian roof.

The middle room opening onto the verandah where they were all sitting at lunch (when Shelley fresh from the sea and having left his clothes in his bedroom hoped to glide past unobserved having nothing on) was a delightful room. Poor Mary Shelley, how she suffered there – writing of it that it was a nightmare of loveliness.

Very tired and very happy we dined in our travelling dress and went to bed. . . . " [7th May 1913 Hotel Regina]

Next day, Jean and Betty went to Pisa and " . . . saw the convent where Shelley's unfortunate Emilio Viviana [Emilia Viviani] was shut up and a wonderful church S. Stefano de Cardieri with Turkish flags and peons [pennons] of Turkish ships – it was very knightly and armorial and we were delighted to have got in. . . . " [8th May 1913 Pisa]

When Jean awoke suffering from asthma she sometimes experienced early morning depression, no doubt from the drugs she took for her asthma, and to help her sleep. Reading her favourite poems cheered her. " . . . I begin to feel happier here this morning; my window is open on a dampish morning – I can see the faint blue hills, and the river reflected in the glass of my open window, also see and hear the rustling of the leaves on the gaen tree, the little birds are flitting in, out and over the balcony at my other window – Chisholm's white pigeons alight – and I am reading 'Ariel' about my beloved Shelley. . . . I am going to love it. . . . " [30th August 1923 5.30 a.m. Deanston]

Creative genius, accompanied by depression, to the point of suicide, inhabited the minds of some poets and writers. It was rather fashionable to be a depressed intellectual. Jean had known the American novelist Henry James, who suffered in this way. During the 1930s and until after World War Two, James' work enjoyed great popularity. " . . . I am reading Desmond McCarthy's 'Portrait' and feel as though I had been talking to him about all those interesting men I know, – Lord Oxford, Lord Balfour, Henry James, George Moore, Walter Raleigh, etc. Had I had more intelligence I would have known them better, or more charm,

push or vim, but with all of them I had moments, precious moments, when I got in touch with them. They were not to me 'ships that pass in the night'.

Henry James describing to Desmond McCarthy the spiral of depression which a nervous illness had compelled him step by step, night after night, day after day, to descend, said he would never have found his way up again had it not been for a life-line thrown to him by his brother William, – he said *'what stages of arid rejection of life and meaningless yet frantic agitation* he had been compelled to traverse'.

That absolutely describes the state I was in for a year when I tried, finally defeated in the struggle to take my own life (I never can understand why I did not succeed). I wonder if Henry James ever reached that extreme lowest step? Oh, if I could add, as he did 'But it has been good' and here he took off his hat, baring his great head in the moonlight, 'good for my genius'.

What a gift of expression he has and what a relief to know a genius like Henry James could feel that arid rejection of life – it eases the loneliness." [10th June 1934]

Jean wrote a series of poems entitled 'The Gallipoli Verses'. Having spent Christmas and the New Year at Deanston with Ian, on Tuesday 1 February 1916 she received a letter from the editor of the *Manchester Guardian*, expressing keen interest in these poems and requesting her to sign them. Ian said **" . . . I'd better not . . . he was afraid Birdwood and Monro would see the verses and be hurt. I said I hoped the Cabinet would, and I intended for years and years to rub Gallipoli into them, whenever I got the chance.**

The verses begin:–

'Your comrades are sadly leaving you now.' "

This line was omitted from the version which Jean sent out to her friends for Christmas 1915, and also from the published book of verses which were inscribed 'Gallipoli 1915, 25th April, 1916 (Anzac Day)'.[9] All Jean's feelings of injustice, anger, and frustration at the betrayal of Ian and his soldiers at the Dardanelles erupted into the 'Gallipoli Verses'. In two of the poems, 'Gallipoli' and 'April in Gallipoli, 1916', Jean made reference to a phenomenon that features in all personal accounts of Gallipoli. In the midst of all the horrors of war, the peninsula was often covered in a blanket of the most beautiful wild flowers, infinitely more colourful than the more famous poppies of Flanders.

Gallipoli

Sleep sound tonight, dear brothers,
Do not listen to those who go with unreturning footsteps.
It is the sighing of the night wind that you hear,
Do not believe it is the sighing of those who return not.

Soon you will hear the footsteps of the returning Spring,
The pink campion, and the yellow clover will stir sweetly about you;
The white orchids and the golden asphodel
Will lift their lovely heads out of your stony graves.
The unforgetting Spring will surely call these forth,
But more lovely spiritual flowers will awake on your graves tonight;
They glow and sparkle with unquenchable splendour,
Though the young eyes of spring will not behold them.

Imperishable Glory has touched their leaves with her bright fingers –
And they will look for ever in radiant immortality.
[Dec. 16th 1915][10]

Winter Dawn

It is not yet full day,
Stars twinkle on the earth,
The moon is still high, crescent shaped and gleaming,
White vapours fly across her.
But the dawn is coming, climbing the dark;
The cold morning light creeps quickly up and up,
Great lakes of clear cold sky appear,
Swimming into the soft brown cloud land.
Golden rose shines the light of the moon,
Below a glimmer of road stretches,
The trees stand out in their blackness,
Through them the mystic horsemen ride.

Every morning in the dawning,
I hear the horseman ride.
[Hyde Park, 1915][11]

April In Gallipoli, 1916

'For lo! the Winter is past: the rain is over and gone:
   The flowers appear on the earth'.

Victorious Spring! Marching so gaily through this bitter land,
Bright conqueror of a thousand battle fields!
Wherefore do you bring here your armies of clover
And your bright battalions of daisies,
Your batteries of red poppies, and glorious asphodel?

Why do you come to this desolate forsaken shore?
Is it to mock our sadness you are here?
Oh! cruel vaunting Spring!

Not so! my brothers! I am thy tender sister Spring,
The banners I bear are the banners of love,
The radiant banners of the Angel of the Covenant.[12]

Jean's tribute to the heroes of the Dardanelles culminated in the politically charged poem 'Anzac'. Those who ordered the evacuation of the Gallipoli peninsula were roundly condemned, and there is a sense of the betrayal of the fallen, a sentiment that was shared by many of the ordinary soldiers who served there, and is felt still to this day. The opening lines of 'Anzac' will remind the reader of William Blake's poem 'The Tyger', which was part of his series of poems, *Songs of Innocence and Experience*. 'Anzac' resonates with 'anvils', and 'On the anvils of war, these heroes were forged' evokes the image of Blake's 'In what furnace was thy brain? What the anvil?' In a flash, the battlefield at Gallipoli is illuminated for us and we see it through the fierce heat and fire of a forge. Like Blake's tiger, the warriors are both 'innocent', in that they are fighting for a belief, and 'experienced', as veteran soldiers.

Anzac

'No prouder name than Anzac will ever warrior bear'

Anzac was struck from the red flame of battle,
     On the anvils of war, these heroes were forged,
Midst the glitter of bayonets; shrieking of cannon,
     A warrior race leaped exultant to birth.

Anzac, the name for a warrior race,
     The flash of a rapier! leaps from its steel,
A shrill cry of battle, the clashing of swords,
     The cheers of the world! resound in the word.

No victor could down them, these heroes of Anzac!
     No foe could expel them, those eagles of war,
Bucklers of England on outpost of Empire,
     Their glory's untouched though Gallipoli fall.[13]

In 1916, the world was not ready for Jean Hamilton's poetic tribute to the ANZAC heroes of Gallipoli, nor for many years to come; perhaps it may be a little more so today!

CHAPTER 14

Grand Ladies and Great Houses

"My diary is still the friend to whom I fly with my complaints and my triumphs . . . I have been re-reading my typed diaries and can re-live many of the scenes again . . . much I can recall . . . so like Pepys I can shake hands with my younger self across the years." [12th May 1932]

Jean was experiencing unwelcome signs of ageing, her eyesight was giving her trouble and she suffered from sensitivity from electric lights. However, she could take some comfort that her contemporaries were ageing at least at the same pace, if not faster, though they coped with it in different ways. Maud Cunard made herself look girlish. " . . . Went to Maud's this afternoon to hear a wonderful violinist play, I wore my daring Aubrey Beardsley dress of black velvet puffed out at the sides and a white leather waistcoat, and felt very unlike myself, but was praised by Mrs. Hulton, who said I never looked so well. Maud was amazing in a little girl's frock of grey crepe, very simple skirt to her knees, and the tiniest of feet. . . . "

Lady Randolph was maintaining her vigorous lifestyle, with her third husband, Montagu Porch. He was forty-three and she was sixty-six, and beginning to admit her age. " . . . I drove Jenny Churchill back – she was very funny and rather pathetic wondering how Ava Ribblesdale managed to keep herself so young, and what a marvel she was; she said: 'Oh, I know I am far older than any of you – I don't care, but it's for Monty's sake I want to keep young.' I said: 'You have far more in your face than Ava has, Jennie,' which is true, and far more in her heart too, I might have added. I said: 'You know exactly how old you are, you told me last year, and you look much younger now all this last year than you did ten years ago.' She said: 'Well, don't tell anyone my age – I don't care, but it's for Monty's sake – he is so sweet to me, and will be waiting for me now.' . . . " [23rd April 1920]

In April 1920 Jean hosted a tea dance at No. 1 HPG, now renowned for its jade green hall and black, cream and gold drawing room, which was written about frequently in the newspapers and magazines. Jean 'looked artistic as ever in a combination of dark velvet embroidered in gold' and a 'floating veil to her high toque'. Lady Randolph wore a dress of 'black and brown'. Mrs Brinton had on a 'turban-shaped toque' and Maud Cunard, flamboyant as ever, was wearing 'one of the fashionable diamond arrows in front of a dark brown velvet hat'. The star attractions for the society columnists were obviously Prince and Princess Obolensky. The Danish Minister, 'little Ian' Hamilton, and his sister, Janet, were there.[1]

Later that month there was an Italian masked ball at Covent Garden and Jean and Ian were in Maud Cunard's box. Jean fancied something different for the ball. " . . . **I went with Heather to Nathan's and hired an Italian page's dress. . . . I also bought two masks – I have always wanted to go to a ball dressed as a page, and I thought if I were masked I would. . . . I eagerly put it on and . . . went up to see little Harry, who was astonished. McAdie was with him in the nursery, and she thought the dress suited me, and to my astonishment was not shocked. Ian was coming up the stairs as I was coming down, and was delighted, and said it suited me better than anything else I had ever worn, as my legs looked so well in tights. . . .**" But Jean lost her nerve and the theatricals ended with the dress rehearsal at home. To the ball, she wore a " **. . . longhi dress, a pretty hat, veil and mask – just a new French model dress with small lace hoops. . . .** " [29th April 1920]

The newspapers reported that the ball opened with a colourful ceremonial procession of the cities of Italy. Each town was represented by its famous citizens and associations: Florence by Dante and Beatrice; Turin by a pageant of the Court of King Victor Amadeus II; Genoa by Christopher Columbus; Verona by Romeo and Juliet and the Capulets; Venice by Othello and Desdemona, and the ladies of Venice; Naples by Masaniello, the fisherman, who strove to overthrow the Spanish domination in 1649, and a group associated with the revolution in Naples in 1799. Rome entered at the end of the procession, surrounded by attendants, to receive the homage of the Italian cities of the world.

The Spanish Ambassador and Mme Merry de Val were there. Maud, Lady Cunard, wearing the beautiful costume of Catarina Cornaro, brought a large party, including the Marchioness of Crewe, the Marchioness of Blandford, the Countess of Dudley and Mrs Austen Chamberlain. Lady Randolph, whom Jean and Ian found in Maud's box, was **"trussed up in**

an Elizabethan dress", of red velvet with slashed sleeves. Lady Ribblesdale looked beautiful in a brilliant gold dress, with a headdress of gold that looked like the rays of the sun at noon. Many people wore masks and it was almost impossible to recognise the wearers. Lord Arlington and his sister, the Hon. Lois Stuart, were dressed as Harlequin and Harlequinade. Mrs Reggie Fellows, formerly Princess de Broglie, and Mrs Parr wore black, pointed masks, studded with circles of brilliants and diamonds that came down in a V-shape over their faces. Mr St Hutchinson in a monk's habit with a long red beard would never have been mistaken for anything but Rasputin. The real excitement of the evening was the entry of four mysterious black figures who were absolutely unknown until the end of the evening.[2]

In August, the Court was in residence at Balmoral, and the Royal Family attended morning service on Sunday at the historic Crathie Church. King George V and Queen Mary, their daughter, Mary, the Princess Royal and Prince Albert, the Duke of York (later King George VI and father to the present Queen Elizabeth II) drove up in an open, horse-drawn carriage. The Right Revd Dr Thomas Martin, Moderator of the Church of Scotland, conducted the service and preached a sermon based on a passage from St John: 'One soweth and another reapeth'. Jean sat amongst the dignitaries: Sir Derek Keppel, Master of the Household, Lady Keppel and the Misses Anne and Victoria Keppel; the Earl and Countess Bathurst; the ladies-in-waiting and the secretaries; and Captain Sir Charles Cust, equerry-in-waiting. The King and the Duke of York wore highland dress with kilts of Rothsay tartan. Queen Mary (formerly Princess Mary of Teck) wore a costume in light blue and a light pink toque, and Princess Mary wore a grey costume with a black picture hat, fronted with roses; both had collars of white fox. As Jean sat through the church service, she pondered the royals. **" . . . Church at Crathie was quite amusing this morning, sitting opposite the King, Queen, Princess Mary and Prince Albert – the Keppels, Sandhursts and Household sitting along side us. I felt sleepy, but did not dare nod as Violet** [Meeking] **had put Lady Bathurst and me in the forefront of the battle. We sang 'Jerusalem the Golden' and I loved that.**

. . . The Queen looked charming if only she would put her hat on at a different angle – she has a charming, capable face and good figure – the King looks nothing at all. . . . "

The King's cousin, the Russian Czar Nicholas II, his wife, Czarina

Alexandra, and their children had been murdered in 1918. " . . . I wondered when I looked at him if he is ever haunted by thoughts of his
cousin, the Czar, and of how a little decision on his part could have
saved them all – Kerensky had arranged for their safe escort to
England when he was in power. . . . " [22nd August 1920 Invercauld]

Death always had a profound effect on Jean. Will Anderson, Norah's
husband, died suddenly in December 1922, and soon after Jean was so ill
she had to be driven by ambulance from Deanston to the Park Lane Clinic
in London. Ian was wearing his years much better and was so popular he
was invited to stand in the general election in a constituency near
Glasgow, but refused. The newspapers were saying he was tipped as the
new Labour War Minister. Jean bounced back and by March 1923 was
well enough to return home. She was deeply conscious of losing her looks,
though her photographs show her looking good for her age and she always
retained her figure. Dining with Boggie Harris, she found Alice Keppel
there, rather plump though she had kept her looks. " . . . Alice . . . looking
very nice and robust. . . . " [21st March 1923]

Electric lights were much brighter and harsher than candle or gas light
and Jean was afraid any lines or wrinkles might be magnified in their glare,
as in the chandeliers of a ballroom: " . . . the Wards' dance at Dudley
House . . . was fun. I loved seeing everyone again; it was a brilliant
scene – the ballroom was gorgeous with its lovely inlaid floor and glorious pictures – Winston Churchill *solemnly*, most solemnly and
painstakingly footing a jazz, Sir Robert Horne gigotting through it
like a pork butcher was quite worth going to see . . . Lady Mainwaring
a vision in crimson and Lady Beatty a faded nightmare – Sonia Cubitt
a *boney* beauty in a lovely frock; Rosie Ridley dancing with Ian in
rather an old-fashioned, very short black gown – her Aunt, Duchess of
Roxburghe, but just in her grave – Flora Guest, Rosie's American sister-in-law did not go to the ball because of this morning. The King and
Queen have however led the fashion in this as they allowed no social
functions to be stopped for Princess Christian's death. Pamela Lytton
looking battered by India, and my beloved Ettie [Desborough] looking
battered by age. . . . Olive Rubens dancing, and I fancy flirting with
Cis Bingham, who looks as if age had hardened him a lot. . . . " [26th
June 1923 London]

Kay's wife, Grace, Lady Muir, died in 1920 and Kay had become very
unhappy. Jean was eager for him to marry again, as Grace, knowing she

was dying, had wished it. There were many women setting their caps for Kay, in his great castle at Blair Drummond. When one in particular, of whom Jean didn't approve, wrote to her saying she was going to stay there, Jean was in despair. But a dreadful kind of fate stepped in to prevent it, when one morning McAdie rushed into the room with the *Daily Mail* in her hand, saying Blair Drummond was burnt to the ground. Kay went, sadly, to live at Deanston until the castle was rebuilt. **[Whit Monday 16th May 1921]**

Sibyl Colefax had a party for Arthur Balfour, and Jean and Kay were invited. Jean, with an eye to a partner for Kay, invited Nadejda Stancioff. Kay fell in love with her and romance was in the air, Jean hoping for a marriage. **" . . . Kay rushed in to see me and told me he was engaged to the fascinating Nada Stancioff – I was delighted as my thoughts have been turning towards her so much of late in my drives past Blair Drummond with Mother – I so long for him to have a delightful wife. I do think he is in luck – she is young, romantic, clever, and I hope he will make her happy – I can't help feeling the life at Blair Drummond may be difficult if she is not fond of sport – shooting, fishing, golf and tennis and in the winter, hunting at Whilton. . . . he wants to be married very quietly and to tell no one. . . . "** [10th December 1923; 2nd February 1924 Deanston]

On Saint Patrick's Day, 17 March 1924, Kay and Nadejda, whose father was a Bulgarian diplomat, were married at the Brompton Oratory in London. Jean and Ian were witnesses at the wedding. Nadejda was a ray of sunshine, reliability and kindness in Jean's life. Harold Nicholson told her that Nada was **" . . . the only woman with real genius he has ever met. . . . "** [31st May 1924]

The war had taken its toll of the rich and Jean mourned the fall of the great houses. Sunderland House, the former home of the Duke of Marlborough, was to belong to the Russians. **" . . . 'The Soviet Embassy' in London is now fixed for *Sunderland House*. Ye Gods! I remember Sonny Marlborough eagerly building it, we lived then in Chesterfield Street and Ian was his special hero. We went to their first dinner party there, the lovely gentle Consuelo presiding. It was then only partially furnished . . . and I think there was some difficulty about spoons or glasses, in spite of the numerous grand flunkies about. It was just as we were leaving our house . . . to go to dine at Sunderland House that night he [Ian] got a letter from Arnold Foster, saying that he could not** bear that a colleague of his should see for the first time the announcement that would be in the newspapers in the morning, and went on to tell him of 'the clean sweep of the War Office' and to assure him he would be offered a good appointment. He opened the letter after we arrived and read it to the astounded party. He was offered South Africa and Lord Roberts told his services would no longer be required.

What gorgeous parties afterwards, all the loveliest, gayest, wittiest that pre-war London could produce filled those rooms. Now they will be filled by coarse brutal new men who will try to still more disintegrate our tottering civilisation.

All the strongholds of Society are gone. Lansdowne House still stands desolately visaging destruction; Dorchester House is demolished entirely, an aching void; Devonshire House a glaring monstrosity; Sutherland House a Museum; Grosvenor House large blocks of flats; only Dudley House still insecurely stands. . . . "

The Hamiltons' old friend of many years, Marie de Rothschild, now only a shadow of her former self, her husband Leo already dead, lived on in the magnificent 'Ascot Wing'. " . . . very warm and cosy in here in my bedroom on the lap of Rothschild luxury. Arrived last night without Ian, as he had a terrific B.L. [British Legion] function on. Found Marie much the same as of yore, a little more wizened and a good deal more nervous . . . adoring her poor old sick dog Chow who was moved on a white cloth from sofa to chair wherever she was. The party are 'confusedly hurled, The remnants of an earlier world.' The lines are from 'The Lady of The Lake' and mother often quoted them, proud she could remember them, as we drove through the mounds and hillocks about Callendar. They well describe us here now.

Seymour Fortescue rather moth-eaten but still retaining the air of the beau Sabreur, the hero of the earlier French novel; Harry Milner of Duchess of Montrose fame; I remember Jennie Churchill whispering to me how the Duchess had cried bitterly, telling her how he went out and left her alone at night, adding bitterly 'and the creature had perfumed himself'. The creature is white-haired and respectable now. . . . He took possession of me at once as an old friend and I pretended I remembered him and we gossiped all last night together while the others played bridge." [9th February 1930 Ascot Wing]

If Alice Keppel had been the belle of the ball in her day, then Lady

Mary Curzon was the star of the world. Adored by millions, Mary was painted by Franz von Lenback in 1901. When Mary died in 1906, aged only thirty-six, 'She was mourned in three continents'.[3] Her husband, Lord George Curzon, died in 1925 and was laid to rest with his beloved Mary, in a white marble crypt, inside Kedleston church in Derbyshire. Jean, rather preoccupied with death, set out to see the place where George and Mary rested. **" . . . Went to Kedleston with Russell and Nance this morning to see George and Mary Curzon's tomb – it is very beautiful and touching – he and she in white marble lying together hand in hand – everything most carefully thought out:**

'Together I and she'

**I would hate to have to lie at Kedleston, a most dreary, vast, grand place. I wonder what Mary Leiter felt about it. I asked Lord Scarsdale who took us over, where her portrait by Lenback was and then I saw it looking like a ghost over one of the doorways. I remember seeing it when it was first painted when we were staying with them, and Evan Charteris saying to her: 'You see you bring your friends one after another to see it and no one likes it. Everyone asks, "Who is it?" '
What a rare and lovely woman she was then – a good imitation of a great lady cruel London said." [30th July 1931 Sandback Park]**

The Curzons had three daughters, but did not produce a male heir to reign at Kedleston. Jean was a friend of a younger Mary Curzon, daughter of Colonel Montagu and Esme Curzon of Garatshay. In 1907, Mary married her cousin, Francis, Viscount Curzon, the son of Earl Howe. Whilst lunching at Claridge's, Jean met Mary's son, and seeing him reminded her of the Christmas and New Year celebrations of 1903/4 at Gopsall with Alice Keppel. **" . . . Lunched with Mabel Corey at Claridge's – a large party to meet the King of Greece. I sat between Lord Elibank and Lord Curzon – I beckoned to him to come beside me . . . I was glad to find he was Mary Curzon's son. . . . We talked much of his lovely mother when she was young and he told me poor Esme, his Grandmother is very ill now in their house, and to-day all the Gopsall pictures are being sold and the old silver. . . . He told me no one ever went to Gopsall now – it was rotting away. How sad! What merry times we used to have there. I went from a gay New Year's Day Party there to stay with Esme when Mary was about 16 and told them about** her cousin . . . and the gay Gopsall party, at which Alice Keppel, at the height of her glory, reigned. . . .

. . . Mary was delighted to have me there to confide in me her love for Lewis Waller, the actor – she was terribly bored at home, she told me, she heard of nothing but scrapbooks and drain pipes there from her Father. Money Curzon her father, had a mania for pasting scraps in books and making poor Esme cry. Mary's ambition then was to have 'a salon'" in London and get to know writers and artists, and when she came to London I tried to help her to meet a few, but Esme would not have it. Mary is still lovely but very far from having 'a salon' she has always been angelic to her Mother." [14th December 1933]

Royalty, the Marlboroughs and the Lansdownes were not untouched by the fall of great houses. " . . . Chesterfield House . . . all the glory has departed and it looks dreary and deserted . . . Princess Mary used to live there. The Marlboroughs' old house . . . in Curzon Street . . . where we used to have such lovely parties in Consuelo's day, is also deserted and only used for exhibitions now. The Lansdowne's house and Dorchester House swept away." [1st Feb. 1934]

Edward, Prince of Wales (later Duke of Windsor, when he abdicated to marry the American divorcee Mrs Wallis Simpson), was much admired by the ladies as the most eligible bachelor in England. Edward was 'obsessively keen on exercise and difficult over food, possessed by the spectre of being overweight like his greedy grandfather, Edward VII.'[4] Maud, Lady Cunard, moved in the same circle as the Prince and Mrs Simpson. Formerly from New York, Maud had married, in 1896, Sir Bache Cunard, third Baronet, of Cunard Shipping fame. Having given herself the colourful nickname of 'Emerald', Maud was a 'short, slight figure, with a receding chin and a high piercing voice' who 'always wore a profusion of jewels and rings'.[5]

Over luncheon at her Grosvenor Square house, Maud told of her first encounter with the Prince of Wales, now in his mid-twenties. " . . . Our luncheon with Maud stands out, at which I sat next Mr. Pringle, a Labour Member – I liked him and his looks. We sat down shortly after 1.30 and never rose till 3.30. Lord Dalmeny was there and Lady Dufferin (Brenda), George Moore and Lady Birkenhead, and the conversation of Maud reached the height of folly, she was certainly 'yapping like a mad poodle', as Billy Grenfell put it.

She did not get command of the entire table, which she loves to do, till nearly the end of lunch – she got the helm by telling George Moore she was going to publish all his letters to her during his lifetime – he was sitting exactly opposite to her. . . . She said they would be on the subject of love, art, letters, music, gossip, as for instance on the subject of Lady Charles Beresford when he travelled to Beyrout with her and she tumbled out of the train in the early morning in a wreath of white roses. She went on from this to denounce religion and marriage, and ended by defiantly praising the overpowering charm of the Prince of Wales.

She had been telling Ian in a short aside that she had asked who the insignificant lame boy was at some party, when he followed the King, and was told he was Prince of Wales, but when he spoke to her she found he was full of magnetism and charm. Ian told her it was the glamour of hearing he was Prince of Wales transfigured him, and I had just been telling Mr. Pringle the same thing about the Queen of Rumania, on the other side. I think she has great charm and radiance, but is not really half so good-looking as most of our mannequins at Reville's or Lucile's or even the meaner shops, but she has the glamour of Queen-ship about her, and it gives her the assurance of pleasing. . . . " [31st March 1919]

Some further colourful stories unfolded about Maud's involvement with Edward and Mrs Simpson and Queen Mary would later blame Maud for encouraging the relationship. " . . . I walked to see Léonie [Leslie] and spent an amusing hour with her. Maud Cunard was there and I heard all the London gossip about Mrs. Vanderbilt's birthday party for the Prince of Wales. He had not wanted a fuss about his birthday, and when he saw a huge three-tier cake with 30 small candles, he said, 'He was damned if he would cut her bloody cake,' and would not go into the supper room, but went off and sat with Mrs. Dudley Ward who has taken him on again. Grace Vanderbilt sent back all the presents hidden in the cake to Carter's the next morning. This probably is untrue, but she is terribly on the war path – very heated in the chase after Royalties. . . . The Americans are funny – titles go to their heads – Society turns them into mere social machines – sort of climbing tanks – funicular tanks. . . . " [3rd July 1924]

Jean's women friends were ecstatic over the handsome Prince Edward. Norah Lindsay and Hazel, Lady Lavery, were part of Maud

Cunard's set and Hazel had been to a dinner Maud had given for the Prince. Over lunch, Jean " . . . **thoroughly enjoyed hearing . . .** " Norah and Hazel " **. . . discuss Maud Cunard and her crew. . . . Hazel had been there and was a brimful of it and Norah was riveted on her words. I egged them on from time to time – poor Ian listened speechless, for once he could not edge in a word. Once when Hazel was describing Emerald's select dinner of eight for the Prince of Wales he tried to say he had talked to the Prince for two hours last night, but neither of our guests removed their eyes from each other's faces – did not make even a movement in his direction so he subsided again into silence, but was much amused and amazed. . . .** " [1st March 1932 London]

The **"rival débutantes"** of the moment were said to be Pamela Smith, (daughter of Lord Birkenhead, formerly Sir F. E. Smith, the Attorney General), and Penelope Dudley Ward. Maud had Penelope to her dinner party " **. . . as the Prince showed her more favour . . .** ", after which they all went on to a dance at the Dorchester. Edward's name was romantically linked with Thelma, Lady Furness (*née* Vanderbilt, wife of the shipping magnate, Lord Furness),[6] with whom he had a 'long-term relationship'.[7] " **. . . The Prince objected to sitting beside the Duchess of Westminster as he wanted to sit beside Lady Furness – that could not be altered. . . .** " [1st March 1932 contd.]

The press had penetrated the situation: " **. . . Emerald will like this article of Castlerosse's I expect, though having now reached the top of the social tree she may see publicity is a mistake though he puts her in the same class as Napoleon and Disraeli. The crème de la crème socially do not go in for publicity, they are a secret society always but I can't help admiring the woman, her career has been amazing and she certainly has vitality courage and determination and they have gained her what she set out to win. Her first ambition was to call three Duchesses by their Christian names, her friends used to say. I expect she found that would not carry her far, but this Débutante stunt has carried her triumphantly to the top twig of the moment – it is quite their moment 'this brave new world' of the blatant ruthless young. . . .** " [1st March 1932 London contd.]

Jean accepted that she was too critical of Maud's lifestyle and though she disapproved of some of the things Maud went in for, she had to admit she was a colourful, entertaining character. As is often the way with peo-

ple who don't play by society's rules, Maud was charismatic and irresistible, a memorable figure. Her husband had died in 1925 and Maud
belonged more appropriately with the era of the deceased King Edward
VII, yet she fitted in with the Prince of Wales and his circle of friends and
the debutantes. " **. . . I must confess (though they would tire me to
death) the gay crowd who revolve round Emerald Cunard make the
rest feel rather dull and flat – London was more amusing when I did
not feel so censorious about her and we went to her parties. Reading
what Horace Walpole wrote of Madame du Defaud's parties when she
was sixty-eight made me think of Maud this morning: 'an old
debouchee of wit.' 'The gayest of all gay people.' 'The most amusing
salver in Paris' – Maud must be that age now yet she triumphantly
leads all the young Debs of the day in the Prince of Wales' set, and
dances with the best of them. . . . " [12th May 1932]**

Jean got her chance to see Maud again, though Ian was not keen on her
and gave her another nickname, 'the yellow canary'. " **. . . We lunched
with Emerald Cunard – Ian wanted me to get out of it, but I would not
as I thought it probably would be good fun, and it was. I sat next Boggie
Harris, who was full of gossip and Lord Allendale on my other side.
Emerald held the table as of yore and was very cruel to Hazel Lavery
who is writhing under the burden of the years but still at times looking lovely and holding her court of boys. She had said across the table
to Emerald, who was discussing Chips Channon's age: 'I know he is
older than I am,' and Emerald had cruelly answered: 'Oh no, Hazel –
I know he is only 42.' Hazel poses as 32, so this was staggering.
Afterwards, Emerald gave us all tickets for Beecham's lovely concert
in the Queen's Hall – we all sat together, Boggie next me, and he was
most agreeable till Ava [Ribblesdale] came and sat on his other side
when he deserted me, the faithless wretch." [11th December 1932]**

On 30 June 1933, the Hamiltons dined with Edward, Prince of Wales.
" **. . . Last night was very exciting – rather formal, all standing in a
row waiting for the Prince's arrival; various Colonial Governors and
their wives, Dorothy and Evan Charteris, Lord and Lady Bute and
Lady Sybil Grant and her husband – she shook hands with me and I
could not think who the enormous fat red woman crowned with
berries and green leaves was, and asked Dorothy who she was; I was
horrified when she told me – the last time I saw her she was a slim girl
at Knowsley.**

I sat by Lord Bute at dinner, and Mr. Clifford, the Governor of the Bahamas – a dull man, but I quite liked Lord Bute.

The Prince was most charming to us both. Ian amuses him and he made him come and sit beside him and after dinner asked me to come into the further room, then asked me to wait a moment while he bustled back and asked some of his other guests to come into the room also, and when he had got them arranged, sat down and had a long talk with me. He adores Ian and was very interested talking about Norah [Lindsay]. I wore my white satin dress – I like it better than my new dress though it's two years old and I am getting rather an old woman to wear white.

I was glad I had seen a cinema of the life of the Prince yesterday so could talk to him about it – I was very interested in it, the Prince is so adventurous and seems to have tried his hand at everything pretty successfully. . . . " [1st July 1933]

The Prince of Wales, now approaching his forty-first birthday, was romantically linked with Mrs Wallis Simpson. " . . . Violet Bonham Carter came to tea with me to-day at 4.30 and stayed till 6 – she was most entertaining and the time passed all to quickly. She was full of gossip which she poured forth in her own very vital way. The Prince of Wales' new mistress is Mrs. Simpson (not so very new either. I first heard her name coupled with his nearly a year ago now) and Violet described the warfare going on amongst the snobs for the entertainment of the Simpsons, as the husband *never* leaves her. Emerald Cunard of course leads, and is the most successful General of that Army – but Sibyl Colefax has had one good score and has had the Prince to dine with her and Mr. and Mrs. Simpson and then she took them all three with her to some evening party where they conspicuously sat Sibyl on one side of the Prince and Mrs. Simpson on the other, Mr. Simpson leaning over her chair, which was flanked by Arthur Colefax. Mrs. Simpson is an American and says *she is disappointed with the Prince of Wales' set.* Violet told me all this news from the Brackenbury front. . . . " [17th June 1935]

Jean went to stay with Lady FitzGerald in the beautiful surroundings of Bucklands Farringdon, where she slept in a " . . . lovely bedroom with a beautiful Chinese flower paper and lovely view of the Park, the deer and the lake. . . ." A large party were staying, including Alice Keppel. They strolled around Lady FitzGerald's model farm and " . . . her lovely little village . . . . "Alice was superstitious and at meal times **" . . . refused to sit down thirteen so we have a small side table where two sit – I sat there last night with Charles Emmott. . . ."** Jean and Alice set out together in the motor to visit Norah Lindsay at Sutton Courtenay, Abingdon. **" . . . It's nice having Alice Keppel here. She is very vital and gay and full of gossip. . . . On the way to Sutton Alice talked of the Prince of Wales and Mrs. Simpson. Alice was very funny over her, saying it was her want of class that mattered so much – she is apparently an excellent cook and has sent off the cook the Prince has had for long at Belvedere, and Alice says the Prince talked to her of nothing but cooking for two whole hours at an evening party the other night!!!. . . . "** [15th December 1935 Bucklands Farringdon]

The romance between Edward and Mrs Simpson remained the focus of curiosity and amusement whilst King George V was still alive but in 1936 it was reported that the King was seriously ill. **" . . . One trembles at the thought of our harum scarum Prince of Wales on the throne – with Mrs. Simpson as his Chief Advisor. I am told she is worried by his overwhelming and possessive passion for her as she is fond of her own husband. I wonder? Emerald Cunard and all her crew are tumbling after her all the time – 'The Royal Racket' they are nick-named an awful lot. . . . "** [20th January 1936 London]

The King died suddenly and the mood changed when the spectre of Edward as King, with the twice-divorced Mrs Simpson as Queen Consort, became a reality. **" . . . The King is dead! It is unbelievable, our good safe king, King George. Yesterday** [sic] **the news hour by hour grew more and more alarming and in the evening bulletins on the wireless were issued every quarter of an hour. . . . "** [22nd January 1936 London]

The new King Edward, as Head of the Church of England, would have found himself in conflict with the church, and the monarchy was now in deep crisis. **" . . . Yesterday Admiral Taylor took me to Westminster Hall where the King lies in State – very beautiful and mediaeval it was. . . .**

. . . London wallows in gloom, everyone in black. I did not think there could be as much black in the world as the shops have suddenly produced." [25th Jan. 1936]

Jean told Ettie Desborough she had been to a party given by Lady Sibyl Colefax, who was a celebrated hostess, and her husband Sir Arthur

Colefax, an eminent King's Counsel. Ettie " **. . . was afraid she might be asked to meet Mrs. Simpson there . . . she** [Sibyl] **with the aid of Mrs. Simpson, has had the King to dine and feels quite 'on the crest of the wave'. I wonder how Emerald likes sharing His Majesty with Sibyl. Of course anyone who can get hold of Mrs. Simpson can now secure His Majesty. Alas! 'The Court' seems only a farce now. Can it last? Emerald and Mrs. Simpson driving to Ascot in the Royal Carriage and the King going about everywhere with a very second-rate crew. Norah** [Lindsay] **tells me Emerald says this is the very first reign she has really enjoyed. She apparently directs the King's visits now and told him he must go to Blenheim. The King has no objection as long as his 'Wally' goes also, and Anne** [Islington] **says she – Emerald – is now going to tell Wally she must try and get the King to marry – as she finds her life with him very strenuous. She possibly may not object (I wonder?). It's too absurd, these ridiculous women planning out the King's life – I do hope he will marry someone nice and suitable and break away from all this crowd who are ruining him. It's too sad. He had such a fine adventurous character.**

   I wonder what the Queen thinks about it all – poor Queen Mary – it must be heart-breaking." [6th July 1936 London]

   Jean heard that Maud had advised Prince Edward to marry and Mrs Simpson was supposedly trying to find him a suitor. From the moment King George V died, Edward was spoken of as King Edward VIII, though he was never crowned. Jean and Ian went to a garden party at Buckingham Palace, where they were greeted by Edward. " **. . . The King looks very inadequate, the Court a joke these days – where apparently Emerald Cunard directs his movements through Mrs. Simpson. They apparently have decided he must marry, Mrs. S. finding her duties rather onerous, but who? . . . "** Edward, whom everyone found charming, was reputed to be an enthusiastic piper and talked to Jean and Ian of the " **. . . Scotch pipers who were marching off swinging their kilts and looking very grand. . . . " [22nd July 1936]**

   The stories about Edward and Mrs Simpson persisted, the affair having become the talk of the nation. " **. . . Frances Horner . . . told me . . . about the King visiting Mrs. Simpson's bedroom at Belvedere while her hairdresser was doing her hair. The King lolled on her bed and finally took the tongs out of the hair-dresser's hands and finished her hair himself." [27th July 1936]**

Alice Keppel made a famous statement about the affair between Edward and Mrs Simpson: 'Things were done much better in my day'. Alice gave Jean another rare glimpse of her views on the subject, when she stayed with her at Lennoxlove Castle, where the Hamiltons were on holiday. "... I motored Alice to Meliston yesterday afternoon.... enjoyed the drive with Alice, she is full of gossip. She told me the King has had a quarrel with Emerald and that she has not gone on the cruise with him after all, and that Diana and Duff Cooper are looking rather glum. I should think they would be horribly bored. Our poor King does seem to be surrounded by a pestiferous gang. Lady Mendl with blue hair and a Pansy called Mullins, I think she said, with blue eyelashes. From these and all other horrors Good Lord, deliver our nice little King. Mrs. Simpson is responsible for Lady Mendl who is furnishing Buckingham Palace, alas from Paris, not London. ... " [11th September 1936]

On Armistice Day 1936, Jean gave a dinner party. " ... Of course everyone discussed the poor little King and Mrs. Simpson, and 'The Royal Racket' as he and his circle are called – it's the one subject of high and low these days.... He certainly has dragged the throne in the dust. ... " [20th November 1936] Norah Lindsay was invited to meet Edward and Mrs Simpson, at a party given by 'Chips' Channon. Prince George, Duke of Kent (Edward's younger brother), and Prince Paul of Yugoslavia were there. " ... Norah had an amazing party at Chips Channon's – the King Mrs. Simpson, the Kents, Prince Paul and Princess Olga, the Duff Coopers, Emerald Cunard – about eighteen to twenty, a very small selected group of the Royal Racket. Victor Cazalet has got himself into it, but was rather pushing, Norah said, and got reproved by the Duke of Kent for lounging when the King was standing up.

There was a small dinner party of about twelve first. Norah arrived about 10.15, and found she was the only woman without a huge tiara. Chips had requested them all to wear tiaras. Diana Duff Cooper had borrowed one. I should have thought the King would have been bored with this at a small informal party. At 11.30 they had a film and the King called loudly for 'Wallis, Wallis,' to come and sit beside him but she was talking to the Duke of Kent and would not, so Diana went instead, which did not please him; he does not like her and he did not talk to her. The film was a Mickey Mouse, News of the

World, and Armistice Day – rather solemn I should have thought, for the party. The King, it seems, always has films every week-end at Belvedere. Chips had selected the film of Mayerling for last night, a curious selection indeed and the King objected to it. . . . " [21st November 1936 London] *Mayerling* was the story of the deaths of the Crown Prince Rudolf of Austria and his mistress, believed to be the result of a romantic suicide pact, at his hunting lodge, Mayerling, because the monarchy did not approve the match.

On Thursday 10 December 1936, Edward abdicated and on the 11th, broadcast his decision live on the radio. The Hamiltons listened to his announcement whilst dining at the Ritz. Edward accepted the title of the Duke of Windsor and went with Mrs Simpson to France, under a cloud of divided sentiments within the nation. Some thought his behaviour scandalous, others admired him for abdicating and marrying the woman he loved and many thought he should have been allowed to marry Wallis and be crowned King. "... **Turia Campbell looked in at 3.30. She has been much with the Kents and told us lots of gossip about the crisis – the Duke of Kent was the first to tell the King a marriage with Mrs. S. was impossible and King Edward was completely astonished, he had always intended to marry her, so her assertions of her intentions never to marry him must have been rot.**

She said Mr. Simpson is behaving like a terrible cad and trying to blackmail the King and Mrs. S. She said he had already filed a petition for divorce in America citing the King as co-respondent months ago, but accepted a large sum of money to withdraw it then. . . . " [13th December 1936 London]

Five days after the abdication, Jean held a tea and cocktail party for Kitty Drummond. Edward and his circle were the popular topic of conversation. " . . . **Poor Alice Keppel is in great trouble, George is so ill at the Ritz, has had pleurisy, and has still four nurses. She is great on Mrs. S. and the King. No one talks of anything else but the Archbishop's rebuke to King Edward and his friends. Emerald and Co. are much abashed though they rage and storm – it will do them all good.**

Col. Bruce Lockhart told me he was writing this [a poem] **for his 'Londoner's Log' in the Evening Standard to-day. His 'faithful to the end' is a hit at Emerald Cunard and Philip Sassoon, who now say they hardly know Mrs. Simpson, and Diana Duff Cooper who now openly**

says horrid things of King Edward, this week is nick-named 'The Rat-trap.'

　　The children's rhyme is –

　　'Hark the herald angels sing
　　Mrs. S. has snapped our King.' "
[16th Dec. 1936]

Frances Horner told Jean of her lunch with Maud Cunard, who was indignant over Edward's demise. Queen Mary was said to have banished Maud from the Palace. **" . . . the Austen Chamberlains were there and they all tried to stop her (Emerald). . . . She actually asked Austen if it was true the Cabinet had turned him** [Edward] **out of England and Austen gave a very wise reply to which they all listened – the tenor of it being that a King had special privileges but also special duties to his people. Emerald, Norah** [Lindsay] **tells me, says: if the Queen** [Mary] **does not invite her to the Court Ball she will get even with her. . . . "**
[March 19th 1937]

The Coronation of King George VI and Queen Elizabeth (the present Queen Mother) took place on 12 May 1937. Ian was honoured by being asked to give the address at the Pre-Coronation Service on the 11th, and the Hamiltons were invited to the Coronation. **" . . . Yesterday was a wonderful day. Our seats in the Abbey surprisingly good and I found myself beside Air Marshall Sir John Salmond and Monica. . . . I stood up on the seat . . . till I got a message from Gold Rod to sit down. That was just before the crowning of the King but I had seen the anointing and Ian was beside me . . . I crept behind Ian and looked over and saw the crowning of the Queen – and wondered what she was thinking and how she felt. She looked very small and sweet, it was impossible to see expressions from where we sat. The Cathedral looked very wonderful and I thought of all the marvellous scenes there. Queen Caroline clambering to be admitted, what did George IV feel then? Anne Boleyn being crowned – how furious many people must have been – Queen Victoria – . It was interesting seeing all the great come crowding in and process to their places – a moving Mediaeval scene – the seven and a half hours did not seem so very long though our seats were small and positions cramped. I had taken a small bottle of Vermouth in my bag and some cocktail biscuits, which greatly revived me and some sandwiches for Ian. My tiara hurt my head but it was** becoming and my dress with its little silver coat made by Annie was quite a success. . . . " [13th May 1937]

At the end of the Coronation service, a large crowd surged out of the Abbey. " . . . **When at last Ian and I emerged into the canvas covered way and saw with dismay the solid crowd in front my heart sank till I saw 'Nancy' in the crowd wearing her lovely tiara. She told me our names had just been called and the car gone on – that hers too had passed . . . . I then told a Gold Rod, who appeared by magic, that our car had just been called and he waved his magic wand and the crowd divided like the waters of Jordan and we passed along on a clear way right into our car." [13th May 1937** contd.]

Good relations now existed between Britain and Turkey and with the coronation spirit still in the air the Hamiltons, Churchills, and Anthony Edens were some of the guests invited to a large and prestigious dinner party at the Turkish Embassy. " . . . **So glad I managed to go to the Turkish Embassy dinner – wore my new brown net dress over gold lamé foundation but didn't feel pleased with my looks. When we entered the drawing room saw at once Blanche Lloyd looking magnificent. She was going on to the Sutherland's wonderful dance for the King and Queen, and so was Lady Keyes, who had felt she was overdressed, she said, till she saw Blanche and me. The little Turkish Ambassadress was charming, so young and friendly, admired my dress and talked about the Coronation. . . ."**

The Winston Churchills were late arriving. " . . . **Finally we went downstairs to dinner without them. We went in pairs, unusual these days except on state occasions and as Anthony Eden was to have taken Clemmie Churchill and Winston, me, I went down with Mr. Eden but alas Winston arrived just as we sat down and took his place beside me, and George Lloyd was on my other side. The lights just beyond him on the wall were so trying to my eyes . . . and I felt I was looking aged in such a glaring light. It would be more comfy I feel, to be frankly an old lady and wear a lace cap or some distinctive dress for the old – then one would have some fun – vying with one's contemporaries – instead of wearing the same kind of dresses as much younger women.**

Winston was grumpy as usual to begin with and eager to talk to Mrs. Eden on his other side, but woke up a bit when I said I had been wondering what the Duke of Windsor was thinking and feeling during the Coronation. Winston is quite sentimental over their love affair

and I am inclined to be but said I thought she must be a vulgar woman to have allowed such a photograph as had appeared in the papers, – they looked like 'Arry and 'Arriet [i.e. a pair of Cockneys] grinning at one another. He excused even that saying it was a gesture. It certainly was but an unlucky one for her, she looked like housekeeper or masseuse and surely must have lost her chic living amongst all those people. I felt I was on dangerous ground with Winston as I thought of his journeys to Belvedere that momentous week and his consultation with Morgan about the marriage.

'Mussolini would not like this dinner party,' Winston said, as he looked round the table and his eyes fell on the Vansittarts. [Vansittart was known to be anti-German.] 'It looks as though we were very friendly with the Turks.'

Thinking this remark too good for me, he turned to remake it to Mrs. Eden and I was rather thankful to remain quiet, my head still feeling confused and my eyes giving me pain. I heard George Lloyd's Turkish lady being very vivacious and saying how beautiful English women were, as she looked at Clemmie C. who did look lovely, George Lloyd was praising the mystery of the Turkish Yashmak. . . . " He told Jean of his " . . . six weeks flight in an aeroplane, spending four days exactly in each wonderful place he visited. He was in Jerusalem at the same time as Betty, [Jean's sister] in March.

Upstairs Clemmie and I sat by the fire in the farthest drawing room, while the others grouped round the fire in the first one. Clemmie looked well but older, I thought, as I saw her nearer. . . . Our nice little hostess soon joined us there with her clever daughter who had sat next Ian at dinner. She has just left Oxford where she won a scholarship. I talked of Fodie to Clemmie and of what she was doing in Vienna and of Priscilla Bibesco who has just been presented, the same day as the Turkish girl we were talking to. . . . " [19th May 1937 London] As Jean and Ian were leaving at 10 o'clock, more guests were arriving at the Embassy, the Rennels, Paravacinis and the Hungarian Ambassador, who had been to the Coronation.

At the July Royal Garden Party Jean met the new Queen. " . . . The Royal Garden Party to-day. . . . The King and the two Queens stopped and shook hands with us. Queen Mary looks so happy – Queen Elizabeth did not look quite so pretty as she has been doing, she is inclined to get too fat. Little Princess Margaret Rose was sweet. The

King looked well groomed and a good figure – very unlike his brother the Duke of Windsor – whom (Louis Lederer when he lunched with us to-day told us) the Hungarians want to have for their King." [22nd July 1937]

On 16 October, Jean and Ian were favoured again at Buckingham Palace by Queen Elizabeth sending for them. When they arrived they went to the room of Captain Richard Streatfeild, the Queen's Private Secretary, where they were received by Lady Katharine Seymour, the Queen's Lady-in-Waiting.[8] " . . . Ian and I stood alone while the Queen walked down the ranks, she wished to take the salute. She walked well and looked very lovely in her daffodil raiment – a very loveable woman – and quite a Queen as she walked slowly and alone to the raised dais. After the review she sent for us and the unkind camera took me thus. Ian brought the picture to me with glee saying 'Witch-like Gypsy is presented to the Queen'. . . . I felt very grand walking in this small company amongst the cheering crowd. . . . " [October 17th 1937]

Next day, photographs of Queen Elizabeth shaking hands with Jean and Ian, separately, made front-page headlines in the newspapers, Jean wearing a floor-length cloak, hence Ian's witty remarks. One heading read: 'A GRACIOUS GREETING – QUEEN'S SMILE OF WELCOME'.

Alice Keppel has been a very special lady in history and interest in her is sustained through her great-granddaughter, Camilla Parker Bowles, friend of the present Prince of Wales. King Edward VII was now seventeen years dead and for most of that period Alice had lived abroad, but Jean saw a good deal of her when she was in England and Scotland. Alice lunched with the Hamiltons and Jean found her " . . . **charming: she has recovered her looks. Norah** [Lindsay] **told me yesterday she nearly committed suicide when King Edward died. . . .** " [25th February 1927]

Sibyl Colefax gave a dinner party and Alice was always amongst the best of company. She was renowned as a bridge player and was difficult to equal. " . . . **Sibyl Colefax's dinner last Monday 18th, was fun. . . . Alice Salisbury was there – Alice Keppel too . . . – Lord Reading – the Oliver Bretts; . . . the Bridge table, at which Alice Keppel immediately seated herself, made everyone uncomfortable, as Sibyl could get no one to play with her. . . finally against her will, Lady FitzGerald was pushed onto the Bridge table, where I am sure Alice Keppel did not welcome her, as she, Lady F., told me the other day she plays very bad Bridge. . . . " [21st March 1929]**

On one occasion when Alice was dining with Jean, she forgot to bring George, her husband, and Jean's table was out, with an uneven number. **"... The Alice Keppel lunch was a great success after all, but gave me a lot of trouble. It came off 28th. Eddie Marsh, Julia Maguire, Beverley Nichols, Violet Bonham Carter, Charles Emmott, Ian – and all attended.**

Alice Keppel seemed to me vulgarised and noisy, rather florid looking. I liked Charles Emmott and disliked Eddie. I was annoyed I had to move him to sit next me instead of George Keppel. Alice K. had quite forgotten to tell him he was invited. . . . " [7th February 1930 London]

Charlie Chaplin and Harry Lauder were popular celebrities in London. **" . . . We are going to see Charlie Chaplin – Norah, Nancy, Eddie Marsh, Chips Channon, Ian and I – and I am sure I will be bored. I have never cared for Charlie Chaplin and simply can't understand London's craze for him or Harry Lauder.**

Yesterday Alice Keppel was telling us all about his first night and the supper party afterwards at the Savoy – she was at his table and he was dancing all the time – wants to marry a girl he has brought with him – Mauritis or some such name. Winston Churchill was also at his table and dancing like mad all night. A.K. puffed herself out to show how fat he looked dancing – she did look awful, this was at Mrs. Higgins' lunch party yesterday. . . . " [31st March 1931 London]

Before Alice Keppel met King Edward VII she was rumoured to have had an affair with Lord Stavordale. During a day out with her girlfriends of the 30 Club, Jean bumped into Alice and 'Stavey', now sixth Earl of Ilchester. **" . . . As the bunch of (30) ladies swept out of the Ritz Grill we passed Alice Keppel seated cosily in a corner with her old love, Lord Ilchester. He looked much like the Stavey who adored her of old but she looks very buxom and overblown, but a jolly woman. I shook hands with her and said it was nice to see her back in England and nodded to her Stavey but Julia [Maguire] stayed and chatted to her. We were all an amazing and unwelcome vision to her, I am sure. . . . " [27th January 1934]**

Jean held an Edwardian-style lunch party and the conversation begun there about ageing continued later that day at Frances Horner's house. **"... Léonie [Leslie] said how old she thought Ettie Desborough looked.**

... I said Lord Hugh [Cecil] **had said Alice Keppel looked 'Georgian' which I thought she decidedly did, when I glanced at her sprawling at the foot of the table. Léonie said: 'I suppose I look older myself.' Poor Léonie, she did indeed, and we began to discuss what our dress ought to be as old ladies. I stoutly declared I did not wish to give up golf, so could not take to wearing long veils yet. . . . "** [21st February 1934]

Some of Jean's friends now seemed to be either bored with their hair or losing it, and at a party Jean studied their new wigs. **" . . . A very grand party at Bath House last night – Russian music of the most exciting kind. . . . I spoke to Alice Keppel who was charming. . . . Ian adored the music. . . . it was amusing to see all the old crew again all in new dresses and new wigs. I studied Alice Keppel's as I sat by her after the concert was over to see some curious dancing, also Julia Maguire's as she sat in front of us.**

Alice Keppel called after me as we were leaving to ask if we would give Sonia [Cubitt, her daughter] **a lift, she lives in Hyde Park Gardens quite near us, which I was glad to do. . . . "** [23rd January 1935 London]

It was little more than sixteen years since the end of the First World War. The rise of Hitler, who had been elected to office in 1933, was not yet seen as a threat to Britain. It had become acceptable again in society to entertain German diplomats. Jean's lunch for Alice Keppel included Lord Gerald Wellesley, Herr von Fries, Julia Maguire, Eddie Marsh, Tottie Holford, George Keppel and Blanche Lloyd. **" . . . We had quite a remarkable lunch party to-day for Alice Keppel and it went so well and they all said it was the nicest party they had been to this year, at least all the women except Star** [Chetwode] **said so and Lord Lloyd and the nice German Ambassador.**

I was terrified in case one would fail and make us 13 and took double precautions with George Keppel as Alice had sailed in without him last year when I was counting on him.

. . . George Lloyd does not approve of the film 'Forgotten Men'[9] and says it has already stopped Recruiting. I find it difficult to defend as I have always hated it and I did not want Harry to see it. As George Lloyd said, why should he want to go and see the horrors of life. We don't depict street accidents and the deaths from disease or old age, etc. That is true but war could be prevented, one feels – and I feel it an 'Anti-War' film and good for politicians. . . . " [11th February 1935]

On 20 March 1935 Jean held a dinner for Ettie Desborough, who was staying with her. Other guests were Rosemary Hinchingbrooke, Lord Stanmore, Lord and Lady Midleton (William and Madeline St John Brodrick), Lord Hinchingbrooke, Lord and Lady Esher, Sir Lancelot Oliphant, Madame Paravacini, Wolkoff, the Swiss Minister, Gooney Churchill and Alice Keppel. At that time, Peter Pollen, Heather's husband, was seriously ill and died on 25 March, by which time Alice Keppel had gone to France. Peter had became a financial adviser when he left the army,[10] and appears to have been a business associate of Alice Keppel's for some years. Jean received a hand-written letter of condolence from Alice, sent from California Palace, Cannes, dated 28 March 1935. The letterhead carried a royal-like crest, i.e. a crown over an ornate A. It was said that on the Continent Alice was treated like royalty.

> So our splendid and beloved Peter has left us and is today laid to his last rest. My thoughts are with you all and I share in your mourning and bitter regret at his loss – I send you my heart's sympathy, dear Jean. As for myself I cannot visualise what I shall do without his steadfast, loyal friendship his wise counsels and ever-ready help in my many perplexities and troubles. I had got to lean on him so and he never in all the years failed me; he was the best and truest type of Englishman as well as a very loveable person. Poor Heather has been through a cruel strain and will now have to take care of herself.
> My affectionate and sympathetic love.
> Alice.[11]

It was during her relationship with King Edward VII that Alice had made her money, when Sir Ernest Cassel was the King's financial adviser, but Cassel died in 1921. Peter Pollen was an equerry to King Edward at the turn of the century, and it is likely that it was then that Alice made his acquaintance. From 1919, Peter had been a member of the Royal Bodyguard, the Honourable Corps of Gentlemen-at-Arms.[12]

The Hamiltons rented Lennoxlove Castle at East Lothian from Mr David Baird, for holidays. Lennoxlove was a former home of Mary Queen of Scots' secretary, Maitland. The Hamiltons had supported the claims of Mary Queen of Scots in the sixteenth century, which explains the choice of 'Mary at Langside' as the subject of a commissioned painting. A lock of the Queen's hair had been handed down as a family heirloom.

Jean and Ian dined with the Courtauld Thomsons. **" . . . We took Tiny [Sword] and Teddy Schuller with us yesterday to lunch with the Courtauld Thomsons and found Alice Keppel there and Princess Victoria – Alice Keppel very charming and Princess Victoria too, though Royalties are always a bore. . . . "** [5th September 1936 Lennoxlove]

Alice Keppel came to stay with the Hamiltons on Monday the 7th. **" . . . Yesterday was unexpectedly delightful. Teddie, Tiny and I played golf in the morning. . . . We had a gay lunch and the sun shone enchantingly. Heather had lent us her lovely new car as a wheel had came off our Humber and at 3 o'clock Alice Keppel, Marie Louise [Maxwell Scott], Teddie Schuller and I set off for Tantallon, where we lay on the ramparts in warm sunshine while Teddie and Tiny climbed to the top of the Tower. . . . "** [9th September 1936 Lennoxlove]

Bridge was Alice Keppel's favourite entertainment and Jean arranged all-night parties of experienced bridge players for her benefit: Sir Walter Lawrence, Tom Bridges, Lord Plymouth and Lord Wemyss. **" . . . Sir Walter was in Edinburgh but returned for their bridge after tea and the four played all night. Tom Bridges is a delightful guest, so clever and interesting. He drove Tiny in his open car yesterday and she is fascinated by him. . . . "** [9th September 1936 contd.]

The press publicised Alice Keppel's visit: 'Mrs. George Keppel, who has lived in Florence for some years, but comes to England periodically, is here now and making a round of country house visits. Tall and graceful with a magnificent bearing, silver hair and dressed richly but simply, this noted Edwardian figure provides an object lesson for women who do not know how to grow old gracefully.' There are three photographs in Jean's diary taken during the holiday: one of Alice seated on the Base Rock; one of Jean, Marie Louise Maxwell Scott and Alice together; and one of Ian and Tiny Sword. The newspapers published a group photograph of a visiting party, taken with Alice, Ian and Jean, on the steps of Lennoxlove Castle: Mrs Kenneth Wagg, Miss Dennistoun Sword, General Sir Tom Bridges, Mr Schuller and Mrs Horlick.[13]

Jean seldom expressed regret when a guest left but she was sorry to see Alice go. **" . . . Alice leaves to-day. Her visit has been a great success and we have all enjoyed ourselves. . . . "** A farewell dinner was given for Alice, with Lord Wemyss and his wife Mary, Tom Bridges, Lord and Lady Plymouth, Tiny Sword and Teddie Schuller. **" . . . Mary looked terribly ill and I found Lord Wemyss very deaf. Alice found Lord Plymouth very slow at Bridge but he and Hugo Wemyss played havoc with her money and Tom's and they looked very blue this morning. I go to bed and leave Alice with her bridge party every night. Mary and Bibs left early last night leaving Hugo to play bridge and Lord Plymouth. . . .**

. . . Sir Courtauld Thomson brought a party of seven to dine here last night including Princess Helena Victoria. We dined in the Banqueting Hall as we were thirteen I put Tiny Sword beside John Fox Strangeways in the alcove. . . .

. . . We did not know how to amuse Princess H.V. after dinner and as she loves jig-saw puzzles we planned to leave a half finished one for her to see and Tiny and Teddie moved into the light and did it with her all evening, bless them. . . .

. . . I took Alice Keppel and Teddie to Dolton Castle and we much enjoyed exploring it. . . . Alice Keppel's visit has been pure pleasure all the time, such a warming interesting personality, no trouble and always ready to be amused and amusing. . . . " [11th September 1936 Lennoxlove]

The following year, the Hamiltons were again holidaying at Lennoxlove and Jean had a dinner party where her guests included Princess Helena Victoria, Sir Courtauld Thomson and Lord Ilchester ('Stavey'), who spoke to Jean of his old love, Alice Keppel. **" . . . Lord Ilchester was nice and prosey . . . all my guests were pleased to meet him. . . . He has just been staying with the Wards now where he met her [Alice] . . . I wonder what he thinks of her now. I wanted her address as I want to get her here now and I am sorry she is not."** [5th September 1937 Lennoxlove]

Alice, possibly prompted by seeing Ian's photograph in the newspaper when he was inspecting members of the British Legion at Aberdeen with the Duchess of Gloucester, wrote Jean a letter dated 9 September 1937, from Alloa House, Alloa, that George was ill but she would like to come and stay.

I have had a *much* better account of George, from the Specialist so supposing I could come which I so want to do could you have me this Thursday 16th mid-day. Will you let me know here, I would go

to Courtauld's on the Monday and come to you on the Thursday –
of course, if the fever is worse I go straight back to London – I so
want to see you both. What a lovely photograph of Ian *quite
overshadowing* the Duchess of Gloucester.

Will you let me know *here*. I am *so* sorry you have not been
well.

Your affectionate
Alice K.

It was too short notice for Jean to get up a team of experienced bridge
players for Alice, who would soon clean less experienced players entirely
out of cash. " . . . **Alice Keppel wanted to come here to-day from
Courtauld Thomson's, but I invented an old aunt and put her off until
tomorrow. I can't get anyone to play bridge with her and dread a
bridge-less visit for her as we have only young people here this week-
end – a party for Harry who arrives tomorrow night for three days
only, poor boy! . . . The Grosvenor girls are dining Saturday night to
play bridge but, Dorothy says, must not play for high stakes – so I am
trying to get Mrs. Horlick to bring Percy Loraine and her son-in-law,
Wagg, tomorrow night.**

**Tiny [Sword] is busy 'phoning to all her smart young men, Lord
Huntley; Lord Haddington's brother . . . and Lord Clydesdale, but
they are all very unresponsive and Ian has produced Lord
Stonehaven's son, Mr. Baird, who wants to rejoin the Gordons and he
comes here from London tomorrow. Teddie Schuller also offered a
visit and arrives Saturday morning for one night only – but I fear
Alice will be bored and it will be collar work for me." [16th September
1937 Lennoxlove]**

Bridge players who would risk playing with Alice could not be found
and Jean was afraid that Alice's visit had not been a success. The only
gambling they could provide for her was roulette. But Jean took her to historic Abbotsford, the home of Sir Walter Scott. " . . . **She has had no
bridge but plenty of company and she says she likes the young. Tiny
has chattered to her ceaselessly and Alice liked Jean Kennerley. . . .**

**. . . I took Alice and Teddy Schuller to Abbotsford on Saturday; it
was a glorious day and the drive across the moor was lovely. We both
enjoyed it, it was my nicest time with Alice.**

The Grosvenor girls were nice on Saturday. We dined in the

Banqueting Hall and played Roulette afterwards. Harry was banker and did it all very well. He is a good host. Our party was: Ian, Beatrice Grosvenor, Harry, Rosemary Grosvenor, Teddie Schuller, Alice Keppel, Mr. Baird, Tiny, Capt. Allfrey, Jean Kennerley and Mr. Collins. . . . " [20th September 1937 Lennoxlove]

Alice Keppel's daughter, Violet, had married Denys Trefusis in June 1919. Gossip was rife about Violet and the renowned woman who would become known as her lesbian lover, Vita Sackville-West, the wife of Harold Nicolson. Jean was on holiday with the children at Lou Casteon in France and Norah Lindsay who was staying at Lou Mas, Saint-Jean-Cap-Ferrat, wrote Jean that 'Alice Keppel came to lunch and regaled us with the amazing details of Violet's divorce. It appears he never *lived* with her, as he married her on those conditions, so naturally *now* they both dislike each other and it is to be annulled. Strange one *always* thought Violet Keppel an improper flirt. . . . '[14] Mary Hunter, who was holidaying in France at the same time, had another version of the story. **" . . . Mary Hunter lunched with me . . . she was interesting only about Violet Keppel and Vita Nicholson and these wives promising to go back to their respective husbands only if they *all* promised not to live with each other, but lead pure lives. . . . " [27th April 1921 Lou Casteon]**

Denys Trefusis died in 1929 and Violet was at last released from her unhappy marriage. In 1937, she stayed with the Hamiltons at Lennoxlove (prior to her mother Alice's visit), and cutting her own visit short, possibly because she did not want to see her mother. When Violet returned to France, she wrote to Jean, on Monday 20 September 1937, enclosing a photograph of her house, 880 La Tour de Saint-Loup.

> Forgive the delay in thanking your for my delightful and altogether too brief stay at Lennoxlove. It was such a pleasure to visit you again. I kept on saying to myself: what a waste! what a waste! I might have enjoyed this delightful friendship all these years! I hope, at any rate, to see a lot of you in future. You *must* come and stay with me when next you come to Paris. Oddly enough, it is rather like an inferior fragment of Lennoxlove, the same period, the same colour.

Thanking you and Sir Ian a hundred times for being so attractive.

I am ever
Yours affectionately
Violet.[15]

Whilst the Hamiltons were holidaying in Monte Carlo in 1939, Alice Keppel's granddaughter made her debut in society. The 'Court and Society' page of the *Sunday Times*, 26 March 1939, which Jean cut out and kept in her diary, reported a debutantes' ball given by the Countess of Elgin and the Countess of Leven at Claridge's. Among those beautiful young girls who danced the hours away amidst the glamour of white gowns, diamonds and tiaras was the eighteen-year-old Rosalind Cubitt, daughter of Sonia and Roland. Rosalind would in turn marry Bruce Shand a few years later and become the mother of Camilla Parker Bowles.

CHAPTER 15

The Later Years

" . . . I have always flown to my diary in my moments of intolerable
depression for comfort, as a safety valve, to get rid of the gloom." [9th
September 1926 Deanston]

On her birthday, Jean " . . . sat for five hours at the hairdressers having
my hair permanently waved, and only just managed to catch the train
. . . and I snatched a hasty bit of delicious Parlett cooked tongue with
wine sauce alone in my Studio. . . . " [8th June 1920 Blair Drummond]
A newspaper portrait by Compton Collier shows her in roaring twenties
style, wearing a slinky dress, her hair shaped and waved, a band round her
head, her eyes made up with eye-liner, long, dangling ear-rings, a rope of
waist-length beads round her neck, and in her hand a huge feather, draped
across her lap. She could have got away with admitting to being thirty-five
but not twenty-nine; she was aged fifty-nine. There was also a newspaper
report entitled 'SIR IAN'S JAZZ'. Ian, Sir Alexander Godley and Sir Archibald
Murray had been to a children's party at Claridge's, and were 'seen con-
templating with considerable satisfaction the jazzing of pretty little flap-
pers.' Of the three, only Ian, aged sixty-seven, 'the ever youthful leader of
the attack on the Dardanelles' had 'ventured to take the floor'.
    In November 1920, Alice Keppel's youngest daughter, Sonia, married
the Hon. Roland Cubitt in the Guards' Chapel in London. The press published photographs of society guests – Jean and Adéle Essex among them
– swathed in furs. John Fane and Hereward Wake were the pageboys and
the Hon. Cecilia Keppel, Lady Bury's daughter, was one of the six brides-
maids. " . . . This is Sonia Keppel's wedding day. I lunched with Adéle
Essex, Ann Islington and Norah Lindsay, and we all went together.
She made a radiant bride, but Mrs. Fane's little boy as page howled
dismally throughout. . . . " [16th November 1920]
    A few days after the wedding, Jean, Harry and Fodie went to France
for the winter to Lou Casteon, a villa situated in beautiful, romantic, pic-

turesque countryside, close to Brooke House, the home of Jean's friend Haller Brooke. Sonia and Roland Cubitt were honeymooning nearby and visited Jean and Haller. Like Jean, Sonia suffered from asthma. "**... Today she [Haller] took the Cubitts back with her to show them her garden. I like Sonia – ... she is pretty to look at, pretty to talk to, but *he* tires me dreadfully. I think she will have a terribly dull life with him – they go back to London tomorrow. ...**" But the weather changed, it rained heavily and all the flowers in the gardens of Lou Casteon died. It was cold and the radiators kept failing. [**29th–31 Nov.; 1st and 14th Dec. 1920**]

Ian and his secretary, Miss Mary Kaye (later Mrs Shield), joined Jean and the children for part of the holiday. While the Hamiltons were in France, several of their friends were there, some of whom owned houses, and it was rather like 'little London'. There was always fear of another war with Germany and war was still much talked about. Jean's attitude towards the beaten enemy was the same as Ian's, that an amicable settlement should be secured to guarantee peace, otherwise a dissatisfied Germany might live to fight another day. Part of the reason the Hamiltons and their circle did not feel very great animosity towards Germany was that before the war they were very friendly with those Germans with whom they identified socially, the moneyed gentry and aristocracy, the intellectual elite. Many English families sent their sons and daughters to the traditional schools in Germany where they themselves had been educated. The royal family were of German descent, some of whom still spoke English with a German accent. Kaiser Wilhelm's London house was in the Mews near 1 Hyde Park Gardens.

"**... I met Lord French with Mrs. Bennett – he looked so old I wondered if it could possibly be Lord French. I told him about Lord Northcliffe going to visit the Kaiser, and he said he thought it only fair the Kaiser should be allowed to make a statement if he wanted to, and he agreed with me the attitude most people take up nowadays to a beaten enemy is most unchivalrous. I said 'I am sure you will agree with me, having lived with soldiers all my life and having heard them say over and over again "We must fight Germany some day, let us fight them at once as the one who starts has the advantage" – we can't now take a high moral stand about the iniquity of the Kaiser – it is too hypocritical and absurd,' and he laughed and said: 'Yes, I have often said it myself.' ...**" [**17th Jan. 1921 Lou Casteon**]

Jean's brother, Sir Alexander Kay Muir, and her cherished friends

Adéle Essex and Norah Lindsay joined them. " . . . **Our long planned Hotel de Paris dinner came off tonight, and was great fun. . . .**" The climax of the holiday was a night's gambling at the Sporting Club. Jean and Norah gambled at roulette and Adéle and Kay played chemin de fer. " . . . **We stayed till nearly one o'clock. I was dead tired, but made some money. . . . I gambled rather high for me, putting about 8 or 9 louis on each time and winning. . . .**" [17th January 1921 Lou Casteon contd.]

Arriving home, a spectacular sight greeted them in the grounds at Lullenden: " . . . **a huge German gun stuck fast and pointing at us – it has been presented to Ian by a grateful Government!!!. . . .**" [2nd May 1921]

The usual round of dinner engagements followed and Jean found out, perhaps thirty-five years too late, that Lord Alwyne Compton may not have been in love with her after all but with her much younger sister, Edie. " . . . **To-night we dined with the Arthur Pollens and after dinner a man with a lovely voice sang. 'We'll go no more a 'roving by the light of the moon' brought back so vividly the moonlight night on the river with Alwyne, and how I wrote him next day and quoted these lines. . . . Mr. Levenson Gower . . . began talking of the Comptons – said they were relations of his . . . he talked of his charm and good looks which pleased me, then went on to tell me how it came about that he married his wife; he said he was really in love with Edie, had proposed to her and been refused, that he confided then in Mollie Vyner, who comforted him by getting engaged to him herself. . . . How thrilling I would have found this once, now, gazing into the fire to-night as I pensively listened, it was a tale that is told of far away unhappy things.**" [5th May 1921 London]

Five months in France had improved Jean's physical and mental health and the children were always a joy to her. She passed her sixtieth birthday quite happily. " . . . **My birthday – and Mother tells me I am sixty years old to-day. I can't believe it. I don't feel sixty, nor look like it, nor can I dress like it, or behave like it. What is to be done? Straightway forget it, I think. [8th June 1921]**

Two days later, she learnt that Lady Randolph Churchill had suffered a sudden, fatal illness. Léonie Leslie, Lady Randolph's sister, phoned Jean to say she could not lunch with her as she could not leave Jennie who was ill. Lady Randolph had fallen down the steps whilst staying with Lady

Frances Horner at Mells Manor, Somerset. After lunch Jean went round in the car to fetch Léonie to go to the theatre to see a play. " . . . **Léonie rushed out obviously terribly upset as we got to the door . . . she then told me poor Jennie's foot will have to be amputated, perhaps to-night, as gangrene had set in from the sprain to her ankle which hap-pened at Mells a fortnight ago, because her maid had not rubbed a pair of new shoes she was wearing. . . . She asked me not to say any-thing about the amputation, as she did not wish a great fuss made. . . . "** [**10th June 1921**] The soles of new leather shoes had to be sandpapered to make them grip. Lady Soames, Lady Randolph's granddaughter, says Jennie's ankle was broken.[1]

The sudden demise of the seemingly invincible Lady Randolph, one of the most beautiful and colourful characters in Jean's life, brought her to a deeper awareness that she was growing old. When she went to stay at Deanston she saw the plight also of her aged mother. " . . . **I think I am getting very old, for I long for the effortless comfort of Deanston, both mental and physical – the long, long drives with Mother every after-noon, in which she repeated again and again . . . the same things and asked the same questions and I gave the same answers, they were soothing, restful drives in monotony amidst such lovely scenes, and I love the frail little old Mother who loves and clings to me – the walks in the well-known, well-loved garden with its jewelled borders of mar-ginal flowers – the comfy luncheons and dinners on the fine and spot-less damask – gleaming silver, exquisite roses, and delicious food – strawberries, raspberries, thick cream, and lovely hot rich soups, and above all my delicious room, with its great balcony, where I stand in my silk nightie, with the summer winds blowing it about, and brush out my fine hair – though short it is very thick, and it's lovely to feel the soft wind through it – this year it grows very grey, and I fear the last lingering remains of what beauty it possessed is leaving me now – more lines appear but I try not to think of the enemy in the glass. . . . "** [**6th August 1921 Cairnoch**]

Ian, by comparison, remained young and sprightly, both mentally and physically, despite being nine years older than Jean, though at times he took too much out of himself and was over-tired. " . . . **His book 'The Soul and Body of An Army' is just coming out – he is very keen about this, and rightly so. I think it is going to be splendid, though I have only just read the first three chapters, it seems to me brilliant and I am** struck again by his sparkle, courage and concentration. As he has this absorbing passion for writing. . . .

. . . I could not sleep last night . . . we seemed to be all riding in the Valley of Death – Mother, me, Ian, Betty, Nora, and all nearing the end – the last fence to face. . . . " [24th August 1921]

Jean could always escape in her mind back to India, and write about her youth as she remembered it then, filling in some of the missing gaps in her life story. " . . . As I lay half awake this morning I planned, as often before, writing out my recollections, the great times in my life that stand out, days and hours that are vivid still. My first adventure going to India, wakening ill with scarlet fever in the awful storm – India, walking in my violet velvet pansy dress with Charlie Muir at the Races. My first meeting with Lord Alwyne at the Park, Ballygunge, and the look he gave me on that Sunday afternoon as he walked away after tea and tennis, and I marked him for my own. . . . " [31st August 1921]

In the years ahead, dear friends and family would die, some of old age and others well before their time. Whilst Jean was still at Deanston, news reached her that Lady Randolph had died, " . . . which distressed me terribly, – that splendid vital woman – I shall miss her very much; I loved having her so near us, and often saw her. . . . " [3rd July 1921] Montagu Porch sent Jean a memento: " . . . Clemmie brought me a fan of Jennie's that Porchie has sent me, poor little man. . . . " [24th October 1921 Lullenden]

In her diaries there are no stories of Jean as a happy little girl and almost nothing is said about her childhood until now. She had a governess named Fletty whom she "adored". But Fletty took to drink and Sir John Muir dismissed her: " . . . the day she was sent away is stamped for ever on my heart in tragic memory. . . . " Jean was Fletty's idol and she loved her. Later, having moved to Australia and reformed, she wrote a book. " . . . Fletty describes in her tragic vivid way how she set up this idol in her heart, saying to God: 'I have loved this idol, and after it I will go,' and how 'it was torn from her in the sweet summer months in a way most humbling, most humiliating, and how she spent days in a horror of great darkness, alone in her room, the sunshine and blue sky being too painful to bear.'

Mother tells me she used to come by train and sit on the Bridge of Allan hill road with a telescope, and watch Deanston to see her come out of the door. Fletty describing some of the nights in the journey she eventually did take to Australia, says: 'And those stars, they seemed to bend down from those still strange heights above and smile pitifully at the sick lonely watcher struggling on alone –....' " [15th February 1920 Deanston]

"... Recollections of childhood are always very dull, except to the recollector ... – mine are a very confusing jumble – being whipped by my nurse for tickling baby Nan with a feather, is the very first, in my old nursery – chasing sheep dressed up in an old coat at Hartree, and pretending to be one – wild plays of slaves and desert islands – delicious readings, full of a fascinated horror of the 'Arabian Nights' in the school room at Deanston seated in a great arm-chair built for two with Nan; I never dared read the 'Arabian Nights' alone, they frightened me so, and gave me a strange feeling of oppression – long afterwards the too luxuriant vegetation in Ceylon gave me the same sinister oppression. Nan was a great help and steadied my nerves – my sister Betty was my boon companion, but Nan was my admirer and comforter ... stealing apples with Nora over a garden wall I remember also, the joy, never, like St. Augustine, with repentance or remorse...." [4th September 1921]

Despite the Hamiltons' advancing years, they were both still ambitious for Ian's chances of obtaining a commission at Gibraltar, though he was approaching seventy years of age. They had been harbouring the idea from the time of their holiday at Lou Casteon, when they went to Monte Carlo for the day to meet Winston and Clementine Churchill. " ... We lunched with Adéle Essex to-day. Winston had just gone, rather a blow to us as Ian wanted to ask him to give him Gibraltar. Clemmie was there, looking rather lovely, but illish. He asked her at once, she said she did not know if it was in Winston's gift, and Ian said 'Oh, yes, it was.' ... " [4th February 1921 Hotel Balmoral] But several months later, Winston's desire to change the way the crown colonies were administered made Gibraltar less attractive to Jean. " ... I want Ian to try and get Gib after Smith-Dorrien gives it up, and so retrieve our shattered fortunes, but I see Winston has a new scheme of Government for the Crown Colonies, and Gib. is to have a High Commissioner stationed at Malta, and I could not go there, and would not like to have that...." [15th September 1921 Lullenden]

The Hamiltons spent Christmas and the New Year at Deanston and early in 1922 tragedy struck again, this time within the family. Jean's brother, Will Muir, of romantic Postlip Hall days, where Jean painted pictures of the house with Winston Churchill, fell from his horse whilst hunting and was badly injured. An operation to his back could not save him and he died on 9 February. Jean almost never attended wakes or funerals, preferring to remember everyone as they were. "... **Ian told me the burial on the hill was one of the most beautiful sights he has ever seen – Will was so loved by everyone....**" [14th February 1922]

Signs of ageing persisted and Jean endured a long period of attacks of bronchial asthma. Throughout her life she had been admired for her great beauty and clever conversation at dinner parties. The prospect of losing her looks was a dreadful experience and she had face massage, "... **a last desperate attempt to save my face....**" [4th March 1922] Her teeth were giving her trouble and she was suffering with pain in her gums. "... **I have been torn with indecision the last week whether to have three of my front teeth out or not ... and I dread to loose the remaining traces of good looks still left me.**" [16th July 1922] With some apprehension she had her front teeth removed and replaced with false ones. Nora reassured her it was "... **an improvement though it seems to me the new teeth look too prominent, but each night since, she has said to me: 'How lovely you look', quite involuntarily, when we have met just before dinner; when I have all my war paint on I suppose my appearance is not ruined yet quite completely....**" [21st July 1922]

Jean got used to her new teeth in time for the Buckingham Palace garden party, where she found her friends, too, were beginning to look and feel their years. "... **The Buckingham Palace garden party was not exciting, but a lovely day and crowds of old friends made it nice. Jack and Anne Islington, Adéle and the Bridges were the most amusing group Ian and I came across; ... Anne ... hates growing old, poor darling, and complains now men don't ask her to dance, and when Victor Cazalet told her the other night that it took courage to ask an elderly woman to dance she was furious, and said she'd never speak to him again; how marvellous all these women are, how can they go on year in year out and never grow weary with the same chatter, the same weary round.**" [23rd July 1922 Trent Manor]

When Harry and Fodie got their summer holidays from school they went with Jean to Deanston, and the children always lifted her spirits. Kay had bought a new Rolls-Royce and Jean, Kay and Betty motored to

Gleneagles and played golf. " . . . It's delicious to be waking up once more in my lovely flower filled room – the scent of pansies everywhere – lovely great scarlet roses on my writing-table and floods of glorious sunshine. . . . writing nice letters and reading 'Moon Calf' . . . Harry was dancing in his blue dressing gown at the door to welcome me when I arrived . . . and I ran up to see Rosaleen, who hugged me . . . she is a loving little pet; they are such a sweet little pair . . . I can't bear a nature incapable of feeling the happiness of gratitude . . . but the attitude of the present day is to resent any effort of the older generation to make their children's path straight, or shed any happiness thereon, they want to owe everything to themselves, to their own unaided astuteness, the trend of the modern novel is to utterly destroy home influence and home comfort." [27th July 1922]

Earlier that month Jean and Nora dined with Sir John and Lady Lavery. " . . . Nora and I called for Adéle Essex in our motor . . . She looked exquisite – fragile, almost brittle, I thought . . . with her lovely finished grace. . . . " [21st July 1922] Adéle promised to visit Lullenden, but it was a promise never fulfilled. " . . . McAdie rushed in with the 'Daily Mail' and a horrified expression, to tell me Lady Essex was dead. I would not believe it, but there was her lovely face, and in cruel hard print the tragic story of the drowning in her bath – darling Adéle, it's unbelievable and unbearable . . . all that sweetness and loveliness gone for evermore. . . .

Adéle's last words to me when she kissed me goodbye were: 'I *must* come to Lullenden in September' . . . I would not for anything have missed that last precious glimpse of Adéle.

London will never be the same to me without Adéle, she was the most reliable and most real friend I had there – one could depend on Adéle. I can't believe she can be gone, all that sweetness and beauty passed for ever – it is too cruel, too sudden a wrench – with Joan married I thought perhaps she would have married again herself, she looked still so young and lovely. . . . " [29th July 1922 Deanston] The newspapers reported that Lady Essex suffered a heart attack and fell into the bath and drowned. Jean sent a heart-shaped wreath of crimson roses to her funeral.

During the 1920s, the Hamiltons were again held in high esteem in society, Ian steadily eroding the attacks made against him over Gallipoli. His *Gallipoli Diary* had been published and he wrote articles and letters to

the newspapers. He was interviewed on the radio, the latest form of mass
communication with the British people, and remained active in the British
Legion.

They were invited to Henry Nevinson's dinner for the new Labour
Prime Minister but when they reached Bellomo's Restaurant they found
he had not arrived, having been detained at the House of Commons. " . . .
**Ramsay MacDonald . . . the Prime Minister was kept at the House
owing to the indiscretion of Mr. Henderson using the word 'revision'
in connection with the Versailles Treaty. . . . However just as I was
carrying Elizabeth Robins off home with me in my motor, a telephone
summoned us all to Downing Street, the Debate being over, so we all
hopped into the motor and drove through sleet and snow to Downing
Street and were received at the door by an efficient and good-looking
young man, in a dark morning dress of some sort. . . . He conducted us
through many dreary chintz covered rooms and finally we arrived at
the Prime Minister, very charming and courteous, but looking utterly
weary after his fight in the House. He had lost his temper, he said, and
gone for Ronald McLean, as he felt he was unfairly trying to make
trouble, just as the Anglo-French strain had been relaxed. He said he
had felt for the last week, that the Conservatives had been doing all
they could to upset them in every way. I could have told him this was
true, as Lord Hugh Cecil lunched with us to-day and told me he was
all for straight dealing, and going for the enemy in the open, and getting rid of them as soon as possible. I felt him small and narrow-
minded, and had a feeling of relief when I turned to talk to Archie
Balfour on my other side, with his visionary eyes, and his real love of
and comradeship with, his poorer brothers. Lord Hugh's mind
seemed fixed only on his Party – quite mediaeval, he is, both in religion and politics. He was sitting by Mrs. Belloc Lowndes, the Harry
Grahams lunched also. I think Lord Hugh had expected a gay Norah
Lindsay kind of luncheon party, and was rather surprised. He said he
hated clever conversation – poor man, he wants his tired mind rested.
Mrs. Belloc Lowndes is clever, ugly, but soothing I think.**

**I was perched on the arm of the vast sofa on which the Prime
Minister and Mr. Nevinson were sunk blotted as these recollections
passed through my mind, and just then Miss Ishbel entered unobtru-
sively and seated herself beside Elizabeth Robins, and I studied her
quietly. Poor child! I wonder how she feels! Certainly she looks as if**

her proper place was the kitchen – her hands swelled and blue as though all her life she had scrubbed floors. She has a nice, sweet, good, homely face, but was paralysed with shyness. On the table beside Ian was the Prime Minister's supper – 4 brown biscuits, and some medicine stuff – a black kettle buzzed on the fire – altogether a strange scene within these walls. I felt it was cruel to stay long, as we were giving no stimulus to the exhausted man beside me. Mr. Nevinson leading him on by a question or a remark from time to time, but Ian was quite silent, sitting on an arm chair near me.

I asked the P.M. which had been the most exciting night – the night before which had been Mr. Wheatley's triumph over Poplar, or to-night? And he said, 'To-night.' I fancy there is a little jealously in his heart about Mr. Wheatley. I know from Mr. Nevinson that he never wanted to include Wheatley in the Cabinet, but could not keep him out. He is there, their great strong man, but last night from being their greatest danger and menace sprung into eminence as their greatest asset and bright star, patted on the back by Mr. Asquith for his clever debating speech.

That rather depresses me, for I feel if this party can gain anything, it must be by simple sincerity and not by clever political debating tricks.

Violet B.C. [Bonham Carter] came to my dinner last night just before her Father spoke – she had left the House she said just after Wheatley's speech. She was very excited over it and said how splendid it was. Margot had turned to a woman beside her and said excitedly, 'That's a splendid speech and will be difficult to answer,' and the woman she said it to, was Lady Joyson-Hicks, whom she did not know by sight, who was heckling Wheatley over Poplar, and who by his speech, was thoroughly ousted." [27th February 1924 London]

At the beginning of 1925 illness and depression once again stalked Jean's life, her mental state doubtless affected by the cocktail of drugs the doctors prescribed: injections of adrenaline, morphine, opium for her asthma; bella donna for hay fever. " . . . I have lain awake a long time, struggling with depression and fear. I have such an agitated feeling of apprehension – I don't know of what. I hope my second childhood is not going to be as painful in this way as my first – one's brain could not stand it – I wonder how I ever struggled through it in childhood. I used to live day after day with the fear of hell fire flaming before my eyes, all day long, from the dreadful Calvinistic teaching I was sub-jected to.

Now the fire is lit, the day breaking, and the electric light pouring over this page I feel better – can almost find a drop of courage to go on with, but the long dark hours crowded with terrible thoughts are awful. . . . " [6th January 1925 Deanston]

Soon after writing these lines, Jean was sedated with morphine, and accompanied by the faithful McAdie, was driven by ambulance back to London to a convalescent home, The Nook, in Hampstead. Little was writ-ten in her diary during those dark days of nervous illness, but nine weeks later Jean returned to No. 1 HPG for Easter. The doctor thought the trou-ble with her nerves was a reaction to having been injected with adrenaline when she'd fainted. A nurse from the convalescent home came to look after her until she was completely well again. Jean was all the more prone to depression now that she no longer had the children in the house with her every day to cheer her up. Harry and Fodie were both at boarding school and only came home during school holidays.

Another treasured friend from the days when Jean was young and beautiful died suddenly.

"... Sargent is dead! ...

'The silence of that dreamless sleep I envy now
Too much to weep.'

He meant much in my life once. I have been thinking and dream-ing all day of the happy days I used to pass with him in his Studio when he painted my portrait, and I used to lunch alone with him in his lovely dining room in his Chelsea house and we had many lovely talks. How restful his Studio where he used to play Wagner and Fauré to me and taught me to love them and books, how much I owe him! I read Alice Maynell's poems and many others as I sat while he painted me. . . . " [16th April 1925]

Employment was a topical subject in the twenties and thirties. The working classes faced the dole queues and soup kitchens during the reces-sion. Jean recognised the importance of work when she took up replanting the gardens at Lullenden. "... A lovely long day's work here in my land girl's dress. I have not felt so happy or well for years as nettle hunting in this dress, and planting rock plants in our new little Dutch garden – probably if all superfluous wealth was got rid of, it would not be the misfortune we now suppose – doing work that counts oneself is what is delightful in life, but the poor have to work *too* hard, and have not good enough conditions and not comfortable enough homes yet. If one were forced to see the wretchedness of some of their lives it would be heart-breaking, I know – one just goes on without thinking, and accepts the existing order, but it is passing away before our eyes to-day and things must be better. . . . " [8th January 1920 Lullenden]

1926 was the year made memorable by the General Strike. Miners, railway workers and many others were on strike, provoked by the mine owners demanding a pay cut. Hyde Park was a central point for strikers' gatherings and Jean could see the crowds from her upstairs windows. The police locked out the strikers: " . . . **The Park gates are closed . . . and guarded by policemen, and some mushroom tents have sprung up in the night and rows of benches to distribute milk, under my window. . . . "** [3rd May 1926] " . . . **The General Strike is upon us . . . and streams of poor work people are pouring along the Bayswater Road . . . as Underground and Tubes are out – some crammed omnibuses still running. . . . "** [4th May 1926 London] The well-to-do opposed the strike and could be seen manning the railways, driving and conducting buses, and attempting manual work to which they had never previously been accustomed. " . . . **Hyde Park is crammed with Society – both men and women – the women feeding all their smart emergency men driving lorries and milk vans, and food stuffs of every description, defended by soldiers in armoured cars, the strikers gazing at these proceedings through the railings." [9th May 1926]**

In the absence of war work, well-to-do women found they had nothing to occupy them save charity work which may not have been as exciting or rewarding as driving ambulances, or making parachutes or munitions in the factories during war time. "**. . . It's sad no employment is to be found for the lonely idle rich women strewn about, with their starving souls. Their bodies are overfed but they eat out their own hearts in despairing isolation. Work, work, work, a panacea for all life's wounds, if only interesting work could be found for all, how many of our problems would be solved.**

At present Maxton & Co. are fighting Ramsay MacDonald and his Government about unemployment, and indeed it's awful. I wonder the Thames these cold stormy nights, is not choked with dead bodies. I can't imagine why they don't end their misery, shivering wretches, unemployed and unemployable. I am reading 'Humanity Uprooted'

just now, a most thrilling and interesting book on Bolshevism by [Maurice] **Hindus. They think they are going to solve the riddle of the universe; as far as I have gone it will only be the survival of the fittest over again, the down-and-outs mentally, physically, morally will be trampled down, only Christianity so far has provided for them. . . . "** [8th December 1929 London]

Since the war, the British economy was less buoyant and Jean did not receive such high dividends on her shares. No. 1 HPG and Lullenden were let when the Hamiltons were not in residence, to raise funds to help pay for their upkeep. Deanston would later be sold. **[25th July; 25th August 1926]**

The advantage of keeping a diary was that Jean could dip into it years later and what she read there could prompt her to examine herself – her faults and failures – and make her see there was room for improvement. **" . . . Mother has been reading pages from my diary 1901–1902 . . . it's rather wonderful to plunge into my diary box and drag days out of my life of twenty years ago – the days live again as I read, I remember it all so vividly – but what a prig I was, and a bore, moaning and whining over nothing – I have always used my diary as a safety valve, and put into it what I kept hidden from the world!" [6th February 1922]**

" . . . On Sunday Mr. Fleming our minister quoted [a] **family motto – 'Who tholes, wins,' so often true. I have been lying thinking over my failures in life because never would I 'Thole'** [tolerate, bear patiently] **anything. I see where I go wrong, but seem unable to change my impatient nature I will thole nothing. How I failed Alwyne when broken by his love for that minx he wanted comfort and help . . . but no! thinking only of myself and my hurt feelings of how he had failed me, I would not stretch out a hand to him in his need and lit no candle for him in his dark surprised misery, and I *could* have helped him, I know, more than anyone else, but was bitter, proud, hard; to Ian I know I am over and over again; though I adore him and mean to be so different – . . .**

. . . I have the diary craze, I suppose, and write because I must express *myself*, not to record facts. . . . " [30th August 1923, 5.30 a.m.]

The glamour of Jean's hey day was in her diary, to be re-lived again, a means of escapism for a fleeting moment. **" . . . Have been reading my old diary of 25 years ago – (a description of a Court ball which I did not much enjoy). I write of many of my old friends that night –**

Alwyne Compton, George Holford, George Wyndham, Charlie Harbord, Riversdale Walrond – all dead – 'All, all are gone – the old familiar faces:' how Tommy Ribblesdale laughed when I quoted that once to him, he said '*how* he wished it were true,' bored as one then was by the monotony of always meeting the same people: Nellie Londonderry – Daisy Warwick – Sarah Wilson – Alice Keppel – lovely Muriel Beckett – I can see them all again as I write, and when I read my diary they live again – the scenes so inadequately described, rise again around me – it was for this I wrote this diary – to be able to go back and look again at what was passing so quickly away. I desired to seize the moments and store them for myself – 'to shake hands with my old forgotten self across the years:' I forget who said that, someone I think before me, and I have loved to do it – enjoy doing it. . . . Ettie Desborough, I remember, once told me, she had always admired the calmness and serenity with which I had gone through these parties, where all the women were running after Ian. She did not say, 'and would have preferred to get him without you,' but I was often acutely aware of it, but Ian would never go anywhere if I were not asked. . . . " [30th January 1927 London]

The particular court ball to which Jean was referring took place soon after the end of the Boer War. She had spent most of the day at a convalescent home with her sister Betty, who was receiving treatment there for her nerves. Jean had found the doctor treating Betty to be very difficult to get on with. When she arrived a Buckingham Palace with Ian, she was tired and out of sorts. " . . . **I had a boring time . . . I felt incapable of cheering up or making an effort but did get five amusing minutes with Lord Harris, such a pompous old darling! Seated in an empty ante-room with him I felt terribly bored and desperate; so, to put life into the situation and amuse myself I suddenly kicked off my slipper, flicking it as far as I could up in the air. It's a trick I am quite good at but I don't think Lord Harris had ever encountered so revolutionary, so riotous an act in the whole of his previous existence as the exhibition of such chamber tricks at a Court Ball with officials and grandees nearby. I did laugh at his face of horror. . . . "** [July 8th 1903]

One afternoon in the spring of 1927 the Hamiltons set out to Lullenden. It was a trip that would end with Jean suffering tremendous personal loss; her maid, McAdie, never arrived. " . . . **McAdie is dead!**

It's fantastic – unbelievable – every minute I feel she must walk in, with the comfort and security she always brings with her.

This morning when I was dressing she came in half-laughing, and said, 'It's awful, my lady, but I don't somehow feel well.' I said, 'Oh, McAdie, don't tell me you are going to be ill.' And she said it was really nothing, a slight pain in her chest, like a lump, and that her right arm felt numb. I made her sit down in the armchair beside my bed, and she shook her arm and hand, and I insisted on ringing for Nurse Mitchell, who was busy over her white washing. McAdie begged me not to call her, but I would and she came and felt her pulse – said it was all right – good and strong. At 3.30 Nurse and she were to motor down with us; Ian on the box and the rest of us inside, but the car was packed so full of boxes and my numerous coats, that McAdie said, at the last moment, she would wait and come by train with Crewe – she waved and smiled to us as we drove off.

I was awaiting the comfort of 'Tadie's' arrival when Ian came and tried to get me back to the house. I would not come, until Ian put his arm through mine, and took me into the little hall, saying he had bad news – 'Not Mother?' I said, terrified. 'No. McAdie.' 'Is she ill?' Where is she?' and he said, 'She is dead'.

I would not, could not believe it, and can't now. When Crewe came she told us 'Tadie' . . . seemed all right in the taxi and took the tickets at the station, and just before Oxted had been admiring the scenery – then fell back and closed her eyes and died without a groan or a struggle – no sadness of farewell for her. She is triumphant in death! Splendid for her, but for me very, very terrible – my friend of 28 years – gone away for ever. She has been like a mother to me in her care, love and pride in me. I feel completely lost without her.

The mainspring of our household is broken! I can't believe the door will not open, and she come in, with her comfortable reassuring presence; she was such a help with the children, so wise in her advice about them both.

'Said not good-night, will she in some brighter clime
Bid me good-morrow'?"

[12th April 1927]

Jean did not go to McAdie's wake or funeral, but Ian went. " . . . Ian says McAdie looked magnificent – like an Egyptian Princess. She was very good-looking – her beautiful thick grey hair, nearly white now, drawn back from her forehead, her face in grand, still repose. I did not want to see her dead. I would rather remember her waving and smiling to me from the front door . . . having seen none of the dread paraphernalia of death – as if my beloved McAdie was just away, and when she returns would take everything up in her capable hands and put things straight for me again." [17th April 1927 Lullenden]

Servants were not usually addressed by their first names and it is not until after McAdie is dead we find out her first name was Helen and then only from the newspaper report of her dying on the train. Her family took her body back to Caithness for burial.[2]

From the time the Hamiltons bought Lullenden, Jean knew she would have to manage on less money, which was not one of her strong points. When the London house was not let it was hired out for functions that raised extra cash. In 1922, Ian's Lullenden farm had lost £1,500, though it later made a profit. They had given up the second car and when Ian went to London on business he travelled round the City on the bus. [31st March; 22nd September 1922]

The employed men at Lullenden gave priority to Ian's instructions for the farm, over Jean's requirements for the garden. " . . . **Woodgate is going to be a bone of contention between Ian and me I can see – the farm against the garden – I thought when I had my own gardener this difficulty would be removed – it was always difficult with Jeffrey between the two of us, if he pleased one he displeased the other. . . . "** [20th May 1923 Lullenden]

After the death of McAdie, life at Lullenden became more difficult for Jean. McAdie had taken care of Jean's health and without her she suffered more frequent asthma attacks. Whilst staying in London, she was " . . . **dreading going to Lullenden without McAdie. . . . "** [17th May 1927 London] She went on holiday with the children for several months each year and when she returned, the garden was in a state of neglect. The romance of the place gradually melted away into smelly pigs, mud, a rotten pond, and the flowerbeds overgrown with weeds. In January 1928 Jean had already decided to give up Lullenden and was again living at No. 1 HPG. By October, Lullenden was on the market for sale. [9th January; 28th October 1928]

Only the house was sold, Ian kept Lullenden Farm and his herd of belted galloway cattle that won prizes in the shows in Scotland. " . . . **Ian**

came back from the Royal Show this morning very cock a hoop as he has won First Prize for his bull 'Concrete' and a lot of other prizes. ...."
[25th July 1929 London] His nephew, 'little Ian', was interested in the belted galloways from he was a boy and visited the farm frequently. Ian left twelve of his cattle in his will to 'little Ian', who in turn passed the herd on to his son Alexander and daughter Helen, who continue the tradition of breeding belted galloways in Scotland today. In 1999 Helen won nine trophies; two of her cattle, mother and son, were named 'Lullenden Abbie' and 'The Abbot'. Alexander remembers 'big Ian' visiting his house when he was a child. 'He came on a Sunday and always gave me sixpence. Once when he was handing me the sixpence he dropped it. We searched the floor but it could not be found. That night, after 'big Ian' returned home and was getting ready for bed the sixpence tumbled out of the turn up of his trousers.'

In 1935, Ian offered Winston Churchill a belted galloway and Winston asked: " ' . . . why this generosity?' and Ian said: 'Because your stock[s] are going up', and Winston said: 'Oh, No! That is not the reason. Your are a foul weather friend.' "[20th October 1935]

The loss of McAdie left a great void in Jean's life and though she now had a new maid, Collins, it was obvious from the start she could not take McAdie's place. At one level Jean was highly accomplished and could converse on many subjects and despite her asthma even excel at sport, golf in particular. At another level, in the absence of any professional training or the discipline of salaried employment, she was so inadequate she could not look after her own spectacles. " . . . motored here with Collins . . . rather disgusted to find Collins had left Despatch case with my specs. in the motor car, and that Martin had locked the car up and gone to the village. Collins had left everything ready I found when I came to bed except the one essential thing, my eyes! so I could not read as I always do. I call her 'Dorothy Perkins', she is just like a rambler rose, after having a sturdy oak to lean on – like my dear McAdie. . . . " [4th July 1927 Sissinghurst]

" . . . Collins tries my temper sadly. I fear I shall grow terribly irritable and will be unable to keep her; she is such a nice girl, I am sad about it, but she makes just the sort of maid I would make myself – vague, dreamy – not on the 'spot'. . . . " [13th September 1927]

In money matters Jean was accustomed to her investments being taken care of by accountants and her brother Kay, and had no experience of handling money, even in the smallest way. "... **Alick McGrigor dined tonight, and I had not enough money to pay the dinner in my purse – Collins had not given me enough, McAdie would never have let this happen; my maids always keep my money, and dole it out as I want it, as I never can keep any account of money – and Ian had to come to my rescue, and as he is very vague too, we had to ask the waiter to count the money we gave him and take his tip, and Moyra** [a niece] **kept producing a silly half crown and being annoying. I felt very humiliated and inadequate. I would soon learn but have always been accustomed to have this done for me.**

After dinner the dancing was fun; I liked dancing with Alick. I long to Charleston, but am afraid to attempt it, and feel absurd at my age dancing at all, but I love it so, and enjoyed dancing with Ian, who adores passionately, prancing; the jazz band is good and haunts me." [20th September 1927 Gleneagles]

Like her women friends, Jean wanted something useful to do, to have some real input into life, or a say in how the country was run, but the social structure barred her in every way. The only sphere in which she could operate was in the field of voluntary, charitable work, feeling herself unsuited to the kind of philanthropy which would have involved going down among the masses in the slums, where the dust and dirt would have caused an asthma attack. "... **I have been lying awake for hours, with the Hallelujah Jazz fox trot drumming away in my head, thinking of life – how futile and aimless it all seems – there ought to be a golden thread – an aim, running through it to hold it together. Ian has found it in his work, and while you pursue an aim you can keep well contented – happy."** [21st Sept. 1927]

Jean was so undomesticated she could not change her alarm clock from summer time to winter time or make herself a cup of tea, and had to have maids to do these things for her. "... **Lawrence Binyon sent me his new Ode to criticise in type, 'A Cry from the Dark Night of the Soul,' – it terrified me and I hastily shoved it back under cover.**

Summer time has been changed to winter time, so when I awoke this morning haunted by the thought of having to get through an extra hour, it was only 3.30 – ... finally after ages I turned on the light boldly – 5.15, but Collins had not changed my little clock, so it was only 4.15; however got up, found the 'Ode' and tackled it ... but got exhausted and cold, and at 8 could bear it no more and called Collins

to tell Joan to bring tea. It was of course only 7 a.m. and Joan arrives grim and furious at being asked to bring tea half an hour earlier, on *Sundays* I have it usually at 7.30. . . . " [Sunday 22nd October 1927 Deanston]

McAdie had been of 'the old school', conscientious almost to a fault. Collins was younger and less subservient. Working-class women had always worked in the cotton mills and factories in the north. Collins was a product of an even newer age, having seen women in large cities like London take over men's jobs in the factories during World War One. By the end of the year, Collins escaped domestic service when she married a Scottish piper and went to live at Chelsea Barracks.

How to cope with growing old had become a pressing problem in Jean's life and that of her contemporaries. An American newspaper reported in 1924 that Lady Diana Manners and her mother, the Duchess of Rutland, were being sued by a Chicago beauty doctor for allegedly not paying a bill for a face-lift. Jean tried to resign herself to Browning's philosophical approach, though he was a man! " . . . A *serene* old age is the picture I want to hold firmly before my eyes, but how can ever one like me attain it? . . . It was easy for Browning, when middle-aged to write:–

> 'Grow old along with me – the *best* is yet to be
> The last of life for which the first was made.'

but when old age did overtake him – 'The Poet's age is sad,' is what he cried – 'the burning bush dead!' " [27th January 1927 London]

In the world of fashion where Jean and her female friends had shone for years, they were now overshadowed by young girls. " . . . I took Louie Godley to Reville's dress show – mannequins parading to slow music – such heat and crowds of ugly old women, with fat bodies, looking on at the slim loveliness of the models, who all have the figures of very young boys and all dresses nowadays are made for figures like this." [15th March 1927] Maud Cunard, whom Jean saw at a party given by the Swiss Minister, M. Paravacini, and his wife, seemed to have overcome ageing. " . . . At Paravacini's we found a wonderful party and wild music – by Stravinsky and Avric, going on. . . . Maud's Eton crop looked somewhat thinned by Father Time, and her very bare back somewhat roughened by the same cruel old fellow, though she defies him with great bravado." [21st March 1927]

Jean and Ian were now playing tennis a lot and Ian weathered the years well, keeping up his dancing, jazzing to the wireless, spurred on by Fred and Adele Astaire, who had taken London by storm with their dancing, "... **London is mad about them. . . .** " [28th May 1926] The Hamiltons were happier than they had ever been, Jean now in her mid-sixties and Ian in his mid-seventies. "**... I said to Ian tonight I wonder if we know how happy and peaceful we are here. We dine together at a small table, in the parlour, drawn up to the wide window, and the wireless is like our own private band, a thing we have always longed to have and said if we were millionaires a band to play to us during dinner we would have.**" [Sunday 1st August 1926 Lullenden] Jean admired Ian's ability to defy ageing: "**... It is his beloved work, his successful work, that keeps him so well balanced, gives him a central resting place. He made me read his Stornoway speech yesterday ... it is very fine and inspiring – he speaks and writes with such facility now – he has gone on so far! Whilst I have stayed 'put' and not developed. . . .** " [Sunday 18th September 1927] Ian's life was always packed with activity and fulfilment and undoubtedly caused Jean to focus on her own lack of confidence. "**... I long to make friends with myself again, to feel my old reckless confidence in Jean. . . .** " [29th January 1928]

Photographs of Jean and Ian taken in the twenties and thirties show they looked at least twenty years younger than their age, still elegant and youthful. Jean's tall, slim figure is dressed in the latest fashion: fitted dresses with a rope of imitation pearls and ear-rings; a picture hat and coat with bell-shaped sleeves, piped with fur and matching fur stole; 1920s shoes. Ian, in morning dress: striped trousers, cut away black jacket and a top hat. Annie Woodger, having been with them many years, had taken over as Jean's maid and was well suited to the job. Annie was an excellent dressmaker and could run up a dress for Jean in which she looked and felt just as good as in one from a leading fashion house, and for a fraction of the cost.

Singer Sargent had summed up Jean's personality accurately as "**un**satisfied". Year on year, she had difficulty accepting she was ageing and tried to grapple with it, 'losing' a year or two along the way. "**...** **Jean, you must face facts – you are** *sixty-five!* **Astounding fact! You are growing very old, and beginning to feel your age however much you may still lightly skip and dance about on your ten toes. What are you going to do about it? Your health is better since you abandoned**

Lullenden, and you may live another ten years; you must get more method into your life, and not just waste your time weeping inwardly over life as you have done the past two years, your heart beating funeral marches to the grave – be up and doing, you silly woman: not much time left." [9th January 1928] She would in fact be sixty-seven on her next birthday.

One way of coping with getting older was to compare herself with her friends who also had been renown for their beauty, and then console herself that she was looking better. " . . . it was amusing to-night to find myself dining with Sibyl Colefax. . . . I was pleased with my own looks and new red shoes and flower, worn with my black velvet and new Russian jewellery. . . .

Austen Chamberlain was the guest of honour, the other men were odds and ends, except Evan Charteris . . .

Alice Keppel, looking large and fat, was there in a short unbecoming frock, her grey hair was tousled all over her head – an unbecoming shingle. Lady [Grace] Curzon plump and common-looking with henna-coloured hair, and mauve orchids worn with white – Julia Maguire covered with beads – Brenda Dufferin looking young and attractive. . . . " [19th March 1928 London]

Ian remained very active in the British Legion and there were frequent functions and celebrations. A more liberal attitude was taken towards the servants. Annie Woodger, who had been called by her first name when she was the children's maid, continued to be called Annie when she was promoted to become Jean's personal maid. At a dance, when there was a shortage of male partners, many men having been killed in the war, Jean found herself dancing with the chauffeur, Henry Martin. " . . . We had more than 350 British Legion with their wives, sisters and sweethearts, dancing in our lovely rooms here tonight. It was a wondrous sight. The Mayfair did the buffet, and we had a *bar*, which rather alarmed me: however the men kept fairly sober. We asked the Prince of Wales, as head of the Legion, to come, and rather against my will, Lord Jellicoe – *he* in fact, was the reason I gave the dance, it was my idea as I wanted to do something for Ian. . . .

I wish I had asked 50 of my own friends, as I longed to dance – there was a lovely band and plenty of room – I was sorry I had not told each of my servants to ask an ex-service man, and made them dance too. . . . I danced with Martin, our chauffeur, who dances well.

How the Legionnaires enjoyed themselves – they danced Paul Joneses to secure partners several times, and really did thoroughly enjoy themselves, and they danced well. They all heartily sang 'For he's a jolly good fellow,' at the end, thanking Ian for the dance and calling for a speech – then for me, 'For She's a jolly fellow,' and we were besieged to write our names on their programmes.

The investitures this morning of Lord Jellicoe, Lord Beatty, etc., was a wonderfully moving sight; the glorious old Abbey never before impressed me so much. I . . . stood on a chair, leaning back on a pillar, so had a grand view, rather to the scandal of my neighbours. Ian looked fine, and I watched his dear, rough crispy head moving up the Abbey in the Procession. . . . " [10th May 1928]

In the house, Ian kept the wireless switched on all the time. He spoke fluent German and very good French and could follow the news and keep abreast of what was happening in Europe. But his great love was jazz bands playing and Jean complained to her diary that the wireless stifled conversation. " . . . Ian adores the wireless and is always playing it, and I have given him a new set a Rees Mace – it cost £35, and he can get Germany, France etc. on it – he is wildly happy with it, and it is put on all through lunch when we lunch together in my sitting room, and all through dinner. After lunch he goes off to rest and have a sleep, and after dinner he lies on the sofa and reads, or works, so there never is any time to talk. . . .

Ian . . . listening and dancing to the wireless jazz: he simply would not go to bed as all those exciting waltzes and fox trots that he loves, were played one after another. I was deadly tired, and said firmly at 10.30, 'I am going to bed,' and he jumped up and went down on his knees, begging me to stay up, saying I did not love him if I would not stay with him. I went however at 10.45, and begged him to go to bed, but he would not – it was with difficulty I got to bed as he kept coming into my room, begging me to dance for him in my nightdress; as the wireless was playing an irresistible little tune we both love, I did, but found my bedroom slippers in the way: he was enchanted with the way my shadow fell on my green bedroom walls as I danced – and I rather loved doing it, but my back hurt, and I had to stop." [Sunday 3rd February 1929 London]

" . . . If years and years and years ago we could have seen in a glass two old people – Ian and me – dancing in my bedroom, I in my night-dress, the wireless on the floor, as we did last night, how we would have laughed.

I had at last firmly said I must go to bed, leaving Ian on his sofa, reading and listening to the wireless, and was washing, when he dragged the wireless into my room – it was playing the airy-fairy tune we both love and always must dance to when it plays. . . . " [Saturday 15th June 1929 London]

On 28 August 1929, whilst Jean was at Deanston, Lady Muir died suddenly. The loss of her mother was a bitter blow to Jean and she wrote on the day of her funeral: " . . . This is the end then to-day, of life here, and my beloved little Mother lies serene, sacred, apart in her refuge in the ground, for the moment so lovely with flowers and flowers, Kay's sweetpea cross tied on to her coffin looked lovely as I looked down at it under the pelting and pitiless rain.

In her coffin she was lovely, still just restfully asleep. I said good-bye to her at 1 o'clock to-day, looked for the last time on her loved face, an exaltation, a vision of beauty. . . . " [30th August 1929 Deanston]

Lady Muir left her cherished ruby ring and diamond necklace to Jean. But the war had caused much poverty in the country and Jean's attitude to expensive jewellery had changed. The only time she wore diamonds was when she presented Nadejda, Lady Muir, Kay's second wife, at Court, and it was customary to wear a tiara. To the Palace Jean wore a glamorous dress of bright orange chiffon, trimmed with silver lace, all glittering with sequins, a diamond tiara and false pearls. " . . . I would hate to hang fortunes round my neck and refuse always to be given them. . . . " [27th June 1929] " . . . I never wear diamonds and have all my own diamonds in the bank; they have been locked up there for fifteen years . . . . " [24th September 1929]

Deanston was to be sold and Jean's mother had lived out her days there, unaware of its fate. " . . . Yes – one's old home, and all the old life is sweeping, sweeping away down the current of time in unreturning waves.

Deanston is to be put up for auction next week – dear, beloved, precious Deanston. . . . " Jean would have to be content to roam through its rooms in her vivid imagination. " . . . I often walk about there, go up the staircase, along the narrow passage with its old prints of boys

playing football and the old battle picture of the warrior Prince lying back in the arms of his comrade. . . . " [8th December 1929]

Judy and Gill Muir, the daughters of Clara and Will and Heather and Jack, were presented at Court. On Wednesday 18 May 1932 their mothers gave a debutantes' ball at Jean's house, which was hired out at a fee of ninety guineas, for dances, balls and coming-out parties. Everything of note the Hamiltons were involved in was announced in the newspapers and the press reports of the ball were retained by Jean in her diary. Other debutantes were: 'Lady Elizabeth Murray, a tall slender figure in a dress of dark blue net worn with a blue velvet coat. . . . Miss Christian Pike, wearing her Court dress of creamy Spanish lace, a tint particularly becoming to her "Magnolia" petal complexion. She is one of the few girls who wear flowers in their hair, and had a couple of gardenias tucked in behind her head. . . . Lord and Lady Darnley were among those who had come with a party.' There was a photograph of Jean, 'a gracious elegant looking figure in pastel coloured lace', sporting a new, short, layered hairstyle. The ball went on all night, and a 'sumptuous supper' was served in the evening and 'in the early hours of the morning', an 'egg and bacon breakfast . . . .'

Ian was making front-page headlines and was photographed accompanying Prince George, the Duke of Kent, on an inspection of the Memorial Parade of the British Legion in Horse Guards Parade, before the Cenotaph service. In another press photograph Ian is seen posing to have a bust of himself made by Professor Strobel. The *Daily Telegraph* reported on *The Memoirs of Marshal Joffre*, which were being reviewed by Captain Basil Liddell Hart, who said: 'A month or two after the Marne, and during the last phase of the Battle of Flanders, in the autumn of 1914, Lord Kitchener . . . proposed that Sir Ian should be put at the head of the British Army instead of Sir John French.' Liddell Hart claimed that Joffre had prevented this move.

With her beloved Deanston sold, Jean and Ian spent Christmas 1932 and the New Year of 1933 with Kay and Nadejda Muir at Blair Drummond Castle. " . . . **Nadejda is very vital and gay and fills the house with light laughter and love. . . . "** They visited Lake Monteith, " . . . **a fairy tale scene . . . it was beauty, transitory, intangible and fragile – every tree and shrub, every twig and withered flower shone in a supernatural glory, outlined by the keen hoare frost, the mountains behind lay bathed in glorious sunshine, a day indeed to be alive and remember forever. . . . "** Ian was eighty on 16 January, and on the 25th went skating on a frozen lake. **[16th and 28th January 1933 Kilbryde]**

Later that year, the Hamiltons dined with the German Ambassador but Jean had just recovered from another illness and had lost weight and was conscious of her thinness. **"... we sallied forth, Ian covered with medals, looking frightfully good-looking.... I wore a new dress of which I felt rather doubtful, of dull black crepe and I wore long black mittens – they looked so odd and rather smart. I wore them to cover my arms which are terribly thin and the skin perished with this last illness which has left me terribly weak. Norah Lindsay arrived and dashed in just as I was fussing over my hair, and she reassured me as to my looks and I found everyone very charming and nice. ... " [20th June 1933]**

Old age, illness and death were taking their toll of Jean's friends, as one by one the precious gems dropped away.[3] When Jean saw Hazel Lavery at a lunch given by Henry Nevinson, she had deteriorated greatly. **" ... Hazel Lavery looking really ill and shockingly badly made up was talking to me when a man – I can't remember his name – came up and said: 'I must talk to two of the most beautiful women in London.' I thought he was making fools of us and Hazel was furious at being coupled with me in that category and said: 'Well, I will leave you with one of them,' – her hair is now bright orange but he evidently still admires her. How lovely she was!!! Alas! to see such beauty fade. ... "** [30th June 1933] Just over a year later, Hazel was dead. **" ... Lovely Hazel Lavery is gone. Byron's poem seems written for her: 'And thou art dead as young and fair as ought of mortal birth.' She was the most exquisite of beings...**" [10th January 1935] Hazel's artist husband, Sir John Lavery, painted her lying in her coffin.

The once great beauty Muriel Beckett had not been well for some time. **"... Muriel Beckett ... has turned her face to the wall and given up living for the last two years. ... It was ghastly to see Muriel look this sinister dark shadow of herself, though throughout it I could still see the outline of the Botticelli Madonna found in the Vatican that was so like her." [29th July 1933]**

During the spring of 1934, Jean, Harry and Fodie went on holiday to Europe. One of the highlights of the holiday was Jean's visit to Alice Keppel at her beautiful villa, Ombrellino, in Florence. **" ... Alice Keppel sent her car and Lady Hood, Arthur Spender, a nice Italian woman and I went to lunch in her enchanting villa at 1.15. I enjoyed it all**

immensely and admire her cleverness, she must have been in a creative mood when she bought and designed it all. The garden is very
Italian, perhaps too many flowers, but they are lovely as she has
arranged them – gay with Spring. May Harcourt was there and
Professor Lindeman. I was glad to see May Harcourt again. I sat next
George Keppel and found him as always, delightfully easy to talk to.
After lunch we wandered round the garden and I stayed till nearly
four o'clock. Alice Keppel sent us back in her car, and I had tea with
the children and went to see 'The Living Dead' by Tolstoi. . . . "
[Sunday 15th April 1934 Florence]

Later that year, back in London, Jean was trying to secure the futures
of Harry and Fodie and was writing her will in their favour. " . . . I must
see Sir Bircham and settle about my will. . . . I . . . sent him [Harry] yesterday his certificate of adoption as he has to fill in papers for
Sandhurst. . . . Kay advised me to apply to the Trustee Department,
Westminster Bank, and to make them responsible for the money I
have put in trust for Harry and Fodie. . . . Kay had been very strong
on the point that Ian should let the children have his name before
Harry went to Sandhurst and Fodie came out. Ian said it was too late
now, and I said: 'Not at all.' It was just the moment, but of course
when he had refused when I adopted them formally I had not wanted
to bother him again. . . . I feel Ian is growing very frail and old and
ought not to be troubled for he is not well and terribly argumentative
and irritable these days, bless him! . . ." [17th and 19th October 1934]

In the next few years several of Jean's friends died. Nellie Sellar, Ian's
loyal secretary of many years, who had been with them from their time in
India, died in 1934. In January 1935, Janet Leeper's husband, Allen, died
young. So many deaths may have prompted Jean to plan a visit to Lord
Alwyne's grave, and stay at Kiftsgate, with her brother Jack and his wife,
Heather. " . . . Compton Wynyates is where he is buried (his brother;
Lord Northampton's place). . . . " [28th May 6. A.M. 1936] Jean was
struggling with hay fever and asthma and it is uncertain whether she ever
saw Lord Alwyne's last resting place.

Mrs Marie de Rothschild of Ascot Wing, with whom Jean and Ian
spent many happy days, died in April 1937. Despite all the illness and
deaths, Jean kept her sense of humour. " . . . Ian and I had luncheon
amongst our contemporaries to-day, a very ageing experience. It was
at the Poulteneys. Pultie, as Kitty D. [Drummond] always calls him,

was standing in the small downstairs room with Lady Tilworth also standing, both so bad with rheumatism they did not wish to sit down, and she could not go upstairs, neither could I, but I sat down and when they had explained their difficulties about their rheumatic legs, I explained about my cough and quoted an epitaph on a grave stone: 'She had two legs and a baddish cough. But the cough it was that carried her off.' . . . " [19th March 1938 London]

Ava Ribblesdale (the former Ava Astor) managed to keep her looks. **" . . . Ava Ribblesdale came to see me, looking I must say lovely still, though I know she is my age. . . . We had much to say to one another about old age and its miseries. She feels dreadfully the loss of her youth, triumph beauty and power. . . "** [24th July 1938] Aileen Roberts whom Jean had known from when they were young girls in their twenties in India had become **" . . . such a pathetic figure now, a little frail old woman. . . . "** [17th February and 26th July 1939]

The spectre of Fascism was rearing its ugly head in Germany. A newspaper report in Jean's diary, dated December 1931, about Hitler, entitled: 'Pen portrait of Germany's Man of Destiny', provides a contemporary view of the Führer. Hitler is portrayed as an enigmatic figure who lives secretively. 'He is known personally to only small groups of friends and political supporters. Of the tens of thousands who have voted for his Party less than a few hundreds have been within more than platform reach of him. In Munich, the city in which Hitler is resident, he lives closely guarded from the outer world. His name figures neither in the street nor telephone directory. . . . It is said in Munich that it is easier to get a private audience with the Pope than with Hitler. . . . His courage was proved in the War and in a hundred ugly political situations since he emerged to become the most powerful force in the Republic. . . .' Hitler planned to visit London and might be 'entertained in the House of Commons. . . .'[4] With hindsight, Hitler is seen today for the monster he was but in the 1930s he was a highly decorated First World War veteran, having been awarded the Iron Cross, First Class, for gallantry. This fact alone may have clouded the minds of both the British and German people as to the real person. When Ian Hamilton was asked, in the event of Hitler's visit, if he would entertain him at No. 1 HPG, he refused. On 1 January, 1933, Hitler became Chancellor of Germany.

Jean kept herself informed from what literature was available, about the situation in Europe and Germany. **" . . . Still more or less laid up with** this tiresome bad throat. I am writing now with such difficulty as half the letters as I write are obliterated. I had to give up reading 'Josephus' by Feuchtwanger, one of the Jews banished by Hitler from Germany, for suddenly as I read I could not see to read any more – half the words went blank. It's very alarming and I think must come from the quantity of bella donna I have to take to stop the virulent hay fever which attacks me. . . . " [13th June 1933 London]

Ian had become a pacifist, believing that potential conflict was best resolved through negotiations rather than war. In his speech, after the unveiling of a war memorial at Reading, he explained his change of mind: 'I unveil war memorials – week after week – and the people who are given the best seats close up to me are the widows and orphans, the mutilated, the blind, and the parents who have lost their sons.'[5]

Good relations with the Germans at an official level continued but on an increasingly difficult basis. Jean, having invited Prince and Princess Otto Bismarck to dinner, took care to let them know that **"the Austen Chamberlains were coming"**, which ensured they declined the invitation – Sir Austen Chamberlain had served at the Admiralty and was known for his anti-German views. Behind closed doors, German political matters could be discussed in some privacy. Others dining were Lord and Lady Allenby, Ettie, Lady Desborough, Lord Stanmore, Lord and Lady Esher, Sir Maurice and Lady Violet Bonham Carter, Mr and Mrs Sacha Sitwell, Evan and Dorothy Charteris, Lord Hugh Cecil and Mrs Ronnie Greville. **" . . . I enjoyed myself sitting between Lord Allenby and Austen last night, which I would not have done had Prince Otto been sitting on my other side as Austen was talking most of the time about France and Lord Allenby about the bad influence of Hitler on Europe. He says Hitler is determined to be Dictator of Europe – that Mussolini confined himself to the re-birth of Italy but Hitler wants to impose his will on the civilised world. Ettie was thrilled talking to General Allenby and rather neglected Lord Stanmore . . . Antoinette Esher was a great bother as I wanted to look after Lady Allenby after dinner as she did not know the women. However, fortunately Violet Bonham Carter, who is staying here, took her in tow and was supported by her in a somewhat violent discussion she had with Maggie Greville over the Jews – Violet feels very strongly about the way Hitler is threatening the Jews. . . . " [29th June 1933 London]**

The Hamiltons invited the German delegation to dine with them separately and British political figures stayed away. " . . . **Von Neurath told Ian the German delegates could not meet Austen** [Chamberlain] **the night they were dining here and Ian had to tell Austen not to come. It was awful having to tell him this after he had accepted. . . .**" At a cocktail party at the Jones' the previous afternoon, " . . . **Ian had a talk with Bernstorff who has been recalled by Hitler to Germany and is terribly sad at leaving – he does not know whether he is going to be imprisoned or what is the reason, and our nice German Ambassador also, it is rumoured, is to be recalled. Princess Otto Bismarck was there wearing a swastika charm on her wrist rather well hidden. . . . I don't like her ugly husband – I had a talk with him and am more than ever thankful he did not come to our dinner. . . .**" [30th June 1933]

The threat and talk of war would continue for the next five and a half years. How seriously anyone took it is uncertain; the prospect of a Second World War was too dreadful to contemplate. Fodie wrote Jean, she was " . . . **frightfully happy in Munich. . . .**" Earlier the same day, Jean noted in her diary: " . . . **There are tremendous things going on in the world – I hear the rumble of world shaking catastrophes in the air, and I hear in Paris the talk is all of war, war, war – it's too awful, if there's another world war it will be the end of civilisation as we know it. . . .**" [7th December 1933]

In London, life continued as normal. Jean had a new dog called little Miss Muffet to walk in Hyde Park. She held out hopes that Harry, now aged seventeen and attending Wellington College, his preparation as a future soldier already underway, would be accepted into the Scots Guards. " . . . **The Scots Guards have sent him a Christmas greeting which sounds hopeful – . . . . How thankful I am I was firm about getting his name put down for Scots Guards by Ian in spite of his opposition and saying it was useless till he went to Sandhurst.**" [12th and 29th December 1933]

Germany had left the League of Nations in October 1933, bringing the threat of war one step nearer. " . . . **Ian dined at his Literary Society Club last night and sat next Douglas Dawson and had a talk with Duff Cooper and Sir Robert Vansittart. He came and sat on my bed on his return and told me Vansittart had said if the Germans won't agree to the note the Foreign Office are preparing now, one condition of which is that they return to the League of Nations, it may mean war. The dread of war is in the air again, it is *inconceivable*.**

Baron Neurath told Ian nothing would induce them to return to Geneva and I don't wonder. . . . " [6th February 1934 London]

Claire Sheridan, niece of the late Lady Randolph Churchill, was a sculptress, living in Paris and making her own way in the world, her husband Wilfred having been killed in the Great War.[6] Claire wrote to Kay's wife, Nadejda Muir, of the riots in Paris and Nadejda sent copies of the letters to Jean:

> . . . 30,000 Anciens Combattants are meeting at the Rond-point des Champs Elysees – the jeunesse patriote before the Hotel de Ville, the Camelots du Roi at the Place de la Concorde, the University Students in the Boul. St Michael. The Communists at all the entrances to all the railway stations, and 20,000 Taxi-Drivers on strike! will swell the ranks of this and that group. Leon Blum has called out the Socialists to fight the Camelots, and all right wing demonstrations. Half the police are Anciens Combattants, so the Government is afraid to count on them, and has brought troops in from the Provinces . . . .[7]

> My God! is it possible that we lived through last night!! From 6-30 p.m. to 1 a.m. my brother [Peter] and I were in the Concorde, swaying back and forth with excited crowds, dodging mounted charges, and seeing men drop around us.

> We marched with the Anciens Combattants, singing the Marseillaise, carrying their silk tricolour. . . . [At the Rue St-Honoré] the mounted Garde Republicaine charged – impossible to go forward; behind 13 police firing, impossible to go back! We were trapped between the high houses in the narrow street. It was a very frightening moment. . . . a little Frenchman speaking perfect English took me by the arm and ran with me up the space more or less opened by the charge. He said: 'Get away from here quick – turn left, go to the Crillion.' . . .[8]

" . . . Frightful things happening in the world – Paris in an uproar, rioting and murder – Vienna in the throes of civil war – unrest, revolutions in the air – Spain having a violent one again. How glad the King must be to be in safe old England – how long will it remain safe? . . ." [12th February 1934]

A newspaper report spoke of bombs in Vienna: 'Dr. Dollfus, the

Austrian Chancellor, was in tears to-night when he spoke to a Press conference on the events that led to the civil war. . . . On a table in front of him lay bombs and grenades seized in raids on Socialist headquarters. It was stated that they were sufficient to blow up all Vienna.' The Germans made much of it, the German Chancellor giving 'the enormous figure of 1,600 dead' in Austria, but Dr Dollfus claimed 'there are only – and that is too many – 211'.[9]

Fodie's friend Princess Priscilla Bibesco, and Violet Bonham Carter's daughters, Cressida and Laura, were in Vienna. **" . . . Terrible things go on happening in the world – Vienna is in a state of civil war now. Cressida, Laura Bonham Carter and Priscilla Bibesco are there with their governess. Violet has got through to them by 'phone and they say they are all right but shut up in the dark. No electric light and the wires cut to the Embassy. It must have been wonderful for them to hear their mother's voice to-day. Paris is almost worse. . . . "** [15th February 1934] Ironically, it was safer in Germany, **" . . . Fodie writes how glad she is she did not go to Vienna as Germany seems to her the only safe place – under the great Hitler's rule. . . . "** [21st February 1934]

Jean and Ian went alone to Lennoxlove Castle on holiday. Another royal romance had brought a ray of sunshine into the lives of the British people. Prince George, the Duke of Kent, and Princess Marina of Greece and Denmark were to be married. **" . . . Today the great Cunarder 534 was launched at the Clyde near Glasgow by Queen Mary. . . . "** It was raining heavily so Jean and Ian **" . . . listened instead to the commentary on the wireless; it was a surprise when the Queen's dear voice christened the ship 'Queen Mary', the name had been kept very secret. Princess Helena said the other day at tea that in talking to an old laddie at Gullam he had said the people thought the ship would be christened 'Princess Marina' – the papers just now are full of the 'Royal lovers' – Prince George and Princess Marina. . . . "** [26th September 1934 Lennoxlove]

In November, Jean was staying with Ettie Desborough at Panshanger and nothing was talked of in society but the impending royal wedding. **" . . . I have the same grand room – the Queen's room, it is called – with its lovely Italian paper, its incongruous furniture and heavy embroidered crimson silk curtains. . . .**

Ettie, bless her, received us yesterday in a gorgeous Nabob tea

gown – long tailed black velvet with touches of crimson, and silver and open at top of sleeves – a lovely dinner gown, I would call it. She was disappointed because I had not brought my Nabob tea gown to wear this afternoon.

Ian and I motored here. . . . all was welcoming brightness here and a delightful comfy house party, just twelve. The Hinchingbrookes, Sonia Cubitt, Tottie Holford, Sir Robert Horne, Tom Mitford, Lord Stanmore.

Tottie is now invited to the evening party at Buckingham Palace – great gossip goes on over the Royal Wedding all the time. It's said Emerald Cunard's name has been sent in from three different sources and been scored out each time by the Queen, but I see she and Mrs. Corey have been busy in the list, I expect, paid for most of the linen. . . . " [26th November 1934]

The marriage of Prince George and Princess Marina on 29 November 1934, at Westminster Abbey, was the highlight of the year. " . . . **Turia Campbell came to tea with me with her hair tightly permed. She was full of excitement about the Royal Wedding. She is a great friend of Princess Marina's and going about everywhere with her. It was great fun hearing about it all and of how happy, how radiant, and how much in love Princess Marina is with Prince George. It all sounded so young, gay and fairy tale-ish from the moment the three lovely sisters alighted in their pretty light garments at our dull foggy Victoria Station and lit up the platform where stood Queen Mary and Princess Mary in their dowdy clothes. I wonder how the Duchess of York** [the present Queen Mother] **likes it. Turia's hairdresser, who is hers, reports the Duchess as being in a '*trés mauvais humeur.*'** [in a very bad mood] **I wonder! She always looks very sweet.**

Betty Moncreiffe dined with us tonight and told us the mink coat Princess Marina has been wearing everywhere was given her by Mrs. Corrigan and cost £800. Mrs. Corrigan wanted to give her a white ermine coat as a wedding present but according to Betty, Queen Mary said she could not accept such a valuable present from a commoner, but of course if the coat were given to her before she married, as a gift to herself, that would surely be all right? Princess M. then said she would prefer mink, which cost double – so Mrs. Coreyagin (which is her nickname here) has the pleasure of paying £800 and is not to be asked to the wedding, it is said, but that I can't believe. I feel sure

Princess Marina will manage to have her asked. . . . " [27th November 1934]

By 1935, the political situation was worsening, with Hitler established in Germany and Mussolini in Italy and no sign of any effective political opposition. **" . . . The clouds of war are gathering on all sides. It is horrible to hear war talked of again. . . . "** [22nd August 1935] **" . . . The fate of Europe meantime trembles in the balance. The smallest mistake may send civilisation up in flames – it's marvellous Mussolini has escaped assassination in every country; so many, so many, pray for his death, but still he fulminates away. . . . "** [9th October 1935 Braco]

Jean organised a lunch and Maud Cunard organised a concert. Sir Edwin Lutyens, Mrs Simon Rodney, Patrick Balfour, Sylvia Oliviera, Léonie Leslie, Tottie Holford, Lord Munster, George Keppel, Norah Lindsay, Wolkoff and Ian, lunched at No. 1 HPG. **" . . . George Keppel . . . is feeling nervous about returning to Italy with Alice next week and as to whether they will be received by the Italians. He is sending me a book on French artists, just a hand book which I am sure I will find useful. . . . "** Maud's concert was a great success but the men did not go on from the lunch to the concert as expected. The singer was Mme Rethberg and Jean **" . . . loved the Ravel music at the end and Emerald's cool green drawing room with its wonderful mirrors and Lawrencin pictures in their glass frames. . . . "** [6th May 1936]

Jean's nephew, John Muir, the son of James Muir, became engaged to Elizabeth Dundas, a descendant of the renowned General Dundas. Jean first saw Elizabeth at the Gleneagles Ball: **" . . . she looked gentle and dignified . . . . "** [2nd October 1936 Blair Drummond] Jean gave John her mother's diamond necklace for Elizabeth to wear on the wedding day and the couple were married in late October of that year. Chattie Muir was a bridesmaid and Harry Knight was an usher. **" . . . had a most happy day and evening. The wedding went off beautifully – everything well arranged. . . . the bride when she came looked gracious and dignified. Her dress was perfect. The sun shone and the wedding group looked lovely. Chattie looked her best. . . . "** [25th Oct. 1936 Bretton Pk] Sir Alexander Kay Muir did not produce an heir and John became the third Baronet. The present Sir Richard Muir (the fourth Baronet) is married to the former Lady Linda Mary Cole, only daughter of the sixth Earl of Enniskillen. Mrs Fiona Goetz, eldest daughter of the late Sir John and Elizabeth, says when she was a baby she was 'dangled on great aunt Jean's knee'.

Harry, who would be twenty-one on his next birthday, was a soldier, having fulfilled Jean's hopes for his career. He had gone to the Royal Military Academy, Sandhurst and been commissioned into the Scots Guards and was stationed at the Tower of London. Like other young men he lived life recklessly. He and his valet drove his new car too fast before it was run in and wrecked the engine. Jean dared not tell Ian! When Harry came home on short breaks, he chain smoked, had a succession of girl friends, went to night clubs and rambled home, up the stairs, at two, three, or four in the morning, though he was always up on time at seven o'clock in the morning to go on duty. Later in 1937, he was stationed at Chelsea Barracks.

Ian's endeavours to foster good relations with Germany continued and he entertained eight hundred German ex-servicemen at No. 1 HPG. It is understandable that, given his experience of the First World War and the terrible death and destruction he had seen then, peace with Germany was preferable, if at all possible. **[19th May 1937]**

By 1938, the threat of war with Germany was closing in on Britain like a shroud. **" . . . This has been a trying week of tension here. No one talks of anything but Austria! Hitler! The Jews – and feeling runs very high as everyone has different views. Ian and I squabble over it a good deal – as I am miserable to think of that wonderful romantic Austria – very nearly my own once country – becoming a German State. . . . "** [18th March 1938] Austrians were fleeing their country and coming to England and Jean counted her blessings that she had not married Count Esterhazy. **" . . . Austria at the foot of Hitler makes me feel sick and weary of the glory of the world, that proud aristocratic country of great traditions being trampled through by goose-stepping Germans makes one feel heartbroken, and Italy, who was to defend her independence, now hastening obsequiously to welcome his baseborn contemporary.**

The world we have known has crumbled to pieces – tradition, glory, romance are dead. Might is now right. Hitler, Mussolini and Stalin the heroes. . . . Thank Heaven my name is not Esterhazy to-day. . . . " [7th April 1938]

The Hamiltons spent their summer holidays at Lennoxlove in 1938, where, in August, they were photographed by the press as a family, probably for the last time. Jean, with little Miss Muffet on her lap, Ian, Harry and Fodie; the Moncreiffes – David, Ian, Elizabeth and Mrs Moncreiffe;

Henry Martin, the chauffeur, visible in his uniform, in the background, standing by the car. As President of the Metropolitan Area Council of the British Legion, Ian had been with a delegation to Germany, to lay wreaths at German war memorials, and Rudolph Hess had taken him to meet Hitler. It was reported in the press that General Sir Ian Hamilton had just returned from his visit to Herr Hitler. The fact that the Hamiltons were staying at Lennoxlove Castle at that time may explain why, when Rudolph Hess parachuted into Scotland in 1941, and asked for the Duke of Hamilton, he may have meant Ian, thinking Lennoxlove Castle was his permanent residence.

The Prime Minister, Neville Chamberlain, went to see Hitler to try to negotiate an agreement. " . . . **The clouds darken. Neville has not been completely successful as first thought and Hitler grows more menacing daily."** [24th September 1938 Lennoxlove] Chamberlain had come back from Munich in October 1938, waving his famous Peace Agreement with Hitler, but it did not last, Hitler could not be appeased. However, it may have lulled the British people into a feeling of false security from war at least for a time.

Harry went to Egypt on normal garrison duty in November, and the following year visited Jean and Ian when they were holidaying at Monte Carlo. Ian had now given up hope of war being averted. " . . . **Ian is now very pessimistic and thinks there will be a war. . . . "** [8th April 1939 Monte Carlo]

Arrangements were taking place for changes in the face of war. Hundreds of Jewish children were arriving as refugees in London. The President of the United States intervened in an attempt to hold on to peace. **" . . . President Roosevelt has sent a message to Hitler and Mussolini asking those two great bullies to 'sign a pact of peace for ten years'. . . . "** [17th April 1939 London]

The country braced itself for another war and people began laying in extra provisions. " . . . **There is a fear that Hitler will enter Danzig on Whit Sunday – and then what?**

Everyone here is preparing for war, laying in stores etc. I have done nothing so far – if it is to be war I feel that will be just 'the end'. . . . " [26th May 1939 London]

" . . . The war news is terrifying. Hitler seems to be in a mad rage and determined to plunge the world into hideous mass murder. Lord Halifax and Neville Chamberlain making useless platitudes speeches.

The King and the Pope broadcasting appeals for peace 'children love one another' sort of thing. . . . " [25th August 1939]

" . . . The blow has fallen on Europe – before 6.00 a.m. Hitler marched yesterday morning into Danzig and has now bombed five towns in Poland and is fighting all along the line so we are at war with Germany. . . . " [2nd September 1939 6.00 am]

The Hamiltons listened to the news on the wireless every day, a means of communication they did not have during the First World War. Ian was writing his memoirs. Janet Leeper and her daughter Katharine, now Mrs Cobbett, were holidaying with the Hamiltons when war was declared. **" . . . Janet and Katharine flew off to London this morning. Janet felt the sooner she got Katharine off to Margot's [Warre] the better, and was right, for now *we* have declared War on Germany. . . .**

At 11 I went . . . to listen to the Prime Minister broadcast. . . . So the curse has come upon us. . . .

. . . This morning Hitler cried 'Havoc and let loose the dogs of war'. . . . " [3rd September 1939 Lennoxlove]

Lennoxlove Castle was converted immediately into a hospital for blind women, who had to be moved from a hospital in Edinburgh that was being commandeered by the government. The Evacuation Officer arrived with the Matron of the Blind Hospital. He told Jean that it was arranged that all of the patients from the hospital would arrive at Lennoxlove the next day, sixty-seven persons, five of them ambulance cases. **" . . . I felt aghast, I had prepared for 30 blind women. . . . " [5th September 1939]**

Every night the wireless brought worse news from Europe. **" . . . Russia has invaded Poland. She marched against her yesterday. We heard this on the 9 o'clock wireless last night. Terrible news, poor, poor Poland. *Why* why did we guarantee her before we had a military pact with Russia which she asked from us over and over again. . . . We wanted to encircle Germany and offered to guarantee the other states who wisely refused our guarantee. How Poland must regret having accepted it. . . .**

It won't be long before Hitler turns his attentions to us now. France and England against Germany and Russia will be war to the annihilation of one or another. . . . Our Government have settled down to a three year war. . . . " [18th September 1939 Lennoxlove]

When the Hamiltons returned to London it was to bleak November weather and a curfew. During that year Jean had lost two further friends: her aunt, Nora Anderson, and Helen Dyck Cunningham. Nora and Will's four sons had all been killed in the First World War. Jean wrote *Easter 1918*, a book of reminiscences, religious thought and photographs dedicated to their memory.[10]

Propaganda films were now being shown to educate the population and convince them that they must dispense with anti-Semitism and show sympathy, understanding and humanity to the Jews and treat them as equal citizens. **" . . . It was a shock going out into the intense dark and the queer ghostly small blue lights, moving along the streets. I was afraid Martin** [the chauffeur] **would never manage it but he did very slowly at first but we were just in time for the Russian Film made about two or three years after the Reichstag fire, very strong anti-German propaganda. 'Professor Mamlock' about a Jewish Surgeon persecuted and killed by the Nazis. It was splendidly acted – filled one with fury against the Nazi regime. I felt to say Heil Hitler was like saying Damn You. . . . coming back . . . I discoursed . . . to Ian on the wickedness of any Christian nation persecuting Jews . . . our Lord and the Virgin were Jewish, our religion Jewish in origin. . . . " [2nd November 1939]**

CHAPTER 16

The Last Romance

'No man alive or dead has ever possessed so brave and devoted a champion in his wife as I in Jean.' [General Sir Ian Hamilton: *Jean: A Memoir*][1]

After years of suffering from asthma and thinking she would die in an asthma attack, Jean had a new illness, which the doctors had difficulty in diagnosing. **" . . . I am always tired in body and mind and in great discomfort this week as I have been having XRay treatment for a nasty lump I have and the two treatments I have had seem to have made matters much worse and I am going to another new doctor in Edinburgh this week.**

I go for a little drive with Ian every day after tea and love having meals alone with him. How happy it is that we have been allowed to grow old together. . . . " [14th September 1938 Lennoxlove]

Surgeons operated on the lump and Jean remained in a private clinic over Christmas. On Christmas Day Fodie visited her and brought all her Christmas cards and presents. By New Year's Day, Jean was home again. **" . . . I have seen nine doctors and they don't seem able to do me much good. . . . " [7th February 1939]** For a time, normal life resumed though Jean was taking chloroform at nights to make her sleep. Fodie was still besotted with the idea of becoming an actress and film star and had been striving, without success, to find work as an actress in London. In the New Year, she went to Europe in the hope of better success there.

There is some inkling that something was amiss with Jean from the emotion with which Winston Churchill received her. The Churchills' youngest daughter, Mary, aged eighteen, the present Lady Soames, was there. **" . . . Clemmie Churchill phoned to ask us to go to tea at Westerham this afternoon. . . . to-day we got a very charming welcome, Winston pressing my hand in both his and calling me 'Dear Jean,' which really surprised me, and placing himself beside me. My voice is rather weak and I had difficulty in making him hear me. After**

tea he took Ian for a long walk to see his fish and his garden and I sat
with Clemmie and Miss Hozier under a tree – Mary's companion –
beside me. I like her and Mary is a charming child. . . . " [Sunday 4th
June 1939 London] Sixty-one years on, Mary remembers that her companion was in fact Miss Maryott Whyte: 'We all called her "Nana" or
"Cousin Moppet".'[2]

Jean was " . . . putting up a great fight against hay fever . . . spray-
ing my nostrils with cocaine. . . . " [7th June 1939] Her seventy-eighth
birthday came round; " . . . Ian and I lead a Darby and Joan existence.
I write letters and he plays the wireless after our little dinner together
in my sitting room . . . " she complained. [8th June 1939]

Despite her fragile state, Jean's engagement book was full. She went
to meetings and kept abreast of the Paddington crèche events, and attended
the opera. " . . . I have taken a box at the opera for Ian for the last three
weeks of the season. Emerald has arranged I get it for half price each
Friday night and we get splendid nights. Last Friday it was Don
Giovanni – Ian's favourite Opera. . . . Ian takes Janet Leeper with him,
she loves and understands music and is a most sympathetic companion – if I depart this life he might have her here to be with him when
he wants her and free to live their own lives as she is a most understanding little woman. I thought Harry and Fodie would be with us to
support and comfort our old age – but 'nous avons changé tout cela'
[we have changed all that] these days and things are better as they are
as old age used to cramp and fetter young lives. . . . " [9th June 1939]

Dr Rossdale, the Hamiltons' family doctor, told Jean the true nature of
the lump and that Ian had known since Christmas. It is likely that Ian confided in the Churchills but kept it from Jean to prevent her worrying, until
she was well enough to be told. " . . . yesterday morning when I had a
heart to heart talk with Dr. Rossdale who confessed to me that at
Xmas when I had the operation in the London Clinic . . ." Ian was told
" . . . that the lump was sceptic and as they thought I was too weak to
have the major operation and could not get the damned thing out by
the roots they had only been able to do the minor operation – and that
the lump would grow again – which it has, large and larger, and also
duplicated itself. . . . " [13th July 1939]

The artist Von Blaas did a chalk drawing of Jean, her figure exquisite,
wearing a tight-fitting waistcoat over a floor-length, full-skirted gown, a
rope of imitation pearls round her neck, elbow-length white gloves, a cane

in her hand; she has the appearance of a fairy queen. Jean and Ian were staying at Blair Drummond with Kay and Nadejda Muir and Jean came down to dinner in the dress she had worn for the drawing. **". . . It has been wonderful for me being here – able still to get about, but the last few days have been difficult – a struggle – last Friday was particularly difficult. We had a family dinner here, Alick McGrigor, Aileen, Monica and Lady Dinny, Aileen's Mother. I felt so bad I had to take two aspirins as the local pain was so tiring and bad and with plenty of champagne I managed to get through dinner. I wore my prettiest dress, the white crinoline one Von Blaas sketched and they were all pleased with it. . . . I played 7 games of back gammon. . . . "** [23rd October 6.15 a.m. 1939 Blair Drummond]

Between the end of 1939 and the beginning of 1940 there is a long gap in Jean's diary when she was ill. **" . . . I have travelled a long dreary road of pain since I last wrote in this book. I grew only more and more ill in the Professor's hands. Luckily Dr. Rossdale came back from the war in time to save me but he said it was just touch and go that he could – but I was not as grateful to him as I ought to have been as I feel my time is now fully up. I have no wish to return to the world though I feel very grateful for the happy times I have had in it, indeed this is not much of a world to return to as this wretched war drags on and on. I listened yesterday on the wireless to Neville Chamberlain's impassioned speech at Birmingham. He is straight and honest but will he be able to master Hitler? Both say we will succeed and many ridiculous boasts are made by Hitler. 'Old desiccated and ossified nonentities who babble of a new order in Europe'. The new order will come he says, but without them.**

England is fighting for world power, our fight is against it . . . later he calls himself a magnet who draws the German people together – this is true enough.

I am glad to live as I feel I am still of some comfort to Ian and our lives together are so peaceful just now. He is very precious." [25th February 1940 London]

During Jean's latest bout of illness, another friend died. **" . . . Dear Frances Horner is being buried this afternoon. . . . "** [5th March 1940]

As Jean lay seriously ill in London, German bombs pounded the city. Ian built a shelter in the basement. Jean moved out of her bedroom and at night and during air raids was sometimes on a sofa downstairs and sometimes in the basement with Ian and the servants. **" . . . The Germans have entered Boulogne, they come terribly near. Heather yesterday when we heard this wanted me to pack and get to Blair Drummond as soon as we could get sleepers – as soon as we can secure them, but I feel very inclined to stay and chance our luck now. We have everything ready in the wine cellar. Annie has bought me a nice warm bombing suit. . . . feeling as I do I can't go to B.D. with two nurses and I can't at present do without the night and day nurse and I would not be able to go to meals and *especially* because I am dying I could not bear to inflict that curse on Kay and Nadejda. Heather says they are most keen to have us – bless them. . . . "** [25th May 1940]

Jean, now fully aware that she had terminal cancer, called her illness 'Barabas', a biblical reference to the thief who was spared crucifixion instead of Jesus. **" . . . We have these horrible raiders over London every night they begin between 8 and 9 p.m. and carry on till 5 or 5.30. Ian has a great belief in our basement being a safe and good shelter. I think it is and as I can't stay in my own beloved bedroom as my bed is too near the window which gets terribly rattled by the bombs which fall thickly around us, I suppose it is the Powder Magazine and Paddington Station they are after. But alas I get asthma every night there and can get little sleep and the asthma combined with the pain of Barabas is more than I can bear so yesterday decided to go to dear Kay and Nadejda they have been so good preparing their best suite of rooms for us all these long months. I have felt I could not leave Ian and he would *not* leave London though there is really nothing to keep him here – he is writing his biography and is President of the Scottish B.L. . . . "** [10th September 8.30 a.m. 1940 London]

In the autumn of 1940 the Hamiltons left London for Scotland. In her heart Jean must have known she would never return to 1 Hyde Park Gardens. At Blair Drummond, Nadejda had all in readiness.

Jean, Lady Hamilton, was one of the most privileged women of her time. She had sacrificed a royal crown at the Court of Vienna to marry the man she loved. Her beauty had turned men's heads.

And now she lay dying . . .

In the stately Blair Drummond Castle, Jean and Ian occupied rooms that Nadejda called 'the royal suite', where King Boris and Queen

Giovanna of Bulgaria had once stayed. Surrounded by grandeur and luxury, Jean entered a finale fit for a Queen. Nadejda was kind to her during her last days. Annie Woodger, her maid, stood by her to the end.

The story of Jean's life, as told through her diaries, concludes with her last entry: "**... This weary wicked war drags on and on. They talk now of a seven years' war. Neville Chamberlain is dead**[3] **– if only he had died when he first returned from Munich triumphantly bringing his message of peace he would have been a 'National Hero' for all time. Now Winston reigns in his stead .....**

The Greeks are showing us what can be done and putting up a wonderful fight against the Italians. At the beginning of the war a German on meeting an Englishman said to him triumphantly, 'We have Italy with us'. 'Yes', said the Englishman, 'You deserve it, we had her last time.'

'Barabas' (the name I call my cancer) because 'Now Barabas was a robber' and certainly all peace and comfort fly before his triumphal approach.

Yesterday my nice Dr. Barnett said he thought I had reached the topmost peak of pain, he says nothing further can be done for me, but Ian has asked him to call in Sir John Fraser. Kay and Nadejda are angelic to us both, books galore and I can read them, one of my most valued blessings. Ian reads to me 'The Forsythe Saga' whenever he can get into my room, and Annie, Eleanor Smith's, which I love.

I don't feel like writing a diary any more. I think I must write Finis to all these records of my Life." [8th October 1940 Blair Drummond]

Ian completed Jean's story in his *Memoir* to her. She still managed to feed the little birds that she loved, on the window ledge of her bedroom. Ian read aloud to her as he saw her through her last days. Jean's wedding day had always been very dear to her and every year she made a special note in her diary on that date. She held on throughout 22 February, their fifty-fourth wedding anniversary, and slipped away on 23 February 1941. Ironically, if Jean had got her wish, the 23rd would have been their wedding anniversary. Ian wrote that the flowers on her grave became encrusted in snow, the orchids and beautifully scented lilies, which were her favourites, remaining perfectly preserved for days after she was buried.

Neither Harry nor Fodie were at home during Jean's last days, Fodie having vanished into war-torn Europe and Harry fighting Fascism with his friend Michael Crichton Stuart in the Libyan desert. Ian wrote to tell Harry of Jean's death, saying he never left her side during the last days and read the Forsyte Saga to her until the end. He had her poem 'The Last Romance' inscribed on her tombstone.

Just as Jean began her married life surrounded by war and soldiering so she went out in the same manner. During the First World War she and her helpers entertained 35,000 wounded soldiers at 1 Hyde Park Gardens. During the Second World War the house was damaged when a bomb fell in a street nearby, a crack in the wall on the stairs remaining into the late 1990s.

Jean's passing spared her the anguish of what would undoubtedly have been the cruellest blow of all – the death of her beloved Harry, her 'knight in shining armour', two months before his twenty-fifth birthday. An acting captain in the Scots Guards, Harry was wounded in the desert in Libya on 15 June and died on 17 June 1941, in the great fight against Hitler and fascism.

Ian returned to the large house in London, though not alone. Mrs Katherine Cobbett says that her widowed mother, Janet Leeper, went to stay with Ian to keep him company. Jean had left Ian as her literary executor. He could now contemplate the letters he had written her, so lovingly and for so long, 'which carefully kept, have tragically come back to their writer now after all these years',[4] tied up with blue silk ribbons. And along with the letters and poems, her life story in a diary. During a bad bout of asthma in 1922, when she thought she might die, Jean had reached agreement with Ian about guardianship of the children and what should be done with her diaries. **" . . . I am feeling quite ready to depart, and whether I live or die it does not much matter, as Ian has promised to look after the children, and to shut all my diaries up . . . for twenty five years . . . ." [9th November 1922]**

Ian, his secretary Mary Shield, and Janet Leeper loyally preserved Jean's life story. Mary Shield typed the diaries and Janet Leeper had the manuscript copied onto microfilm by Kodak in 1948. General Sir Ian Hamilton died in London on 12 October 1947, aged ninety-four. Janet Leeper and Mrs Shield were two of his literary executors. Some time after the twenty-five-year embargo expired, the reels of film containing the diaries were placed in the Liddell Hart Centre for Military Archives at King's College, London.

Ian is buried beside Jean at Doune, near Deanston in Scotland. There is a commemorative plaque to Captain Harold Knight on the wall close by which was unveiled by Ian in a memorial service in 1944. Of Jean Ian said: 'in no other woman have I felt at the core of her mantle of social grace so wise and helpful a counsellor, so splendid a courage . . . Death, which she called "The Last Romance" has claimed him [Harry] as it claimed her and here my memoir must come to a full stop. But something tells me that my memory of Jean will surely march on into Eternity'.[5]

Throughout her life, Jean had a preoccupation with death that had now enveloped her. " . . . **'Old age flowing free with delicious assurance of death.**

That line of Walt Whitman's is a comfort to me, one of the crutches of my old age. It smoothes away many worries but not the one of on whom am I going to lay the heavy weight of these endless and meaningless diaries of mine. Ian insists that I am not to allow them to be destroyed – that there are many interesting things to be found in them. I have only written them for myself because I wanted a friend or confidante by my side and I pictured reading them with Ian in our old age, but so seldom is there 'the time, the place and the diary all together'." [6th March 1938 London]

Possessing an ordered mind in matters of the intellect, Jean had already written her own epitaph in the poem 'The Last Romance'. In conversation with Walter Sickert, she had noted he " . . . **knew a little of Mallarmi** [sic] . . ." [14th May 1904] Stéphane Mallarmé, the French poet (1842–1898), was known as the master of French symbolism. He devised a theory that a poem's form and content could be as one, as in a dance. W. B. Yeats, whom Jean admired, adopted Mallarmé's technique and crafted what is probably the perfection of the theory in his poem, 'Among School Children'. The dancer and the dance are at one – each exists because of the other and the poem exists independently as an art form, like a painting or a vase. Yeats boasted of his achievement in the last two lines of the poem:

O body swayed to music, O brightening glance,
How can we know the dancer from the dance?[6]

Yeats, too, had a preoccupation with death and in two of his poems, 'Byzantium' and 'Sailing to Byzantium', he envisaged existing in the hereafter in a state of the highest form of art, like that present in the golden statues of ancient Byzantium (Constantinople/Istanbul), when that once great city was at the height of its power. In 'The Last Romance', there are echoes of Yeats' poems: 'the dancer' and 'the dance', become 'song and dance' and 'golden' becomes 'silver' and 'gilded'. As the art form preoccupied Yeats, so romance preoccupied Jean, and formed the basis of how she would exist in the 'holiness' of her after life.

The Last Romance

O! I'm homesick for romance,
For life-long devotion
    Fired by a glance;
For the beauty of tenderness,
For the mystical passion of holiness.

But it's over – youth's romance,
The quick intoxication
    Of song and dance;
Over the delicious thrill
Of new love; over the hush of rapture still!

Yes, ''tis over, sweet Romance,
No more I'll wander through the spring
    In dreamy trance;
On perfumed mornings by the sea,
No more radiant wakenings
    Thinking of Thee.

Over! over! Life's Romance
but still before me gleams
    The last romance;
Before me still, Death's great adventure lies,
And hope sets silver sail for gilded skies.[7]

Notes

Foreword

1. Frank Prochaska, *Women and Philanthropy in Nineteenth Century England* (Oxford, **1980**), p. **1**.

1. A Whirlwind Romance

1. Hamilton, Ian B. M., *The Happy Warrior* (Cassell, 1966), p. 72.
2. A history of James Finlay & Co., Finlay House, 10–14 West Nile Street, Glasgow was provided with the kind permission of Sir Richard Muir of Blair Drummond.
3. Hamilton, Ian B. M., from an unpublished manuscript by kind permission of Alexander V. Hamilton.
4. Ibid.
5. *The Happy Warrior*, p. 83; Hamilton, General Sir Ian, *Listening for the Drums* (Faber, 1944), pp. 201–2.
6. Jean is quoting from Oscar Wilde's *The Importance of Being Earnest*.
7. Beckett, Professor Ian, *Women and Patronage in the Late Victorian Army*, p. 28. By kind permission of the author.
8. *The Happy Warrior*, pp. 78–9.
9. Hamilton Archives 1/2/9.
10. Interview with Elizabeth, Lady Muir, May 1999.
11. *Listening for the Drums*, p. 188.
12. *The Happy Warrior*, p. 72.
13. Hamilton, General Sir Ian, *Jean: A Memoir* (Published privately, 1941: by kind permission of Elizabeth, Lady Muir), letter of 3 November 1886 from Ian to Jean Hamilton.
14. *Listening for the Drums*, p. 187.

15. *The Happy Warrior*, pp. 75–6.
16. *Jean: A Memoir*, p. 2.
17. *Listening for the Drums*, p. 197.
18. *The Happy Warrior*, p. 76.
19. Ibid.
20. *Listening for the Drums*, p. 186.
21. Hamilton Archives 20/4/1, 2, 3, 4 and 5.

2. A Soldier's Wife

1. Hamilton, General Sir Ian, *Listening for the Drums* (Faber, 1944), p. 199.
2. Ibid., pp. 199–200.
3. Ibid., p. 200.
4. Ibid., p. 201.
5. Ibid., pp. 208–10.
6. Ibid., p. 216.
7. Ibid., pp. 210–12.
8. Ibid., pp. 203–10.
9. Ibid., pp. 203–10
10. Hamilton, Ian B. M., *The Happy Warrior* (Cassell, 1966), p. 85.
11. Aileen, Countess Roberts to Mrs Janet Leeper, 25 November 1942. Hamilton Archives 25/12/26.
12. Roberts, Field Marshal Lord, of Kandahar, *Forty One Years in India* (Macmillan, 1898), pp. 252, 268, 309, and 315.
13. *The Happy Warrior*, pp. 90–91.
14. Ibid., pp. 110–11.
15. Clephane, Irene, *Our Mothers* (Gollancz, 1931) gives a fascinating insight into the lives of women at the turn of the century.
16. The term was made memorable by Sheila Rowbotham's *Hidden from History* (Pluto Press), 1973.
17. Hamilton, Ian B. M., unpublished manuscript, by kind permission of Alexander V. Hamilton.
18. Interview with Elizabeth, Lady Muir, May 1999.

3. Edwardian High Society

1. Hamilton, Ian B. M., unpublished manuscript, by kind permission of Alexander V. Hamilton
2. Sandys, Celia, *Churchill Wanted Dead or Alive* (HarperCollins, 1999) gives brilliantly the full story of this exciting episode.
3. Fitzroy, Sir Almeric, *Memoirs* (Hutchinson, 6th edn., no date), vol. 1, pp, 161–2. Fitzroy was Clerk to the Privy Council.
4. History of James Finlay & Co., by kind permission of Sir Richard Muir.
5. Graham, Caroline, *Camilla: The King's Mistress* (Blake, 1944), p. 3.
6. Wilson, Christopher, *A Greater Love: Charles and Camilla* (Headline, 1994), p. 13
7. Martin, Ralph G., *Lady Randolph Churchill: Vol. 2* (Cardinal/Sphere Books, 1974), p. 246.
8. Hamilton, General Sir Ian, *Listening for the Drums* (Faber, 1944), p. 238.
9. Souhami, Diana, *Mrs Keppel and her Daughter* (HarperCollins, 1996, p. 22.

4. Japan

1. Hamilton Archives 3/2/3. Ian to Jean Hamilton, 7th February 1904.
2. Ibid., Ian to Jean Hamilton, 8 February 1904.
3. Ibid., Ian to Jean Hamilton, 9 February 1904.
4. Ibid., Ian to Jean Hamilton, 10 February 1904.
5. Ibid., Ian to Jean Hamilton, 15 February 1904.
6. Ibid., Ian to Jean Hamilton, 22 February 1904.
7. Ibid., Ian to Jean Hamilton, 5 March 1904.
8. Ibid., Ian to Jean Hamilton, 7 March 1904.
9. Ibid., Ian to Jean Hamilton, 10 March 1904.
10. Ibid., Ian to Jean Hamilton, 24 March 1904.
11. Ibid., Ian to Jean Hamilton, 4 April 1904.
12. See Jean's Diary for 2 September 1902 and Hamilton, General Sir Ian, *The Soul and Body of an Army* (Edward Arnold, 1920), Chap. 1.

5. Tidworth

1. Hamilton Archives 3/2/3. Ian to Jean Hamilton, 4 April 1904.
2. Nicholson, Nigel, *Mary Curzon* (Weidenfeld & Nicolson, 1977), pp. 108–9.
3. Hamilton, Ian B. M., *The Happy Warrior* (Cassell, 1966), p. 129.

6. Malta

1. Jean was quoting again from one of her favourite writers, Oscar Wilde.
2. Hamilton, General Sir Ian, *Compulsory Service* (John Murray, 1910).
3. Hamilton, Ian B. M., *The Happy Warrior* (Cassell, 1966), p. 249.
4. Hamilton, General Sir Ian, *Jean: A Memoir* (Published privately, 1941: by kind permission of Elizabeth, Lady Muir).

7. The Beginning of World War One

1. Hamilton, Ian B. M., *The Happy Warrior* (Cassell, 1966), pp. 258–260 for a description of Jean's work at what the family call 'No. 1 HPG'.
2. See Jean's diary for copies of articles from *The Queen*, 30 December 1916, and Rosa Stuart in *Every Women's*, 25 September 1917.
3. Maurice, Maj.-Gen. Sir Frederick, *Haldane 1856–1915* (Faber, 1937), p. 357.
4. Ibid., pp. 361–4.
5. Ibid., p. 360.
6. Ibid.
7. Hamilton, General Sir Ian, *The Commander* (Hollis & Carter, 1957), p. 100.
8. Simkins, Peter, *Kitchener's Army* (Manchester University Press, 1988), p. 36.
9. Anecdote related by Ian Hamilton at a press party for the Celia and John Lee biographies of the Hamiltons, organised by Mrs Barbara Hamilton, 29th February 2000.

8. Gallipoli – The Battle that Would Never End

1. Gilbert, Martin, *Winston S. Churchill: Companion Vol. 3 Pt. 1* (Heinemann, 1972), pp. 340–42.

2. Gilbert, Martin, *Winston S. Churchill: Vol. III 1914–16* (Heinemann, 1971), pp. 230–31.

3. The casualties on the first day numbered about 5,000. The total Allied losses for the campaign (including sickness) were nearly a quarter of a million, of whom nearly 50,000 died.

4. Wilson, Trevor, *The Myriad Faces of War* (Blackwell/Polity Press, 1986), pp. 410–11.

5. Ibid., p. 203.

6. Grigg, John, *Lloyd George: From Peace to War 1912–16* (Methuen, 1985), p. 254.

7. Ibid., p. 256.

8. *Myriad Faces of War*, p. 208. *The Myriad Faces of War* is strongly recommended as a background to the political dimensions of the campaign and the war.

9. Hamilton Archives 20/1/3. The letter is added to Jean Hamilton's diary for 24 June 1915.

10. This is an important example of Jean going back into her diary to add extra information. While she might have known in advance about the offensive (another case of lax security in London) she could not have known in August that the attack at Loos would fail in September.

11. Lee, John, *A Soldier's Life: General Sir Ian Hamilton* (Macmillan, 2000), pp. 189–91.

12. *Myriad Faces of War*, p. 274.

13. *Winston S. Churchill: Vol. III*, p. 555.

14. Hamilton, General Sir Ian, *Jean: A Memoir* (Published privately, 1941: by kind permission of Elizabeth, Lady Muir), p. 18.

15. Lloyd George, David, *War Memoirs: Vol. 1* (Odhams 'New Edition'), pp. 866–7.

16. Hamilton, General Sir Ian, *The Soul and Body of an Army* (Edward Arnold, 1921), p. 189.

17. Ibid., p. 194.

18. Hamilton Archives 5/3/14.

19. Hamilton Archives 5/3/23. *Report by the Inspector-General of the Oversea Forces on the Establishments and Distribution of Troops in Oversea Garrisons.* 1913, Appendix 1, p. 23.

9. Lady Hamilton's Gallipoli Fund

 1. Hamilton, General Sir Ian, *Jean: A Memoir* (Published privately, 1941: by kind permission of Elizabeth, Lady Muir), p. 16.
 2. Imperial War Museum BO2/12 Women's Work Committee. 12/3 First Report 12 July–30 September 1915.
 3. Ibid., 12/3, 12/4, 12/5–11.
 4. Ibid., 12/3.
 5. Ibid., cutting from the *Observer*, 25 September 1915.
 6. Hamilton Archives 7/4/26.
 7. Ibid., cable from Ian to Jean, 24 July 1915.
 8. Imperial War Museum BO2/12. First and Final Reports.
 9. Hamilton Archives 7/4/26.
10. Imperial War Museum BO2/12. Final Report.
11. Hamilton, *Jean: A Memoir*, p. 16. The 'bright blue kit' was the hospital uniform of wounded men at home.
12. Ibid.

10. The Dardanelles Commission of Inquiry

 1. PRO CAB 19/29 Memorandum by Sir Ian Hamilton on a letter from Mr K. A. Murdoch to the Prime Minister of the Australian Commonwealth, gives the text of the letter and Hamilton's refutation of it, 26 November 1915.
 2. See the article by Nicholas Hiley, 'Enough Glory for all: Ellis Ashmead-Bartlett and Sir Ian Hamilton at the Dardanelles', *Journal of Strategic Studies*, vol. 16 no. 2, June 1993, pp. 203–56.
 3. Hamilton Archives 20/1/2 Ian to Jean Hamilton, 3 June 1915, added to Jean's diary.
 4. Lister, Charles, *Letters and Recollections with a Memoir by his father Lord Ribblesdale* (Fisher Unwin, 1917), pp. 189–215.
 5. Ibid.
 6. PRO CAB 19/29 Murdoch to Fisher, 23 September 1915. See note 1 above.
 7. Hamilton Archives 20/1/3. Ian Hamilton to Walter Braithwaite, 12 July 1916, added to Jean's diary.

8. Martin Gilbert writes: 'Hamilton kept no diary while at Gallipoli. In June 1916, more than seven months after his recall, and over a year after he had gone to Gallipoli, he began to dictate the "Private Diary of General Sir Ian Hamilton" to his secretary.' (*Winston S. Churchill: Vol. III 1914–16* (Heinemann, 1977), p. xxiv.) In fact the diary was dictated daily to Staff-Sergeant Stuart during the campaign and it was work on this that Jean read in September 1916.

9. Hamilton Archives 20/1/3 Braithwaite to Hamilton, 5 November 1916, added to Jean's diary.

10. Hamilton, General Sir Ian, *Listening for the Drums* (Faber, 1944), p. 257.

11. Hamilton Archives 20/1/3, 29 June 1916.

12. Grigg, John, *Lloyd George: From Peace to War 1912–16* (Methuen, 1985), Chapter Two.

13. Hamilton Archives 20/1/3, Ian to Jean Hamilton 7 January 1917, added to Jean's diary.

14. Hamilton Archives 20/1/3; Stuermer, H., *Two War Years in Constantinople: sketches of German and Young Turkish ethics and politics* (Hodder & Stoughton, 1917).

15. Moseley, Sydney, *The Truth about the Dardanelles* (Cassell, 1916), p. 165.

16. Hamilton Archives 20/1/3, Ian Hamilton to Lord Derby, 17 January 1918, added to Jean's diary.

17. Ibid., Sir Francis Davies to Ian Hamilton, 1 February 1918.

18. Ibid., Hamilton to Lord Derby, 6 February 1918.

19. Ibid. The cutting from the *Pall Mall Gazette* of 31 March 1919 is added to Jean's diary.

20. PRO CAB 19/31. Cables presented as evidence to the Dardanelles Commission. Cable No. 465.

11. And Now The War Is Over

1. Asquith, Lady Cynthia, *Diaries 1915–18* (Century, 1987), p. 512.

2. Hamilton Archives 20/4/14.

12. Love, Sex and Children

1.   Hamilton, Ian B. M., *The Happy Warrior* (Cassell, 1966), p. 438.
2.   Hamilton, General Sir Ian, *Jean: A Memoir* (Published privately, 1941: by kind permission of Elizabeth, Lady Muir), pp. 21–2.
3.   Ibid.
4.   Soames, Lady Mary, *Clementine Churchill* (Cassell, 1979), p. 121.
5.   Ibid., p. 122.
6.   Ibid., p. 123.
7.   Ibid., p. 188.
8.   *The Happy Warrior*, p. 437.
9.   *Clementine Churchill*, p. 188.
10. Ibid., pp. 127, 328 and 369.
11. 'Dark Rosaleen' is the English translation of the title of an old Irish ballad called 'Roisin Dubh'. Ostensibly about a love affair, it is said to be in reality a veiled reference to colonised Ireland, and Jean was obviously familiar with the song. A translation from the Irish was published in a book edited by Stopford Brooke. See 'Dark Rosaleen', a ballad translation from the Irish by James Clarence Mangan, a Dublin poet; printed in Brooke and Rolleston *A Treasury of Irish Poetry* (Smith Elder & Co., 1905), pp. 250–52.
12. Souhami, Diana, *Mrs Keppel and her Daughter* (HarperCollins, 1996), p. 48.

13. Jean: Artist and Poet

1.   'In the Great World: Lady Hamilton', *The Sketch* magazine, 21 April 1915.
2.   Walter Sickert to Jean Hamilton, undated Venice, inserted into Jean's May 1904 diary.
3.   Walter Sickert to Jean Hamilton, undated London, inserted in Jean's July 1914 diary – obviously slightly out of place as the war started in August!
4.   Undated article by T. Austen Brown in Jean's 1925 diary.
5.   Newton, Eric, 'Sickert and Wood: Lyric Poetry in Paint' – newspaper article inserted in Jean's 1938 diary.

6. Hamilton, General Sir Ian, *Jean: A Memoir* (Published privately, 1941: by kind permission of Elizabeth, Lady Muir), pp. 17–18; Hamilton, Ian B. M., *The Happy Warrior* (Cassell, 1966), pp. 83–4.
7. Soames, Lady Mary, *Winston Churchill: His Life as a Painter* (Collins, 1990), p. 114.
8. Winston Churchill to Jean Hamilton, inserted in Jean's 1921 diary.
9. Hamilton Archives 20/4/12 Lady Hamilton's Poems; Published Privately 1916.
10. Ibid.
11. Ibid.
12. Ibid.
13. Ibid.

14. Grand Ladies and Great Houses

1. A newspaper report of the event is inserted in Jean's April 1920 diary.
2. Newspaper reports dated 27 and 29 April in Jean's April 1920 diary.
3. Nicholson, Nigel, *Mary Curzon* (Weidenfeld & Nicolson, 1977), p. 212.
4. Bradford, Sarah, *Elizabeth: A Biography of Her Majesty the Queen* (Heinemann, 1996), p.16.
5. Martin, Ralph G., *Lady Randolph Churchill: Vol. 2 1895–1921* (Cardinal, 1974), p. 232.
6. *Elizabeth*, pp. 44–5.
7. Allen, Martin, *Hidden Agenda* (Macmillan, 2000), p. 14.
8. The author thanks Lady Frances Campbell-Preston, Lady-in-Waiting to Queen Elizabeth, The Queen Mother, and Miss Pamela Clark, Deputy Registrar, The Royal Archives Windsor for points of clarification in letters of 28 March 2000 and 11 May 2000 respectively.
9. Ian Hamilton is on film introducing Sir John Hammerton's *Forgotten Men*, a fiercely anti-war documentary made in 1934, re-released by DD Video in 1999.
10. Interview with Mrs Fiona Goetz (*née* Muir), Lady Hamilton's great-niece, April 2000.

11. Letter from Alice Keppel to Jean Hamilton in Jean's March 1936 diary.
12. The obituary notice is inserted in Jean's March 1935 diary.
13. See newspaper cuttings inserted in Jean's September 1936 diary.
14. Nora Lindsay to Jean Hamilton, then holidaying in Lou Casteon, inserted in Jean's 1921 diary.
15. Letter from Violet Trefusis to Jean Hamilton in Jean's September 1937 diary.

15. The Later Years

1. Soames, Lady Mary, *Clementine Churchill* (Cassell, 1979), p. 200.
2. *Yorkshire Evening Post* report, 11 July 1927.
3. A reference to Thomas Moore's ballad 'The Last Rose of Summer'.
4. From a newspaper cutting inserted in Jean's 1931 diary.
5. From a newspaper cutting of 26 April 1935 inserted in Jean's diary; Ian Hamilton repeated these words and phrases at every opportunity in press interviews in the 1930s.
6. Martin, Ralph G. *Lady Randolph Churchill: Vol. 2* Cardinal/Sphere Books 1974, p. 250,323,339–340
7. Letter of 6 February 1934, inserted in Jean's 1934 diary.
8. Letter of 7 February 1934, inserted in Jean's 1934 diary.
9. Cutting from *Sunday Express* in Jean's 1934 diary.
10. Hamilton Archives 20/4/13.

16. The Last Romance

1. Hamilton, General Sir Ian, *Jean: A Memoir* (Published privately: 1941: by kind permission of Elizabeth, Lady Muir), p. 18.
2. Lady Mary Soames to the author, 2 June 2000.
3. 8 October 1940 is the last date in the diary. At that time Jean was at Blair Drummond battling bravely with terminal cancer. She may have written that date in error or have added to it later without changing the date. This must be since we know Chamberlain died on 9 November 1940.
4. Hamilton, General Sir Ian, *Listening for the Drums* (Faber, 1944), p. 188

5. *Jean: A Memoir*, pp. 18, 21–2, 24.

6. Yeats, William Butler 'Among School Children', from *The Tower* (1928) in *Collected Poems of W. B. Yeats* (Macmillan, 1979), p. 245.

7. Hamilton Archives 20/4/12. Lady Hamilton's Poems, published privately 1916.

Sources and Bibliography

Jean, Lady Hamilton's Diaries

Lady Hamilton's printed diaries, Oct **1901** to Aug **1903** by kind permission of Mr Ian Hamilton, Literary Executor of General Sir Ian's and Lady Hamilton's papers.
Lady Hamilton's diaries, on microfilm at King's College London, Liddell Hart Centre for Military Archives, Reference Hamilton **20/1/1–8** Diaries of Jean Miller Hamilton, Lady Hamilton, **1886–1940**.

King's Reference

Hamilton	Volume Number	Dates
20/1/1	Vols 1–4 and part of vol 5	1886 Aug 1–1887 Mar 2, 1903
		Aug 11–1908 Apr 17
20/1/2	part of vol 5, vols 6–8	1908 Apr 18–1915 Jun 8
20/1/3	Vols 9–11 and part of vol 12	1915 Jun 13–1919 Dec 31
20/1/4	part of vol 12 and vols 13–15	1920 Jan 1–1926 Dec 31
20/1/5	Vol 16	1927 Jan 1–1928 Sep 28
20/1/6	Vols 17–21	1928 Sep 30–1935 Sep 22
20/1/7	Vols 22–24	1936 Sep 22–1938 Feb 15
20/1/8	Vols 25–26	1938 Mar 6–1940 Oct 8

Manuscript Sources

Jean Hamilton – writings: **20/4/1–14**
Ian Hamilton Papers, Liddell Hart Centre for Military Archives, Kings' College, London
Ian Hamilton (son of Vereker Hamilton and Gen. Sir Ian's nephew) unpublished writings on Lady Hamilton and her family, the Muirs and on the family of Gen. Sir Ian Hamilton, by kind permission of his son Alexander Hamilton

The History of James Finlay & Company by kind permission of Sir
Richard Muir

Dardanelles Commission of Inquiry papers, CAB **19**, Public Record
Office, Kew

Women's Work Committee papers, BO2/**12**, Department of Documents,
Imperial War Museum, London

Published Sources

All published in London, unless otherwise stated

Amery, Leo, *The Leo Amery Diaries* (volume one 1896–1929), edited by
John Barnes and David Nicholson Hutchinson 1980

Asquith, Lady Cynthia, *The Diaries of Lady Cynthia Asquith 1915–18*
Century 1968

Asquith, Margot, *The Autobiography of Margot Asquith* Eyre &
Spottiswoode 1962

Bonham Carter, Violet, *Winston Churchill As I knew Him* Eyre &
Spottiswoode 1965

Bott, Alan and Clephane, Irene, *Our Mothers* (2nd edition) Victor
Gollancz 1932

Bradford, Sarah, *Elizabeth A Biography of Her Majesty The Queen*
Heinemann 1996

Churchill, Randolph S. *Winston S. Churchill: Youth 1874–1900*
Heinemann 1966

Churchill, Randolph S. *Winston S. Churchill: Companion Vol. 2 Pt. 1
1901–1907* Heinemann 1969

Churchill, Winston S., *Ian Hamilton's March* Longmans 1900

Clarke, Mary, *Diana One Upon A Time* Sidgwick & Jackson 1994

Fitzroy, Sir Almeric, *Memoirs* (Volumes 1–2) Hutchinson, no date

Gilbert, Martin, *Winston S. Churchill Volume 3: 1914–1916* Heinemann 1971

Graham, Caroline, *Camilla The King's Mistress* Blake 1994

Grigg, John *Lloyd George: from peace to war 1912–1916* Methuen 1985

Hamilton, General Sir Ian, *Gallipoli Diary* (2 volumes) Edward Arnold
1920

— *Jean. a Memoir* published privately 1941 by kind permission of
Elizabeth, Lady Muir, from her personally inscribed copy

— *The Soul and Body of an Army* Edward Arnold 1921

— *When I was a Boy* Faber 1939

— *Listening for the Drums* Faber 1944

Hamilton, General Sir Ian (ed. Major A. Farrar-Hockley) *The Commander* Hollis & Carter 1957

Hamilton, Ian B. M., *The Happy Warrior: A Life of General Sir Ian Hamilton* Cassell 1966

Hamilton, Vereker, , *Things That Happened* Edward Arnold 1925

Jenkins, Roy, *Asquith* Collins 1964

Judd, Dennis, *Edward the Seventh* Futura 1975

Lee, John, *A Soldier's Life: General Sir Ian Hamilton 1853–1947* Macmillan 2000

Lloyd George, David *War Memoirs* (Volumes 1 and 2) Odhams Press

Martin, Ralph G., *Lady Randolph Churchill A Biography* (volumes 1 and 2) Cardinal/Sphere Books 1974

Maurice, Major-General Sir Frederick, *The Life of Viscount Haldane of Cloan 1856–1915* Faber & Faber 1937

Morton, Andrew, *Diana Her True Story* (revised edition) Michael O'Mara 1997

Nicholson, Nigel, *Mary Curzon* Weidenfeld & Nicholson 1977

Roberts, Field Marshal Lord *Forty-One Years in India* Macmillan 1898

Sandys, Celia, *Churchill Wanted Dead Or Alive* Harper Collins 1999

Simkins, Peter *Kitchener's Army: The Raising of the New Armies 1914–1916* Manchester University Press 1988

Soames, Mary, *Clementine Churchill* Cassell 1979

Soames, Mary *Winston Churchill: His Life As A Painter* Collins 1990

Souhami, Diana, *Mrs Keppel And Her Daughter* Harper Collins 1996

Wilson, Christopher *A Greater Love: Charles & Camilla* Hodder 1994

Wilson, Trevor *The Myriad Faces of War* Blackwells/Polity Press 1986

Annotated Index

Varney, Ellen, JH's head house maid 211–2, 216, 220–1

Venice 31, 64, 223–30, 247

Ventnor 225

Verschoyle, Miss 186

Victoria, Princess 269

Victoria, Queen 25, 34, 188, 262

Vienna 264, 303–4

Villiers, Sarah, Lady 3

Vincent, Capt., ADC to IH at Tidworth, married (1906) Kitty Ogilvy, daughter of Lady Mabell Airlie 78–9, 84–5

Vincent, Sir Edgar, Conservative MP 36, 44, 120

Vincent, Lady Helen, wife of Sir Edgar Vincent 28, 36, 45–7

Vincent, Kitty (née Ogilvy), daughter of Lady Mabell Airlie and the late David William Stanley Ogilvy, 11th Earl of Airlie 85

von Blaas, artist 223, 312

von Fries, Herr 267

von Lenback, Franz, artist 252

Vyner, Mary, Lady, see Compton, Lady

Wagg, Mrs Kenneth 269

Wagner, Richard 36, 284

Wake, Hereward 274

Waller, Lewis 253

Walrond, Riversdale 287

Wantage, Harriet, Lady (née Jones Lloyd), daughter of Baron Overstone, married 1st Baron Wantage (Robert James Lloyd-Lindsay), an equerry to Edward Prince of Wales (later King Edward VII) 87

Ward, Mrs Dudley 249, 255

Ward, Humphrey 44, 249

Warre, Barbara (1920–90), daughter of Maj. Felix Warre and Marjorie (Margot) (née Hamilton) 218

Warre, Felix (1897–1953), fifth son of Edmund Warre, Head Master and Provost of Eton College, Capt. in the King's Royal Rifle Corps, married (1915) Marjorie, second daughter of Vereker Hamilton and Lilian (née Swainson) 20, 108

Warre, Marjorie (Margot) (1894–1959), educated Kensington High School and the Royal College of Music, ballet dancer, married (1915) Felix Warre, five children, Ursula, Richard, Barbara,

Michael and Griselda (Mrs Maffett) xix, 20, 90, 108, 309

Warrender, Lady Ethel (Maud) (1870–1945), daughter of the 8th Earl of Shaftesbury, married (1897) Sir George Warrender; opera singer 127, 147–8

Warrender, Margaret 64, 66, 95, 99

Warwick, Countess of, Frances (Daisy) 52, 287

Wedgewood, Maj. 175

Weininger, Otto 195

Wellesley, Lord Gerald 267

Wells, H. G. 223

Wemyss, Lady Mary 269–70

Wemyss, Lord Hugo 113, 269–70

Werner, Lady 182

West, Mrs George, see Churchill, Lady Randolph

Westbrook, Harriet 239

Westminster Abbey 34–5, 262, 295, 305

Westminster, Duchess of 255

Wheatley, Mr 283

Wheelband, Mrs 78

Wheeldon Trial 164

Whistler, James McNeill 225, 227

White, Lady 22

White, Nurse 202, 213

White, Sir George 14, 24

White, Harry 48

Whitman, Walt 228, 317

Whyte, Maryott 312

Wigram, Col. Clive 166

Wilde, Oscar 76, 319, 322

Wilhelm II, Kaiser 38, 96, 113, 178, 182, 193, 275

Williamson, Mr 225, 227, 233

Williamson, Phyllis 184

Wilson, Miss 68, 70, 81

Wilson Mr 29

Wilson, Adm. Sir A. 99

Wilson, FM Sir Henry 109, 177, 188

Wilson, Muriel 30, 184

Wilson, Lady Sarah (née Spencer-Churchill) (1865–1929), daughter of the 7th Duke of Marlborough, married Lt.-Col. Gordon Chesney Wilson 29, 41–2, 45, 49, 51, 129, 200, 287

Wilson, Trevor 123

Wimborne House 44

Wimborne, Lady (Cornelia Guest) (née Spencer-Churchill) 44–5, 49, 92, 200